Building Sustainable Competitive Advantage

To my family Pushpa, Roli, Atish, Leela and Ishani who have the patience and humor to survive my work, for their support and encouragement.

Building Sustainable Competitive Advantage

Through Executive Enterprise Leadership

DHIRENDRA KUMAR

Routledge
Taylor & Francis Group

LONDON AND NEW YORK

First published 2015 by Gower Publishing

2 Park Square, Milton Park, Abingdon, Oxfordshire OX14 4RN
52 Vanderbilt Avenue, New York, NY 10017

Routledge is an imprint of the Taylor & Francis Group, an informa business

First issued in paperback 2020

Gower Applied Business Research
Our programme provides leaders, practitioners, scholars and researchers with thought provoking, cutting edge books that combine conceptual insights, interdisciplinary rigour and practical relevance in key areas of business and management.

British Library Cataloguing in Publication Data
A catalogue record for this book is available from the British Library.

The Library of Congress has cataloged the printed edition as follows:
Kumar, Dhirendra, 1942-
   Building sustainable competitive advantage : through executive enterprise leadership / by Dhirendra Kumar.
      pages cm
   Includes bibliographical references and index.
   ISBN 978-1-4724-7031-7 (hbk) -- ISBN 978-1-4724-7032-4 (ebook) -- ISBN 978-1-4724-7033-1 (epub)
   1. Total quality management. 2. Leadership. 3. Sustainability. I. Title.
   HD62.15.K8547 2016
   658.4'092--dc23

                                                                                    2015018101

ISBN 13: 978-1-4724-7031-7 (hbk)
ISBN 13: 978-0-367-60607-7 (pbk)

Contents

List of Figures

List of Tables

About the Author

Dr. Dhirendra Kumar is retired from the North Carolina (NC) State University in the USA. He has worked as an engineer, technical adviser and program manager for Outboard Marine, John Deere, Pratt & Whitney, and Pitney Bowes. Since turning to academia, Dr. Kumar has been a researcher, senior lecturer, and visiting and adjunct professor, holding different posts at the universities of Iowa, Nebraska, Hartford, Central Connecticut and New Haven and NC State University. He has written books, instructional manuals and many conference and journal papers and was a member of a number of advisory boards and scholarship committees. In his last assignment he advised undergraduate and graduate students on industrial projects and led projects in organizations external to NC State University. Dr. Kumar developed and taped courses for distance learning on topics such as Enterprise Growth Strategy, Resources Transformation and Continuous Improvement.

List of Abbreviations

3E	Equitable, Ecologically sound and Economically viable
AAUP	American Association of University Professors
AICPA	American Institute of Certified Public Accountants
AIG	American International Group
AMA	American Management Association
AMA	American Marketing Association
AFP	Association of Financial Professionals
ANAC	Association of Nurses in Aids Care
ABEF	Australian Business Excellence Framework
AQC	Australian Quality Council
BSC	Balanced Scorecard Concept
BCBS	Basel Committee on Bank Supervision
BHAG	Big Hairy Audacious Goal
BCG	Boston Consulting Group
BRICS	Brazil, the Russian Federation, India, China and South Africa
BP	British Petroleum
BEE	Business/Enterprise Excellence
BE	Business Excellence
BEF	Business Excellence Framework
CAS	Casualty Actuarial Society
CRM	Catastrophic Risk Management
CEO	Chief Executive Officer
CFO	Chief Financial Officer
CIO	Chief Information Officer
COO	Chief Operating Officer
COSO	Committee of Sponsoring Organizations of the Treadway Commission
CA	Competitive Advantage
CPSC	Consumer Product Safety Commission
CI	Continuous Improvement
COBIT	Control Objectives for Information and Related Technology
COPQ	Costs of Poor Quality
CSF	Critical Success Factor
CSC	Cross-Sector Collaboration
CCS	Customer-Centric Systems
EPS	Electric Power Steering
EM MNE	Emerging Market Multinational Enterprise
EE	Enterprise Excellence
EGS	Enterprise Growth Strategy
ERM	Enterprise Risk Management
ET	Enterprise Transformation
ERP	Enterprise Resource Planning
ERM	Enterprise Risk Management

ESAT	Enterprise Strategic Analysis and Transformation
ES	Enterprise System
ESE	Environmentally motivated Social Enterprise
EDD	Equality, Diversity and Discrimination
EDOD	Equality, Diversity, Opportunity and Discrimination
E3	Ethical, Effective and Efficient
EADS	European Aeronautic Defense and Space Company
FAA	Federal Aviation Administration
FERMA	Federation of European Risk Management Associations
FY	Fiscal Year
FDA	Food and Drug Administration
FDI	Foreign Direct Investment
GTF	Geared Turbofan
GE	General Electric Company
GSM	Growth-Share Matrix
HD	Harley-Davidson
HDTV	High Density Television
HRM	Holistic Risk Management
HR	Human Resource
HPS	Hydraulic Power Steering
ISACF	Information Systems Audit and Control Foundation
ICT	Information and Communication Technology
IBM	International Business Machines
ICF	International Coach Federation
IIF	the Institute of International Finance
ILFC	International Lease Finance Corporation
IP	Intellectual Property
IRM	Integrated Risk Management
ISO	International Organization for Standardization [not an acronym, common short name]
IT	Information Technology
IW	Information Warfare
KPI	Key Performance Indicator
KRI	Key Risk Indicator
KN	Kilo Newton
LEAP	Leading Edge Aviation Propulsion
LOF	Liability for Foreignness
MIT	Massachusetts Institute of Technology
MEM	Mechanical and Electrical Manufacturers
M&A	Merger and Acquisition
MPH	Miles per hour
MNE	Multinational Enterprise
NASA	National Aeronautics and Space Administration
NQA	National Quality Award
NPD	New Product Development
NYSE	New York Stock Exchange
NGO	Non-Governmental Organizations
OSFI	Office of the Superintendent of Financial Institution
ORM	Operational Risk Management
OA	Organizational Assessment

OECD	Organization for Economic Co-operation and Development
OPEC	Organization of the Petroleum Exporting Countries
OEM	Original Equipment Manufacturer
PTP	Piedmont Triad Partnership
PW	Pratt & Whitney
P&G	Procter and Gamble
P&L	Profit and Loss Statement
PRINCE2	Project in Controlled Environment
R&D	Research and Development
ROI	Return on Investment
RUPD	*Revealed Unit Price Differential*
RC	Risk Control
RMC	Risk Management Culture
RR	Rolls-Royce Holdings, Plc.
SIOP	Sales Inventory and Operations Planning
SOX	Sarbanes–Oxley Act of 2002
SEC	Security and Exchange Commission
SEE	Social-Ecological Enterprise
SEI	Social-Ecological Innovation
SOA	Society of Actuaries
SNECMA	*Société nationale d'études et de construction de moteurs d'aviation* [National Company for the Design and Construction of Aviation Engines]
S&P	Standard and Poor
SRM	Strategic Risk Management
SCA	Sustainable Competitive Advantage
TQM	Total Quality Management
TBL	Triple Bottom Line: People, Planet and Profit
TTL	Triple Top Line: Equity, Ecology and Economy
UN	United Nations
UNDP	United Nations Development Program
UPS	United Parcel Service
UTC	United Technologies Corporation
VA	Value Alignment
WEF	World Economic Forum
WIRED	Workforce Innovation in Regional Economic Development
WWII	World War Two

Introduction

The Enterprise Excellence (EE) philosophy is a holistic approach for leading an enterprise to total excellence under the executive leadership by achieving a sustainable competitive advantage, significant growth in revenue and profitability, and a reduction in business cycle time while strategically managing the enterprise risk and primarily focusing on the needs of the customer. There are various organizations within an enterprise but they all focus on meeting or exceeding customer needs. Therefore, enterprise excellence is an integrated approach affecting every employee, every functional area and strategy within the organization. This principle applies to all sizes of enterprises (large or small), as well as to all types of enterprises (commercial or government, private or public). To address the EE philosophy, organizations must be focused on producing products and/or services using a variety of processes to meet or exceed customer demand, while simultaneously increasing profitability or margin. These processes occur in all functional areas including product conception, engineering, sales and marketing, financial, operations and services.

Businesses regardless of industry are innovating and trying to grow/survive in a global economy. The rate of change in today's competitive world is constantly increasing and the competition is forcing businesses to be well funded and at the same time, customers are becoming unpredictable. These constantly changing hurdles are creating unfamiliar conditions for leadership. As business leaders develop their growth strategy proposal, they would need to identify, assess and prioritize risk in their strategy to execute and achieve goals. Every business leader must strategize in ways not previously expected in the hope of meeting or exceeding customer demand, while retaining and attracting new customers.

Enterprise Excellence is achieved through developing and executing a sustainable growth strategy as well as analyzing and minimizing risk through Enterprise Risk Management (ERM), while building sustainable competitive advantage to:

- support markets and products growth;
- acquire new or expand business;
- improve margin;
- increase revenue and profitability;
- reduce business cycle time.

The top level elements of EE philosophy are the enterprise growth strategy and the enterprise risk management. Therefore, enterprise growth strategy must be developed concurrently while strategically analyzing and managing risk.

Enterprise Growth Strategy (EGS)

It is important to note that successful enterprise growth is likely to require significant investments in skills, processes, organization and technology. Enterprise growth initiatives may be driven by external opportunities such as market segment/customers which will force the development of strategies such as targeted market, value proposition, or new/upgraded product/service offerings.

Enterprise growth calls for more than superficial change. These changes can be in response to marketplace events or to address underperformance but enterprise growth is quite different from a company's turnaround in financial difficulties. It will inevitably be the biggest single internal program that any enterprise undertakes. There are several questions that have to be answered during development and execution of enterprise growth, such as:

- What must enterprise do to grow?
- What do leaders transform?
- What product, market, and/or service do they need to grow?
- What are the vital signs that growth is underway?

Enterprise growth is a C-level (CEO, CFO, business president, etc.) leadership initiative towards corporate growth and/or renewal, constituting a range of competitive strategies impacting the key elements of an enterprise thus resulting in a sustainable competitive advantage.

Growth strategy initiatives may also be driven by competitors' initiatives which will force the development of operations-oriented strategies such as supply chain restructuring (simplifying supply chains, negotiating just-in-time relationships, developing collaborative information systems), outsourcing-domestic and/or off-shoring, process standardization, and process re-engineering (identification, design, and development of value-driven processes, identification and elimination of waste and minimization of non-value-adding activities). There are many approaches to enterprise growth, especially those that are operations-oriented, are pursued in the context of information technology (IT) related solutions such as Enterprise Resource Planning (ERP), Customer Relationship Management, and Supply Chain Management (SCM). Ideally, these types of enterprise solutions are viewed *as just a part of the enterprise growth process*.

The execution of these strategies is to bring about transformational results. Examples include Airbus, Toyota, Wal-Mart, and so on. The following are the key characteristics where enterprise growth is the best strategy:

- When C-level and executive leadership are required to be involved.
- Where primary aspects of enterprise are usually impacted.
- When the basis of enterprise competition has changed.
- When overall performance needs to be enhanced, renewed and sustained with leadership in the marketplace.
- When drastic increase in market share and/or market responsiveness is required.

Growth strategy goals tend to significantly differentiate initiatives. The approach, and the resources utilized for business growth, relates to both the goal pursued and the nature and competencies of the enterprise. Therefore, the need for enterprise growth entails a fundamental change in the way enterprises are started to optimize the probability to flourish. Those that succeed eventually must face the challenges of change, which some master and succeed in enterprise growth strategy. Most enterprises fail to transform or grow.

Enterprise Risk Management (ERM)

Enterprise risk must be identified, assessed and prioritized as developing growth strategy proposal which leadership has to execute to achieve goals. As business leaders lead the efforts, they have to minimize, monitor and control the probability and/or impact of unfortunate events and maximize the realization of opportunities. Risk is not just as threat but also as opportunity. Risk can come from various areas: project failure (at any phase of the project – from development through sustained life cycle), financial markets, credit risk, accidents, legal liabilities, natural disaster, etc. Several institutions have developed risk management standards: Project Management Institute, the National Institute of Science and Technology and actuarial societies. Risk calculating methods, definitions and goals vary widely according to whether the risk management method is in the context of project management, security, engineering related activity, industrial processes, financial portfolios or public health safety. Therefore, ERM is the discipline by which an organization in any industry assesses controls, exploits finances and monitors risks from all sources for the purpose of increasing the organization's short- and long-term value to its shareholders. There are various risk areas in any enterprise including equality risk, operational risk, political risk, customer risk, ethical risk, technology/product and competitive risk.

What are the Key Achievements of Enterprise Excellence (EE)

The achievements in enterprise excellence can range from greater cost efficiencies, improved market perceptions, fundamental changes to markets, to new product and service offerings. There may also be significant upgrades in skills, technology and business strategies. The scope of enterprise excellence can also range from operations activities, to business functions, to overall organization, to the enterprise as a whole. For example, Dunkin' Donut stores sell sandwiches but are still known as donut shops, IBM's business concentration moved from computers and servers to providing integrated technology services, Honda's business moved from motorcycles and automobiles to commuter planes.

Therefore, the need for enterprise excellence entails a fundamental change in the way enterprises are started every day; some flourish. Those that succeed eventually must face the challenges of change; some succeed in achieving the enterprise excellence by building sustainable competitive advantage. Most enterprises fail to transform and/or grow. This book provides the study of enterprise excellence with a focus on understanding the challenges of change and determining what practices help to address change through the executive enterprise leadership and successfully achieve enterprise excellence.

The revolution in IT and the rapid growth in global competition have resulted in an increasing need for enterprise excellence to maintain or gain competitive advantage. This increased need raises important issues concerning how enterprise excellence is best understood and pursued. This text outlines the enterprise excellence model and guides the development and implementation process. A variety of industries and corporate vignettes are used to illustrate the model. The book detail by chapter is as follows:

Chapter 1, "Enterprise Excellence Model" – logically developing the enterprise excellence model using the historical model as the starting point. Identifying as well as resolving the issues in the historical model with the new model through the executive enterprise leadership. Developing the structural relationship of the model elements as well as identifying, defining and presenting an overview of these elements.

Chapter 2, "Enterprise Growth Strategy (EGS)" – identifying the elements of EGS (Business vision and mission, Innovative growth ideas, market growth strategy and core competency) and presenting the literature research with discussion. Various models on these elements are presented with discussion. Discussion on various sub-level elements is also presented including:

- Diffusion of innovation research which was first started in 1903 by researcher Gabriel Tarde. Tarde defined in 1903 that the innovation-decision process as a series of steps that include:

  1. First knowledge.
  2. Forming an attitude.
  3. A decision to adopt or reject.
  4. Implementation and use.
  5. Confirmation of the decision.

- Market growth is the interface across the business which supports the flow of products, services, money, and information. These flows across the business boundary are a consequence of interactions within the business, within the market and between the two. The positive change in demand for products or services or both is defined as market growth for the business. These increases in demand could be for:
  - existing products or services or both;
  - new products or services or both;
  - combination of existing and new products and services.

Chapter 3, "Enterprise Risk Management (ERM)"– identifying the elements of ERM such as strategic risk management (SRM), holistic risk management (HRM) and integrated risk management (IRM) and presenting the literature research with discussion. Also discussing why ERM is important and what the characteristic forces of ERM are, and how to quantify the enterprise risk. Various other enterprise risk topics are discussed including risk management guidelines.

Chapter 4, "Enterprise Transformation (ET)" – as technology and processes are changing, enterprises may go through transformation before their growth strategy can be executed. Identifying the elements of ET and presenting the literature research with discussion. Four case studies are presented with discussion: business transformation at John Deere Tractor Division, Manufacturing transformation at Pratt & Whitney, Business transformation at IBM, and small business transformation.

Chapter 5, "Strategy Execution and Measurement" – it does not matter how well the enterprise growth strategy is developed if it is not executed and measured. Execution provides life to developed strategy and the measured results are recognized, appreciated, and advertised. Several approaches to strategy execution and measurement are presented in this chapter. There is some discussion about strategy derailment, and the safeguards that must be in place to achieve success.

Chapter 6, "Enterprise Excellence Case Studies" – two major case studies are discussed: case study of two commercial airplane businesses (Boeing and Airbus); case study of three aerospace manufacturing companies (General Electric Company, Rolls-Royce Holdings, Plc. and United Technologies Corporation). These case studies are clearly validating the structural concept of the enterprise excellence model as well as demonstrating the enterprise success through the measuring elements: growth in revenue and profitability and reduction in business cycle time.

This text can be used in several ways: as a one-semester class for a senior/beginning graduate level course, a three-to-five-days seminar based on selected topics with case studies, or as a great reference book for practicing professionals, teaching faculty and students.

Enterprise Excellence Model

The Enterprise Excellence (EE) philosophy is a holistic approach for leading an enterprise to total excellence by focusing on the needs of the customer whether within the state, the nation, or the world while building sustainable competitive advantage. As global competition is increasing, anything less than EE is not enough. Many US companies have already started setting up their pursuit of excellence under the executive leadership to meet the Asian threats (Japanese, Chinese, Koreans, etc.). They are also preparing for increased competition from the Economic Community (Shore, 1990). Shore is identifying three key elements in building sustainable competitive advantage to achieve the EE:

* complete customer satisfaction;
* minimum cycle time;
* minimum resources consumed.

This is achieved by changing the way the business is run, i.e., business transformation is a necessity and not a luxury. The central constructs of the theory are value, work processes, decision-making, and social networks (Zhongyuan et al., 2011). *Value* is a measure of the extent to which an enterprise provides a market that the consumers in this market want. Increasing variations of offerings from what consumers want results in decreasing value. Value can also accrue from providing customers an offering they did not expect, e.g., Apple's iPhone. This leads to innovation whereby the market changes its desires. Market innovators are usually not transformers; their innovations cause the other players in the market to have to transform. Thus, for example, Macy's innovated in the retail marketplace; JC Penny was thereby forced to transform.

Other companies have been driven to pursue excellence through visionary executive enterprise leadership. This includes activities such as strategic visioning, innovating products, core competency and strategic marketing. Hence, look at excellence from a different perspective. For example (Zink, 2007) tried to come up with a new definition for excellence, based on a review of the historical development of the total quality movement. Dahlgaard-Park and Dahlgaard-Park (2007) proposed, on the basis of a review of eight excellence frameworks, a new model called the 4P model that depicted the factors for sustainable excellence, and Komashie et al. (2007) identified the different factors for creating excellence in the health-care and manufacturing industries. As reviewed in the articles in the special issue of the *Journal of Management History*, it became clear that among these and other authors there was no agreement on which factors (elements) create sustained enterprise performance. This agreement is all the more important as the times have changed considerably since the special issue was published. In 2007 the credit crisis hit, causing the most severe recession since the 1930s (Colvin, 2009). At the same time a wave of trends and developments, including globalization (Bakker et al., 2004; Starbuck, 2005; Schuster and Copeland,

2006; Sirkin et al., 2008; Ramamurti and Singh, 2009), new technology (Malone, 2003; Light, 2005), ascension of Asian markets (especially China and India) (Backman and Butler, 2007; Nath, 2008; Nobrega and Sinha, 2008), environmental, demographic and other issues were sweeping the business world and reshaped the world economy. Additional discussion is presented in Section 1.2 – Excellence Models' Evergreen Characteristics.

Therefore, the following sections are presented in this chapter:

1.1   Historical Enterprise Excellence Models
    1.1.1   Innovation
    1.1.2   International Business Excellence Statistics
1.2   Excellence Models' Evergreen Characteristics
1.3   Development of the Enterprise Excellence (EE) Model
    1.3.1   Enterprise Growth Strategy (EGS)
        1.3.1.1   Business vision and mission
        1.3.1.2   Innovative growth ideas
        1.3.1.3   Market growth strategy
        1.3.1.4   Core competency
    1.3.2   Enterprise Risk Management (ERM)
        1.3.2.1   Strategic risk management (SRM)
        1.3.2.2   Integrated risk management
        1.3.2.3   Other risk areas
    1.3.3   Enterprise Transformation (ET)
    1.3.4   Strategy Execution and Measurement

1.1   Historical Enterprise Excellence Models

There is no uniformly accepted definition of enterprise excellence. Initially business leaders were concentrating their efforts on operations, and then moved on to business and finally concentrating their efforts on the enterprise. Variety of EE models are discussed in the literature including the following.

Edgeman and Eskildsen (2014) have documented a skilled use of an enterprise excellence system to significantly boost performance across an array of key domains, including financial, human capital, and operations including supply chain, but social and environmental performances are not included. The Triple Top Line (TTL): Equity, Ecology and Economy, and the Triple Bottom Line (TBL): People, Planet and Profit are intended to communicate the crucial nature of connecting these to drive alignment between, and hence convergence of, sustainability and enterprise excellence. The relationship among these various elements is very complex, but Edgeman and Eskildsen (2014) are presuming that ethical, effective and efficient (E3) are enterprise governance driven equitable, ecologically sound and economically viable (3E) strategy producing positive TBL (People, Planet and Profit) for the enterprise performance. They have presented their conceptual model (not mathematical equation) in the following expression:

$$\iint [(E3 \text{ Governance}) \times (3E \text{ Strategy})] dGdS \rightarrow 3P \text{ Performance}$$

The use of "∫" integration symbol from calculus is to emphasize the importance of integrating enterprise strategy with enterprise governance to produce 3P (People, Planet and Profit) performance. To accomplish sustainable EE, the integrated approach to organizational design function emphasizing superior performance with various domains including innovation, business intelligence and analytics, operational including supply chain, human capital, financial, marketplace, societal and environmental.

Environmental and social elements establish enterprise boundary conditions or constraints that are influenced by competitive environment, and legal and regulatory requirements. The enterprise-level strategy and governance that jointly optimize resilience and robustness must also regard sustainability. In turn these promote sustainable superior performance across the environmental, societal and economic sustainability dimensions of the TBL (Elkington, 1997). Sustainability is a business imperative (Lubin and Esty, 2010) that stimulates enterprise innovation strategies and tactics (Nidumolu et al., 2009) which are capable of providing the next big source of competitive advantage (Laszlo and Zhexembayeva, 2011). Inclusion of sustainability in enterprise strategy and governance is now common practice (Fowler and Hope, 2007). Corporate governance is vital to both corporate sustainability (Aras and Crowther, 2008) and organizational resilience (Avery and Bergsteiner, 2011), especially in high-intensity enterprise environments marked by the need to integrate and govern complex human capital and technological interfaces (Smith et al., 2005).

Some of the business/enterprise excellence (BEE) models are derived from Total Quality Management (TQM) theory and practice. The BEE models supporting America's Baldrige National Quality Award and the European Quality Award are globally dominant. Effective implementation of BEE models and strategies correlates positively with improved performance in emphasized model areas (Balasubramanian et al., 2005). Inclusion of intelligence and analytics in sustainable EE is driven by rapid evolution of data-driven decision-making toward vastly more complex and computationally intensive "big data analytics," LaVelle et al. (2011) that support sophisticated transformation and translation of information into actionable enterprise intelligence and foresight.

The following specific characteristics are recognized in these models:

- Executive enterprise leadership in BEE model defines, refines and deploys enterprise mission, vision and strategy in order to fulfill organizational objectives and continuously improve performance in areas of competitive importance, including enterprise innovation and agility, Bou-Llusar et al. (2009).
- Both Total Quality Management (TQM) and BEE models practice innovation, but it is not strongly linked (Sun and Zhao, 2010; Teece, 2010) yet curiously, BEE models have not explicitly attended to innovation's role in BEE and assessment of its impact on BEE progress.
- Social-ecological enterprise (SEE) model stresses E3 (ethical, effective, efficient and transparent) strategy and governance as causal to enterprise performance of all sorts. SEE thus focuses on integration of E3 governance with 3E (equity, ecology and economy) triple top line (TTL) strategy, while McDonough and Braungart (2002) are emphasizing that (3E) social equity, ecological responsibility, and economic soundness are along with innovation, resilience and robustness.
- Specifically, SEE emphasizes social-ecological innovation (SEI) resulting from strategic integration of sustainable innovation and innovation for sustainability (Edgeman, 2013). Sustainable innovation manifests in enterprise cultures characterized by rigorous, regular, systematic and systemic innovation throughout the enterprise and is central to its strategy, financial performance, and other key performance domains (Wolpert, 2002).
- Gunester et al. (2010) are also emphasizing that eco-efficiency of enterprise governance is positively correlated with operational and supply chain robustness as well as to value differential that increases over time between more and less eco-efficient enterprises.
- Analyzing and assessing both the models carefully, innovation in SEE differentiates SEE from BEE and, while effectively implemented ecologically and socially responsible enterprise governance and strategy has been positively associated with enterprise value (Al-Najjar and Anfimiadou, 2012; Jo and Harjoto, 2011).

- The combination of governance and strategy with innovation capability and capacity that most strongly drives enterprise value (Hart and Dowell, 2011).
- Hence, the critical elements to these models are governance and strategy, enterprise intelligence and analytics, foresight, innovation, reliance and robustness. For example, enterprise intelligence and analytics: Atkinson et al. (2000) and Galbraith (2012) have acknowledged that organization design components enable pursuit of continuously relevant and responsible performance – an effort further aided by appropriate organizational structure. Among the above-listed elements, innovation is one of the most critical elements in achieving the EE and building sustainable competitive advantage, therefore, some literature research on innovation is necessary to discussed.

1.1.1   INNOVATION

Every product will have a life cycle with an infant period, growth period and then the maturity/decline period (Figure 1.1). This product curve is also known as "S" curve. Tarde (1903) defined the "S" process as the innovation-decision process. Once innovation occurs then the innovations generally spread from the innovator to other individuals and groups in the organization. The S-curve maps growth of revenue or productivity against time. In the early stage of a particular innovation, growth is relatively slow as the new product establishes itself. At some point customers begin to demand and the product growth increases more rapidly. New incremental innovations or changes to the product allow growth to continue. Towards the end of its life cycle growth slows and may even begin to decline. In the later stages, no amount of new investment in that product will yield a normal rate of return.

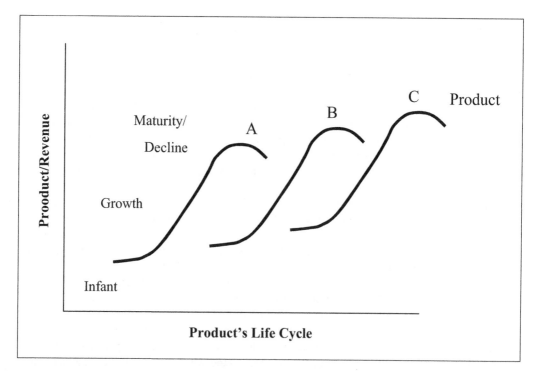

Figure 1.1   Product life cycle "S" curve

Innovation is critical to support the sustainability, resilience and robustness of the enterprise excellence model. Therefore, some additional research on innovation is as follows:

- Reinmoeller and van Baardwijk (2005) have documented that enterprises with the greatest diversity in their innovation strategies portfolio are also the most resilient ones with four key innovation strategies: exploration, knowledge management, entrepreneurship and cooperation.
- Innovation has a documented positive impact on environmental and social performance and is inextricably connected to sustainability (Melville, 2010; Terjesen et al., 2011), while leadership innovation has a deep impact on enterprise governance (Birkinshaw and Mol, 2006).
- Hoffmann (2012) provides a means of deeply embedding customer needs in design of sustainability-oriented products, while Edgeman and Eskildsen (2012) provide a means of integrating societal and environmental considerations into the innovation process.
- To support the enterprise intelligence and analytics, organizations with greater technological and market intelligence absorptive capacity are better able to navigate competitive turbulence and are hence more robust (Lichtenthaler, 2009). This is critical to innovation, assimilation and transfer of intelligence, and subsequent mobilization of resources that contribute to improved performance across an array of key enterprise performance dimensions, including innovation and leverage of social capital across the enterprise supply chain and its broader ecosystem (Maurer et al., 2011).
- Human capital is one of the most critical elements in innovation. Hence, their talent and skills be enriched and optimized to drive innovation. Similarly, a better engagement be cultivated between the enterprise and the people for whom the organization innovates, including direct users of its innovations, to yield more fruitful co-creation (Edgeman and Eskildsen, 2012; Hoffmann, 2012).
- Eskildsen and Edgeman (2012) very positively express that social-ecological innovation contributes to enterprise value creation through: revenue growth; cost, risk and waste reduction; strategic redesign of products, processes or business functions; and differentiating the enterprise value proposition.

1.1.2 INTERNATIONAL BUSINESS EXCELLENCE STATISTICS

Business excellence frameworks (BEFs) and national quality awards (NQAs) are administered by national organizations ("custodians") responsible for a wide range of activities, including promotion and creation of awareness of the national BEF within that nation's business community. The Australian BEF (the Australian Business Excellence Framework – ABEF) was one of the first four worldwide, developed independently in 1987, SAI Global (2007). It was administered by the Australian Quality Council (AQC) until 2001 when custodianship passed to SAI Global, an ASX 300 company and one of the world's leading business publishing, compliance, training and assurance organizations. SAI Global is the only privately owned organization currently administering a BEF (Grigg and Mann, 2008). While such a situation could potentially lead to concerns about whether their primary affiliation is to the promotion of the framework or to their shareholders, SAI Global are uniquely well positioned, being also the national standards body in Australia, to market and promote the framework exactly as it does the standards.

According to Grigg and Mann (2008), awareness of the ABEF is lower than was previously estimated in Australia, with under 10 percent of randomly sampled organizations being aware of the model. ABEF evaluators perceived the methods of promoting the ABEF to be relatively ineffective. Worldwide, custodians of business excellence (BE) models reported that awareness of BE had generally increased in their country in the last three years. Miguel's (2004) research has identified 76 nations which administer a national BEF, although Grigg and Mann (2008) estimate that figure has increased to over 80, with around 50 of these using the Malcolm Baldrige NQA (MBNQA) Criteria and a further 25 having adopted the EFQM European Excellence model (EFQM, 2007). The remaining BEFs are unique and tailored to suit the particular business and cultural context of the nation to which they apply. These include frameworks used in Australia, Malaysia, Singapore, Japan, Mexico, Brazil, South Africa and Canada. Despite this prevalence, there is relatively little in the literature on the subject of promoting and creating awareness of BEFs and awards.

A study on BE awareness levels was conducted by the Australian Quality Council and Deloittes-Touche-Tohmatsu (2000) in Australia and reported high levels of framework awareness and use, with between 70 percent of Australian organizations (and around 90 percent of its public sector organizations) reportedly being aware of the ABEF, and around 34 percent making use of it.

Grigg and Mann (2008) are reporting their global survey statistics: international custodians were asked to assess the extent to which BE awareness had changed in their country over the last three years. Most custodians (75 percent) indicated a "slight" or "substantial" increase, with one (UK) indicating levels remaining the same, and three (Sweden, Australia and Ireland) indicating that levels may have "decreased slightly." Two countries (Brazil and Canada) indicated that awareness had increased substantially and were asked to provide reasons why this may be the case. Brazil put the increase down to an increased number of national, regional and sectoral programs/awards (now 49 awards in total), and to "the increase of the number of universities that have used BE in administration." Canada cited their "healthy workplace framework," which has "led to more organizations being aware of business excellence in general."

Despite the prevalence of national BE awards and frameworks, awareness among organizations of their national framework may be lower than is estimated. Grigg and Mann's (2008) awareness survey in Australia reported lower levels of BE awareness than had been indicated in previous studies. Custodian organizations generally report that awareness is increasing in their countries, although SAI Global is one of three custodians who felt that BE awareness was on the decline. Grigg and Mann (2008) findings support that view. As a custodian's role is typically to increase BE awareness and use levels, they concluded that substantially more had to be done to raise awareness of the ABEF throughout Australia, and recommended that SAI continue to undertake BE awareness and use surveys in future, so that the ongoing impact of its BE strategies can be assessed.

Therefore, the recommendations include providing a high priority to forming strong relationships/partnerships with organizations that have a vested interest in the success of BE such as the government and industry/membership-based associations (for example through formation of a steering group to achieve their buy-in); marketing to CEOs and senior business executives; improving the website; providing low-cost guides and literature on the framework and its use; and increasing the pool of evaluators (traditionally quite static) to foster more widespread promotion.

1.2   Excellence Models' Evergreen Characteristics

The *Journal of Management History* published a special issue titled "Our dreams of excellence" at the year's end on the topic of excellence with the guest editor Dahlgaard-Park (2007). She stated in her editorial that research into excellence had taken a high flight in recent years despite the fact that there was no unanimity yet about the definition of excellence, let alone about the factors that influence sustained excellence. She also proposed a definition of the notion of excellence in the context of quality management, referring to it as "upgrading the level of organizational management to a level of excellence, which is necessary to provide excellent results, i.e. products and services which delight the customers." Dahlgaard-Park ended her editorial by expressing the hope that the content of the special issue would provide readers with building blocks for future excellence.

The following statement is quoted from Warren Bennis and Burt Nanus, from their book "Leaders" published in 1985 (Bennis and Nanus, 1985):

> This is an era marked with rapid and spastic change. The problems of organizations are increasingly complex. There are too many ironies, polarities, dichotomies, dualities, ambivalences, paradoxes, confusions, contradictions, contraries, and messes for any organization to understand and deal with. One can pick up a paper any day of the week and find indications of this inordinate complexity. Traditional information sources and management techniques have become less effective or obsolete. Linear information, linear thinking and incremental strategies are no match for the turbulence of today's business climate.

The following second statement is a more recent description from the 2009 book *The Death of Modern Management* by Owen (2009). He is stating that there are five major "strands of revolution" emerging:

1. There is the strategic revolution in which competitors no longer play to the rules of the game but create their own market place.
2. There is a shift of power revolution in which power goes from shareholders to managers, from the West to the rest of the world, from producers to consumers, and from the unskilled to the skilled.
3. In the knowledge revolution, having ideas is far more important than having capital.
4. In the organizational structure revolution, traditional organizational boundaries are blurring and even collapsing, giving way to more "fluid" structures.
5. Finally, because of the freedom revolution, employees are no longer at the mercy of an all-powerful employer.

Instead they can move their "human capital" around to workplaces they like. Managers think that the times they are living in are unique and that the things they need to do to achieve excellence are special, but is this really true? In the book *Managing* by Mintzberg (2009), the section "Managing in times of less change than you think" states:

> For all the fashionable management hype about leadership, it is unfashionable management that is being practiced and its fundamental characteristics have not changed.

Managers deal with different issues as time moves forward, but not with different managing. The job does not change. Despite the great fuss we make about change, the fact is that basic aspects of human behavior – and what could be more basic than managing and leading? – remain rather stable.

Tengblad (2006) also claims that the empirical data show that new work practices are combined with older practices, both in complex and context-specific ways. Several other researchers have found in a number of empirical studies of middle managers that only small changes in managerial work had taken place over the years as managers were basically still responsible for the results of their organizational units and their focus was therefore on monitoring and managing performance (Hales, 1990; Hales and Tamangani, 1996; Hales and Mustapha, 2000). Watson (2001) also found that managerial behavior is of a relatively stable nature. Tolmie et al. (2003) utilize the concepts of "virtual organization" and "virtual teamwork" in their study by managers in a major UK retail bank and found that there is recognizable change in the work of such managers at the level of content and resources, but there is no fundamental change in the interactional competences involved. They conclude that even with changing organizational objectives, requirements and roles, the primary resources that managers and employees use to deal with these changes are not so much new "virtual" ones but rather the old, trusted ones.

Many authors have started proclaiming from the later part of the twentieth century that organizations would significantly change and as a result managerial practices to achieve excellence would also have to be adapted (Drucker, 1988; Handy, 1989; Kanter, 1989; Peters, 1989; Morgan, 1993). Later researchers indeed found changes. For example, Worrall and Cooper (2004) found in their study that the changing nature of managerial work in England and the impact of different forms of organizational change on managers' perceptions of the organizations they work in, and some forms of notable change such as redundancy and flatter organization that have had particularly damaging effects on managers' experiences in the workplace and on their behaviors within and beyond their organizations. Clarke (1998) has also described the changing role of middle managers because of the reorganizing, rationalization and change management programs sweeping through modern-day organizations. Quinn et al. (2000) listed that the pressing problems in modern organizations keep us up at night and proclaimed the need for new managerial styles to cope with these problems.

The above contradictory findings in the literature raise questions about the validity of the outcomes of studies into excellence which have become increasingly popular in the past three decades. In the wake of the landmark books *In Search of Excellence* by Peters and Waterman (1982), the best sellers *Built to Last* by Collins and Porras (1994), *Good to Great* by Collins (2001), and *The World is Flat: A Brief History of the Twenty-First Century* by Friedman (2006), there has been a strong interest among academics and business leaders in identifying the factors of high performance (O'Reilly and Pfeffer, 2000; Hess and Kazanjian, 2006; Porras et al., 2007; Thoenig and Waldman, 2007; Gottfredson and Schaubert, 2008; Simons, 2008; Tappin and Cave, 2008; Spear, 2009). During review of these articles, specific attention has been paid to enterprise resources which can create sustainable success. Pitelis and Teece (2009) noticed that it is widely recognized that intra-enterprise factors are more important in explaining the enterprise profitability than industry-level factors. Therefore, the resource-based view of the enterprise has been researched into the factors that create excellence and provides sustainable competitive advantage (Lockett et al., 2009) and the theory of dynamic capabilities (Peteraf and Barney, 2003; Easterby-Smith et al., 2009; Teece, 2009).

When reviewing these articles and books written on excellence, it is very surprisingly noticed that – although many authors claim universal validity of their findings – many different elements which potentially create excellence are found. Which of these elements are found seems to depend on the personal views and interests of the researchers, the time period when the research was conducted, or the values assigned to these elements. Hence, this can validate the contradictory findings on the changing properties of the enterprises, business executives' responsibilities and activities and the structure developed for excellence. At the same time, it is difficult to distinguish an overall set of elements which describe excellence in general and through time. Therefore, it is imperative that a clear excellence model is constructed so that generalization can take place. The developed model would utilize the literature review, whether the elements (factors) that create excellence, as found in the literature, are constant over time, i.e. have been valid in the past decades or so and therefore may be assumed to be predictive for the future. Utilizing the basic definition of Dahlgaard-Park (2007) and building on it: achieving enterprise excellence which should lead to a high-performance enterprise achieving sustainable competitive advantage, financial and non-financial results that are better than those of its competition over a period of time of at least five years (de Wall and Frijns, 2009; de Wall, 2013) as well as managing the enterprise risk. These characteristics are always critical for creating and sustaining the enterprise excellence, and the executive enterprise leadership must always has to take the leading actions in their enterprise to excellence and superior results.

1.3   Development of the Enterprise Excellence (EE) Model

Research articles are identifying various elements including innovation, products, people, intelligence and market to compete customer satisfaction, while expecting financial growth in revenue and profitability and reduction in a business cycle time. Businesses have to have their vision and mission, and market growth strategy to support the enterprise growth strategy. Customer needs are changing with technology, therefore enterprises have to innovate and produce products to meet or exceed customer needs as well as core competency to support the innovated products. With innovated products and changing technologies, enterprises have to be transformed to stay competitive. These activities support the development of growth strategy, but without executing these strategies, enterprises would not achieve their goals and sustain their competitive advantage. There are various supportive activities including business structure, continuous improvement and business assessment. These activities must also support the growth strategy. Executive enterprise leadership has to lead as well as support these activities to achieve the enterprise growth strategy.

Another critical element which is not generally discussed in these articles is "enterprise risk." Risk management in general can encompass a wide variety of risk that any enterprise faces. Some risk exposures may be harmful, but will not threaten the overall health of the enterprise or its ability to ultimately meet its business objectives. For example, a temporary electricity outage or a chemical spill in the manufacturing facility can result in a short-term problem or customer dissatisfaction, but once recovered, the enterprise can quickly be back on track. Other more significant risk events can be catastrophic, resulting in losses that can not only impair the ability of the enterprise to meet its objectives, but may also threaten the survival of the enterprise – for example, the credit crises of 2007. These more significant risk exposures have given rise to the enterprise risk management (ERM).

Therefore, the top elements of the EE are the enterprise growth strategy and the enterprise risk management (ERM). There are various elements under each top level elements, e.g., business vision and mission; innovative growth ideas; market growth and core competency are some of the elements under the enterprise growth strategy. Business vision and mission, and innovative growth ideas give birth to innovative product(s) to meet or exceed the customer needs and provide sustainable competitive advantage. These innovated products are then developed through various elements of enterprise excellence and at the same time minimizing the enterprise risk elements. For example, after WWII, Boeing was the main source of commercial airplanes manufacturer in the non-communist world. During 1950s and 1960s, energy was not the issue and the airlines were very much interested in having a larger plane for the long-distance flights. With Boeing's vision and mission, product innovation ideas, their core competencies and the market demand which helped the company in mitigating their risk factors and developed the product known as

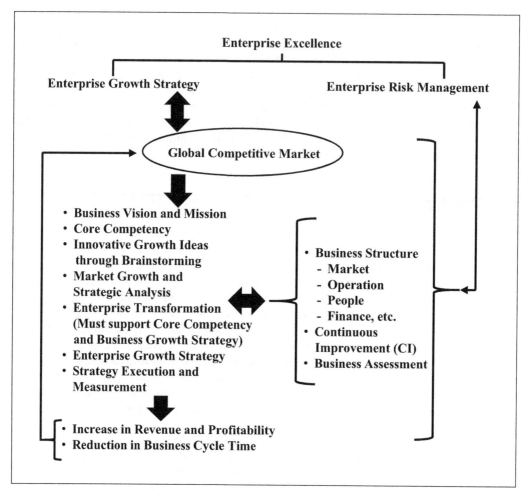

Figure 1.2   The initial conceptual EE model

Boeing 747 (Jumbo jet) plane during late 1960s and the plane went in flights in 1970s (Kumar, 2014).

The initially developed conceptual model of the EE (Figure 1.2) was based on the above-identified elements by Kumar (2009). The model was utilized on the commercial side of the Boeing business and the Airbus companies to validate the model structure (Kumar, 2014). This is a "C" level model where the executive enterprise leadership works with the board of directors to accomplish the EE. Some major issues were recognized with this model (Figure 1.2):

- Global Competitive Market should be a part of Market Growth and Strategic Analysis. In the current global economy, almost all industries are participating globally and to develop their market growth strategy, they would have to participate globally. Therefore, global competition is one of the critical elements in market strategy and not a separate issue.
- The key elements linked to Enterprise Growth Strategy (EGS) are:
  - Business Vision and Mission.
  - Innovative Growth Ideas.

- Core Competency.
- Market Growth Strategy.

- When an enterprise is innovative and developing products to meet or exceed market needs, its core competency must also meet or exceed the product requirements. As customer needs and technologies are changing while the enterprises want to grow, they would need to innovate and produce products to meet or exceed the market demand; this would require the enterprise transformation to support the enterprise growth strategy. Therefore, the enterprise transformation must support the enterprise growth strategy as a separate element.
- Enterprise Execution and Measurement is not required to develop the enterprise growth strategy, but the execution process helps to achieve the growth strategy goals and building sustainable competitive advantage while measurements tell the enterprise executives how well the growth strategy goals are achieved. Hence, the activity "strategy execution and measurement" is the most critical activity and should be beyond the planning phase of the enterprise growth strategy.
- Business structure, Continuous improvement (CI) and Business assessment have a direct relationship with the enterprise growth strategy, but the "C" level (executive enterprise) leadership generally does not directly participate in day-to-day activities, and the operational leadership leads these responsibilities. Therefore, these elements should not be included in the "C' level EE model.
- The "C" level leadership believes that they can exploit risk to their advantage and generate value to the enterprise. Risk management concept is to operate in an environment in control, not a controlled environment (Lam, 2003). Risk is vital to the business world so that those organizations that are able to overcome their challenges can show the rest how it is done (Wade, 2010). For example, historically validating the concept where auto companies like Ford and General Motors in the 1930s and 1940s, computer hardware companies like IBM in the 1950s and 1960s and Dell in 1990s, software companies like Microsoft and Intel in the 1980s and 1990s, and new companies like Google, Apple and Facebook in the twenty-first century. Therefore, enterprises face the parallel challenges of growing revenue and earnings, and managing risk. A thriving enterprise must identify and meet or exceed customer needs with quality products and/or services; and correctly make business and investment decisions that will lead to future revenue and profit opportunities.

Hence, enterprise risk management (ERM) is an emerging high-level requirement at enterprises and organizations where the management of risk is integrated and coordinated across the enterprise as a whole. ERM takes a holistic approach to risk management – moving from a fragmented methodology to integrated and broadly focused. ERM expands the process to include not just risks associated with unintended losses, but also financial, strategic, operational and other risks. The high-level elements which are directly linked to enterprise risk management (ERM) are:

- Strategic Risk Management (SRM);
- Integrated Risk Management (IRM); and
- Other Risk Areas.

The upgraded enterprise excellence (EE) model is presented in Figure 1.3.

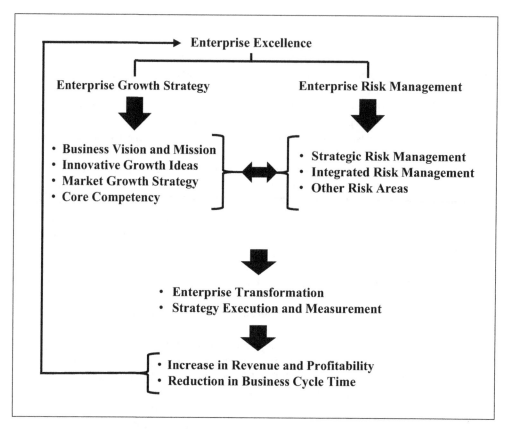

Figure 1.3   The upgraded EE model

Therefore, EE would be achieved by developing and executing a sustainable growth strategy while minimizing the enterprise risk, which also provides sustainable competitive advantage (Kumar, 2010a) to:

- support markets and products growth;
- acquire new or expand business;
- improve margin;
- increase revenue and profitability;
- reduce business cycle time.

The quantitative values for revenue, profitability and business cycle time as well as risk management would vary from industry to industry, but could be compared within the same industry. Every business offers products for the selected market based on their vision and mission, innovation, core competency, market competition and risk management. Risk Management is the identification, assessment and prioritization of risk followed by coordinated and economical application of resources to minimize, monitor and control the probability and/or impact of unfortunate events or to maximize the realization of opportunities (Hubbard, 2009). Therefore, risk is not just as threat but also as opportunity. Risk can come from various areas including project failure (at any phase of the project – from development through sustained life cycle), financial markets, credit risk, accidents, legal liabilities and natural disaster.

1.3.1   ENTERPRISE GROWTH STRATEGY (EGS)

Enterprise growth is an integrated approach affecting every employee, every functional area and strategy within the organization. It relies on transformational change management. It is very different from implementing the firm's business strategies or executing process changes in isolation (Kumar, 2010a).

Enterprise growth calls for more than superficial change. These changes can be in response to marketplace events or to address underperformance, but enterprise growth is quite different from a company's turnaround in financial difficulties. It will inevitably be the biggest single internal program that any enterprise undertakes. It is expected to disrupt the existing business model (Kumar, 2010a). There are several questions that have to be answered during development and execution of enterprise growth, Kumar (2010b), such as:

- What must enterprise do to grow?
- What do leaders transform?
- What product, market, and/or service do they need to grow?
- What are the vital signs that growth is underway?

It is important to note that successful enterprise growth is likely to require significant investments in skills, processes, organization, and technology. Enterprise growth initiatives may be driven by external opportunities which will force the development of strategies such as targeted market (emerging markets or pursuing vertical market), value proposition (providing integrated solution), product and/or service offerings (changing the products and services provided) (Kumar, 2009). Key elements of the enterprise growth strategy are:

- Business Vision and Mission.
- Innovative Growth Ideas.
- Market Growth Strategy.
- Core Competency.

1.3.1.1   Business vision and mission

"Vision" is one of the most important concepts for developing and motivating any type of enterprise. Vision can, however, be easily confused with strategy, mission, values or purpose. Companies that enjoy lasting success have core values and a core purpose that stays fixed while their enterprise strategies and practices are continuously adjusted in the changing world (Collins and Porras, 1996).

The dynamics of preserving the core while stimulating progress is the reason that companies such as United Technologies Corporation (UTC), General Electric Company (GE), Caterpillar, Hewlett-Packard, and Motorola became superior corporations able to renew themselves and achieve outstanding long-term performance. For example, GE continually questions its structure and revamps its processes while preserving the founding ideals the company believes in (to become the most competitive enterprise in the world by being number one or number two in market share in every business the company is in – John F. Welch, Jr., CEO 1981–2001). UTC was recognized as an environmental leader in 2009 while UTC's CEO George David's vision of early 1990s was to be environmentally friendly enterprise.

A mission statement should provide a clear and concise description of any firm's (or individual's) overall purpose. Key characteristics of a mission statement are:

- Entity/organization/enterprise must have a reason for existence.
- It embodies its philosophies, ambitions, qualities, etc.
- Mission statement should be clear and no complex and awkward wording.
- Mission statement should be concise: The fewer words the better; prefer less than 25 words.
- Measurable goals with some deadline.
- Catchy and memorable: easy to recall and also easy to explain.

The mission statement should also be able to answer the following questions:

- *What business are you in?* Ask yourself this question and do not narrow yourself down. One of the classic business examples is automobiles, where the US manufacturers lost a chance to grow in the beginning of the twenty-first century because they mis-defined themselves. They thought they were in the business of running cars on roads and highways. They did not understand that they were in the business of transporting people and goods. When foreign competition grew, the US manufacturers were left behind.
- *Are your customers satisfied?* Leading experts look for customer satisfaction goals in the mission statement. Developing customer care program depends on communicating and spreading the idea, as well as identifying the importance within a company.
- *What is your workplace philosophy?* Your company's stand in fundamental issues such as maintaining creative work environment and building respect for diversity.
- *Does your company believe in value-based marketing?* Value-based developed marketing framework helps business leaders and their associates to understand business better. This framework starts with a business value proposition, which states what benefits a business offers, to whom, and at what relative price level. For example:
  - This automobile manufacturer offers a reliable and safe automobile for families at a relative price premium.
  - This supermarket offers variety of fresh fruits and vegetables at low prices.
- What does the organization do?
- How does the organization do it?
- For whom does the organization do it?

Therefore, the mission statement should enable large groups of individuals to work in a unified direction toward a common cause (goal), passionate, and energizing. It should be compelling, as well as risky and challenging.

1.3.1.2 *Innovative growth ideas*

Innovation is the development of new product/value/idea through solutions that meet or exceed existing and/or new customer requirements (needs) (Kumar, 2009). "Innovation generally refers to renewing, changing or creating more effective processes, products or ways of doing things," Australian Government Initiative (business.gov.au). For businesses, this could mean implementing new ideas, creating dynamic products or improving existing services. Innovation can be a catalyst for the growth and success of any business, and help businesses to adapt and grow in the marketplace (Kumar, 2014).

Innovation strategy helps companies in three ways: exciting its customers, outperforming competitors and building a new product portfolio (Bowonder et al., 2010). IBM was involved in transformation from computer maker to e-business servers for a large-scale, open systems computing during 1990s which required courage, focus and commitment at all levels of the enterprise (Meyer et al., 2005). There are various innovation approaches in the literature, for example, end-user-innovation, Von Hippel (1988), chain-linked model of innovation (Kline, 1985), companies' growth through innovation (Davila et al., 2006) and research and development innovation model (Mark et al., 2008). Robotic engineer Engelberger (1982) strongly believes that innovation requires three things:

1. A recognized need.
2. Competent people with relevant technology.
3. Financial support.

1.3.1.3 Market growth strategy

A simple definition of market growth is when demand for a particular product and/or service increases over time. Market growth is considered slow if consumer is not ready to adopt the product and/or service, the product and/or service is not meeting customer needs or the customer is not ready to pay the asking price. Market growth is considered rapid when the demand is high and customer finds the product and/or service useful for the price level as well as meeting customer needs. For example, a new technology might only be marketable to a small group of customers, but as the price of the technology decreases and its usefulness in daily life increases, more customers would increase demand. From business perspective, the goal of any business growth is to increase revenue and profitability with a reduced business cycle time that is more productive, innovative and export-led, delivers high-value products and/or services for customers and markets around the world.

Kumar (2010a) has defined a product-market growth relationship. Marketers have to consider four ways of relationship between product and market via present and/or new markets, existing and/or new products. This relationship can be written as follows which creates four possibilities:

1. Present (existing) market and existing product-market growth can be achieved through:
   - gaining competitors' customers;
   - attracting non-users of your product;
   - current customers to use more of your product.
2. Present (existing) market and new product-market growth can be achieved through:
   - attracting new customers through new products;
   - meeting additional needs of present customers.
3. New market and existing product-market growth can be achieved if customers in the new market buy your existing product against your competitors.
4. New market and new product–this may be diversification in your business. If market research is done properly, this will open a new market and would provide market growth.

1.3.1.4 Core competency

History reveals that before the term was coined, it was known as special skills developed within an organization based on the skills, knowledge and the experience of employees along with the available equipment and the market requirements. For example, during the 1980s when aerospace industry was machining very hard titanium and nickel alloy parts then the special machining skill was known as special skill.

Prahalad and Hamel (1990) coined the term "core competency" and identified it as the collective learning and coordination skills behind the firm's product lines. They made the case that core competencies are the source of competitive advantage and enable the firm to introduce an array of new products and services. Several measures have been proposed to identify unique resources and capabilities: resources and capabilities are important for understanding the sources of sustained competitive advantage for firms (Barney, 1991); when formulating business strategy, resources-based strategy provides the competitive advantage (Grant, 1991); resources competence provides the competitive advantage (Hamel, 1994); and competitive advantage is due to assets, processes and evolutionary methods (Teece et al., 1997).

The generalized terms such as resource, asset, capability and competence are not clearly explained in connection with competence theory; they become an obstacle in understanding many contemporary management concepts (Hafeez et al., 2002). They are categorizing resources into physical, intellectual and cultural assets and showing relationships between assets, capabilities, competencies and core competencies. There are several definitions in the literature: Knowledge view, Leonard-Barton (1992), Network view, Klein and Hiscocks (1994) and Harmony view (Sanchez et al., 1996).

Therefore, core competency is the fundamental knowledge, ability, or a specific subject area or skill set. It can take various forms, including technicality of subject matter know-how, a reliable process and/or unique understanding of material flow from supplier to manufacturer to end customer. It requires technically qualified and dedicated employees with a deep commitment to working across organizational boundaries, good market coverage, leadership support, etc. Core competencies are the collective learning in organizations, and involve how to coordinate diverse skills: marketing, product design, production, distribution, etc. and integrate multiple streams of technologies. These are the skills that the organization possesses and sets it apart from its competition. These skills are the sources of competitive advantage as well as the building blocks to future opportunities (Kumar, 2014).

1.3.2   ENTERPRISE RISK MANAGEMENT

Risk management is a process where risk has to be identified, assessed and prioritized so that proper resources could be utilized economically to minimize the impact of unfortunate events and/or to maximize the realization of opportunities. Pullan and Murray-Webster (2011) have set out a very practical approach where risk management process can deliver value through effective facilitation. This developed process utilizes the human aspects of risk and risk attitude and the facilitation capacity of the individual. They have identified five areas: avoiding pitfalls, understanding of risk management, understanding your role, tried and tested tips for each step of the risk management process and running risk workshops.

Growing revenue and earnings are the expected goals of any enterprise growth strategy, but at the same time managing risks. The following key risk elements are discussed:

* Strategic Risk Management.
* Integrated Risk Management.
* Other Risk areas.

1.3.2.1   Strategic Rsk Management (SRM)

Strategic Risk Management (SRM) is a business discipline that drives deliberation and action regarding uncertainties and untapped opportunities that affect an organization's strategy and strategy execution. The importance of SRM cannot be overemphasized. As technology and the world are changing, risks to enterprises grow ever more prevalent. To maintain a strong SRM philosophy, it is imperative that business leaders are taking initiative to remaining prepared to handle emergencies that might arise. SRM elements could include such diverse areas as examining the possibility of poor business decisions to failing to grab growth opportunities that might present themselves. Every element of a business should be incorporated in a successful SRM philosophy, including every level of enterprise personnel. For example, when a new product or service comes along that can help the enterprise and also can lower risk elements, such as a new form of security, the SRM leadership would incorporate the new technology.

The strategic risk assessment process should be designed such that it can be tailored to an organization's specific needs and culture, and the resultant reporting must reflect and support an enterprise's culture so the process can be embedded and owned by business leaders. Ultimately, if the strategic risk assessment process is not embedded and owned by the leadership as an integral part of the business processes, the risk management process will rapidly lose its impact and will not add to or deliver on its expected role. Business leadership teams and boards of directors must challenge themselves and their organizations to move up the strategic risk management learning curve. Developing strategic risk management processes and capabilities can provide a strong foundation for improving risk management and governance. Boards may want to consider engaging independent advisers to advise and educate themselves on these matters.

1.3.2.2   Integrated Risk Management (IRM)

Integrated risk management is a relatively new concept and there is no one standard model. Each enterprise must design a framework which should be tailored according to their business mix, industry sector, organizational structure, goals and risk tolerance. Senior business leaders must take the ownership of the concept to integrate risk management in their enterprise. The concept can align the corporate and risk management objectives, set the organization's risk culture and institute a process to ensure its full integration. The integrated risk management structure should set a clear control infrastructure, establishing policies, procedures and authority limits for each area of the organization (Nottingham, 1996). Further, the structure should clarify the train of reporting relationships and the division of accountability, risk and ownership.

Integrated risk management is quickly becoming one of the critical tools which leading organizations are adopting to steer them through turbulent and volatile operating environments (Nottingham, 1996). Just as organizations have come to recognize that business processes cannot be separated, so too they are realizing that risk must be managed on a holistic basis.

For example, Singla and Sagar (2012) have conducted a research utilizing the concept of integrated risk management service for agriculture, as well as identifying different risk management practices that may be offered in conjunction with crop insurance, to address the various problems and challenges being faced by farmers and by insurance companies. They have used an inductive approach of developing theory from case studies using within-case and cross-case analysis. However, apart from exploring different elements from case studies, some of the existing concepts have been reviewed from the literature for their application in agricultural risk management. *They have found that* an integrated framework for risk management in agriculture has been developed by inductively exploring the various elements that may be successfully interlinked with the crop insurance to tackle the various agricultural risks more efficiently and effectively. Their research could be used as a basis for new product development in agricultural risk management through the use of this integrated approach of risk management and the different elements that have been identified to improve the effectiveness of crop insurance.

1.3.2.3   Other risk areas

There are various risk areas in any enterprise including equality risk (Morden, 2011); operational risk; political risk (McKellar, 2010); Customs risk (Truel, 2010); ethical risk (Patetta Rotta 2010); technology/product and competitive risk. Some of these are briefly discussed below:

Equality: The concepts of equality is concerned with ensuring that people are not discriminated against unfairly, but are instead given the same and equal opportunities. In a global ongoing economic crisis, any growth resource should be fully utilized to pull out of the crisis. Nevertheless, despite advanced domestic legislation and extended international regulation, women's labor is a resource of growth still not fully utilized globally. Different reasons explain this fact. Often, domestic decision-makers and international organizations are held responsible for it. Less attention is paid to the effect on labor conditions globally, and on women's labor utilization particularly, of two hidden players acting behind the curtains: multinational enterprises (MNEs) and non-governmental organizations (NGOs) supporting women's rights, Munin (2013).

Diversity: the concept of diversity involves the valuing and respecting of difference, whether this difference (for example, race, disability, gender, etc.) is visible or not. There is a need to recognize that people are not all the same and that they have different but equally valuable life experience, knowledge and skills to offer.

Ethics and environment: Stainer and Stainer (1997) have argued that corporate responsibility must span over the legal, social, economic and technological domains. Placing environmental system standards and auditing in their business strategic roles and gives a stakeholder approach to environmental management with its relationship to sustainability, economic growth and improved quality of life. They have also outlined the importance and relevance of "green" yardsticks in non-financial performance measurement terms. Their analyses of ethical dimensions, stressing that, by developing an ethical corporate culture, enterprises can create both a competitive advantage and environmental excellence.

Risk-mitigating in IT value: To create IT value as well as mitigating risk, the company's mission and strategic direction must be distilled into business needs for IT applications. This requires alignment of the company's business, operational, and IT strategies. Mechanisms should be in place to ensure that the respective planning functions cross-pollinate and remain synchronized, so that business needs are met on an ongoing basis. An IT investment and prioritization process should be in place, facilitated by an IT strategy or steering committee, to provide a way to assess the cost/benefits of the IT investment (Robinson, 2005).

1.3.3   ENTERPRISE TRANSFORMATION (ET)

In today's globally competitive market, enterprises are trying to achieve their excellence through executing their growth strategy while managing risk. As technology and market requirements are changing, enterprises need to transform and create meaningful changes, including modification/upgrading/new products and services, and similarly modification/upgrading/new processes before executing the growth strategy while managing risk. Contemporary enterprises face enormous uncertainties. For example, defense procurements in twenty-first century may no longer be dominated by traditional weapon systems. Health-care delivery may transition from pay for services to payment for health outcomes. Intelligent sensing and control technology may morph the energy ecosystem. Similarly, there are many examples of substantial uncertainties in other industries such as education, finance and food (Rouse and Basole, 2010). There are, at least, two types of uncertainty (Zhongyuan et al., 2011). First, the enterprise may not be sure of the nature of the impending change. For example, the direction of the change may be clear, but its timing and magnitude may be uncertain. The second type of uncertainty concerns how best to respond to change. What should one's offerings and processes become? Given insights into or answers of these questions, how can one best allocate resources between the enterprise one has and the enterprise one is striving to become? Thus, the leaders of these enterprises must wrestle with the question of whether they should invest in becoming better at what they are currently doing versus investing in doing new things that will better match emerging market desires. In other words, should they focus on business process improvement or enterprise transformation? Schumpeter (2009) reported that the Fortune 500 has seen a 200 percent turnover in the past 25 years. Thus, the challenge of enterprise transformation has been, and continues to be, very significant.

There is another part of the world where there have been dramatic changes since 1990. Among all the changes, the transition from a command economy to a market economy has been one of the most important peace events of the 1990s. For example, the developments after the fall of the Berlin Wall in 1989 and the dissolution of the Soviet Union in 1991 sharply accelerated this process of transition. The three important aspects of economic reform in transition economies (i.e., former socialist countries including Russia) are:

(a) liberalization;
(b) privatization; and
(c) globalization.

Privatization remains a key step in the policies of transition economies to form a viable market-oriented economy. There are various methods of privatization such as restitution, direct sales, equity offerings, management–employee buy-outs and mass/voucher privatization. This process of reform and privatization has brought about a certain transformation of enterprises in Russia.

Business transformation is the key executive leadership initiative that attempts to align people, process and technology initiatives of an organization more closely with its business strategy and vision to support and help new business strategies and meet long-term objectives. Therefore, enterprises need to make continuous fundamental transformations – such as improving current business processes, performing entirely different tasks and conducting automated business processes – to maintain or gain competitive advantage. These transformations may increase value or decrease business cycle time, costs and uncertainties. However, it is difficult to choose transformations that deserve major investment without assessing the relative value of alternative transformations. Analyzing and redesigning business processes to ensure consistency with business requirements and information technology (IT) specifications is a critical factor for successful enterprise transformation (Cheng et al., 2012). The university setting contains a variety of research teams that specialize in solving specific technical problems, developing new products, or leading to new patents. Specifically, for small and medium-sized enterprises typically do not have sufficient resources to explore research and development. Thus, universities can play a role as their strategic partners. For example, the applications of the integrated information system with the partnership between university and businesses would provide the flexibility needed to achieve the best return via the use of an efficient database/IT solutions.

Social alliances are voluntary collaborations between business and social enterprises addressing social problems too complex to be solved by unilateral organizational action. Hence, social, economic and environmental dimensions of development continue to be the greatest challenges in the twenty-first century. Governments, international organizations, business and civil society can fulfill only one-third of the need to realize international goals focused on human and sustainable development, World Economic Forum (2004). Many countries are caught in a dilemma of implementing a model that promises strong economic growth with a social vision that incorporates their poor millions into the system and its benefits (Hartigan, 2004).

The convergence of economic, social and political pressures is fostering collaboration across various sectors of society (Gray, 1985; Austin, 2000) as a viable and necessary approach to dealing with complex social problems (Trist, 1983). Cross-sector alliances between business and social enterprises are formed explicitly to address social issues and causes that actively engage the partners on an ongoing basis (Selsky and Parker, 2005). These partnerships have become more prevalent in the recent years. United Nations Office for Partnerships alone partially funded about 500 cross-sector projects in 2009 with a total value of more than $1 billion (US) (United Nations Office for Partnership, 2009).

Most research on social alliances has been conducted in developed country contexts (e.g. Austin, 2000 and Berger et al., 2004). Even though there are numerous examples of studies on commercially derived cross-sectors collaborations targeting the poor as consumers at the base of the pyramid (Whitney and Kelkar, 2004; Prahalad, 2005b; London et al., 2006; Singer, 2006; Johnson, 2007; Sanchez et al., 2007; Seelos and Mair, 2007; Weiser, 2007; Perez-Aleman and Sandilands, 2008; Rashid and Rahman, 2009; Crawford-Mathis et al., 2010; Dahan et al., 2010; Webb et al., 2010), research on social alliances in subsistence marketplaces is limited.

1.3.4   STRATEGY EXECUTION AND MEASUREMENT

Enterprise transformation leads to strategy execution to achieve the strategy goals and build sustainable competitive advantage. Measurement provides the information about how well the strategy is executed and should the execution be considered as achieving the enterprise excellence. Therefore, strategy execution is followed by the enterprise transformation, which is a connecting link between the strategy development and execution.

The criticality of executing strategy effectively has been realized at every walk of strategic leadership evolution (Hrebiniak and Joyce, 1984; Wooldridge and Floyd, 1992; Kaplan and Norton, 1996a; Bossidy and Charan, 2002a; Higgins, 2005; Brenes et al., 2008; Martin, 2010; Kaplan and Norton, 2013). However, many scholars (Hrebiniak, 2006; Noble, 1999) reviewed that focus on formulating a unique strategy has been the dominating feature of research in strategic leadership. Several scholars, especially since last decade, questioned the proposition of brilliant strategy and underlined the importance of execution (Bossidy and Charan, 2002a; Martin, 2010). They argued that even a simple strategy brilliantly executed could bring enterprise success. However, scholars also demonstrate that enterprises cannot successfully execute strategy if strategic analysis and formulation is poor (Hrebiniak, 2006).

Effectiveness of strategy depends both on the formulation and execution. Though multiple frameworks are available for strategy formulation as well as execution, but the emphasis on the execution is lacking. The majority of firms fail to execute because they do not focus resources on priorities – and in a majority of cases, employees have not been informed of the strategy. The fundamental business goal remains constant: increase revenue and profit, and return value to shareholders. Therefore, the objective is straightforward: sell a product or a service to customers to meet or exceed their need. Executing a strategy to achieve this objective in today's unforgiving business environment is not nearly as straightforward. Global markets, intense competition, compliance constraints, disruptive technologies, and talent shortages are all pressuring companies to become more agile so that they can constantly adjust to a world of accelerated change. This condition of constant adjustment forces enterprises to embark on a non-stop cycle of strategy development, execution, measurement and refinement. Enterprises that can effectively manage their performance within this steady cycle of change are well positioned for success; enterprises that cannot are likely to suffer a less fortunate fate.

Various topics impacting strategy execution are discussed in Chapter 5, including organizational resources alignment, organizational behavior, researchers' approaches for strategy execution and elements impacting strategy execution.

The industrial-age competitive advantages of the nineteenth century and many of the twentieth century businesses were achieved through their investment and management of tangible assets such as facility, equipment and inventory (Chandler, 1990). In tangible assets dominated economy, financial measurements were adequate to support the growth strategy. Income statements could capture the expenses associated with the use of these tangible assets to produce revenues and profits, but by the end of the twentieth century, intangible assets became the major source for competitive advantage. Literature search and proposed methods on measurements are discussed as well as proposed the measurement metrics.

Enterprise Growth Strategy (EGS)

2

Enterprise growth is an integrated approach affecting every employee, every functional area and strategy within the organization. It relies on transformational change management. It is very different from implementing the firm's business strategies or executing process changes in isolation (Kumar, 2010a). Growth emerges as an inevitable necessity especially under the global competition and contemporary economic conditions. The results of activities such as acquisition, joint venture and merger are not just merger, acquisition and joint venture but very specifically are growth, staying power and sustaining competitive advantage. Gumus and Apak (2011) suggest that the enterprises to achieve business success and to acquire growth, staying power and sustaining competitive advantage. It is underlined that in order to achieve these goals, the enterprises should analyze their corporate and financial structures and settle their strategies in line with the results of the analyses.

Enterprise growth calls for more than superficial change. These changes can be in response to marketplace events or to address underperformance, but enterprise growth is quite different from a company's turnaround in financial difficulties. It will inevitably be the biggest single internal program that any enterprise undertakes and it is expected to disrupt the existing business model (Kumar, 2010a). There are several questions that have to be answered during development and execution of enterprise growth, Kumar (2010b), such as:

- What must enterprise do to grow?
- What do leaders transform?
- What product, market, and/or service do they need to grow?
- What are the vital signs that growth is underway?

It is important to note that successful enterprise growth is likely to require significant investments in skills, processes, organization and technology. Enterprise growth initiatives may be driven by external opportunities which will force the development of strategies such as targeted market (emerging market or pursuing vertical market), value proposition (providing integrated solution), product/service offerings (changing the products and services provided) (Kumar, 2009).

Multinational Enterprises (MNEs) and their international locations: There is little theoretical or empirical research on the influence of firm characteristics on the specific location choices of MNE subsidiaries (McCann and Mudambi, 2005; Beugelsdijk et al., 2010). More specifically, the attraction of MNEs to "global cities" has been largely overlooked by international business scholars. At the same time, economic geographers have carefully studied the concept of location, one strand of economic geography research has been preoccupied with the propensity of firms and employees to cluster in geographic space as regions become more integrated, whereas another has focused more specifically on the emergence and evolution of global cities (Jacobs, 1984; Friedmann, 1986;

Beaverstock, 2002). Primary research focus is on the characteristics of economic agglomeration, however, with less attention to the behavior of multinational firms, and the way in which their heterogeneous capabilities and strategies interact with location.

When researching the literature in international business scholarship, on topics such as those on geographic scope (Goerzen and Beamish, 2003; Asmussen, 2009), culture (Makino and Neupert, 2000), expatriates (Belderbos and Heijltjes, 2005), and entry mode (Tihanyi et al. 2005), just to name a few, has been to use the nation state – defined by national political boundaries – as the basic unit of analysis when examining location. But some authors argue that these large geographical units are often too coarse to provide an accurate picture of the role of MNEs in economic globalization, since the trends of outsourcing and new technologies as well as economic policies of liberalization, have made nation states less significant as units of analysis (Krugman, 1991; Brown et al. 2010). Ultimately, firms choose a specific place within a country as the location for their investments, and at the country or even the regional level of analysis these micro-location decisions are obscured. In fact, recent research on MNE location strategy has already begun to consider the subnational level, including industry clusters (Pouder and St John, 1996; Gordon and McCann, 2000; Porter, 2001) and regions (Ma et al., 2012). At the same time, international leadership scholars are focusing their attention on "global cities." The prominent example of these cities are New York, Tokyo, London, Frankfort and Chicago; and these cities are characterized with high degree of centrality, influence in the world economy and also interconnected in global networks that provide an infrastructure for the global economy (Sassen, 1991 and 2012; Wall and van der Knaap, 2011).

There are some observers who have suggested that cities are becoming obsolete (Scott et al., 2001). This concept is based on the information that MNEs are among the most significant forces in the global economy and are acting as centrifugal forces for "offshoring" their operations (Bhagwati et al. 2004; Harrison and McMillan, 2006), expanding their worldwide networks of alliances and subsidiaries (Goerzen and Beamish, 2005; Goerzen, 2007), and moving their back-office operations from urban centers to outlying suburbs (Sassen, 2001). At the same time, state-of-the-art infrastructure and the specialized leadership expertise are required to make international systems and processes function which appear to be assembling in "global cities," and these emerging urban phenomena are providing a countering centripetal force in the global economy (Sassen, 1991, 2012). These global linkages are connecting these cities together and at the same time, network technologies such as the Internet have only accelerated this force (Sassen, 2001). These observations have provided an impetus to re-examine the relationship between global cities and MNE location strategy to shed new light on the MNE in geographic space.

Buckley and Ghauri (2004) have examined globalization in terms of conflicts between markets and economic leadership and suggested that the differential pace of globalization across markets presents a number of challenges to policy-makers in local, national and regional governments and in international institutions. They analyzed the changing location and ownership strategies of MNEs and they found that the increasingly sophisticated decision-making leadership in MNEs is slicing the activities of enterprise more finely and in finding optimum locations for each closely defined activity, the business leadership is deepening the international division of labor.

Local stakeholders in global cities are more likely to be exposed to international stimuli, therefore, tend to be more cosmopolitan – for example, through personal relationship transcending geographic space or expatriate (Sassen, 2002; Lorenzen and Mudambi, 2013). Riefler et al. (2011) have defined and operationalized cosmopolitanism with three secondary-type attitudes: open-mindedness to other countries and cultures, appreciation of diversity, and preference for international consumption. Such attitudes will lead foreign firms to be seen as more legitimate to the customers, suppliers, prospective employees and so on, many of whom themselves are foreign or have international experience and connections (Beaverstock, 2002). These MNEs also deal with various professional service providers including advertisers, accountants, lawyers and bankers who often have global reach, specializing in serving MNEs, and who may, in turn, lend local credibility to these MNEs, just as government institutions and policies in global cities may be more conducive to inward investment (Wu, 2000; Saito, 2003).

In the early research findings (Kindleberger, 1969) and Hymer (1976) found that foreign firms in host country markets face costs over and above those faced by their incumbent competitors, and several empirical studies have conducted after the initial findings and have provided evidence of such costs (Zaheer, 1995; Zaheer and Mosakowski, 1997; Mezias, 2002). These costs in the international business literature are known as liability of foreignness (LOF), and economic geographers are broadly define as "border effects," McCallum (1995) and the "frictions of distance," Appold (1995). In reference to MNE strategy, these liabilities are likely to affect both pre- and post-decisions by MNEs performance implications (Zaheer, 1995; Asmussen, 2009).

Study sample of Goerzen et al. (2013) had 77 percent MNEs to locate their foreign operations within global cities, which was clearly pointing to the importance of considering subnational levels when analyzing investment location decisions. Their results show that the MNE in geographic space is clearly attracted toward global cities that provide specific micro-locational advantages that appear to help mitigate the negative effects of the LOF. They have also identified the incremental costs (i.e., "friction") (international connectedness, advanced producer services, and cosmopolitan environment) associated with the "uncertainty," "discrimination," and "complexity" of doing business in a foreign environment. While global city attributes reduce the costs associated with the LOF for MNEs that locate within them, but this relationship varies with the underlying motive of the MNE (Nachum and Zaheer, 2005; Goerzen et al., 2013) and they also support their findings. A demand-driven market-seeking and market-serving activities, such as sales and distribution, are more likely to locate in global cities, supply driven efficiency-seeking and asset-seeking activities, such as production and R&D, are more likely to be located outside the global cities, either in the metropolitan areas surrounding these cities, or in the peripheral rural areas. Together, these findings provide further evidence for the importance of accounting for the nature of activities of subsidiaries in conjunction with locational attributes when studying subsidiary location (Enright, 2009) with the contention that MNEs invest on an activity-by-activity basis.

Hence the extent to which MNE headquarters contribute with positive value-added resources to the subsidiary (Mudambi and Swift, 2011) may impact its ability to overcome location-specific LOFs, thereby putting a premium on parent – subsidiary relations in location decisions (Dellestrand and Kappen, 2012). The initial work of Sassen (1991, 1994 and 2001) and others along with the later work of Goerzen et al. (2013) suggest clearly that urban agglomerations such as global cities have a significant impact on the location strategies of MNEs. Not only does this have a bearing on the global movement of capital; these findings also have implications for the international movement of people. Therefore, it is important, both for MNE business leaders responsible for the location strategy of their subsidiaries and for scholars interested in international business, to develop a better understanding of the influence of global cities as well as the opportunities to use the micro-locational attributes to advantage.

Environmental and Social strategies for the enterprise growth: The challenges and concern created by social needs, environmental changes and financial crises of 2007 have reinforced requirements to realize the potential of alternative business forms and social innovation (Murray, 2009; Scott-Cato and Hillier, 2010). Value-driven enterprises or social enterprises that operate in the incorrectly defined space between the for-profit and non-profit worlds – are seen by some to have particular strengths in simultaneously addressing social, environmental and economic needs (Pearce, 2003; Amin, 2009; Boyd et al., 2009).

The term "social enterprise" is contested and unclear, but it is used to refer to a set of organizations with primarily social purpose. These organizations generate a significant amount of their income from trading in goods and/or services (Chell, 2007; Bridge et al., 2009). The categories included are community enterprises, employee-owned businesses, development trusts, cooperatives, the trading divisions (arms) of charities, social firms and housing associations. Teasdale (2012) is pointing out that these are significant tensions inherent in the concept of social enterprise within recent policy discourses, specifically due to the diversity of organizational forms, motivation and expectations around their role and potential. One of the key dimensions of the traditional not-for-profit civil organizations is "social" to address social needs that the state and private sectors are either unwilling and/or unable to meet and also the notions of "alternative economic spaces," democratic governance and accountability. At the same time, according to Sepulveda (2009), the term "enterprise" lends itself to emphasizing business opportunities, neoliberal perspective, the efficiency of unfettered markets and a need to restrict the role of state, including transferring responsibilities to the private sector and civil society. Vickers and Lyon (2014) have examined some recent experiences of contrasting types of social enterprises, which claim to integrate economic, social and environmental objectives.

Environmentally motivated business executives/entrepreneurs can encompass a diverse range of measures to conserve resources, biodiversity and ecosystems, and therefore, protecting the life support and other economic functions of the environment (Shepherd and Patzelt, 2011). The provision of environmentally related sectors, for example, waste management and low-carbon technologies or services in the products/services of an enterprise can produce economic value in the form of monetary or employment outputs. This should also provide the growth of local or regional systems of production and consumption (Marsden, 2010). Additionally, the business leaders' activities can contribute to the social dimension of sustainability as well as strengthening the web of relationships and cultures that bind groups of individuals, places and communities of interest (Shepherd and Patzelt, 2011; Maclean et al., 2012). There would be a great potential for multiple forms of social value creation, for example, the growth of communities and individuals through self-actualization and achievement, and greater economic outcomes (Korsgaard and Anderson, 2011). Government plays the critical role in enabling the sustainability and shaping the regulatory environment as well as the structure of incentives facing businesses and consumers (Vickers, 2010). Dominant responses to promote sustainable development have centered on the progressive "ecological modernization" of the existing economic, political and social institutions (Hajer, 1995; Murphy, 2000).

The post-capitalist vision of sustainability "deep-green" involving radical reconceptualization of prosperity and wealth, and a more egalitarian and less materialistic society (Scott-Cato, 2009). This type of reconceptualization underpinned the alternative technology of the 1970s and 1980s, with its advocacy of community-level initiatives in areas such as renewable energy, organic food and autonomous eco-housing (Smith, 2005). Vickers (2010) has summarized these activities which are diverse in nature and originating motivations are known as "Environmentally-motivated social enterprise (ESE)." Therefore, ESE activity can be understood as a product of the interplay between top-down ecology modernizing policy actions and institutional change opening-up opportunities as well as bottom-up visions and energies informed by critical environmental politics and social movements (Pepper, 1996).

There has been a significant interest in these models and strategies to enable the scaling-up of social enterprises and their beneficial impacts. These activities can involve the business leaders and/ or organizations working in or developing "green niche" markets (Seyfang and Smith, 2007), and these activities are geographically replicating a successful concept, such as through a franchising operation (Litalien, 2006; Johnson et al., 2007; Tracey and Jarvis, 2007), growth through alliances (Sharir and Lerner, 2006), and joining or forming consortia to tender for public contracts, for example, waste recycling (Rowan et al., 2009). Olson (2008) is pointing out that many businesses have already made significant progress with initiatives that fit within the scope of an enterprise-level green strategy. However, very few companies have taken the broadest view of the green possibilities that are available today and the enormous potential those possibilities have when considered in the context of the whole enterprise.

Enterprise Systems (ESs) and Business Strategy: The enterprise resource planning (ERP) systems are also known as enterprise systems (ESs), which were developed to meet the functional requirements of an organization. Traditionally, these systems integrated information from disparate sources such as customers, supply chain, human resources, and financial accounting to make up the value chain of the enterprise enabling an organization to become significantly flexible and efficient (Davenport, 1998). Companies such as SAP and Oracle offer these systems as standardized software packages allowing organizations to procure them off-the-shelf and align to their business needs (Allen et al., 2002).

In today's digital economy, ESs have become part of the business and support tactical movements and strategic direction. A successfully integrated ES can enhance operational efficiency by supporting a firm's business processes as well as create sustainable competitive advantages by facilitating innovative practices (Chen et al., 2009). ESs promise not only information integration but benefits of re-engineered and improved business processes as well. McFarlan (1984) suggested that an organization might be able to realize strategic benefits in the business environment with the use of information and communication technology (ICT). Sharma and Gupta (2003) also saying that only the most strategically intelligent businesses will remain competitive and thrive in global, Internet-worked economy – those that have an enterprise-wide view of key business operations and have the tools to link business strategy with operational execution. Ragowsky and Gefen (2008) have found little evidence in support of this empirically, specifically in the case of ESs, where ICT is expected to impact significantly. They say it depends on the "specific operational characteristics of each company" (2008: 33) and the usability of ES.

To understand the real impact of ESs on realizing business strategies would be of utmost importance to both academics and practitioners, especially those organizations considering new or upgraded ESs. Several research studies have been conducted to understand the critical success factors (CSFs) for ES implementations (Bancroft et al., 1998; Holland and Light, 1999; Allen et al., 2002; Chen et al., 2009) as well as benefits from ES investments (Deloitte Consulting, 1998; Davenport, 2003; Ittner and Larcker, 2003; Yang and Seddon, 2004). However, there has been little research to evaluate the effects of ESs on realizing business strategies in the post-implementation phase (Hedman and Borell, 2002; Ifinedo and Nahar, 2006). This makes it difficult to draw conclusions on the utilization of ESs in enhancing organizational effectiveness (DeLone and McLean, 1992; Hedman and Borell, 2002; Ifinedo and Nahar, 2006).

Mathrani et al. (2013) findings are based on interviewing and data collection from two large- and one medium-size organizations. They found that strategic benefit realization from an ES implementation is a holistic process that not only includes the essential data and technology factors, but also includes factors such as digital business strategy deployment, people and process management, and skills and competency development. Although many companies are mature with their ES implementation, these firms have only recently started aligning their ES capabilities with digital business strategies correlating data, decisions, and actions to maximize business value from their ES investment.

Large US businesses may have significant levels of internal resources to support the growth strategy concept, but definitely small to medium-sized businesses would need the consulting help. Therefore, the US businesses would need a network of consulting partners to transform them quickly than they would progress on their own. Consulting organizations are generally separate businesses and can provide customized consulting to US businesses to make significant improvements to their products and/or services, revenue, profitability and within their value chain. These consulting organizations must also share the same commitment to improving US businesses as the US business executives are thinking. This partnership would produce an extraordinary reward in terms of return on investment (ROI) for the US businesses and stakeholders. This partnership will accelerate the US position in the global market at this critical time. Hence, the key elements of the enterprise growth strategy are:

• Business Vision and Mission.
• Innovative Growth Ideas.
• Market Growth Strategy.
• Core Competency.

And therefore, the following sections are presented in this chapter:

2.1   Business Vision and Mission

In the recent history, two time periods are comparable for wrong reasons. The prominent graft cases involving executive business leaders of many corporations during the dot-com years of early

2000s and years 2008–2009 for some well-known corporations. During 2008, prominent financial enterprises like Bear Stearns and Merrill Lynch were forced to sell, while Lehman Brothers went bankrupt; additionally, venerable enterprises like Citigroup and AIG found themselves on the brink of bankruptcy. Later in 2009, enterprises such as Toyota and British Petroleum (BP) were found themselves in serious public relations and structural problems. The problems that engulfed the corporations like Enron, Tyco, WorldCom, and HealthSouth during the early 2000s were different, but the results were almost identical. Several of these corporations passed through severe crises from which some survived while others did not. The common denominator in all these crises was widespread perception by the stakeholders of deep mistrust in executive business leaders of these corporations. Mission and Vision statements provide identity and roadmap of future for a corporation. Corporate vision and mission should be drafted such that during times of crisis, it can be used as a guiding tool for successfully navigating the troubled water faced by executive enterprise leaders.

Initial understanding of these terms came from Cummings and Davies (1994). Mission and vision are in fact two sides of the same coin in a manner which draws on the advantages of both, and negates the disadvantages of each. Their definitions of vision and mission are:

Vision conceptualizes something seen which is not actually present or historical, something which may be – a notion of the future which can provide something to anticipate and aim towards or away from.

Mission as the intent, sprit, or rallying cry which constitutes the organization's, and its members' primary duty or way behaving, the foundation and force which throws, sends, or casts itself into the future towards its goals and targets.

Therefore, mission and vision means quite different things. Both can inspire as well as can provide an individual or a group with motivation, inspiration, and a purpose. Khalifa (2011) noted that the failure of mission statements to improve performance may be related to a confusion of concepts, but he recommends organizations distinguish between mission, vision, values, and identity and deal with each separately.

2.1.1 VISION

Visioning is a practical process of business leadership whose responsibilities and authorities stems from the facilitation of strategic conversations among stakeholders and the reflexive engagement of business leaders (Finkelstein et al., 2008). Visioning works best when grounded in the knowledge and understanding of existing leadership teams. Visioning also works because it stimulates reflexivity, opening up the conversational space needed to challenge existing assumptions and introduce fresh possibilities. The power of visioning, whatever the process employed, stems from reflexive engagement of business leaders in past-present-future thinking. According to California Management Review (1995), reflexivity is the practice of self-consciously distancing oneself from the immediate to consider fundamental questions and generate, through discourse, alternative answers. Finkelstein et al. (2008) approach breaks down the vision into its component parts, lending simplicity and structure to the visioning process. They worked with senior leadership of Harley-Davidson Company and the leadership recognized the need for a vision that was comprehensive, inclusive and dynamic, but also realistic and grounded in the history and present circumstances of the business. The visioning process at the company was transformational because it ignited a strategic conversation that went beyond the boardroom to include employees, customers, partners and financiers. Therefore, visioning is not a magical process and cannot be removed from business realities.

A well-conceived vision consists of two major elements – "*Core ideology*" and "*Envisioned future*" as per Collins and Porras (1996) which is also known as "Big hairy audacious goal – BHAG." Certainly one of the stranger business terms introduced in the 1990s, but BHAG serves a very important purpose: to unify an enterprise and provide an easily understood compelling focus. The *American Heritage Dictionary* defines ideology as "the body of ideas reflecting the social needs and aspirations of an individual, a group, a class, or a culture."

2.1.1.1   Core Ideology

In *Built to Last*, Collins and Porras (1996) have noted that a core ideology is made up of a set of "*core values*" and a "*purpose*" that drive an individual or organization forward, set of principles that guide them to success and through tough times. Core ideology provides the glue that holds an organization together as it grows, diversifies, decentralizes, expands nationwide/globally, and develops workplace diversity.

Core values: These values are essential for an organization and are composed of enduring tenets as well as a small set of general guiding principles. Core values reflect the deeply held values of the organization and are independent of the current industry environment and management fad. Do not relate with specific cultural or operating guidelines; and also not to be compromised for financial gain or short-term growth. Core values have intrinsic value and are critical to those inside the organization. The following are the examples of core values (generally not more than 4–5):

*   excellent product/service;
*   pioneering technology;
*   creativity;
*   providing an enjoyable work environment for employees.

Purpose: An organization's fundamental reasons for existence, beyond making money, is to represent the true motivation of employees to work for a company, but is not to be confused with business strategies or specific objectives. It also does not represent the company's throughput and/or selected customers. It keeps the organization alive. Unlike the core values, the core purpose is relatively unchanging and for many organizations endures for decades or even centuries.

Visionary corporations prefer to function with a foundation steeped in their core ideology. It may not be reasonable or acceptable in the thinking of shareholders, customers or the public. It does not change direction to follow trends or market conditions that are not allowed to affect core ideologies. In fact, most core ideologies do not identify their products/services or markets served through their respective organizations. There is no defined "right" ideology, but as per Collins and Porras (1996), there are some specific ideological contents that are essential to a visionary organization. They found that the authenticity of the ideology and the extent to which an organization attains consistent alignment with the ideology counts more than the content of that ideology.

A variety of questions should be answered when analyzing the core ideology of any organization including: Who created it? Why does it exist? How long has it been in existence? Has it been modified for financial or marketing growth? Do individual groups/departments align their operations to the organization's core ideology? Therefore, many associates in every profession are struggling to convey their values and worth to the leaders in their organizations. To effectively communicate such value, these individuals need to make sure that their values are aligned with, and meet, the requirements of the organization's core ideology. It is also critical to communicate correctly. Hence:

Core Values + Purpose = Core Ideology

The following are some of the samples of core values from several corporations:

- Sony Corporation:
  - to be a pioneer, not following others, but doing the impossible;
  - to elevate the Japanese culture and national status;
  - to respect and encourage each individual's ability and creativity.
- Wal-Mart Stores, Incorporated:
  - to provide value to our customers;
  - to be in partnership with employees;
  - to work with passion, commitment, and enthusiasm;
  - to run lean;
  - to pursue ever-higher goals.
- Walt Disney Company:
  - no cynicism allowed;
  - fanatical attention to consistency and detail;
  - to celebrate, nurture, and promulgate "wholesome American values";
  - continuous progress via creativity, dreams, and imagination;
  - fanatical control and preservation of the Disney magic.

2.1.1.2 Envisioned Future

The second key component of the vision structure is an envisioned future. This is made up of two key elements:

- A 10 to 30 years audacious goal; and
- Some descriptions of what it will be like to achieve that goal.

Every company has a goal, but there is a great difference between simply having a goal and being committed to the goal. The BHAG process is not about slogans, but it is about setting goals. It is about deciding on a goal that will stimulate change and progress and then making a true commitment to it. When business leaders are developing BHAG, they have to think about the following points positively:

- must be exciting;
- must be easy to grasp, clear and compelling;
- must be exciting to a broad base of workers in the organization;
- must be like a dream vision;
- a great percentage of organization must believe that the BHAG would be achieved if the organization is fully committed to it;
- the organization must believe that they would be recognized in 25–30 years when they would achieve the BHAG.

For example, NASA's moon mission continued to unite people even though President John F. Kennedy (the leader who set the goal) died several years before its completion. Organizations are required a certain level of unreasonable confidence and commitment to achieve an effectively envisioned future. It is not unreasonable for a small package handling company to set the goal of becoming "the most serviceable package handling, the most far-reaching around the world package handling company that has ever been," as the United Parcel Service (UPS) did in 2006. Boeing not only envisioned a future dominated by its commercial jets; it bet the company on the 747 and, later on the 777, and now on the Dreamliner 787. The following listings are "Envisioned Future" goals of some organizations:

SCNetwork – Canada
SCNetwork is recognized as the leading thought community in Canada that brings all stakeholders together to develop strategic capabilities to maximize business success.

Lion Precision
Lion Precision will be the worldwide, preeminent authority in sensing solutions.

ANAC – Association of Nurses in Aids Care
Become a globally recognized association that is the preeminent source of nursing expertise related to all dimension of HIV disease.

Finkelstein et al. (2008) believe that a comprehensive, inclusive and dynamic vision can be developed through the employment of a process they call it "vision by design." This involves critical reflection on each of the four main dimensions of the enterprise – organization, culture, markets and relationships. Each dimension has three critical elements, and the developed true vision should be both inward looking (organization and culture) and outward looking (markets and relationships):

- organization – processes, systems, and structures;
- culture – values, management style, and employees relations;
- markets – customers, products, and locations;
- relationships – regulations, supply chain, and competitors.

For example, a Harley-Davidson (HD) motorcycle is for many the ultimate symbol of American individualism and few would deny the company's special place in US cultural history, but during the late twentieth century, Harley-Davidson almost went out of business. The company had retained its iconic status, but by the early 1980s found its market share slipping and product quality deteriorating. It was not long before the company became a laggard in an industry it had helped found. What caused such a dramatic decline in the fortunes of one of America's great companies? Many specific errors and oversights can be pinpointed, but underlying all was one dominant problem: HD had lost touch with the needs and aspirations of its customers. Finkelstein et al. (2008) coordinated a series of strategic initiatives, HD subsequently revolutionized its product offering and forged a new identity as a lifestyle company. In the process, it revitalized its vision and re-directed its energies, improving quality, productivity and employee relations. By extending its brand into related businesses, HD was propelled from industry laggard to leader. By pursuing a vision that excited its customers and employees, the company re-established itself as one of the USA's most dynamic corporations.

The HD case is illustrative of the crucial roles of vision and visioning in enterprise regeneration. Vision lent direction and a renewed sense of purpose. Customers, employees and other stakeholders were inspired and their confidence in the business restored. The vision of a modern, stylish and efficient lifestyle company, with its roots in a glorious past and at the hub of a worldwide biker community, was the bedrock for numerous strategic initiatives. It served to unite and make sense of the whole. The process of visioning addressed the individual and collective interests of all stakeholders. It is hard to imagine that without a renewed vision, HD could have bounced back from near bankruptcy in the mid-1980s to become the corporate force it is today.

Despite its widespread use, the term vision remains ill-defined and inconsistently applied (Finkelstein et al., 2008). It has been conceived variously as a form of charismatic leadership, an approach to scenario planning, a set of organizational values, a logic underlying action, and a projected business image (Christenson and Walker, 2004). Collins and Porras (1991) believe that the most commonly held view is that vision encapsulates the ideology or guiding philosophy of a business; expressing values, purpose and direction through a mission statement and set of corporate objectives. Core values and purpose are held to remain constant, whilst all else may change. The essential principle is that the vision should be both constant and adaptive. Finkelstein et al. (2011) endorse this approach, but in most writings on the subject, little is said about how a vision might be formed, communicated and applied. The methods proposed are unsystematic at best and arbitrary at worst. The general tendency is to suggest ways of projecting more widely the goals and aspirations of the present leader. There is a reluctance to apply visioning more deeply as a means of conducting strategic conversations. According to *Harvard Business Review* (1996), many executives equate visionary with impractical, a source of lofty ideals and unattainable goals. Before vision can be taken seriously as a tool of strategic leadership, it must be released from the grip of negative perceptions, and the best way to do this is to demonstrate how visioning works in practice and what it is capable of delivering.

2.1.2   MISSION

Mission statements define the nature, purpose and role of organizations; focus resources; and guide planning (Keeling, 2013). Some theorists maintain that mission statements drive strategic planning, while others claim they merely reflect institutional reality.

A mission statement is a statement of the purpose of a company, organization or person, its reason for existing. The mission statement should guide the actions of the organization, spell out its overall goal, provide a path, and guide decision-making. It provides "the framework or context within which the company's strategies are formulated." It's like a goal for what the company wants to do for the world (Hill and Jones, 2008).

Business communication researchers have described mission statements as persuasive communication devices (Williams, 2008). Others document a belief that the process of developing a mission statement fosters communication and commitment to a shared organizational purpose (Stemler et al., 2011).

Educational missions reflect sponsors' goals, describe present reality, and communicate how the institution delivers what constituents want (Morphew and Hartley, 2006; Williams, 2008). Mission statements in K-12 education reflect community priorities and typically include themes of cognitive, social, and civic development. The effect of mission statements on performance is unclear, but some suggest that the degree of commitment to shared purpose distinguishes high-performing schools from failing schools (Williams, 2008; Khalifa, 2011; Stemler et al., 2011). Mission statements serve two purposes in communication. First, the act of crafting a mission statement brings people together to negotiate and clarify roles and responsibilities. Second, the mission statement communicates an intent to serve the community by defining an understanding of the needs of its members; the skills, resources and capacity needed to fulfill those needs; and an expected outcome that will benefit the community (Keeling, 2013).

A mission statement should provide a clear and concise description of any organization's or individuals overall purpose. Key characteristics of a mission statement are:

- entity/organization/enterprise must have a reason for existence;
- it embodies its philosophies, ambitions, qualities, etc.;
- mission statement should be clear and no complex and awkward wording;
- the fewer words the better; prefer fewer than 25 words (concise);
- measurable goals with some deadline; and
- catchy and memorable which should be easy to recall and explain.

And the mission statement should be able to answer the following questions:

- *What business are you in?* Ask yourself this question and do not narrow yourself down. One of the classic business examples is the automobiles, where the US manufacturers lost a chance to grow in the beginning of the twenty-first century because they miss-defined themselves. They thought they were in the business of running cars on roads and highways. They did not understand that they were in the business of transporting people and goods. When foreign competition grew, the US manufacturers were left behind.
- *Are your customers satisfied?* Leading experts look for customer satisfaction goals in the mission statement. Developing customer care program depends on communicating and spreading the idea as well as identifying the importance within a company.
- *What is your workplace philosophy?* Your company's stand in fundamental issues such as maintaining creative work environment and building respect for diversity.
- *Does your company believe in value-based marketing?* Value-based developed marketing framework helps business leaders and their associates to understand business better. This framework starts with a business value proposition, which states what benefits a business offers, to whom, and at what relative price level. For example:
  - This automobile manufacturer offers reliable and safe automobile for families at a relative price premium.
  - This super market offers variety of fresh fruits and vegetables at low prices.
- *What an individual or organization does?*
- *How the individual or organization does it?*
- *For whom the individual or organization does it?*

Therefore, the mission statement should enable large groups of individuals to work in a unified direction toward a common cause (goal), passionate and energizing. It should be compelling, as well as risky and challenging.

A company mission statement should define the underlying goals (such as making a profit) and objectives in broad strategic terms, including what market is served and what benefits are offered. The following are some sample mission statements:

General Electric (GE)
Imagine, solve, build and lead - four bold verbs that express what it is to be part of GE - and should serve to energize ourselves and our teams around leading change and driving performance.

Walmart
To give ordinary folks the chance to buy the same thing as rich people.

Apple Computer
To offer the best possible personal computing technology, and to put that technology in the hands of as many people as possible.

IBM
We strive to lead in the invention, development and manufacture of the industry's most advanced information technologies, including computer systems, software, storage systems and microelectronics.

We translate these advanced technologies into value for our customers through our professional solutions, services and consulting businesses worldwide.

Keeling's (2013) experience confirms the value of a mission statement as a communication device that reflects, affirms, and inspires while communicating the current reality in practice. Biloslavo (2004) analyzed the mission statements of 50 top Slovene enterprises which are published on the companies' websites. His analysis has three goals:

1. to establish the degree to which the Slovene enterprises make use of their websites to convey their mission to various stakeholders;
2. to identify the stakeholder groups that are mentioned in mission statements;
3. to analyze the contents of these statements.

His research has shown that there are some significant differences between these mission and those of other European or American companies. The reason for these differences is culturally, institutionally and historically embedded. His research indicates that, despite the processes of globalization and regionalization, convergence of various contents or roles of the mission statement is questionable. Instead, a kind of borrowing of individual elements among different cultural and economic systems, in quest of their own ways, could be considered.

Despite widespread recognition of its importance, very little empirical research has been conducted on strategy documents, particularly Mission or Vision statements (Cady et al., 2011). They developed a database containing 489 organizational statements from 300 different organizations. They analyzed their statements to determine how many distinct concepts could be identified and the most commonly used concepts. Statements were carefully read to determine if multiple use of a term within a single statement indicated multiple meanings. The results indicate that while traditional titles are most often used to label such statements, there is a wide variety of terms used to express the ideas contained in them. Many organizational statements contain so many unique concepts that they begin to suffer from high density.

Nature (2010) asked a selection of leading researchers and policy-makers where their fields will be ten years from now. They invited them to identify the key questions their disciplines face, the major roadblocks and the pressing next steps. Some of those are presented here:

Topic: Search by Peter Norvig, Director of Research at Google
Internet search as we know it is just one decade old; by 2020 it will have evolved far beyond its current bounds. Content will be a mix of text, speech, still and video images, histories of interactions with colleagues, friends, information sources and their automated proxies, and tracks of sensor readings from Global Positioning System devices, medical devices and other embedded sensors in our environment.

An experimental minority of search queries will be through the direct monitoring of brain signals.

The majority of search queries will be spoken, not typed, and an experimental minority will be through direct monitoring of brain signals. Users will decide how much of their lives they want to share with search engines, and in what ways …

Topic: Synthetic Biology by George Church, Professor of genetics, Harvard Medical School
In the past decade, the cost of reading and writing DNA has dropped a millionfold, outstripping even Moore's law for exponentially increasing computer power. The challenge for the next decade will be to integrate molecular engineering and computing to make complex systems. The development of engineering standards for biological parts, such as how pieces of DNA snap together, will permit computer-aided design (CAD) at levels of abstraction from atomic to population scales. Biologists will have access to tools that will allow them to arrange atoms to optimize catalysis, for example, or arrange populations of organisms to cooperate in making a chemical ...

Topic: Drug discovery by Gary P. Pisano, Professor of Business Administration, Harvard Business School

No one should be surprised to see the emergence of a major Chinese multinational drug company.

The next ten years will witness an acceleration of the upheaval in the pharmaceutical industry. Profound changes in drug research and development, competition, government policies and markets will continue to challenge existing business models and strategies. Many established players will not make the transition. Some venerable companies have already disappeared through acquisitions. The industry will bifurcate into firms that pursue a long-term commitment to creating novel drugs and those that focus on marketing. The latter may do better in the short term but are doomed to failure eventually. The development of effective treatments is the only sustainable source of value for the pharmaceutical industry. Given the paucity of therapies for many serious diseases and the mediocre efficacy of many existing drugs, the opportunities are huge. There are risks in trying to discover new drugs, but the risks of backing away from that commitment are higher ...

2.2   Innovative Growth Ideas

An enterprise that offers higher-quality, lower- or competitive-price products (goods and/ or services) over a sustained period of time is an "innovative enterprise." The objective of the business enterprise is to offer competitive products that customers want or need at prices that they are willing or able to pay. Therefore, the innovative enterprise is the one that generates the higher-quality, lower- or competitive-price products that provide better than the industry average profit margins as well as give households with employment incomes and with enough consumer choice on product markets.

Innovation is defined as the act which endows resources with a new capacity to create wealth (Drucker, 1985). While Lieberman and Montgomery (1988) suggest that innovative firms enter the market first will be able to develop a stronger base for building sustainable competitive advantage. Therefore, innovation is the basis of wealth creation, and by implication the future success of firms is driven through innovation. There are some other definitions of innovation:

- Innovation can be viewed as the application of better solutions that meet new requirements, in-articulated needs, or existing market needs (Maranville, 1992). This is accomplished through more effective products, services, processes, technologies, or ideas that are readily available to markets, societies and governments. The term innovation can be defined as something original and, as a consequence, new, that "breaks into" the market or society. A definition consistent with these aspects would be – an innovation is something original, new and important in whatever field that breaks in to a market or society (Frankelius, 2009).

- Kline (1985) model is a chain-linked model of innovation and he places emphasis on potential market needs as drivers of the innovation process and describes the complex and often iterative feedback loops between marketing, design, manufacturing and R&D. Research and development (R&D) helps spur on patents and other scientific innovations that lead to productive growth in such areas as industry, medicine, engineering, and government (Mark et al., 2008). If employees recognize their experiences while exchanging ideas would develop innovative ideas which could be less formal on-the-job business growth ideas. The revolutionary and unique innovations tend to emerge from R&D while more incremental innovations may come from practice, but there are many exceptions to each of these situations.

- There are various sources for innovative ideas outside the business: consumer (user) centered approach; supplier centered approach. A great deal of user innovation is done by those actually implementing and using technologies and products as part of their normal activities. The majority of the time these users' innovators have some personal record motivating them which may lead to their becoming entrepreneurs. Entrepreneur means selling their products, may choose to trade their innovation in exchange for other innovations, or their supplier may be adopting their innovation. Davila et al. (2006) notes "Companies cannot grow through cost reduction and reengineering alone … Innovation is the key element in providing aggressive top-line growth, and for increasing bottom-line results." Innovation programs in organizations (firms) are generally tightly linked to their market competitive positioning, and goals and objectives of the business plan. One of the drivers of innovation is to achieve business growth strategy.

- Innovation is a collective, cumulative and uncertain process (Lazonich, 2014). It is collective because it requires the skills and efforts of variety of resources in hierarchical and functional areas of resources to generate the organizational learning that results in competitive products. It is cumulative because the developing and utilizing process of these value-creating capabilities must occur continuously over extended periods of time before competitive products are developed. And it is uncertain because a firm that seeks to be innovative may be incapable of transforming the technologies and accessing the markets that enable a product to be higher-quality and/or lower-price than those of its competitors. Therefore, the collective, cumulative and uncertain characteristics of the innovative process have profound implications for understanding the relationship between value creation and value extraction.

- A very simple definition, innovation is finding a better way of doing something (Wong, 2013).

Tucker (2001) strongly believes that innovation is the only sustainable source of growth, competitive advantage and new wealth. He studied the Arthur D. Little's survey conducted of 669 global company executives found fewer than 25 percent of the companies believe their innovation performance is where it needs to be if they are to be successful in the competitive marketplace. They have tried an endless array of alternatives, company leaders are now accepting enterprise-wide innovation as a key operational discipline, just as in the past they adopted the disciplines of quality, planning and management.

While something novel is often described as an innovation, in economics, management science, and other fields of practice and analysis it is generally considered a "process" that brings together various novel ideas in a way that they have an impact on society. Bowonder et al. (2010) visualize innovation strategies in 12 ways: platform offering, co-creation, cycle time reduction, brand value enhancement, technology leveraging, future-proofing, lean development, partnering, innovation mutation, creative destruction, market segmentation, and acquisition. End-user-innovation is widely recognized in current economy. This is where the individual/group develops an innovation for their use because existing products do not meet their needs.

Tucker (2001) suggesting that twenty-first century promises to bring more change, more complexity, and more competition. As a result, enterprise-wide innovation will become a required operational discipline. Leading innovation in this environment involves four key principles: the approach must be comprehensive; innovation must include an organized, systematic and continual search for new opportunities; organizations must involve everyone in the innovation process; and every enterprise must work constantly on improving its climate for innovation.

The twenty-first century industrial enterprises which are in the pursuit of innovation and sustained competitive advantage involve in a set of processes which support the transformation of knowledge into new processes and products, goods and services, and which provide the enterprise with particular strength and superior value relative to other enterprises. In such a perspective, innovation is a key source of customer benefits and sustainable competitive advantage (Tidd et al., 2005; Nobre et al., 2011).

However, more recently there are those who now argue that being a "fast second" or imitation in general is potentially a more profitable and lower risk route to competitive advantage. Imitation avoids costly investments in research and development, and reduces the risk of failure, the concept support the imitator in finding out which ideas are ultimately accepted by the market (Markides and Geroski, 2005; Chittoor et al., 2009; Shenkar, 2010).

Discovery/Invention/Innovation – one popular way to frame the innovation process is to break it down into discovery (new knowledge), invention (new technologies) and innovation (useful things like products and services) as per Satell (2013b). However, it does not take much thinking to realize that this is not very useful because it confuses work products with work processes. For example, both penicillin and the discovery of DNA were both the products of discovery (and eventually, by Heidegger's definition, became technologies), but in one the process was accidental (penicillin) and the other the process was innovative (DNA), combining new techniques in chemistry, biology and physics in ways no one had thought of before, and that is a very crucial point. It is absolutely senseless to argue what constitutes a commercial product or service (it is, after all, a matter of context rather than of quality), but finding novel solutions to important problems is a crucial component of modern business life.

2.2.1   INNOVATION MANAGEMENT MATRIX

Satell (2013a, 2013b) presented the Innovation management matrix in *Harvard Business Review* and applied to some situations in his blog on innovationexcellence.com in Figure 2.1. Each of the four quadrants represents an area of innovation, and in each quadrant requires finding novel solutions to important problems as well as the opportunity to create new products and services.

By arbitrarily determining that Netflix and the iPhone are innovations and the discovery of the structure of DNA and quantum teleportation are not, this would be unnecessarily limiting the classifications and therefore missing opportunities. After all, one man's purpose is another man's folly. They do, however, require separate and distinct innovation processes and that's where the discussion becomes important. In order to manage innovation effectively, leaders need to focus on one set of processes or their organizations will become hopelessly muddled.

However, leaders will still need to gain some competence in other quadrants or they will miss opportunities (as Apple is doing now). Finding the right mix of research, partnering, mining the organization for disruptive ideas and engineering improvements is essential for every organization.

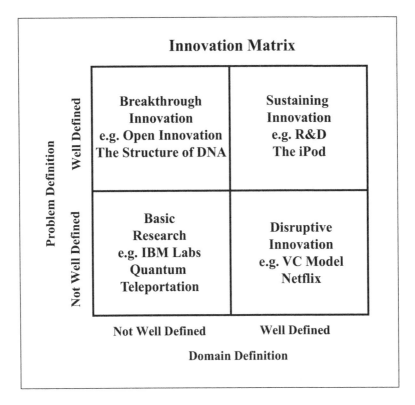

Figure 2.1   Innovation management matrix

Therefore, innovation can help businesses to adapt and evolve to survive and grow. Innovation is generally driven by the need to solve a problem or capture a new opportunity. Businesses could improve old products or services are used, find new uses for them, or even create new ones. Innovation also includes changes that business executives would like to make to run their business – business leaders can create new processes or a new business model. There are many ways to be innovative. Business leader could implement a big change, a small change, or gradual changes over time.

There is a general miss-understanding that innovation deals with new products only, but actually it can be applied to any business area. According to Davila et al. (2006) study, large number of manufacturing and service organizations ranked the following activities in decreasing order of popularity for innovation: improved quality, creation of new markets, extension of the product range, reduced labor costs, improved production processes, reduced materials, reduced environmental damage, replacement of product/service, reduced energy consumption and conformance to regulations. To achieve successful goals through innovation depends greatly on the environment prevailing in the business (Khan, 1989).

2.2.2   DIFFUSION OF INNOVATION

The concept of product "S" curve (Figure 2.2) came from "Diffusion of innovation research" which was first started in 1903 by researcher Gabriel Tarde. Tarde (1903) defined the innovation-decision process as a series of steps that include:

1. First knowledge.
2. Forming an attitude.
3. A decision to adopt or reject.
4. Implementation and use.
5. Confirmation of the decision.

Once innovation occurs then the innovations generally spread from the innovator to other individuals and groups in the organization. This process has been proposed that the life cycle of innovations can be described using the "S-curve" or "diffusion curve." The S-curve maps growth of revenue or productivity against time. In the early stage of a particular innovation, growth is relatively slow as the new product establishes itself. At some point customers begin to demand and the product growth increases more rapidly. New incremental innovations or changes to the product allow growth to continue. Towards the end of its life cycle growth slows and may even begin to decline. In the later stages, no amount of new investment in that product will yield a normal rate of return.

The S-curve derives from an assumption that new products are likely to have "product life," i.e. a start-up phase, a rapid increase in revenue and eventual decline. In fact the great majority of innovations never gets off the bottom of the curve, and never produce normal returns. As innovations are made that will eventually replace older ones, successive S-curves will come along to replace older ones and continue to drive growth upwards. As shown in Figure 2.2 that the first curve shows a current technology and the second S-curve shows an emerging technology that currently yields lower growth but will eventually overtake current technology and lead to even greater levels of growth. As Rogers (1962) pointed out, the length of life will depend on the many factors – for example, the life of a software program versus an automobile engine.

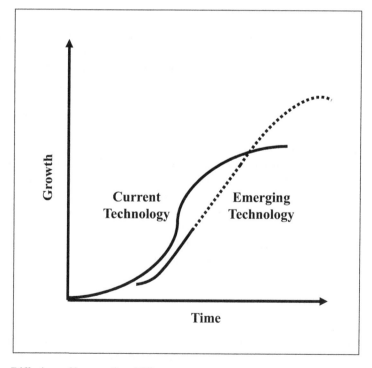

Figure 2.2   Diffusion of innovation "S" curve

2.2.3   INNOVATION REPORT

Ernst & Young (2012) has developed an "Innovation report" which is based on the qualitative research with special focus on business model innovation. They conducted a series of face-to-face and telephone interviews with 45 participants (professionals, academic and business leaders) from Europe, the US, Africa, Brazil, China, India and Russia. The developed report is divided into seven sections. A short overview of each section is presented following the list:

1. Introduction.
2. Overview.
3. The model.
4. External environment.
5. Business model.
6. Business outcomes.
7. The next step.

Introduction: Most people will think about innovation as an extraordinary invention creation activity by solitary geniuses, but currently majority of business innovations are quite the opposite of people thinking. The businesses that generate these ideas thrive on collaboration, a free exchange of ideas and regular interactions with customers and other stakeholders. They innovate not necessarily to revolutionize their industry – although that may happen to a lucky few – but to meet specific objectives and carve out a competitive edge.

Overview: Innovation is the successful development of an idea that generates business value for sustainable growth. Innovation is not a strategy; it is a way of being. In the current environment, innovation is not a linear process for most of the businesses. It is a continuous cycle with ups and downs, inputs from different places, repetitions, failures and several steps back and forth. By adopting this approach, the most innovating businesses are able to:

- take advantage of changes in the external environment;
- continually revamp their business models to achieve and sustain competitive advantage;
- innovate to obtain specific business outcomes, such as increased agility or productivity.

The model: The conceptual structure of the model is presented in Figure 2.3. The model is based on the research work done by Ernst & Young. Typical areas of innovation are products and service, processes and business model. According to Ernst & Young research, product and service innovations certainly help businesses to obtain a competitive advantage, but business model innovation tends to confer more lasting benefits.

External environment (left side listing): Identifies the major market and economic elements that affect business as well as offer major opportunities that can transform whole industries. Innovative businesses know how to capitalize on the external environment. These elements are identified in Figure 2.3. Sometimes business conditions may not be totally favorable, but if a business is truly innovative then the business will be able to turn a challenging situation to their advantage. For example, iPad and iPhone have radically changed the notion of computer size and the ease of communication.

Business model: Ernst & Young research findings have confirmed that companies who alter their business model – and do so more than once – are more likely to achieve a sustainable competitive advantage. It is much more difficult for a competitor to copy a business model than it is to replicate products or services. One of the examples of Ernst & Young is of sharing risk and reward; Boston-Power business model is based on traditional contract manufacturing agreements but on a business partnership with shared risk and reward. Ernst & Young have presented several types of models in their report.

Business outcomes (right side listing): Shows that businesses innovate to achieve five outcomes: profitable growth, customer engagement, business sustainability, productivity and business agility. The challenge to business executives is to focus on all of these outcomes together, rather than favoring one over another, which compromises the ability to anticipate change and drive growth.

The next step: Companies from emerging markets are coming up with breakthrough products and services all the time. Business size is no longer important to gain the market share, even small businesses grab market share in niche areas. Engaged customers, aided by social media, are changing traditional R&D; Ernst & Young still believes that spiral approach is the robust process for innovation that, if followed carefully, can provide flexibility and structure for businesses of all types, regardless of size or industry sector.

The input elements (external environment) have to work with an innovation enabler, external collaboration and an innovation process with identified innovation areas to achieve competitive advantage which results in achieving business outcomes.

Innovation enabler: These are the internal elements necessary for the innovation spiral to work.

- leadership mindset and culture;
- people and skills;
- technology;
- infrastructure;
- organization and governance;
- risk management;
- measurement and KPIs (key performance indicators);
- funding.

Organization leaders must be innovative and ready to take risks to achieve competitive advantage. Once innovation becomes a part of their culture, the other seven elements need to be aligned to allow innovation to flourish.

External collaboration: The most innovative organizations collaborate throughout the process to access diverse internal and external expertise:

- customers;
- investors;
- suppliers;
- government;
- financial institutions;
- competitors;
- academics;
- other companies.

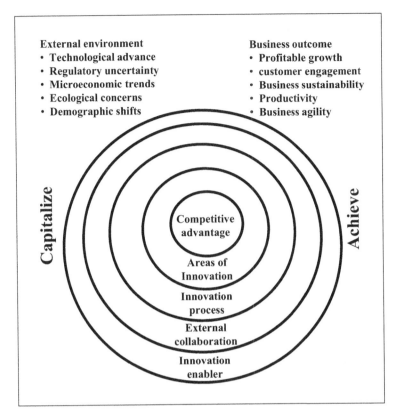

External environment
- **Technological advance**
- **Regulatory uncertainty**
- **Microeconomic trends**
- **Ecological concerns**
- **Demographic shifts**

Business outcome
- **Profitable growth**
- **customer engagement**
- **Business sustainability**
- **Productivity**
- **Business agility**

Competitive advantage

Areas of Innovation

Innovation process

External collaboration

Innovation enabler

Capitalize

Achieve

Figure 2.3   Innovation spiral: A spiral approach to business innovation

2.2.4 INNOVATE OR IMITATE

Schumpter (1934) suggests that the successful innovation is the driver for growth, and therefore imitation becomes inevitable as successful firms are imitated by others seeking to gain a share of excess profits. From this perspective Nelson and Winter (1982) found that firms who wish to grow (or avoid decline) have no option but to imitate. Therefore, the concepts of incremental and radical innovation can be considered as points along this continuum, which differentiate between a pure "copy" of another firm's innovation as the definition of imitation, an adaptation of existing ideas relating to incremental innovation (Henderson and Clark, 1990) and radical innovation – adoption of new and distinctive concepts not found in existing competitors – as the opposite pole to imitation.

Lippman and Rumelt (1982) describe situations where the links between actions and performance are unclear, therefore the factors responsible for performance differentials are difficult to identify and create stable inter-firm differences in profitability. Teece (1986) suggests a number ways firms can protect their innovations from imitation and refers to legal documentations such as patents, trade secrets and copyright, which includes the level to which competitors can understand the competences needed to create it. If the basis of innovation is not clearly defined then it is referred to as "casual ambiguity." If the casual ambiguity concept is linked to the resource-based view of the firm, where firms are able to acquire or develop valuable resources which are difficult for competitors to imitate or obtain and are therefore a potential source of competitive advantage (Barney, 1991). These valuable resources may develop core competency within the firm to support the innovation (discussed later in the chapter – section 2.4). Much of the work in this area emphasizes the importance of firms investing in competences which are causally ambiguous in order to protect competitive advantage. Reed and DeFillippi (1990) suggest that there are three characteristics of competences that can be simultaneous sources of advantage and ambiguity:

1. tastiness, where the competences are based on tacit knowledge;
2. complexity, within and between a firm's competences;
3. specificity, where the competences are highly specific and interdependent with internal and/ or external relationships.

Podolny (1993) asserts that firm behaviors are influenced by the relationship status with other manufacturers and proposes that sociological approaches to markets can help to explain strategic decisions at the firm level. Such perspectives are valuable contributions to understanding firm level behaviors in competitive and institutional contexts. Similarly, Gemser and Wijnberg (2001) suggest that the fear of losing an innovative reputation will inhibit firms from engaging in imitative strategies.

The implication of the linkage between belief in competence and innovation is that organizations will develop collective positions as to whether they should be innovating or imitating, or potentially some combination of the two (Jankins, 2014). This gives rise to three interrelated propositions as Jankins describes:

1a: Where there is a collective belief in the competences of the organization, firms will focus on innovating from these competences rather than imitating competitors.
1b: Where there is a lack of a collective belief in the competences of the organization they will tend to focus on imitating competitors rather than generating innovation from their own internal competences.

The role of organizational performance is important, which provides clear feedback as to whether or not such competence can create successful performance. Therefore, the business leadership would interpret that as a consequence of the success of the product strategy. Hence, the possible relationships between performance, belief in competences and innovative or imitative strategies are:

2a: Where innovative strategies lead to performance improvement then this will increase collective belief in competences, which in turn will increase the focus on innovation.
2b: Where innovative strategies lead to performance reduction then this will reduce collective belief in competences, which in turn will increase the focus on imitation.

Similarly, in the case of imitation, business leaders can articulate the relationships as follows:

3a: Where imitative strategies lead to performance improvement then this will increase belief in collective competences, which in turn will increase the focus on innovation.
3b: Where imitative strategies lead to performance reduction then this will reduce collective belief in competences, which in turn will increase the focus on imitation.

Jankins (2014) is suggesting that both successful and unsuccessful imitation will stimulate a move toward innovation either because of the increased belief in firm competence created by success, or the reduced belief in the value of following competitors' strategies created by failure. In both cases, it is more likely that business leaders will shift to innovation as the focal strategy of the firm to seek their own innovative path in response to the competitive advantage of a competitor. This suggests that, contrary to the belief that competing firms will constantly seek to imitate sources of advantage implied by a focus on the importance of inimitability. Powell et al. (2006) noted that the impact of causal ambiguity, an underpinning concept of inimitability, is potentially overblown as a source of competitive advantage and it is possible that causal ambiguity, broadly and objectively considered, has no net effect on firm performance.

Jankins (2014) research implicate that both innovation and imitation are effective strategies to bring about a performance turnaround, particularly where there are opportunities to either add value to a competitor's innovation, the so-called innovative imitation, or, to create innovations that undermine a competitor's competence in a particular domain, by substituting this for a competence in which the firm has a particular expertise. This implies that in situations of poor performance firms should consider both innovative and imitative approaches, but carefully assess the value of both based on the level to which they really understand the basis of imitation and the extent to which their innovative focus creates a potential for substituting for competitors' competences. Jankins' (2014) research model suggests that in cases of both successful and unsuccessful imitation firms will tend to move inexorably towards innovation. This is because either their confidence in their own competences is boosted by successful imitation, or, in unsuccessful imitation, they put more faith in their own innovations as the basis for improving their performance. Therefore, the research implies that attempts to imitate will ultimately lead to a greater focus on innovation whether or not the imitations are successful.

2.2.5   ADAPTATION AND INNOVATION DYNAMIC CAPABILITIES

The concept of dynamic capabilities is still under-developed. Researchers are trying to define exactly what dynamic capabilities are composed of because it is unclear on which micro-foundations they are built (Kraatz and Zajac, 2001; Felin and Foss, 2005; Teece, 2007; Wang and Ahmed, 2007; Ambrosini and Bowman, 2009; Easterby-Smith et al., 2009). Zollo and Winter (2002) are trying to address the source of dynamic capabilities and their underpinning routines generation and evolvement. Teece (2007) is providing a theoretical concept of dynamic capabilities by defining them as "distinct skills, processes, procedures, organizational structures, decision rules and disciplines."

The ability of an organization to perform a coordinated set of activities utilizing organizational resources, for the purpose of achieving a particular objective is defined as organizational capability (Helfat and Peteraf, 2003). These capabilities are classified as either operational or dynamic (Winter, 2003). Operational capabilities are named as "substantive" capabilities by Zahra et al. (2006), facilitate efficient and effective use of existing resources. Winter (2003) describes operational capabilities as zero-level capabilities, or "how a business leader can earn a living now."

When a company is implementing a value-creating strategy not simultaneously being implemented by competitors as well as it cannot easily be imitated could provide a competitive advantage (Barney, 1991). Competitive advantage could also be achieved if a business is developing operational capabilities along with the dynamic capabilities (Teece et al., 1997). These capabilities enable organizations to adapt, integrate and reconfigure skills, resources and functional competences. They are "dynamic" in the sense of enabling the organization to renew its competences to achieve congruence with the changing environment. Therefore, dynamic capabilities are the foundation for a firm's ability to respond to environmental change.

Helfat et al. (2007) define dynamic capabilities as the capacity of an organization to purposefully create, extend or modify its resource base, and distinguish two functions of dynamic capabilities – the deployment function, and the search and selection function. Wang and Ahmed

(2007) have attempted to disaggregate and clarify the component factors of dynamic capabilities such as adaptive, absorptive and innovative capability; while Teece (2007) is sensing and shaping opportunities and threats, seizing opportunities, maintaining competitiveness through enhancing, combining, protecting and reconfiguring assets; Bowman and Ambrosini (2003) are reconfiguring, leveraging, learning and creative integration; and Ambrosini et al. (2009) are incremental, renewing and regenerative capabilities. Researchers have also identified some specific types of dynamic capability, e.g., architectural innovation (Galunic and Eisenhardt, 2001); absorptive capacity (Zahra and George, 2002; Hotho et al., 2012); and Bruni and Verona (2009) are focusing on a specific function of dynamic capabilities, such as marketing.

Therefore, two distinct types of dynamic capabilities in the literature that are pivotal for organizational transformation and growth: adaptation dynamic capabilities and innovation dynamic capabilities. Meyer and Day (2014) are defining these dynamic capabilities:

> Adaptation dynamic capabilities relate to routines of resource exploitation and deployment, which are supported by acquisition, internalization and dissemination of extant knowledge, as well as resource reconfiguration, divestment and integration.

These capabilities alone are not sufficient to sustain a competitive advantage in relation to top performing global competitors. Organizations also need to develop unique capabilities through experimentation as well as the development of new internal routines rather than just importing routines from others (Kogut and Zander, 1996). For example, Taiwan industry (photovoltaic) first engaged in fast followership of their Western counterparts through acquiring technological capabilities and then moved from imitation to technological innovation (Mathews et al., 2011).

> Innovation dynamic capabilities relate to the creation of completely new capabilities via exploration and path-creation processes, which are supported by search, experimentation and risk taking as well as project selection, funding and implementation.

These capabilities provide guidance to business leaders for creating an appropriate organizational environment to facilitate exploration and path creation. This also provides the basis on which to develop new and unique capabilities. Innovation dynamic capabilities are the source of unique capabilities (Prahalad and Hamel, 1990; Barney, 1991), and these capabilities may lead to sustainable competitive advantage. However, the latter is not guaranteed, due to the inherent risks associated with innovation (Helfat et al., 2007). Therefore, innovation dynamic capabilities of an organization are those which business executives need to nurture to create the potential for competitive advantage, whilst recognizing that there is a risk that some projects will fail.

The sequencing these two types of dynamic capabilities would help the organization to secure short-term competitive advantage as well as to create the basis for long-term competitive advantage. Meyer and Day (2014) have examined the process of organizational transformation in a Russian oil company and developed an understanding of two critical types of dynamic capability – adaptation and innovation. The speed and radical nature of the change in the Russian oil industry highlights these processes, which they maintain are also relevant for mature Western organizations seeking sustainable competitive advantage in turbulent environments.

2.3   Market Growth Strategy

All businesses are under increasing pressure to deliver effective solutions with fewer resources that will produce results over shorter time frames. The market growth strategy team can help business executives, and their support team members facing today's challenges through providing processes, guidance, solution and tools that will support the planning, designing, and implementing the market growth strategy. The risk element increases as businesses move further away from known markets and existing products. Thus, new products and new markets typically create greater risk of penetration than the existing products in present markets.

2.3.1   MARKET RESEARCH

The twenty-first century is the information age. Every business requires accurate and timely market information to be successful. Whether a business is large or small, correct information about equipment, facility, material, technology, experience and financing alone is not enough to succeed without a continuous flow of the right business information. Large corporations can support very sophisticated and lengthy market research processes. These processes reveal almost everything possible about their customers (Kumar, 2010a). For example, Kotler's (2002) research states that Coke knows that their customers put 3.2 ice cubes in a glass, customers watch 69 of their commercials every year and prefer cans to pop out of vending machines at a temperature of 35 degrees.

All successful businesses must know their markets, competitors and customer needs and wants. It is required for all businesses to be competitive. In today's competitive market, it is not enough for business leaders to know the answers to the what, where, when and how questions about their business, but they also need to know why customers are buying their products/ services. Every business has to have at least a minimal amount of time and budget for market research.

Market Research Needs and Objectives: Before starting market research, every business needs to decide what they need to investigate. The kind of information they seek should determine the type of research they will do, but most of the time market research is constrained due to budget limitations. Therefore, businesses need to obtain general information about how key customers think about their products, brands, buying frequency, etc. One of the easy ways to collect information is to interview groups of target customers in focus areas. However, this type of research indicates only directional trends, and may not be statistically reliable. These businesses also need outside information services, industry trade associations, and industry experts for advice.

Market Research Procedures: Generally there are two types of market research: primary and secondary:

- Primary research involves the actual data collection for the defined usage patterns, liking and disliking of product features and so on, of target customers of their products.
- Secondary research takes place when marketing information is collected from a third source like periodicals, business magazines, etc. This type of research is generally less expensive and takes a shorter time than primary research.

A breakdown of these two types of research information collection is presented in Figure 2.4 (any marketing text book can be used to get further details). However, small businesses may not be able to afford, or appropriate enough funds for, their businesses to collect market research information. Leadership of small businesses has to be more creative and productive in:

- setting affordable budgets and deciding to do a limited amount of necessary research;

- working with outside experts or market research specialists (could be in-house) to define research issues to work on;
- accepting market research data at a lower confidence level due to smaller budget and sample size, and the randomness of the selected sample.

Sometimes outside sourcing at a reasonable price is very useful, and one reliable source is The American Marketing Association (AMA), located in Chicago, Illinois which can be reached at 1-800-262-1150.

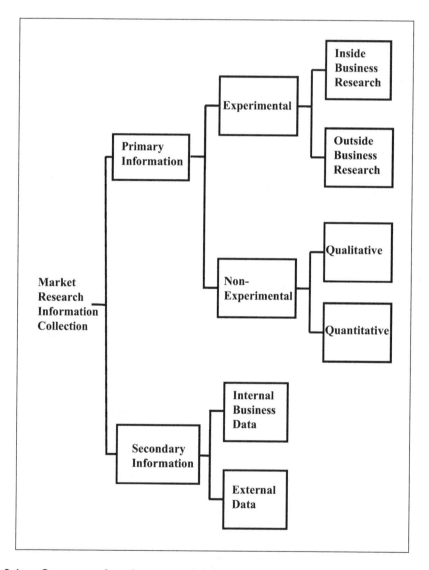

Figure 2.4   Structure of market research information collection

Finding New Customers and Markets: Finding new customers to grow is not just about finding more customers and markets; it is about finding the right customers and markets. The priority is not just sales (revenue) dollars, but how to identify the best customers/markets. The next question is "how to achieve this?" The following is a brief guideline to businesses to support the concept:

- Analyze business information (internal data):
  - lost orders, late, and not properly developed orders (not developed as per customer specifications);
  - customer complains;
  - customers not paying for delivered products/services;
  - identify best customers for now and in the future.
- Analyze both internal and external elements:
  - Where are current and future market niches?
  - What kind of products/services would current customers like in the future?
  - Can businesses compare their products/services to competitor's products/services in terms of price, delivery, services (support), and key features by model?
  - What is their profit margin by product or service job?

The above analysis and the answers to those questions will help lead the businesses to new markets and products growth. Next is to develop a marketing plan for the business and see how customers fit into the developed plan. Key elements in the developed plan should be:

- business profile with core competencies and services expertise;
- marketing niche with a listing of the most valuable customers;
- sales goals for the most valuable customers for 2–4 years as applicable;
- marketing strategy and plan for new businesses and customers;
- identify sales force (internal and/or external);
- information needed to achieve sales goals – competitors' information, regular customers, prospective customers and so on.

Once a business has sold some product/service to a new customer, they would need to analyze their competition and the market segment. Relate this information to firm's core competency and business strategy. If the sale supports both (core competency and business strategy) then this is a great sale for business growth, if not, it is not critical for firm's business. These new customers may need different kinds of products/services in the future. This sets the stage for developing the right products/services that firm's business will sell.

2.3.2 MARKET GROWTH AND ANALYSIS

Market is the interface across the business which supports the flow of products, services, money and information. These flows across the business boundary are a consequence of interactions within the business, within the market and between the two. The positive change in demand for products or services or both is defined as market growth for the business. These increases in demand could be for:

- existing products or services or both;
- new products or services or both;
- combinations of existing and new products and services.

Numerous market growth models are available in the literature and some interesting models are presented below.

2.3.2.1   The Whetstone Group's approach for market growth

The Whetstone Group (2005) believes that business growth starts with an overall business strategy, identifying business customers and serving those customers. It is critical that everybody in the business be on the same page to develop a market growth strategy. This supports the next step of marketing and sales analysis along with budgeting and accounting processes. The process steps can be linked as presented in Figure 2.5.

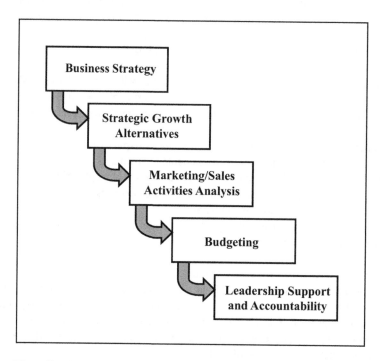

Figure 2.5   **The effective market growth process**

Once the business strategy is defined, the market growth alternatives can be developed. The Whetstone Group (2005) identifies four growth alternatives which are presented in the matrix form in Figure 2.6 opposite. Each business has to analyze these alternatives for their growth potential, allocation of business development time, other resources and budgeting process to achieve their market growth goals. The next step is to implement the market growth strategy.

Implementing the market growth strategy: Businesses need to recognize the difference between marketing and sales. The Whetstone Group (2005) has developed a qualitative graph (Figure 2.7) which shows how marketing and sales efforts work together to produce business growth. The marketing group must first be engaged in the market to position the business to generate orders

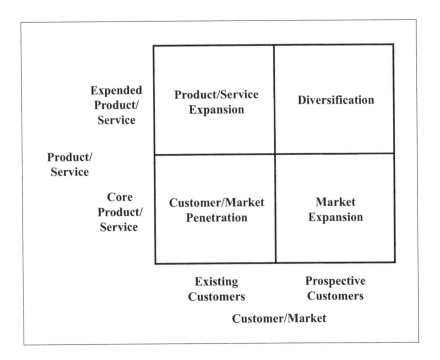

Figure 2.6   Market growth alternative matrix

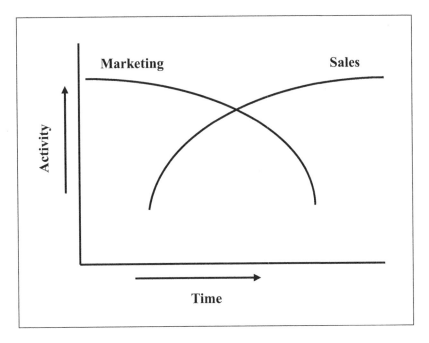

Figure 2.7   Qualitative relationship between marketing and sales activities

and the sales activity must begin and continue through the sales cycle. It is important for any business that does a lot of direct mail to do follow-up: set appointments and have face-to-face contact with prospective customers to begin the sales cycle. Do not try to get into sales without having done the marketing.

2.3.2.2   Charan's approach for market growth

Charan (2004) outlines his approach and points out that for many businesses growth is about "home runs" – the big bold idea, the next new thing and the product that will revolutionize the marketplace. Even though these ideas are great, home runs do not happen every day and frequently come in cycles. A sure and more consistent path to profitable revenue growth is through "singles and doubles" – small day-to-day wins and adaptations to changes in the marketplace that build the foundation for substantially increasing revenues. The impact of singles and doubles can be very significant. They are the basis for sustained revenue growth as well as the foundation for home runs. Singles and doubles provide the discipline of execution which is an absolute necessity for successfully bringing a breakthrough technology to market or implementing a new business model.

According to Charan (2004), business growth is every employee's business and not limited to the sales force and top business leadership. Just as every employee participates in cost reduction, so must every employee be engaged in the growth agenda of the business. Every contact of each employee with a customer is an opportunity for revenue growth. This concept does not exclude anybody, from the employees working in a company's call center handling customer inquiries and complaints, to the top leader CEO.

Charan (2004) lists 10 building blocks as tools that can put a business on the path of sustained and profitable growth:

1. Make revenue growth everyone's business.
2. Hit many singles and doubles, not just home runs.
3. Seek good growth and avoid bad growth – good growth means an increase is in both revenue and profit, is sustainable over time and does not require unacceptable levels of capital. It is also primarily organic and based on differentiated products and services that meet new or unmet needs and creating value for customers.
4. Dispel the myths that inhibit both people and organizations from growing – confront excuses such as; "We are in a no-growth industry and no one is growing"; "Customers are buying only one price"; or "The distributors are the ones in direct contact with retailers and there is not much I can do."
5. Turn the idea of productivity on its head by increasing revenue productivity – the old saying, "We have to do more with less." The problem, though, is that the focus is generally on the "less" and the "more" rarely happens. Revenue productivity is a tool for getting that elusive "more" by actively and creatively searching for ideas for revenue growth without using a disproportionate amount of resources.
6. Develop and implement a growth budget – every business has a budget and it is surprising to discover how little detail about revenue and sources of revenue growth are available. Almost all the detail in the budget is cost related. Few, if any, identify resources specifically identified for growth. The growth budget provides a foundation that will allow a business to increase revenues instead of just talking about it.
7. Beef up strategic marketing – one of the key missing links for generating revenue growth at most businesses is strategic marketing. Most business leaders visualize marketing as tactical tools such as promotion, advertising and brand-building. Strategic marketing, on the other

hand, takes place at a much earlier stage by identifying and defining precisely which customer segments to focus on. It analyzes how the end user uses the product or service and what competitive advantage will be required to win the customer and at what price.

8. Understand how to do effective cross-selling – cross-selling can be a significant source of revenue growth, but most businesses approach it from exactly the wrong perspective. They start by saying; "What else can we sell to our existing customer base?" Instead of looking inside-out their business, they need to look outside-in. Successful cross-selling starts by selecting a segment of customers and then working backward to define precisely the mix of products and services customers need and creatively shaping a value proposition unique to them.

9. Create a social engine to accelerate revenue growth – every business organization is a social system, the center of which is a way of thinking and acting that sets both day-to-day activities and the long-term agenda. When an organization has an explicit growth agenda understood by every employee, growth becomes a central focus – a social engine – during formal meetings and informal discussions. This tool is closely linked to tool number 1: Make revenue growth *everyone's* business.

10. Operational innovation by converting ideas into revenue growth – innovation is not the private property of some exceptional intellectual working away from the mainstream of the business. In any business of reasonable size, innovation is a social process that requires collaboration and communication for idea generation, selecting those ideas for revenue growth that are to be funded and shaping those ideas into product and/or service prototypes and launching them into the marketplace.

Too many businesses focus narrowly on cost reductions, but to survive long term they need to have the growth engine running as well.

2.3.2.3   *Boston Consulting group's (BCG) approach for market growth*

Henderson (1970) adopts a chart approach known as the growth-share matrix (GSM), which was originally created in the 1970s to help corporations analyze their business units or product lines. This helps the company to allocate resources and is used as an analytical tool in brand marketing, product management, strategic management and portfolio analysis.

The GSM chart is presented in Figure 2.8 on the following page, where business data are plotted into four quadrants. Each quadrant is defined below:

*   *Cash cows* are units with high market share in a slow-growing industry. These units typically generate cash in excess of the amount of cash needed to maintain the business. They are regarded as staid and boring in a "mature" market and every business would be thrilled to own as many as possible. They are to be "milked" continuously with as little investment as possible, since such investment would be wasted in an industry with low growth.
*   *Dogs* – more charitably called pets – are units with low market share in a mature, slow-growing industry. These units typically "break even," generating barely enough cash to maintain the business's market share. Though owning a break-even unit provides the social benefits of providing jobs and possible synergies that assist other business units, from an accounting point of view such a unit is worthless, not generating cash for the company. They depress a profitable company's return on assets ratio, used by many investors to judge how well a company is being managed. Dogs, it is thought, should be sold off.

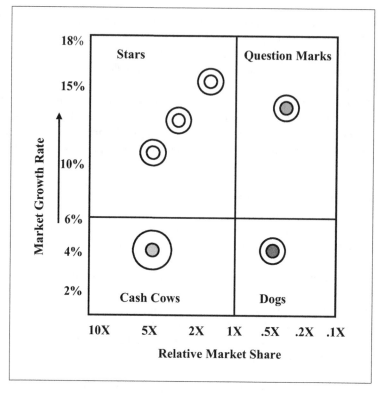

Figure 2.8   Growth-Share matrix (GSM)

- *Question marks* are growing rapidly and thus consume large amounts of cash, but because they have low market shares they do not generate much cash. The result is large net cash consumption. These units are also known as "problem child": they have the potential to gain market share and become a star and eventually a cash cow when the market growth slows. If the question mark does not succeed in becoming market leader then perhaps after years of cash consumption it will degenerate into a dog when the market growth declines. Question marks must be analyzed carefully to determine whether they are worth the investment required to grow market share.
- *Stars* are units with high market share in a fast-growing industry. The hope is that stars become the next cash cows. Extra cash may be required to sustain the business unit's market leadership, but this is worthwhile if that is what it takes for the unit to remain a leader. When growth slows, stars become cash cows if they have been able to maintain their category leadership, or they move from being stars to the dog category.

As a particular industry matures and its growth slows, all business units are either cash cows or dogs. The overall goal of this ranking was to help corporate analyst to identify which business units to fund and how much; and which units to sell. Business leaders were supposed to gain perspective from this analysis which allowed them to plan with confidence to use money generated by the cash cows to fund the stars and, possibly, the question marks. This was the original application of this matrix in 1970s.

This matrix was utilized by a diversified company with a balanced portfolio for its growth opportunities. The balanced portfolio has:

- Stars whose high share and high growth assure the future.
- Cash cows that supply funds for that future growth.
- Question marks to be converted into stars with the added funds.

For each product or service the "area" of the circle represents the value of its sales. The GSM chart offers a very useful map of the organization's product and/or service strengths and weaknesses in terms of current profitability and the likely cash flows. One of the main indicators of cash generation is "relative market share," and one which pointed to cash usage is that of "market growth rate."

Relative market share: This indicates likely cash generation, because the higher the share the more cash will be generated. As a result of economies of scale, it is assumed that these earnings will grow faster the higher the share. The exact measure is the brand's share relative to its largest competitor. Thus, if the brand had a share of 25 percent, and the largest competitor had the same, the ratio would be 1:1. If the largest competitor had a share of 50 percent, however, the ratio would be 1:2, implying that the organization's brand was in a relatively weak position. If the largest competitor only had a share of 5 percent, the ratio would be 5:1, implying that the brand owned was in a relatively strong position, which might be reflected in profits and cash flow.

The reason for choosing relative market share, rather than just profits, is that it carries more information than just cash flow. It shows where the brand is positioned against its main competitors and indicates where it might be likely to go in the future. It can also show what types of marketing activities might be expected to be effective.

Market growth rate: In a fast-growing market, businesses would like to strive for rapidly growing brands, but business leaders have seen, the penalty is that they are usually net cash users and require investment. The reason for this is often that the growth is being "bought" by the high investment and the reasonable expectation is that a high market share will eventually turn into a sound investment in future profit. The theory behind the concept is that a higher growth rate is indicative of accompanying demands on investment. The cut-off point is usually 10 percent per annum. Determining this cut-off point, the rate above which the growth is deemed to be significant, is a critical requirement of the technique; once again makes the use of the GSM in some product areas. In this concept, market growth rate is linked to brand position, not just its cash flow. It is a good indicator of that market's strength, of its future potential and also of its attractiveness to future competitors. It can also be used in growth analysis.

Risk and criticisms: The BCG's growth-share matrix ranks only market share and industry growth rate and only implies actual profitability. In some businesses, it is certainly possible that a particular dog can be profitable without cash infusions required, therefore should be retained and not sold. The matrix also overlooks other elements of industry attractiveness and competitive advantages.

With this or any other such analytical tool, ranking business units has a subjective element involving guesswork about the future, particularly with respect to growth rates. Unless the rankings are approached with rigor and skepticism, optimistic evaluations can lead to a "dot com" mentality in which even the most dubious businesses are classified as "question marks" with good prospects; enthusiastic leaders may claim that cash must be thrown at these businesses immediately to turn them into stars before growth rates slow and it is too late. The poor definition of a business's market will lead to some dogs being misclassified cash bulls, which would mean they provided good cash flow, but in reality that is not true.

It is a foolish vendor (supplier) who diverts funds from a "cash cow" when these are needed to extend the life of that product. Although it is necessary to recognize a "dog" when it appears (at least before it bites you), it would be foolish in the extreme to create one to balance up the picture. The supplier, who has most of their products in the "cash cow" quadrant, should consider them self-fortunate and an excellent marketer; although they might also consider creating a few stars as an insurance policy against unexpected future developments and, perhaps, to add some extra growth.

2.3.2.4   Ansoff's approach for market growth

Ansoff (1957) created the marketing tool known as the "Product-Market Growth Matrix" (Figure 2.9). This matrix allows marketers to consider ways to grow the business via existing and/or new products in existing and/or new markets – there are four possible product/market combinations, and the matrix helps businesses decide what course of action should be taken given current performance. The matrix consists of four strategies:

Market Penetration: In order to penetrate existing markets, businesses are offering existing products. One of the best ways to achieve this is by gaining competitors' customers. Other ways are attracting non-users of firm's product or convincing current customers to use more of their products/services, via advertising or other promotions. Sometimes brand products provide market penetration, for example, BMW in automobile market.

Market Development: This involves finding a new market for the existing products. An established product in the marketplace can be tweaked or targeted to a different customer segment, as a strategy to earn more revenue for the business. For example, bottled water consumption was started in communities where public water supply was not good, but bottled water is now

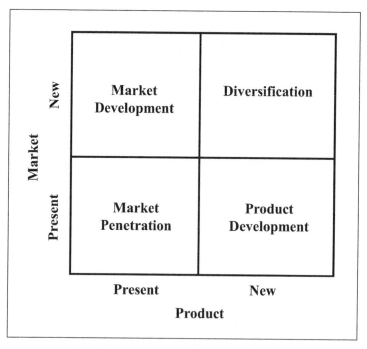

Figure 2.9   Ansoff's product-market growth matrix

consumed everywhere. A marketing manager has to think about the following questions before implementing a market development strategy: Is it profitable? Will it require the introduction of new or modified products? Is the customer and channel well enough researched and understood? Market managers also need to analyze and focus to the market segments: existing customers, competitors' customers, non-buying in current segments, and new segments.

Product Development: Businesses try to develop new products in the existing markets. A business with a market for its current products might embark on a strategy of developing other products catering to the same market. For example, McDonald's is always within the fast-food industry, but frequently markets new food items – chicken, salad, etc. Frequently, when a business creates new products, it can gain new customers for these products. Hence, new product development could be a crucial business development strategy for businesses to stay competitive (topic is discussed in more detail later).

Diversification: Here, product and market are both new. This results in the company entering new markets where it had no presence before. For example, Honda is entering into the small six-seat airplane manufacturing business. The following are some special definitions of diversification:

- Diversification is a corporate strategy that takes the organization away from both its current markets and products, as opposed to either market or product development.
- Diversification in finance involves spreading investments around into many types of investments.
- Diversification from demographics point of view is a measure of the commonality of a population. Greater diversification denotes a wider variety of elements within that population.

As business strategy moves away from existing products and existing markets to new products and new markets, the element of risk increases significantly. Thus, product development and market extension typically involve a greater risk than penetration; and diversification – new product and new market – generally carries the greatest risk of all. Diversification usually requires new skills, new technologies and new facilities. As a result it almost invariably leads to physical and organizational changes in the structure of the business which represent a distinct break with past business experience (Kumar, 2010a).

New product development (NPD): The term commonly used to describe the complete process of bringing a new product or service to market. The process is divided into two parallel paths: one involves the development of the idea, product design, and detailed engineering through manufacturing; the other path involves market research and marketing analysis. Businesses generally see new product development as the initial stage in generating and commercializing new product within the strategic process of product life cycle management used to maintain or grow their market share. There is a period ahead of the new product development period that is generally known as "fuzzy front end": however, these activities are not fuzzy, as explained below.

Fuzzy front end: A distinct period in the new product development process. It is at the front end that the firm formulates a concept of the product to be developed and decides on whether or not to invest resources in the further development of an idea. Koen et al. (2001) and Kim and Wilemon (2002) describe this phase as existing between the first consideration of an opportunity and when it is judged ready to enter the structured development process. This front end includes all activities from the search for new opportunities through the formation of an idea to the development of a precise concept. The fuzzy front end is complete when the firm approves and begins formal development of the concept.

Fuzzy front end is a critical decision period and the product's whole future depends on it. The time is always limited between the product concept and the production. If a company utilizes almost half of this available time up-front for the activity known as "fuzzy front end" they must then accomplish the rest of the activities in the remaining time, which will generally create problems. This leads to late product delivery. According to Smith and Reinertsen (1998), the fuzzy front end need not be an expensive part of product development; however, it can take up to 50 percent of the development time, and it is where major commitments are typically made involving money, time, and the product's nature, thus setting the course for the entire project and final end product.

Consequently, this phase should be considered as an essential part of the development rather than something that happens before development, and its cycle time should be included in the total development cycle time. Koen et al. (2001) have identified five different front-end activities; these are listed in no particular order:

- Opportunity identification.
- Opportunity analysis.
- Idea genesis.
- Idea selection.
- Concept and technology development.

Opportunity Identification: In a large or incremental business, technological chances are identified in a more or less structured way. Based on the guidelines established here, resources will eventually be allocated to new projects which then lead to a structured new product and process development (NPPD) strategy.

Opportunity Analysis: This translates the identified opportunities into implications for the business- and technology-specific context of the company. Business invests a great deal of time and effort in aligning ideas to target customer groups and in market studies and/or technical trials and research.

Idea Genesis: An evolutionary and iterative process progressing from birth to maturation of the opportunity into a tangible idea. The process of the idea genesis can take place internally or come from outside inputs, for example, a supplier offering a new material/technology or from a customer with an unusual request.

Idea Selection: To choose or not to pursue an idea by analyzing its potential business value.

Concept and Technology Development: At the front end of the business, development is based on estimates of the total available market, customer needs, investment requirements, competitive analysis and project uncertainty. Some firms consider this step as an initially required step before NPPD process.

Types of new products: There are several general categories of new products:

- Some are new to the market, for example, high density television set (HDTV) in the home entertainment, and iPhone in the individual and business communication.
- Some are new to the company, for example, digital camera for Kodak.
- Some are completely novel and create totally new markets, for example, new commercial/commuter jet plane of different capacity (a small six-seat plane).

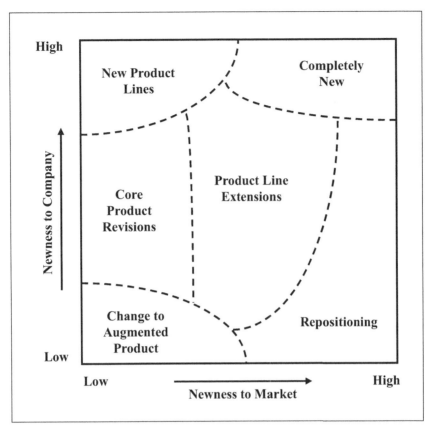

Figure 2.10   New products and market relationship

When analyzing against a different criteria, some new product concepts are merely minor modifications of existing products while others are completely innovative to the company. These different characterizations, presented in Figure 2.10 above and can be from low to high categories.

New product development (NPD) Process: There are several stages in the new product development process, but they are not always followed in the same order. These process stages are briefly described below:

Idea generation: Ideas for new products can be obtained from various sources – customers, employee-user innovation, the company's R&D group, focus groups, regular employee, sales people, competitors, trade shows, or through the innovation policy. Customer/user needs and habits are also good sources for product lines and product features. Formal idea generation techniques can be used, such as attribute listing, brainstorming, morphological analysis or problem analysis.

Idea screening: It is important to eliminate cost ineffective ideas before allocating critical resources, therefore, follow some basic guidelines. The objective is to eliminate unsound concepts prior to devoting resources to them. Those screening new ideas must ask at least three questions:

1. Will the customer in the target market benefit from the product?

2. Is it technically feasible to manufacture the product?
3. Will the product be profitable when manufactured and delivered to the customer at the target price?

Concept development and testing: At these early stages of product development, try to answer as many as possible of the following marketing and engineering questions. Try to prove product feasibility through virtual computer modeling and rapid prototyping.

*   Who is the target market and who is the decision-maker in the purchasing process?
*   What product features must the product incorporate?
*   What benefits will the product provide to consumers?
*   How will consumers react to the product?
*   How will the product be produced most cost effectively?
*   What will be the production cost?

Business analysis: Once the initial design is complete and the manufacturing process and cost have been identified, complete the business analysis.

*   Estimate the likely selling price based upon competition and customer feedback.
*   Estimate sales volume based upon market size.
*   Estimate profitability and break-even point.

Beta testing and market testing: Before the product is introduced to the open market, perform some controlled tests and analyze the product performance results as well as its acceptance in the defined customer areas.

*   Produce a physical prototype or mock-up.
*   Test the product in typical usage situations.
*   Conduct focus group customer interviews or introduce at trade show.
*   Make adjustments where necessary.
*   Produce an initial run of the product and sell it in a test market to determine customer acceptance.

Technical implementation: Once the product is proved to be acceptable in the controlled environment and looks profitable then the next step is technical implementation. The key steps of technical implementation are:

*   new program initiation;
*   program resource estimation;
*   requirement publication;
*   engineering operations planning;
*   operations (manufacturing side) planning and scheduling;
*   supplier collaboration;
*   program review and monitoring;
*   contingencies-what-if planning.

Commercialization: This step generally starts at the tail end of the technical implementation. Whatever is commercialized must be delivered on time and meeting or exceeding customer expectations based on the commercialization.

- Launch the product.
- Produce and place advertisements and other promotions.
- Fill the distribution pipeline with product.
- Critical path analysis is most useful at this stage.

Some of these steps may be combined, eliminated, or run at the same time (referred to as "concurrent engineering" or "product time to market"). In most industries, business leaders see new product development as a proactive process where resources are allocated to identify market changes and new product opportunities are seized upon before they occur. This concept is in contrast to a reactive strategy in which nothing is done until problems occur or the competitor introduces an innovation. Many industry leaders see new product development as an ongoing process and is generally known as continuous development in which the entire organization is always looking for opportunities.

For the more innovative products, as indicated in Figure 2.10, a greater amount of uncertainty and change may exist, which makes it difficult, if not impossible, to plan the complete project before starting it. In this case, a more flexible approach may be advisable.

Since the NPD process typically requires engineering (product design and manufacturing), materials, financial and market expertise; cross-functional teams are a common way of organizing projects. The team is responsible for all aspects of the project, from initial idea generation to final commercialization, and they usually report to senior management within the organization. In those industries where products are technically complex, development research is typically expensive, and product life cycles are relatively short, strategic alliances among several organizations help to spread out the costs, provide access to a wider set of skills, and speeds the overall process.

Protecting new products: When developing a new product, many legal questions may arise and some of these questions are:

- How do I protect the innovation from imitators?
- Can the innovation be legally protected?
- For how long can I protect the innovation?
- How much will this cost?

The answers to these and other questions are complicated and several legal concepts may apply to any given innovation, product, process, or creative work. These include patents, trademarks, service marks, trade names, copyrights, and trade secrets. It is critical to know which are applicable and when each is appropriate. This varies somewhat from jurisdiction to jurisdiction. The advice of a lawyer who specializes in these matters and is knowledgeable with corporate philosophy regarding intellectual property (IP) protection is essential.

Generally, copyrights are fairly easy to obtain, but are applicable only in certain instances. Patents on the other hand, tend to involve complex claims and approval processes, are expensive to obtain and even more expensive to defend and preserve.

2.3.3   NEW PRODUCT GROWTH AND INVESTMENT STRATEGY

A technological innovation may create a new industry or market. For example, Internet technology has created a new industry of websites. Industry offers products and/or services in the market to meet or exceed customer needs. Every product's *life cycle* can be divided into three phases (Figure 1.1): infancy, growth and maturity/decline. Products of Internet technology are going through the growth period during the early part of twenty-first century. Similarly with computer or television industries, both of which have had periods of rapid growth after WWII. The growth phase is characterized by high levels of investment, rapid and accelerating growth in sales, and relatively high levels of both entry and exit. When product prices started to decline is a good indication that the product is reaching at maturity or declining stage of its life cycle.

The strategic interaction among enterprises occurs during these products *life cycle* along several dimensions: pricing, capacity, product policy and R&D. Most of these strategies involve substantial investments and the investments are largely irreversible. They represent commitments to the industry by the enterprises and are an integral part of the process of establishing the relative position of the enterprises – in terms of market share, costs and products.

The growth phase of an industry is of interest to both the business leaders and the economist (Spencer, 1979). The evolutionary process in the business strategy development should improve the quality of predictions about the consequences of strategic investments, most of which take place in the growth phase. The opportunities for changing one's market position are much more limited in a mature product. The evolutionary process determines the returns to a variety of kinds of investment, including that in R&D, which have implications for the dynamic aspects of the performance of the economy.

Spencer (1979) argues that constraints on growth and the timing of entry put enterprises in asymmetrical positions with respect to investment. Those enterprises fund themselves in the more favored positions exploit the advantage by preempting the market to some extent. The result is an analysis of the optimal preemptive investments for the enterprises that are similar in spirit to the German economist Heinrich Freiherr von Stackelberg model of oligopolistic interaction (in which the leader enterprise moves first and then the follower enterprises move sequentially). The roles of the enterprises, however, are determined by the constraints on growth and the history of the industry. The equilibrium with investment paths as the objects of choice seems to Spencer (1979) a less plausible assumption about behavior than the asymmetric approach.

Spencer (1979) has developed the capital investment behavior model with the constraints on investments as the central features of the model. For example, investment is irreversible; business can be shut down but it cannot withdraw its capital on a dollar-for-dollar basis. There are several types of investments: for example, plant and equipment, R&D, advertising, etc., with revenue and margin growth is as rapid as possible. However, there is the additional of the composition or mix of investments. The enterprise invests in the capital with the highest marginal product net of interest cost, unless and until their marginal products are equal; then it invests so as to keep them equal until it hits a sequence of optimal stopping point, one for each type of capital.

2.3.4   EMERGING MARKET – MULTINATIONAL ENTERPRISES WITH INTERNATIONAL GROWTH

Emerging economy enterprises have benefited tremendously from internationalization at home through cooperation via original equipment manufacturers (OEMs) and joint venture in particular with global enterprises which have provided technological and organizational skills, allowing emerging market enterprises to grow internationally. The BRICS countries (Brazil, the Russian Federation, India, China and South Africa) continued to be the leading resource of FDI (foreign direct investment) among emerging investor countries. Capital flow from these five countries rose from $7 billion in 2000 to $145 billion in 2012, accounting for 10 percent of the world total (UNCTAD, 2013), although, developed countries multinational enterprises (MNEs) remain the major source of outward FDI today.

Luo and Tung (2007) define emerging market multinational enterprises (EM MNEs) as international companies originated from emerging markets and are engaged in outward FDI, where they exercise effective control and undertake value-adding activities in one or more foreign countries. Their definition excludes the following:

- Import-export companies without outward FDI.
- Investing mainly or exclusively in tax-haven countries, for example, Cayman and Virgin Islands.
- State-owned enterprises to completely pursue political objectives designated by their respective home governments, for example, Indian Oil Corporation's acquisition of oil and gas resources in West Africa; or undertake foreign aid investment programs to strengthen the political and diplomatic ties between home and host country governments, for example, China's state-owned construction companies, which built bridges, stadiums, railroads and hospitals in Africa. These EM MNEs neither compete in global markets nor do they perform tasks to benefit enterprise gains.

Luo and Tung (2007) have also analyzed the uniqueness of these EM MNEs, including their rationale and motives, activities and strategies, propelling and facilitating forces as well as risks and challenges in the course of international expansion. Dumming's (1981, 1988 and 2001) concept of EM MNEs international expansion is especially in other developing countries, in search of location-specific advantages by leveraging their unique capabilities. Similarly, the evolutionary process theory of Johanson and Vahlne (1977) where EM MNEs do not necessarily follow the incremental approach in internationalization, but they still attend carefully to the importance of organizational learning and global experience.

Luo and Tung (2007) believe that EM MNEs are at present much less path-dependent (e.g., the ethnic network is no longer the key) and much more risk-taking (e.g., through aggressive acquisitions and mergers) than "third world" multinationals in the 1980s; the two groups still share same home strengths (e.g., cost advantage) and weaknesses (e.g., limited knowledge of overseas markets).

The following are some examples where EM MNEs aim at accomplishing their goal of opportunities:

- Where companies are taking advantages of their reputation and size, for example, Brazilian banks including Banco do Brasil and Banco Bradesco achieved their objectives through investments in Europe and South America.
- Some home and/or host countries' governments are offering preferential financial and non-financial treatments; for example, the Chinese government has given Lenovo some support, such as financial underwriting, and privileged access to domestic government and educational markets.
- Some MNEs are tapping niche opportunities in advanced markets that complement their strengths; for example, India's top software companies including Infosys, Satyam and Wipro all benefited from new clients and rapid growth in North America.
- Utilizing the opportunities in other developing countries to leverage their cost-effective manufacturing capabilities; for example, several Chinese companies invested in South East Asia to utilize their excess production capacity; and a similar concept is also applicable in South America.
- Some South American companies have made real estate investments during 1980s in the US, especially in the states like Florida and New York.

Some EM MNEs often undertake several strategies/activities associated with international spring-boarding (Luo and Tung, 2007), including:

- cumulative benefits from inward investment before undertaking outward FDI;
- leapfrog trajectory;
- simultaneous competition and cooperation with global players.

Entrepreneurial leadership is also an important driving force behind the springboard activities. For example, when both state-owned and non-state-owned enterprises interact between institutional legacies of emerging economies and dynamic capabilities of their corporate entrepreneurs is crucial for understanding their internationalization strategies (Child and Rodrigues, 2005).

EM MNEs are proactive in international markets, which are often led by business leaders who have sharp vision and have adopted pragmatic measures to tap into foreign markets that provide resource-seeking or market-seeking opportunities (Andreff, 2002; Tsang, 2002). Luo and Tung (2007) reviewed EM MNEs and providing examples of some leading EM MNEs, such as China's Lenovo and Haier, and India's Tata and Wipro Technologies, reveal just that: their corporate leaders have a strong appreciation of the core of global competition – serve worldwide customers, including those in advanced markets, quicker, better and inexpensively. To maintain this position, they aggressively expand their scale and scope by investing present capital in new projects and/or reinvesting accumulated-retained earnings in existing or new projects.

Quick changes in the technological and market landscapes, and heightened integration of the global economy during the starting period of the twenty-first century have propelled EM MNEs to enter on to the world stage. While international spring-boarding presents many opportunities, it also involves many risks. Therefore, all multinationals have to contend with risks as discussed in Chapter 3 (Enterprise Risk Management).

2.3.5   FOREIGN AND/OR NEW MARKET AND GROWTH STRATEGY

When enterprises enter to a new market then they must grow quickly to reach a size at which their operations are cost-competitive with incumbent enterprises to survive (Porter, 1980; Shane, 1996; Garnsey, 1998). The enterprise growth has attracted significant interest, both theoretically and empirically, but the literature does not provide enough documented research (Gilbert et al., 2006). Research on domestic enterprises cannot be fully generalized to foreign enterprises, partially because domestic investors are typically more financially constrained than their foreign counterparts (Mitchell et al., 1994; Li, 1995). Additionally, the growth dynamics of domestic enterprises differ from those of foreign enterprises (Mata and Portugal, 2002). There is not enough literature to compare external growth, that is, acquisition, with internal growth – green field investments.

Empirical findings are generally mixed, with all suggesting that the relationship between mode of foreign entry and post-entry growth may be more complex than previously understood (Woodcock et al., 1994; Pennings et al., 1994; Li, 1995; Shaver, 1998; McCloughan and Stone, 1998; William, 2003; Mata and Portugal, 2004; Slangen and Hennart, 2008). According to Tan's (2009) literature search, only two studies examined the importance of entry strategy on post-entry growth (Williams, 2003; Portugal, 2004), both of which found that acquisition entrants have lower employment growth rate than do green field entrants. Empirical work on international entry mode choice, which typically hypothesizes that enterprises attempting to pursue speedy entry will choose acquisition (Hennart and Park, 1993; Andersson and Svensson, 1994; Barkema and Vermeulen, 1998; Brouthers and Brouthers, 2000; Chang and Rosenzweig, 2001; Chen and Zung,

2004). Therefore, the international business literature has argued that acquisitions provide a means of rapidly entering new market, but some case studies and the enterprise histories do not support such philosophy (Hasting, 1999; Zook and Allen, 1999).

Multinational enterprises consist of corporate offices and subsidiaries. Enterprise-specific leadership capabilities within MNEs can be developed at both the corporate offices and subsidiary levels, with subsidiary-level leadership capabilities being specific to a particular subsidiary. It stands to reason, then, that leaders of MNEs entering foreign markets through new subsidiary, that is, green field entries, which will not yet possess such subsidiary-level capabilities. Therefore, the enterprise can recruit experienced business leaders, but the team experience within the new venture can be accumulated only within that venture. However, interdependence between subsidiaries within a multinational network can sometimes be strong and complex. For example, an MNE may encounter the same customers or competitors in different national markets. This requires behavior coordination among the subsidiaries involved. Moreover, maintaining competitive advantage requires frequent exchanges between subsidiaries to achieve scale and scope economies, and to promote innovation.

Coordinating highly independent subsidiaries within MNE requires corporate-level business leadership capabilities (Verbeke and Yuan, 2007). Since leadership policies and procedures governing interactions between subsidiaries may not be consistent with the best interests of individual subsidiaries, O'Donnell (2000), but the design and implementation of such policies and procedures must address the interdependence between the corporate office and the subsidiaries (Hennart, 1991). Business leaders must have an unbiased appreciation of the role and responsibility of individual subsidiaries and must remain loyal to the enterprise, Bartlett and Ghoshal (1989).

Greenfield and acquisition strategies differ in their use of business leadership resources (Tan, 2009). While acquisition brings in subsidiary-level leadership resources, they consume more corporate-level leadership resources if interdependence within MNE is strong and complex. Consequently, strong and complex interdependence negatively affects post-entry growth of acquired business venture. In contrast (Tan, 2009) argues that although greenfield business ventures need to accumulate subsidiary-level leadership resources, they consume fewer corporate-level resources in the presence of strong and complex interdependence within the MNE network. The negative impact of strong and complex interdependence on post-entry growth is smaller for greenfield business ventures. Hence, MNEs with weak and modifiable interdependence are more likely to choose acquisitions; conversely, those with strong and complex interdependence are more likely to choose greenfield investments. Tan (2009) suggests that the marketing intensity of the MNE facilitates post-entry growth of acquired business venture, whereas this positive affect is weaker or absent in greenfield business venture. Hence, weather a particular type of entry strategy allows a subsidiary to grow quickly depends on the characteristics of its parent company and of the industry it enters.

2.3.6   COMPETITIVE DYNAMICS THROUGH ACQUISITIONS

Keil et al. (2013) have analyzed 1,316 public software enterprises in the United States between 1980 and 2005, and their findings are consistent with the prediction of the competitive dynamics research, that acquisitions of rivals in a product segment of an enterprise negatively affects the enterprise performance. A focal firm's acquisition in another segment is the only response to an acquisition by a new entrant that has positive effects. Therefore, results of Keil et al. (2013) suggest that the optimal response strategies depend on the source of the competitive pressure and the acquisition response may not be the best strategy.

Many software enterprises use acquisitions to execute their competitive growth strategies. For example, software enterprises such as Google, Facebook, Microsoft, Oracle, etc. have attracted significant media attention due to acquisition programs. They have used to grow and defend their market positions. Therefore, some serious questions should be answered: what are the effects of these acquisitions on rivals? How should an enterprise respond to an acquisition in its industry by a new entrant or by one of its existing rivals? There is an extensive body of research on acquire performance and the performance of individual acquisitions, but there is not enough research on the effects of acquisitions on rivals (Fosfuri and Giarratana, 2009). Acquisitions generally create consolidation, therefore, acquisitions by rivals will lead to decreased competitive intensity. Competitive dynamics research, on the other hand, regards acquisitions as competitive moves that are difficult to match due to their implementation difficulties and are therefore likely to have negative effects on rivals (Chen et al., 1992).

The acquisition of an established competitor by a new entrant is often performed by a larger enterprise that has already been successful in another industry segment and is now expanding its scope to other industry segments. The new entrant is likely to have superior financial resources and scale, which it can use to enhance the competitive position of the acquired business (Keil et al., 2013). For example, a new entrant in the software industry may benefit from complementary products between their own offering and the offering of the acquired business. Microsoft has been accused of using its de facto monopoly in the software industry to unfairly conquer new segments of business. This may not be true all the time. Some new entrants may face serious issues in entering new segments of a business. A new entrant may not be very familiar with the specifics of business logics. There are some of the elements associated with the acquisition of a business in a new area.

2.4   Core Competency

There are several definitions of core competency in the literature including the following:

- The knowledge view suggests that core competence is a knowledge system embodied in technology, human resources, information and organization (Leonard-Barton, 1992).
- The network view advances the idea that core competence is a network of skills and can be found out through cluster analysis of skills (Klein and Hiscocks, 1994).
- The harmony view thinks that core competence is the development of assets and skills in a harmonious fashion (Sanchez et al., 1996).

Some examples of core competency are: Walt Disney World's efficient operation of theme parks; Apple Computer understands the customer needs: iPhone, iPad, etc. Core competency needs to fulfill three key criteria:

1. It must not be easy for competitors to imitate.
2. It can be reused widely for various products/services and markets.
3. It should lead to core products which must contribute to the end products to meet or exceed customer needs.

Core competencies can represent a set of tacit and collective knowledge which is developed through learning processes and which provides the enterprise with particular strengths and superior value relative to other enterprises. They are sources of innovation, customer benefits and sustainable competitive advantage (Lei et al., 1996). Espinoza et al. (2011) offer insights regarding the core leadership competencies in leading the workforce. They state that millennials are making its significance in the organizational agenda wherein US Bureau of Labor Statistics reveals that millennials constitute almost 25 percent of the workforce in the US. Espinoza et al. (2011) also mentioned that efficient business leaders should start with the millennials' experience and suspend their own bias. A proactive reaction to perceived millennial orientations and millennial intrinsic values are core competencies that effective business leaders need to master and cites several required leadership competencies which include motivating, directing, and engaging.

Nobre (2011) emphasizes that customer-centric systems (CCS) are enterprise type which strategically organize their resources and competencies around customers' values and needs, in order to involve customers into their business. Once customers are involved into their task environments and business, CCS-based enterprises have the chance to understand their clients' real needs and to produce the appropriate products (goods and services). Nobre (2011) believes that the enterprises attempt to master, analyze and integrate technological, leadership and organizational perspectives of past and current manufacturing organizations, which contribute to illuminate features and to identify core competencies of future industrial enterprises, which are in the pursuit of innovation and sustainable competitive advantage in the twenty-first century.

The concept of CCS was first touched by Nobre and Steiner (2002) and later was further developed by Nobre et al. (2008, 2009). Briefly CCS represents new organizational needs with capabilities to:

- manage high levels of environmental complexity;
- operate through high levels of mass customization;
- pursue high degrees of organizational cognition, intelligence and autonomy, and consequently high degrees flexibility and agility.

Every organization requires certain competencies to operate effectively and carry out their mission. These fundamental competencies are called "table stakes" (McIntire 2008). These stakes define the standard level of competency needed to sustain operations. Some of the basic competencies are marketing; product design, development and manufacturing; human resources; fund raising; financial; administration, and so on. Sample detail of some of these activities is presented below:

Marketing skills where personnel would have knowledge and experience in:

- the activities needed to identify the customer needs and the product characteristics and service offerings that can meet or exceed customer needs and how to package these into the product and/or service offering;
- determining the price for the product and services offered including discounts, sliding scale fees, etc. and how payment will be accepted;
- determining how and where the product and services will be offered and by whom;
- promoting the products and services, communicating with the prospective customers, and selling.

Human resources skills where personnel with knowledge and experience in:

- interviewing prospective employees, managers and business leaders;
- hiring and introducing new hires;
- determining the compensation for the new hires and establishing the process to pay them;
- determining their training requirements to perform their jobs and providing or making arrangements to provide this training;

- reviewing performance and discharging ineffective personnel.

Therefore, how to determine the organization's core competency? As pointed out earlier that core competencies require continuous improvement as technology and customer needs are changing. Demands on organizations continue to change and today's core competencies may be tomorrow's table stakes. Organizations that provide standard services and are in high demand; organizations that do not operate in a highly competitive environment or enjoying monopolies will usually do not possess or need core competencies. Table stakes are more than sufficient for their success. The examples of these organizations are some basic services such as homeless shelters and soup kitchens. It is almost impossible to find an example of a monopolistic business due to government regulations. The only time some elements of monopolistic philosophy are found is in a small bank or airline serving a small city.

Organizational competencies require the integration of skills across the functional lines. A core competency is a bundle of skills that enables an organization to provide a particular benefit to customers. Each competency listed in any organization must be associated with a customer benefit or a significant contribution to the financial health of the organization. For example, the design core competency of Boeing resources are providing the Dreamliner plane (Boeing 787) to meet customer needs and providing significant financial benefits to Boeing.

2.4.1   RESEARCH AND DEVELOPMENT (R&D) PROFESSIONALS AND CORE COMPETENCY

The ability of R&D technical professionals has emerged as a critical factor in creating and maintaining a company's technological competitiveness. This is because a company's sustainable competitive advantage largely depends on R&D technical professionals' capabilities that enhance the company's effectiveness and performance in developing new products and processes. To meet the impact of technological change, most companies have an ongoing need for competent technical professionals. Hence, the technological competitive advantage of a company is contingent on identifying and maintaining an adequate number of qualified technical professionals. To hold on to a sufficient number of capable professionals, most companies must effectively help them to identify and to cultivate their competencies.

Mansfield (1996) states that a competency model is a detailed description of those behaviors which are required in order for employees to be effective in a job, i.e., excellent performers on the job demonstrate these behaviors much more consistently than average or poor performers (Schoonover et al., 2000). Although a variety of competency models have been developed, there are few specific competency models appropriate for technical professionals. Spencer and Spencer (1993) provide in-depth explanations for the development and application of competency models, together with several generic competency models including technical professionals, salespeople, managers and entrepreneurs. The generic competency model presented for technical professionals (Spencer and Spencer, 1993) contains 12 necessary competencies, including achievement orientation, conceptual thinking, analytical thinking, initiative, self-confidence, concern for order, information-seeking, teamwork and cooperation, expertise, and customer service orientation.

The Works Institute (2003) suggests that it is best to implement the competency model gradually and involve fewer than eight competencies at one time. Dive (2004) emphasizes that it is difficult to implement a model comprising too many competencies, and that six is the practical maximum. In order to maintain technical competitiveness, companies have an ongoing need to identify and foster core competencies for technical professionals in the area of research and development (R&D). Exploring core competencies is, however, a qualitative problem. The rough set theory (RST), which has recently become well known as a data-mining technique, is a good tool for data reduction in qualitative analysis. Wu (2009) utilized the rough set approach, which he considers is a suitable approach for dealing with the problem of exploring competencies. Wu (2009) applied the model in semiconductor manufacturers in Taiwan in mining the critical competencies for R&D technical professionals, and he successfully demonstrated a reduction of the numerous essential competencies into a more compact set. He arrived at six core competencies which can be regarded as the indispensable attributes for the design of competency development programs for R&D technical professionals. These six core competencies for R&D technical professionals are: Objective management, Technical improvement, Achievement orientation, Team-working, Relationship building, and Willingness to learn. Among these six core competencies, the most significant competency is the "willingness to learn." This reveals that the most critical competency for technical professionals is a willingness to learn new things to meet future changes.

2.4.2   MANUFACTURING ORGANIZATION'S CORE COMPETENCE

Core competence is a dynamic knowledge system, which interacts with three critical elements:

* Business environment (external).
* Inner environment.
* Technology.

These elements are integrated with core competence. These components and the architecture are the elements which are the sources of sustainable competitive advantage. Core competence elements support the development of core products which are not sold directly to end users. These products are generally utilized in wide array of end products. The business units of the company tap into a few core products to develop a variety of end products (the concept is presented in Figure 2.11 on the next page). The core competence concept can be summarized as follows:

* It is a knowledge system constituted of a competence component and the competence architecture.
* Interaction with business environment (external), inner environment (firm) and technology.
* It is the source of sustainable competitive advantage.
* It is dynamic.

The interaction of market opportunities with core competencies develops the basis for launching new businesses. A company can launch a vast array of businesses if it combines a set of core competencies in different ways and matches them to market opportunities. A large corporation is simply a collection of discrete businesses without core competencies. Core competencies serve as the glue that binds the business units together into a coherent portfolio.

Core competencies tend to be rooted in the ability to integrate and coordinate various groups within the company. A company may be able to hire a group of brilliant scientists in a particular technology, but in doing so it does not automatically gain competence in that technology. It is the effective coordination of all the groups involved in bringing a product/service to market that result in a core competence.

According to Prahalad and Hamel (1990), core competencies are developed from the integration of multiple technologies and the coordination of diverse manufacturing skills. For

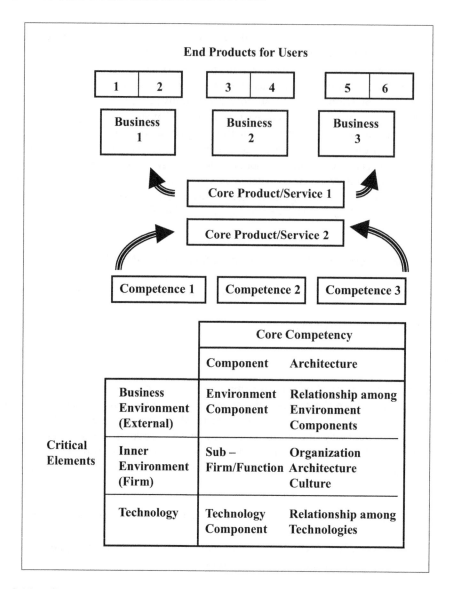

Figure 2.11   Core competencies to end products

example, Sony's ability is to miniaturize electronics. The following three tests are commonly utilized for identifying a core competence:

- It should provide access to a wide variety of markets.
- It should contribute significantly to the end-product benefits.
- It should be difficult for competitors to imitate.

An expensive undertaking is not necessary to develop core competencies. Often the missing element of a core competency can be acquired at a low cost through alliances and licensing agreements. In many situations, an organizational design that facilitates the sharing of competencies can result in much more effective utilization of those competencies at a small to no additional cost.

According to Prahalad and Hamel (1990), core competencies are not necessarily about:

- sharing costs among business units;
- outspending rivals on R&D;
- integrating vertically.

Core competencies help to develop core products and/or services that serve as a link between the competencies and end products/services. For example:

- Honda – gasoline powered engines: in automobiles, motorcycles, lawn mowers and portable generators.
- Black & Decker – small electric motors in small home appliances and tools.
- Canon – laser printer system.
- NEC – semiconductors.

Once a company has successfully developed its core products, it can expand the number of uses to gain the cost advantage via economies of scale and economies of scope.

2.4.2.1   The loss of core competencies

Sometimes cost-cutting activities destroy the ability to build core competencies. For example, when a company decentralizes its businesses, it becomes very difficult to build core competencies because autonomous business units rely on outsourcing critical tasks. This outsourcing prevents the company from developing core competencies in those tasks because it no longer consolidates the know-how that is spread throughout the company.

If businesses fail to recognize their core competencies, then this may lead to decisions that result in their loss. For example, during the 1970s when electronic (radio and television) manufacturing businesses were mature, and high-quality lower-cost products were available from Far East manufacturers, many US manufacturers divested themselves of these businesses. In the process, they lost their core competence for the next-generation product – video – and this loss resulted in a handicap in the newer digital television industry. A company can make better divestment decisions if it recognizes its core competencies and understands the time required to build them or regain them.

2.4.2.2   Implications of corporate leadership

Prahalad and Hamel (1990) recommend that a corporation should be organized into a portfolio of core competencies rather than a portfolio of independent business units. Business unit leaders tend to focus on getting immediate end products to market rapidly and usually do not feel responsible for developing corporate-wide core competencies. Consequently, without the incentive and the direction from corporate leadership to do otherwise, strategic business units are inclined to under invest in building core competencies. For example, if an autonomous business unit does not manage to develop its own core competencies over time then it would not have its core competencies to share with other business units. One possible solution could be for corporate leadership to utilize their capability not only to allocate cash but also core competencies among business units. Business units that lose key employees for the sake of a corporate core competency should be recognized for their contributions.

2.4.3   COACHING CORE COMPETENCIES

It is critical to understand the skills and approaches used by coaches within today's coaching profession. These coaches must support clients in calibrating the level of alignment between the client-specific training expected and the training client has experienced.

International Coach Federation (ICF) (2006) is a coaching organization in which the coaching process is grouped into four clusters where the coaching elements fit together logically based on the common ways of looking at the competencies in each cluster. The competencies are neither prioritized nor weighted. All the competencies are treated as core or critical for any competent coach. The four defined clusters are:

- setting the foundation;
- co-creating the relationship;
- communicating effectively;
- facilitating learning and results.

Setting the foundation: Initial meeting must discuss ethical guidelines and professional standards as well as how to apply these elements appropriately during coaching sessions. This should lead to establishing the coaching agreement.

Co-creating the relationship: The coach has to establish trust and intimacy with the client. This will create a safe and supportive environment which should produce ongoing mutual respect and trust. The coaching process must create a spontaneous and conscious relationship with the client with the expectation that it is open, flexible, and confidential.

Communicating effectively: The coach has to be an active listener and focus completely on what the client is, and is not, saying. It is critical for the coach to understand the meaning of what is said in the context of the client's desires, and to support the client's self-expression. The coach has to ask powerful questions. These questions will reveal the information needed for maximum benefit to the coaching-client relationship. Coach has to ask direct questions to communicate effectively during the coaching sessions and use language that has the greatest positive impact on the client.

Facilitating learning and results: The coach has to integrate and accurately evaluate all sources (single or multiple) of information, and to make interpretations that will help the client to gain awareness and thereby achieve agreed-upon results. The coach should have the ability to create ongoing opportunities for the client during coaching and in work-life situations. The coach should be able to develop and maintain an effective coaching plan and should also be able to recognize and pay attention to what is important for the client, but also leave responsibility with the client to take action.

2.4.4   COMPETITIVE ADVANTAGE

Competitive advantage is a position that an enterprise occupies in its competitive environment and it also represents the organization's capability to create superior value for its customers and superior profits for itself (Porter, 1998). Therefore, a business is considered to have a competitive advantage (CA) over its competitors when the business maintains profits that exceed the average for its industry. Most business strategies have a goal to achieve a sustainable competitive advantage. Two types of competitive advantages are commonly used:

*   cost (also known as minimum cost);
*   differentiation.

A business that is able to provide the same product/service as competitor but at a lower cost is defined as having cost advantage, for example Southwest Airlines. A business that delivers a product/service that exceeds the competing product/service is defined as having a differentiation advantage, for example BMW automobile. Therefore, a competitive advantage enables the business to create a superior value product/service for its customers and superior profits for itself.

The resources and capabilities of a business provide distinctive competencies to create a competitive advantage in the form of cost or differentiation. These advantages ultimately result in superior value creation and the concept is presented in Figure 2.12.

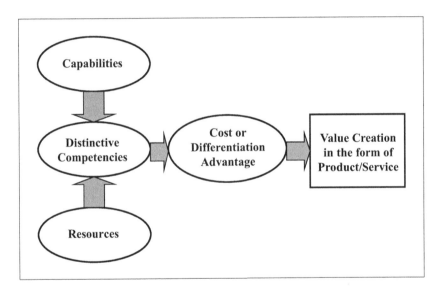

Figure 2.12   Competitive advantage model

The business must have superior resources and capabilities to those of its competitors to develop a competitive advantage. Without this superiority, the competitors could simply replicate what the business was doing and any advantage would quickly disappear. Resources are those critical assets of the business used for creating a cost or differentiation advantage which are not easy for competitors to acquire. These typical resources are:

*   proprietary know-how (may be processes);
*   patents and trademarks;
*   customer base;
*   business reputation;
*   product/Service brand.

Capability refers to the effective utilization of resources. For example, a business must have the ability to bring a product to market faster than its competitors. Such capabilities are ingrained in the routines of the organization and are not easily documented as procedures and so are difficult for competitors to replicate. Resources and capabilities together form the distinctive competencies for the business. These competencies create opportunities for innovation, quality, efficiency and satisfaction, all of which can be leveraged to create a cost advantage or a differentiation advantage.

2.4.4.1   Sustainable competitive advantage

A business processes is a Sustainable Competitive Advantage (SCA) when it has value-creating processes that cannot be duplicated or imitated by competition while also maintaining a profit that exceed the average for its industry. Lei et al. (1996) also suggest that the organization's competitive advantage becomes sustainable when its value evolves with basis on the strategic resources leading along with the development of learning processes and dynamic core competencies. However, it is possible for some businesses to make profits above industry average for a time without sustainable competitive advantage.

The key difference between competitive advantage (CA) and SCA is that the processes and positions a business may hold are non-duplicable and non-imitable when a business processes a SCA. Hence a sustainable competitive advantage is one that can be maintained for a significant amount of time even in the presence of competition. Therefore, what is a "significant amount of time"? A competitive advantage becomes SCA when all duplication and imitation efforts have stopped and the rival businesses have not been able to replicate the same value (products/ services) that the said business is creating. The source of SCA is core competency. For example, Southwest Airline is maintaining its sustainable competitive advantage with above-average business profit while other airlines are either losing money or making relatively lower profit.

2.4.4.2   Building sustainable competitive advantage

Three types of assets help to build on SCA and these assets are exhaustive:

1. Organization and Leadership Process: *Team coordination* is the key to organizational success. Breaking down interdepartmental silos, coordination and resources sharing must be fundamental to creating value. *Integrating resources* is critical to business success. *Learning* processes must be a part of resource integration. Enterprise executives must decide how to collect, distribute, interpret and respond to market-based information, and how to incorporate changes in the environment. These changes in the environment could be customer-based changes, technological developments and legal or government restrictions. Businesses have to develop robust market awareness and expand capabilities to effectively collect information. Businesses have to incorporate market collected information in the products/services they produce. The environment for businesses is constantly changing and constant *reconfiguring and transformation* is very important to forming SCA. Learning and transformation is the key to producing innovative products/services. Innovative capacity of a business determines how it learns from and reacts to market information.
2. Positions: Market positions are the assets to a business and key assets are:
   - financial;
   - technological;
   - reputation;

- business structure: it determines business performance. Business leadership can influence its culture, processes and routines.

3. Path: At the start of a business usually followed with certain *orientations*. This process generally stays with the business for a long time. The path the business takes then determines the development of its competencies. *Technological development* at this time can determine how a business can exploit opportunities to form SCA. Very often it is possible that several technological factors converge into a capability to form a SCA. For example, the rise of a company such as Microsoft with the development of Windows™ operating software.

3

Enterprise Risk Management (ERM)

Business executives expose the enterprises to risk because they believe that they can exploit these risks to their advantage and generate value to the enterprises. This may be one of the reasons why firms embark into emerging markets that have significant political and economic risk and into technologies especially during the latter part of twentieth century and in the twenty-first century where ground rules and information are changing very rapidly. History validates the concept where auto companies like Ford and General Motors in the 1930s and 1940s, computer hardware companies like IBM in the 1950s and 1960s and Dell in 1990s, software companies like Microsoft and Intel in the 1980s and 1990s and now companies like Google, Apple and Facebook in the twenty-first century. These companies have achieved their success by seeking the risk and not avoiding it.

Risk management concept is to operate in an environment in control, not a controlled environment (Lam, 2003). Hubbard (2009) is identifying risk management is the assessment and prioritization of risk followed by coordinated and economical application of resources to minimize, monitor and control the probability and/or impact of unfortunate events or to maximize the realization of opportunities. Tattam (2011) provides a context for risk management in terms of regulation and guidance through a critique of the Basel II regulatory framework, and basing the characteristics of risk management processes around ISO 31000. It is true that risk exposes a firm to potential losses but risk also provides the firm with opportunities. A simple vision of successful risk-taking is that the firm should expand their exposure to upside risk while reducing the potential for downside risk.

Risk, for lack of a better word, is good. Without it, there would be no successful businesses, or, rather, there would only be successful business, as being successful would be so easy that any start-up would have an idyllic path to quarterly revenue bonanzas. Risk is vital to the business world so that those organizations that are able to overcome their challenges can show the rest how it is done (Wade, 2010).

Literature also provides the evidence that risk-taking can sometimes hurt companies and that some risk-taking, at least on average, seems foolhardy. Bowman (1980) uncovered a negative relationship between risk and return in most sectors, a surprise given the conventional wisdom that higher risk and higher returns go hand-in-hand, at least in the aggregate. This phenomenon, risk-taking with more adverse returns, has since been titled the "Bowman paradox" and has been subjected to a series of tests. In follow-up studies (Bowman, 1982) argued that a firm's risk attitudes may influence risk-taking and that more troubled firms often take greater and less justifiable risks. A later study broke down firms into those that earn below and above target level returns (defined as the industry average return on equity) and noted a discrepancy in the risk/return trade-off. Firms that earned below the target level became risk seekers and the relationship between the risk and the return was negative, whereas returns and risk were positively correlated for firms' earnings above target level returns (Fiegenbaum and Thomas, 1988).

According to the Corporate Treasurers Council of the Association for Financial Professionals (AFP 2006), there is an increasing focus on risk management at the highest levels within organizations and it has been used as the catalyst for broad financial transformation initiatives. Jeff Glenzer, Executive Director of the Corporate Treasurers Council of the AFP, said: "There is an increasing dialogue and accountability at the executive management and board levels for enterprise risk management, and treasury's role has grown in the process." There is a growing movement toward enterprise risk management (ERM) in organizations. The statistics are as follows:

- 25 percent are currently managing an ERM program.
- 30 percent are planning to launch an ERM initiative within the next two years.

Approximately three-quarters of organizations conduct risk management with the objective of reducing the variability of earnings and/or cash flow.

Historically, most companies that have grown into household names (some of them are listed in the beginning of the chapter) have managed their risks well. Well enough anyway. The thriving company has mitigated its true, existential threats through a business model that ensures that, say, manufacturing costs, no matter the occasional unforeseen price spike, will never outpace earnings or through vigilant leadership that ensures that a rival will not dominate the market to the point that the company can no longer compete (Wade, 2010). There are excellent observations about the organization's risk management; and without management sponsorship, risk management will not become embedded in the "way of doing business," and may therefore be seen as interference, or an optional add-on, to managing the business. The aim must be to develop risk management in an organization to a point where, perhaps controversially, Risk Management becomes so embedded in the way or working that it is no longer discussed as a separate subject. O'Rourke (2010) is providing some risk statistics as he surveyed business executives: Of the risks that private companies were most concerned with in the near future, 92 percent pointed to the weak economy and the threat of another recession. Rising costs, heightened competition, unstable capital markets, the possibility of increased taxation to offset public deficits and overregulation were also cited by 60 percent or more of respondents as viable concerns.

Stern School of Management at New York University is also providing five possible sources to exploit risk:

- If a firm is having more timely and reliable information when confronted with a crisis, which will allow the business leaders to map out a superior plan of action in response.
- The speed of response to risk is not the same in all firms, even when provided with the same information. Their response may not be equally effective, timely and appropriately.
- The institutional memories as well as the individual business leaders' experience of how the crises unfolded may provide an advantage over competitors who are new to the risk.
- Any firm's advantage is grounded in resources, since firms with access to capital markets or large cash balances, superior technology and better trained personnel can survive risks better than their competitors.
- Finally, firms that have more operating, production or financial flexibility built into their responses, as a result of choices made in earlier periods, will be able to adjust better than their more rigid compatriots.

Pullan and Murray-Webster (2011) have set out a very practical approach where risk management process can deliver value through effective facilitation. This developed process utilizes the human aspects of risk and risk attitude and the facilitation capacity of the individual. They have discussed the following five areas:

- Avoiding pitfalls – how to make sure you are better prepared, better able to use your knowledge with groups and better able to avoid unsupported or skewed results.
- An understanding of risk management – to refresh your own knowledge and provide the basis for knowledge and ideas you can share with your group(s).
- Understanding your role – whether you are a fulltime facilitator or a line manager with the need to improve risk management, you will learn the skills you need and gain an understanding of how best to develop them.
- Tried and tested tips for each step of the risk management process – proven practices showing how you can use the right mix of workshops, small groups and individual work to keep people engaged and get results.
- Running risk workshops – the whole area of making workshops work.

Literature research on risk management approaches were analyzed based on calendar timings and these approaches can broadly be classified into two categories:

- Traditional approach which was generally followed through late twentieth century. The standard management practice was to identify and prioritize risk based on foresight and/or disaster history and transfer the risk through insurance and/or financial products.
- Changed approach was started at the tail end of the twentieth century. Firms treat the holistic view of risk instead of treating individual risks separately which is considered as managed in "silo." Therefore, business leaders are planning, analyzing and executing the risk at the business level and treating individual risk separately is considered as inefficient approach. The concept is not uniformly practiced in all industries, but business leaders are trying to practice the enterprise risk management (ERM) in the twenty-first century.

Therefore, the following sections are presented in this chapter:

3.1 ERM – Introduction and Definition

Businesses face the parallel challenges of growing revenue and earnings, and managing risks. A thriving business must identify and meet or exceed customer needs with quality products/ services, and correctly make business and investment decisions that will lead to future revenue and profit opportunities. However, the pursuit of new opportunities means that the business must take on a variety of risks. All of these risks must be effectively measured and managed across the business enterprise, otherwise today's promising business ventures may end up being tomorrow's financial disaster. If risks are not managed properly in the long term then the only alternative is crisis management – and the crisis management is much more expensive, time and resources consuming, and embarrassing. Business leaders might have experienced one or more crises in their time, hence this is a message that rings true.

Every business decision involves an element of risk. Hence, there are risks involved in making investments, hedging with derivatives, or extending credit to a customer or business entity. There are also risks involved when developing and pricing new products, hiring and training new employees, aligning performance measurement and incentives with business objectives, and establishing a culture that balances revenue and profit growth and risk management. COSO (2009) has identified that the role of the board of directors in enterprise-wide risk oversight has become increasingly challenging as expectations for board engagement are at the all-time high. Hence, the challenge to the boards is how to effectively oversee the organization's enterprise-wide risk management while adding value to the organization. However, especially for non-financial companies that may be relatively new to these topics, enhancing risk management can be a somewhat daunting task and COSO has shade some light on the topic. Enterprise Risk Management (ERM) is an emerging model at companies and organizations where the management of risks is integrated and coordinated across the organization as a whole. ERM takes a holistic approach to risk management – moving from a fragmented methodology to integrated and broadly focused. ERM expands the process to include not just risks associated with unintended losses, but also financial, strategic, operational and other risks.

The Society of Actuaries (2006) is recommending and organizing the activities of ERM into four themes: Risk Control (RC), Strategic Risk Management (SRM), Catastrophic Risk Management (CRM) and Risk Management Culture (RMC).

- Risk Control is the process of identifying, monitoring, limiting, avoiding, offsetting and transferring risks.
- Strategic Risk Management is the process of reflecting risk and risk capital in the strategic choices that an enterprise makes.
- Catastrophic Risk Management is the process of envisioning and preparing for extreme events that could threaten the viability of the enterprise.
- Risk Management Culture is the general approach of the enterprise to dealing with its risks.

The literature has introduced and discussed concepts under various titles including "integrated risk management (IRM)," "strategic risk management (SRM)" and "holistic risk management (HRM)," Casualty Actuarial Society (CAS 2003). These concepts are synonymous with, ERM where all these concepts emphasize a comprehensive view of risk and risk management, and identifying the movement away from the "silo" approach of leading the variety of risks within an enterprise separately and distinctly. Enterprise risk management (ERM) is a "critical requirement" in achieving the enterprise excellence (EE) while building sustainable competitive advantage. ERM addresses critical business issues such as growth, margin, consistency and value creation as well as the clear linkage between the business fundamentals and the growth strategy. Hence, risk is not just a threat but also an opportunity. Risk management can be a value-creating as well as risk-mitigating process. Risk can come from various areas: project failure (at any phase of the project – from development through sustained *life cycle*), financial markets, credit risk, accidents, legal liabilities, natural disaster, etc. Several institutions have developed risk management standards: Project Management Institute, the National Institute of Science and Technology and actuarial societies. Risk calculating methods, definitions and goals vary widely according to whether the risk management method is in the context of project management, security, engineering related activity, industrial processes, financial portfolios or public health safety.

A couple of definitions from the literature are presented here with some discussion. The Casualty Actuarial Society (CAS) Committee (2003) on Enterprise Risk Management has adopted the following definition of ERM:

> ERM is the discipline, by which an organization in any industry assesses, controls, exploits, finances, and monitors risks from all sources for the purpose of increasing the organization's short- and long-term value to its shareholders.

In order for the ERM to be a discipline in any enterprise, this has to be recognized as a standard procedure with a series of activities and must have full support and commitment of the enterprise leadership which influences corporate decision-making and ultimately becomes part of the culture of that enterprise. This definition applies to all industries and the specific mentioned of exploiting risk is a part of the risk management process which demonstrates that the intention of ERM is to be value-creating as well as mitigating all types of risk (hazard risk, financial risk, etc.). The ERM must consider all stakeholders of the enterprise, which includes shareholders and financial institutions, enterprise leadership, employees, customers, and the community within which the enterprise resides. Frigo and Anderson (2011a) have developed the ERM definition for the Committee of Sponsoring Organizations of the Treadway Commission (COSO):

> Enterprise risk management is a process, effected by an entity's board of directors, management, and other personnel, applied in strategy setting and across the enterprise, designed to identify potential events that may affect the entity, and manage risk to be within the appetite, to provide reasonable assurance regarding the achievement of entity objectives.

These definitions can be compared and contrasted, but ERM is different from traditional risk management. It is the holistic approach of the enterprise that makes the difference – the contribution of the enterprise risk, rather than the risk associated with each individual investment. Hence, it is important to recognize "where and how" to start the ERM process. This is a challenging question to every business due to the complexity of ERM and/or a lack of understanding of its strategic benefits which they may be derived from the ERM system. In this globally competitive market, there are organizational pressures where risk may not get the fair priority (where it is expected to reduce cost) which might set the stage for unmanaged risk exposure that could seriously threaten the viability of the organization.

Organization culture plays a critical role in managing the enterprise risk. Developing a risk culture is a basic and critical element to implement good ERM practices (Farrel and Hoon, 2009).

The importance of risk culture is also evident in the COSO – ERM Integrated Framework, which considers the internal environment is the basis for a correct functioning of the control system, including the ERM. The risk culture influences decisions at all levels of the organization and therefore the possibility of reaching the strategic goals, thus influencing enterprise value (IIF, 2009). Brooks (2010) argues that the risk culture is not an intangible concept but it can be measured using the level of consistency between the decisions about risks and the existing policies and the desired risk profile. Organizations lacking a strong risk culture may find themselves operating against their own policies which might be resulting in the inability to reach their strategic, tactical and operating goals as well as their reputational and financial losses (IRM, 2012). Risk culture regards values, norms and behaviors shared by all members of an organization, which determines how they act towards the enterprise risks (Abrahim et al., 2012).

ERM is a holistic business approach, hence, decisions, guidance and responsibility lies with the board of directors and executive business leaders. It can be time-consuming, but, like success, it touches the whole enterprise. It is important to see managing risk as a central business need, woven throughout the fabric of the organization (Carroll and Webb, 2001; Lam, 2003; COSO, 2004; Lawrence, 2005; Beasley and Frigo, 2007; Farrel and Hoon, 2009; IIF, 2009; Thompson, 2012)).

Holistic risk management helps insurers support strategic decisions and execute rigorous risk management analysis, such as the development of sound loss reserves and the leadership of underwriting and pricing risk. Hence, the foundation of holistic risk management is the quantification of risk and its inherent uncertainties for the insurer. Quantification calls for high-quality, reliable, appropriate and timely data to be used by actuaries, other analytical professionals, and the company's chief risk officer to provide business leadership and the insurer's board of directors with an unbiased view of the risk and opportunities the enterprise faces (Prevosto, 2008).

Internal auditors can develop a holistic approach to their roles in enterprise risk management initiatives, while remaining mindful of the need to maintain independence. The goal is to maintain their effectiveness in the traditional internal audit activities of compliance, control testing, and providing independent assurances with a degree of consultation with executive business leaders that is appropriate. In so doing, however, internal auditors can provide substantial support and advocacy for all elements of risk management, including those that are the responsibility of the executive business leaders (Schneider et al., 2012). Hespenheide et al. (2007) specifically argue that internal auditors should expand their focus on and proficiency in risk management by adopting a holistic view of their role in the process. Internal auditors are especially well qualified to participate in the development of key risk indicators (KRIs) and in designing systems to monitor them (Steinberg, 2011). Many internal audit staffs have information technology specialists who can play key roles in the system development initiatives (Deloitte, 2011) and internal auditors' training in assurance reporting can help them frame the output in ways that are especially useful for the executive business leaders and the board of directors (Moeller, 2009).

Zwaan et al. (2011) conducted a study with the auditors' involvement in ERM and analyzed the strength of the relationship between internal audit and the audit committee. They selected 117 certified internal auditors, collected information and performed statistical analysis. The study indicated that a high involvement in ERM impacts the perception of internal auditors' willingness to report a breakdown in risk procedure to the audit committee. However, a strong relationship with the audit committee does not appear to affect their perceived willingness to report. The study also finds that the majority of organizations have recently adopted ERM. Internal auditors are involved in ERM assurance activities but some also engage in activities that could compromise objectivity. Hopkin's (2002) approach of holistic risk management in practice is largely based on five steps. He recognizes that risk is best managed where it is created.

1. Identify core dependencies of each distinct business operation.

2. Identify key risks to each core dependency.
3. Measure and treat key risks.
4. Embed controls in work practices and create accountabilities.
5. Measure compliance.

It is a very critical responsibility of the executive business leaders to clearly communicate the business objectives, policies, risk tolerance thresholds throughout the organization (COSO, 2004; Deloitte, 2008; KPMG, 2008; Cendrowski and Mair, 2009; ISO, 2009a, b; Ernst & Young, 2010; Rittenberg and Mattens, 2012).

The executive leadership also has the responsibility to clearly use, and share and communicate risk information in a common risk language throughout the organization (CAS, 2003; COSO, 2004; Aabo et al., 2005; Beasley and Frigo, 2007; Shenkir and Walker, 2007; Frigo, 2008; IIF, 2009; Rochette, 2009; ISO, 2009a and 2009b; Frigo and Anderson, 2009; Lai and Samad, 2010; Abrahim et al., 2012; Deloitte, 2012; IRM, 2012; Zurich and HBRAS, 2012). Organizations must provide continuing education opportunities to employees (Lam, 2001; Lam and Associates, 2008).

A general argument gaining momentum in the literature is that the implementation of an ERM system will improve firm's performance (Barton et al., 2002; Lam, 2003; Stulz, 1996 and 2003; COSO, 2004; Nocco and Stulz, 2006). Even in the health-care industry, the company's (CAREMARK International Inc.) board of directors recognized that ERM is the process by which the board of directors and the business executives can define the firm's strategies and objectives so as to strike an optimal balance between growth and return goals and related risks (Bainbridge, 2009). It encompasses determining an appetite for risk consistent with the interests of the firm's equity owners and identifying, preparing for, and responding to risks.

3.2 Why ERM is Important

There are eight drivers to support the title question of the ERM discipline as per the Society of Actuaries (2006):

1. Regulatory developments [Basel I and II, COSO Commission, Cadbury Code 1992, Australia/ New Zealand (AS/NZS) Risk Management Standard of 1995 which was updated in 1998, Sarbanes–Oxley Act of 2002, SEC added requirements in 2010, Dodd–Frank Wall Street Reform and Consumer Protection Act 2009–2010].
2. Rating agency views.
3. The COSO Report.
4. Basel.
5. Economic Capital.
6. Conglomerates.
7. Convergence of financial products, markets, globalization.
8. Board attention due to public's demands for certain assurances.

Regulatory developments became one of the most critical drivers in the ERM discipline; therefore, some of those key drivers of change and development are discussed here. These series of developments and acts went through in the past several decades including the following drivers:

• The Basel Committee on Banking Supervision was formed in 1974 from among central bank governors and regulators from major industrialized countries. In 1988 meeting in Basel, the "Basel Capital Accord" was reached to set the new framework for minimum risk-based capital requirements for internationally active banks which has been adopted by over 100 countries worldwide. Basel Capital Accord of 1988 is known as Basel I, as per Investopedia. A set of agreements set by the Basel Committee on Bank Supervision (BCBS), which provides recommendations on banking regulations in regards to capital risk, market risk and operational risk. The purpose of the accords is to ensure that financial institutions have enough capital on account to meet obligations and absorb unexpected losses. The second Basel Accord, known as Basel II, is to be fully implemented by 2015. It focuses on three main areas, including minimum capital requirements, supervisory review and market discipline, which are known as the three pillars. The focus of this accord is to strengthen international banking requirements as well as to supervise and enforce these requirements.

- In 1985, COSO formed an independent, national commission to undertake a private study of factors that causes fraudulent financial reporting. The COSO framework set forth recommendations for internal controls needed to identify and monitor risks. The recommendations followed by the practice workshop of senior executives to utilize risk registers or risk maps to rate and track the likelihood and impact of risks.
- In 1992, the London Stock Exchange introduced new regulations following a series of high-profile corporate frauds and accounting scandals. The new rules are based on the Cadbury Committee's code of best practices covering financial aspects of corporate governance that would apply to publicly held companies. Adrian Cadbury (1992) chaired the committee. The current UK rules are contained in the Hampel Committee's "Combined Code," (January 1998) whereby UK listed companies are required to evaluate their internal controls covering all types of risks.
- Australia/New Zealand (AS/NZS) Risk Management Standard of 1995, which was updated in 1998 (AS/NZS 3931: 1998) creating a generic framework for the risk management process as part of an organization's culture. This presaged similar standards in Canada (Dey report, 1997) and Japan, and in the UK (2000). The ISO (International Standards Organization) is working with other countries and regions in Europe who are considering similar standards, particularly in the area of common terminology.
- A string of corporate accounting scandals had profound implications in the US and worldwide, and led to the passage of the Sarbanes–Oxley Act of 2002 or SOX (Kimmel et al., 2011). This is a United States federal law that set new or enhanced standards for all US public company boards, management and public accounting firms. It is named after sponsors US Senator Paul Sarbanes (D-MD) and US Representative Michael G. Oxley (R-OH). The new law included risk management processes aimed to keep internal controls up to date. One of the key provisions requires that SEC (Security and Exchange Commission) registered companies evaluate the effectiveness of internal controls over information issued in the capital markets and have such evaluation audited and made public. SOX increased the independence of the outside auditors who review the accuracy of corporate financial statements, and increased the oversight role of boards of directors.
- Securities and Exchange Commission (SEC) added requirements in 2010: these requirements are related to proxy statement discussion of company's board leadership structure and role in risk oversight. Companies are required to disclose in their annual reports the extent of the board's role in risk oversight, such as how the board administers its oversight function. For example, does the risk oversight is on the board's process and whether and how the board or board committee monitors risk? Whether the risks oversee leadership report directly to the board as whole, such as on the audit committee, or to one of the other standing committees of the board? Most board delegate oversight of risk management to the audit committee, which is consistent with the New York Stock Exchange (NYSE) rule that requires the audit

committee to discuss policies with respect to risk assessment and risk management (Lipton et al., 2010).

- The Dodd–Frank Wall Street Reform and Consumer Protection Act (Public Law 111–203, H.R. 4173; commonly referred to as Dodd–Frank) was signed into federal law by President Barack Obama on July 21, 2010 at the Ronald Regan Building in Washington, DC, Dodd–Frank (2010). Bill passed as a response to the recession of late-2000s and it brought the most significant changes to financial regulation in the United States since the regulatory reform that followed the Great Depression (Yahoo! News, 2010; Paletta and Lucchetti, 2010; *The Washington Independent*, 2010). The Bill also made changes in the American financial regulatory environment that affect all federal financial regulatory agencies and almost every part of the nation's financial services industry (The Harvard Law School Forum on Corporate Governance and Financial Regulation July 21, 2010).

- There are some information technology security management-related systems including COBIT (Control Objectives for Information and Related Technology) framework developed by ISACF (Information Systems Audit and Control Foundation). COBIT provides guidance for executives to govern the information technology within the enterprise. There is also an effective project management system, PRINCE2 (Project in Controlled Environment) which is widely recognized in the UK and internationally.

- There are several financial services industry systems including:
  - Canada's OSFI (the Office of the Superintendent of Financial Institution);
  - The United Kingdom's Financial Services Authority system of risk-based supervision;
  - The United States, S&P (Standard and Poor's) with their risk-based capital adequacy model for financial products companies and Moody's Financial Institutions with their ERM model to deal with corporate governance guidelines for the general industry.

3.3   ERM through Strategic Risk Management (SRM) and Holistic Risk Management (HRM)

The top level elements of enterprise excellence are growth strategy and risk management. There are strategic objectives as "high-level goals" which are aligned with as well as supporting the vision and mission of an enterprise. These strategic objectives are the core for any organization's growth strategy. There may be internal and/or external events and scenarios that can inhibit the organization's ability to achieve its strategic objectives are known as strategic risks which must be the focus of strategic risk management (SRM). Therefore, SRM is a critical element of any organization's overall ERM process. It is not separate from ERM but is a critical and important element of it. The focus of SRM issues should be on the most consequential and significant risks to shareholder value and these issues clearly deserve the time and efforts of the executive leadership and the board of directors. It is possible for business leaders to prepare for major future risks and this type of preparation is generally useful. If enough information is available, it is also possible to turn risks into opportunities.

According to COSO (2004), an organization's ERM system should be geared toward achieving the following four objectives:

1. Strategy: high-level goals, aligned with and supporting the organization's mission.
2. Operations: effective and efficient use of the organization's resources.
3. Reporting: reliability of the organization's reporting system.
4. Compliance: organizational compliance with applicable laws and regulations.

These four objectives of ERM clearly incorporate COSO's (1992) narrow framework for internal control (IC). The COSO's (2004) notion of ERM also includes a strategy objective not included in its IC framework. Audit Standard No. 5 (AS No. 5), published by the Public Company Accounting Oversight Board (2007), is also emphasizes the importance of a broad view of risk management for companies listed with the US Security Exchange Commission.

In developing its ERM framework COSO (2004) recognizes that the appropriate ERM system will likely vary from organization to organization. In essence, COSO suggests a contingency perspective toward the appropriate ERM system for a particular organization. The fact that there is no universally ideal ERM system is, of course, intuitive and has been suggested elsewhere, for example (The Financial Reporting Council's Report, 2005; Beasley et al., 2005; Moeller, 2007).

In the last 20 years of the twentieth century, there has been a dramatic decrease in the number of stocks receiving a high-quality rating by Standard and Poor's and a dramatic increase in the number of low-quality stocks (Slywotzky and Drzik, 2005). Their analysis indicates that from 1993 through 2003, more than one-third of Fortune 1,000 companies – only a fraction of which were in volatile high-technology industries – lost at least 60 percent of their value in a single year.

Strategic management of risk is part of the business landscape. Companies do not exist in vacuums, and need to monitor factors that can influence the business model, both internally and externally. Strategic management of risk examines any factor that can affect a business, seeking to reduce any risks to as low a level as possible. The global financial crisis of 2007–2009 has taught several things to business leaders and one of them is that they need to clearly link growth strategy and risk management, and be able to identify and manage risk in a highly uncertain environment to achieve their enterprise excellence while building sustainable competitive advantage. The key focus must be that risk management creating value (in terms of new revenue and profitability) as well as protecting value.

According to the Society of Actuaries (2006), strategic risk management is only effective if it is applied universally throughout the enterprise. In fact, uneven application of SRM can actually hurt the risk-adjusted return of the enterprise by thwarting options with moderate risk reward profiles in areas that are practicing SRM while allowing areas without SRM discipline to pursue plans that have poor risk-adjusted returns. Some risk control process should be used in conjunction with the SRM process to ensure that risks that are retained by the enterprise do not exceed expectation during implementation of the enterprise's plan.

Miller (1992) was one of the early researchers who used the term "strategic risk" and has identified a number of strategic moves that can potentially mitigate the risks associated with the uncertainties. For example, Miller has identified five "generic" responses to environmental uncertainties: avoidance, control, cooperation, imitation, and flexibility. Slywotzky and Drzik (2005) have described that SRM is a technique that can be used for devising and deploying a systematic approach for managing strategic risk, the array of external events and trends that can devastate a company's growth trajectory and shareholder value. The authors have identified seven classes of Strategic Risk: Industry, Technology, Brand, Competitor, Customer, Project, and Stagnation. Frigo and Anderson (2011b) have developed a definition of SRM: "Strategic Risk Management is a process for identifying, assessing and managing risks and uncertainties, affected by internal and external events or scenarios, that could inhibit an organization's ability to achieve its strategy and strategic objectives with the ultimate goal of creating and protecting shareholder and stakeholder value." It is a primary component and necessary foundation of ERM and is also based on six principles.

1. It is a process for identifying, assessing, and managing both internal and external events and risks that could impede the achievement of strategy and strategic objectives.
2. The ultimate goal is creating and protecting shareholder and stakeholder value.

3. It is a primary component and necessary foundation of the organization's overall enterprise risk management process.
4. As a component of ERM, it is by definition effected by boards of directors, management, and others.
5. It requires a strategic view of risk and consideration of how external and internal events or scenarios will affect the ability of the organization to achieve its objectives.
6. It is a continual process that should be embedded in strategy setting, strategy execution, and strategy management.

Tonello (2012) also defines strategic risk management: "Strategic risk management is the process of identifying, assessing and managing the risk in the organization's business strategy – including taking swift action when risk is actually realized." Strategic risk management is focused on those most consequential and significant risks to shareholder value, an area that merits the time and attention of executive leadership and the board of directors.

Standard and Poor's (2008) press release on strategic risk management announcement that it would apply enterprise risk analysis to corporate ratings: management's view of the most consequential risks the firm faces, their likelihood, and potential effect; The frequency and nature of updating the identification of these top risks; the influence of risk sensitivity on liability management and financial decisions, and the role of risk management in strategic decision-making. Clearly the potential impact of strategic risks is significant enough to deserve the attention of the board and its directors. Hence, strategic risk management is a necessary core competency at the board of directors' level.

Charan (2009) is listing questions in his book which all board members needs to ask themselves to focus on the risk that is inherent in the strategy and the strategy execution. For example, one of the questions is, "Are we addressing the risks that could send our company over the cliff?" Risk is an integral part of every company's strategy; when boards review strategy, they have to be forceful in asking the CEO what risks are inherent in the strategy. They need to explore the sensitivity of the risk with executive leaders in order to stress-test against external conditions such as recession, currency exchange movements, or the political stability in the foreign country. Regarding risk culture, Charan provides the following insight: "Boards must also watch for a toxic culture that enables ethical lapses throughout the organization. Companies set rules – but the culture determines how employees follow them." Corporate culture plays a significant role in how well strategic risk is managed and must be considered as part of a strategic risk assessment.

Sedlacek (2008) is providing a guideline to view and analyze risk activities with time horizon, see Figure 3.1 on the next page. These policies should be reviewed annually. For example, asset allocation is a very long-term activity; risk guidelines and performance relative to benchmark should be analyzed annually; while liquidity and market reaction should be analyzed very frequently.

Business planning and IT leadership are becoming an integral part of enterprise-wide risk management and business resilience frameworks at a growing number of organizations (Someren et al., 2012). This creates both challenges and opportunities for business leaders and IT security specialists and risk leadership executives. These professionals can adopt a number of strategies to leverage their knowledge when they are invited to participate in broader discussion:

• Focus on business goals.
• Seek out common ground.
• Speak the language of the business.
• Bring something new to the table. For example, how developed tools will support the IT security management; how quantitative methods and process-driven approaches will be adopted to mitigate variety of risks.

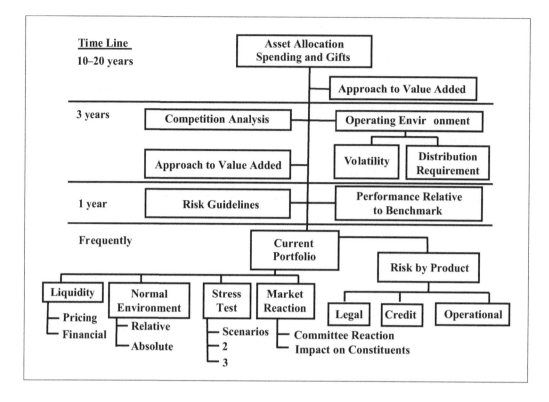

Figure 3.1   Risk analysis guideline chart

It is critical for the executive business leaders and the board of directors to understand the organization's strategic risks and related risk management processes. Therefore, one of the first necessary steps for boards is to understand their strategic risks and how their executive leaders are managing and controlling those risks is a strategic risk assessment process. Frigo and Anderson (2009) are defining as a systematic and continual process for assessing the most significant risks facing an enterprise. It is anchored and driven directly by the organization's core strategies. Breasley et al. (2011) have also stated that linkage of top risks to core strategies helps pinpoint the most relevant information that might serve as an effective leading indicator of an emerging risk. Tonello (2012) is stating as well that conducting an initial assessment can be a valuable activity and should involve both executive leadership and the board of directors. The executive leadership should take the lead in conducting the assessment, but the assessment process should include input from the board members and, as it is completed, a thorough review and discussion between executive leadership and the board. These dialogues and discussions may be the most beneficial activities of the assessment and afford an opportunity for the executive leadership and the directors to come to a consensus view of the risks facing the company, as well any related risk management activities.

The risk assessment process would be most useful if the risk management process and the resultant reporting must reflect and support an enterprise's culture, and hence, the process can be embedded and owned by the business leaders. Ultimately, if the strategic risk assessment process is not embedded and owned by the business leaders as an integral part of the business processes, the risk management process will rapidly lose its impact and will not add to or deliver on its expected role.

3.3.1   STRATEGIC RISK ASSESSMENT AND MANAGEMENT PROCESSES

3.3.1.1   *Strategic risk assessment process*

Strategic risk management increasingly is being viewed as a core competency at both the executive business leadership and the board levels. The exact steps that an organization should take will depend on the level of maturity of its overall ERM processes. For some organizations that have already started to implement ERM, the focus on strategic risks will be a refinement and evolution of their activities. For those just starting or just considering an ERM effort, an initiative focused on strategic risks may be a good starting point. Tonello (2012) is presenting a simple strategic risk assessment process, which is based on the conference board's notes series by Mark L. Frigo and Richard J. Anderson. This process is based on seven steps:

1. Achieve a deep understanding of the strategy of the organization:
   a) To gain a deep understanding of the key business strategies and objectives of the organizations.
   b) To develop an overview of the organization's key strategies and business objectives. This step is critical, because without these key data to focus around, an assessment could result in a long laundry list of potential risks with no way to really prioritize them. This step also establishes a foundation for integrating risk management with the business strategy/business growth strategy.
2. Gather views and data on strategic risks:
   a) To gather information and views on the organization's strategic risks. This can be accomplished through interviews of key executives and directors, surveys, and the analysis of information such as, financial reports and investor presentations. This data gathering should also include both internal and external auditors and other personnel who would have views on risks, such as compliance or safety personnel.
   b) To frame discussions or surveys and relate them back to core strategies. This is also an opportunity to ask what these key individuals view as potential emerging risks that should also be considered.
3. Prepare a preliminary strategic risk profile:
   a) To combine and analyze the data gathered in the first two steps.
   b) To develop an initial profile of the organization's strategic risks. The level of detail and type of presentation should be tailored to the culture of the organization. For some organizations, simple lists are adequate, while others may want more detail as part of the profile. At a minimum, the profile should clearly communicate a concise list of the top risks and their potential severity or ranking.
   c) To color coded reports or "heat-maps" may be useful to ensure clarity of communication of this critical information.

Steps 4 and 5 should be processed simultaneously and their output would be utilized in step 6.

4. Validate and finalize the strategic risk profile: the initial strategic risk profile must be validated, refined and finalized. Depending on how the data gathering was accomplished, this step could involve validation with all or a portion of the key executives and directors. It is critical, however, to gain sufficient validation to prevent major disagreements on the final risk profile.
5. Develop a strategic risk management action plan: while significant effort can go into an initial risk assessment and strategic risk profile, the real product of this effort should be an action plan to enhance risk monitoring or management actions related to the strategic

risks identified. The ultimate value of this process is helping and enhancing the organization's ability to manage and monitor its top risks.

6. Communicate the strategic risk profile and strategic risk management action plan: building or enhancing the organization's risk culture is a communications effort with two primary focuses.

a) The first focus is the communication of the organization's top risks and the strategic risk management action plan to help build an understanding of the risks and how they are being managed. This helps focus personnel on what those key risks are and potentially how significant they might be.

b) A second focus is the communication of management's expectations regarding risk to help reinforce the message that the understanding and management of risk is a core competency and expected role of people across the organization. The risk culture is an integral part of the overall corporate culture. The assessment of the corporate culture and risk culture is an initial step in building and nurturing a high-performance, high integrity corporate culture.

7. Implement the strategic risk management action plan: The real value resulting from the risk assessment process comes from the implementation of an action plan for managing and monitoring risk. These steps define a basic, high-level process and allow for a significant amount of tailoring and customization to reflect the maturity and capabilities of the organization.

Strategic risk assessment is an ongoing process as presented in Figure 3.2 below, not just a one-time event. Reflecting the dynamic nature of risk, these seven steps constitute a circular or closed-loop process that should be ongoing and continual within the organization.

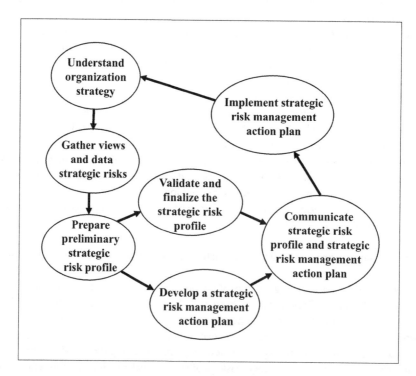

Figure 3.2   Strategic risk assessment process flowchart

3.3.1.2   *Strategic risk management process*

Slywotzky and Drzik (2005) and Frigo and Anderson (2011b) have presented a high-level process for strategic risk management and could be used as good working guidelines:

- Identify and assess risks based on key elements such as severity, probability, timing, likelihood over time and then create a strategic risk map.
- Quantify risks in a common measurement currency, for example, economic capital at risk, market value at risk.
- Identify potential positive consequences of risks. If enough information about any risk activity is available then turn the risk into an opportunity.
- Assess the maturity of the organization's ERM efforts relative to its strategic risks. Consider whether the executive business leadership and the board feel that they have an excellent understanding of the organization's strategic risks and the related risk management processes. Develop action plans to move to a high level of ERM maturity.
- Conduct a strategic risk assessment as identified above and then prioritize the organization's strategic risks. Consider both internal and external risks and events.
- Review the process for strategy setting, including the identification of related risks. Review the organization's process for setting and updating its strategies and strategic objectives. Ensure that the process requires the identification and assessment of the risks embedded in the strategies. Develop risk mitigation action plans wherever applicable.
- Review the strategic risk management processes to measure and monitor the organization's performance. Expand the processes to include the monitoring and reporting of key performance indicators (KPIs) related to strategic risks. Embed risk monitoring and reporting into the organization's core processes for budgeting, business performance monitoring, scorecards and performance measurement systems.
- Develop an ongoing process to periodically update the strategic risks assessment and the strategic risk management processes.

3.3.2   STRENGTHS AND LIMITATIONS OF STRATEGIC RISK MANAGEMENT

Strengths include:

- Preparation and analysis for a major risk enables mitigation of that risk and makes sense to protect company stability.
- SRM is an excellent tool for thinking systematically about the future and identifying opportunities.
- Strategic risks can be converted into opportunities which would change from defensive risk strategy to offensive risk strategy.
- Probably the benefits of SRM outweigh those of other, less strategic forms of managing risk.
- Could provide better opportunities to utilize capital and reduce its cost.
- SRM supports the better organization of systems and processes that would increase the risk-adjusted return on capital of the company.
- SRM would help to mitigate/control/eliminate risk, which should protect company reputation.
- Helps companies to incorporate any additional regulatory and legislative regulations on how they run their businesses.
- Helps executive business leaders to defend themselves against legal lawsuits.

Limitations include:

- SRM is not a simple exercise; there are substantial efforts and cost involved in the SRM process.
- In light of Sarbanes–Oxley, Dodd–Frank Wall Street Reform and Consumer Protection Act (Public Law 111–203, H.R. 4173; commonly referred to as Dodd–Frank) and others, companies may likely view SRM as simply another regulation being imposed on them rather than new "ground rules" that, if followed enthusiastically, have the potential to provide global competitive advantage and enhance shareholder value.
- It is almost impossible for any company to anticipate all risk events.
- Certain risks may occur and cause irreparable damage despite anticipation and preparation: tornado, hurricane, earth quack.

3.3.3   ERM PRACTICE STATISTICS

The relation between ERM and firm performance is contingent upon the appropriate match between ERM and the following five factors affecting a firm: environmental uncertainty, industry competition, firm size, firm complexity, and board of directors' monitoring. Based on a sample of 112 US firms that disclose the implementation of their ERM activities within their (year 2005) 10Ks and 10Qs filed with the US Securities and Exchange Commission, empirical evidence confirms the above basic argument (Gordon et al., 2009). The implication of these findings is that firms should consider the implementation of an ERM system in conjunction with contextual variables surrounding the firm.

Hoyt and Liebenberg (2011) performed a study to measure the extent to which specific firms have implemented ERM programs and then, to assess the value implications of these programs. They focused their attention in this study on US insurers in order to control for differences that might arise from regulatory and market differences across industries. They simultaneously model the determinants of ERM and the effect of ERM on firm value and estimated the effect of ERM on Tobin's Q, a standard proxy for firm value. They found a positive relation between firm value and the use of ERM. The ERM premium was roughly 20 percent which is statistically and economically significant. One of the major challenges researchers are facing is how to identify firms that are engaged in ERM. Sometimes researchers would need to perform a detailed search of financial statements, press reports, newswires and other media for evidence of ERM use.

Wade (2012) is reporting the Federation of European Risk Management Associations (FERMA) survey that only one-third of companies in Europe are embedding risk management into strategic decision-making. About 66 percent of companies have only a "moderate" or "emerging" capability to use risk management for strategic decisions including major projects, investments, contracts, acquisitions and budget allocations. FERMA is also reporting that nearly three-quarters (74 per cent) of companies that have an earnings growth rate of more than 20 percent have mature or advanced risk management practices. Wade is also quoting FEMRA President Jorge Luzzi "We have long believed that good risk management contributes to sustainable corporate growth and now we have clear evidence that there is a correlation."

3.3.4   DISCUSSION EXAMPLES SHOWING RELATIONSHIP BETWEEN ERM AND EGS

The following are some discussion examples showing the relationship between the enterprise risk management (ERM) and the enterprise growth strategy (EGS).

Academics and industry researchers argue that ERM benefits firms by decreasing earnings and stock price volatility, reducing external capital costs, increasing capital efficiency, and creating synergies between different risk management activities (Miccolis and Shah, 2000; Cumming and Hirtle, 2001; Lam, 2001; Meulbroek, 2002; Beasley, Pagach, and Warr, 2008).

Most of the literature search information is about the analysis of the elements that influence the ERM adoption and its effects on firm's performance, but recently some research work has been done to evaluate the quality or maturity of the ERM programs implemented by firms (Monda and Giorgino, 2013). They have developed a Delphi scoring model that can be used to assess the maturity of an ERM program by administering a questionnaire composed of 22 closed-end questions to firms: answers are collected and scored, and all scores are combined in a single final score, the ERM Index (ERMi). They have tested the robustness of the model on a small sample of firms.

Lafley and Martin (2013) are discussing in their book about "how strategy really works." They believe that good companies are thinking hard about what constitutes enterprise risk and they also think that the enterprise risk depends significantly on what industry and business they try to play. Lafley [Retired CEO from Procter and Gamble (P&G)] talked about his own company where they were a manufacturer of everyday branded products. It was a company that had $6–8 billion food and beverage business which is regulated by the FDA and others, that presents a different profile from household cleaning products and at the same, P&G was also in the health-care products business. P&G made a big push into China and Southeast Asia, and a big move into Eastern Europe and Russia, Middle East and Africa. The company felt that they had to make those moves because their business was driven by demographics: where are the babies born, where do the households' form, where does economic growth drive a rising middle class? There is a huge middle class growing in emerging markets, and the business leadership felt like that the company had to be there since that is the biggest part of company's market. P&G serves middle-class families, therefore, that was a risk the company felt was worth taking.

For a company like General Motors that has gone under a prolonged consumer confidence crisis, its problems were rooted in labor costs and benefits, and poor manufacturing. But whereas in the past the main fallout of these failings might have been legal liabilities resulting from the labor strikes and court cases, and the costs of conducting a product recall, the greatest asset at risk today is General Motors reputation after going through the bankruptcy. The lawsuits can be covered and the recalls can be paid for, but if the typical customer (car buyer), someone who has a wider selection of safe cars to choose from than ever before, decides that General Motors is a brand they no longer trusts, and if auto sales do not return to the company's prior expectations, then even a seemingly sound business strategy of domestic and international market share acquisition and forward-thinking hybrid innovation may not make a difference.

Such reputation concerns are among the most frightening risks that companies are just now learning how to manage – just ask AIG or BP – but they are far from the only major emerging threat. Supply chain disruptions, climate change and extreme weather, global and local regulatory uncertainty, counterparty default and dozens of other risks now pose greater challenges to companies than ever before.

3.4   ERM through Integrated Risk Management (IRM)

During the latter part of the twentieth century, scenario planning gained prominence as a strategic management tool. Scenario planning encourages executive business leaders to envision likely future states of the world and consider how to take advantage of opportunities and avoid potential threats. In the last decade of the twentieth century, finance researchers have developed real option analysis as a way to value investments under uncertainty. Scenario planning and real option analysis have complementary strengths and weaknesses as tools for executive business leaders making strategic investment decisions under uncertainty. Miller and Waller (2003) have combined these two approaches in an integrated risk management process. This process involves scenario development, exposure identification, formulating risk management responses, and implementation steps. They advocate a corporate-level perspective on managing risk that takes into consideration the full range of exposures across a firm's portfolio of businesses. There are several definitions in the literature with similar concept:

- Miller (1992) has developed an approach of treating uncertainties in isolation from one another is known as integrated risk management. The integrated risk management perspective – takes a general management view giving explicit consideration to numerous uncertainties.
- Nottingham (1996): "Integrated risk management calls for a framework that allows the organization to identify, anticipate and effectively respond to the multiple events that may affect its ability to fulfill strategies and achieve objective."
- Tatum (2014): "Integrated risk management is a process that takes into consideration the degree of risk that is found at all levels within a given organization."

A major strength of the integrated risk management perspective is that it facilitates explicit recognition of trade-offs between exposures to various uncertainties. The reduction of uncertainty in one dimension may result in increased to another uncertainty. For example:

- Level of R&D expenditures in relation to product and process innovation.
- Environmental uncertainties in firm's country versus foreign countries.
- A firm's product sale in foreign currency may wish to hedge its foreign exchange exposure. Such a hedge can be undertaken by selling forward the foreign currency to be received for home country currency or fixing the exchange rate.

Miller (1992) has also pointed out that uncertainty trade-offs can occur across three levels of analysis: general environment, industry and firm-specific uncertainties. Several authors in the literature have utilized the concept of integrated risk management and applied to their specific situations including some of those presented here:

- Over the years, risk management has developed separately in both the insurance and financial fields. Today, the two are finding value in each other's tools and techniques. Integrated Risk Management combines the best of the two notions of risk management, insurance and financial, to develop solutions ideal for today's complex risk environment (Doherty, 2000).
- Strategy and tactics are connected through project objectives, which are both affected by uncertainty, leading to risk at both strategic and tactical levels. An integrated approach to risk management can create significant strategic advantage by bridging the strategy/tactics gap, and dealing with both threats and opportunities, to enable both successful project delivery and increased realization of business benefits (Hillson, 2006).
- A positive link is found between the extents to which departments other than the finance department are involved in the management of exchange rate risks; and second, the extent to which the firm is likely to speculate – whether in the form of selective hedging or active speculation – on the foreign exchange market (Aabo et al., 2012).

The general understanding of economist about integrated risk management is that the management of business risks defined as "the threat that an event or action will adversely affect an organization's ability to achieve its business objectives and execute its strategies successfully." Therefore, when use the integrated risk management effectively; it is a very proactive process. As the first step to the process, it is necessary to identify risk as it exists at various levels within the business and then risk must be assessed in terms of what that risk means to each phase of the business. Once the assessment is completed, it is essential to address risk at each step in the business process, and determine what options are viable for dealing with that risk factor. Finally, steps are taken to reduce risk within each area of the business, which in turn leads to increased efficiency and productivity, while at the same time limiting the potential for losses.

The key concept in business ethics has changed from "corporate social responsibility" to "integrated risk management." This change has first brought by American laws that have been extended to other countries through globalization. The most important laws concern corruption, anti-trust, consumer safety, environmental protection and insider-trading. The "Federal Corporate Sentencing Guidelines" have particularly been helpful in identifying and valuing business risks. Sison (2000) proposes a next-generation business ethics integrating personal, professional and organizational ethics in the context of an institutionalized, country-sensitive "corporate culture."

Nottingham (1996) has developed a check list for the executive business leaders when planning to implement the integrated risk management philosophy:

- Does the business leadership thoroughly understand all the risks facing the corporation?
- Have they quantified these risks? How are unquantifiable risks handled?
- How do they know that the risk management actions they intend to take are in the best interests of shareholders?
- Are their risk management practices and procedures well-articulated, all-encompassing and enforceable? Do they meet industry standards?
- Do they have a mechanism to monitor and measure their success in achieving risk management objectives?
- Are risk limits set, and is the company operating within them?
- Do they have adequate resources and capability to manage the risks of the business; how are these assets being deployed?
- Have they promoted and fostered an appropriate risk culture? Is accountability for managing risks clearly identified?

Integrated risk management addresses risks across a variety of levels in the organization, including strategy and tactics, and covering both opportunity and threat. Effective implementation of integrated risk management can produce a number of benefits to the organization which are not available from the typical limited-scope risk process. Hillson (2006) is identifying some of the key benefits specifically linking to strategy/tactics:

- Bridging the strategy/tactics gap to ensure that project delivery is tied to organizational needs and vision.
- Focusing projects on the benefits they exist to support, rather than simply on producing a set of deliverables.
- Identifying risks at the strategic level which could have a significant effect on the overall organization, and enabling these to be managed proactively.
- Enabling opportunities to be managed proactively as an inbuilt part of business processes at both strategic and tactical levels, rather than reacting too little and too late as often happens.
- Providing useful information to decision-makers when the environment is uncertain, to support the best possible decisions at all levels.

- Creating space to manage uncertainty in advance, with planned responses to known risks, increasing both efficiency and effectiveness, and reducing waste and stress.
- Minimizing threats and maximizing opportunities, and so increasing the likelihood of achieving both strategic and tactical objectives.
- Allowing an appropriate level of risk to be taken intelligently by the organization and its projects, with full awareness of the degree of uncertainty and its potential effects on objectives, opening the way to achieving the increased rewards which are associated with safe risk-taking.
- Development of a risk-mature culture within the organization, recognizing that risk exists in all levels of the enterprise, but that risk can and should be managed proactively in order to deliver benefits.

3.5   Risk Areas

There are various risk areas in any enterprise to analyze and then minimize/mitigate risk to achieve an excellence as well as providing support in building sustainable competitive advantage including the following:

- Equality risk.
- Operational risk.
- Political risk.
- Customs risk.
- Ethical risk.
- Technology risk.
- Product risk.
- Competitive risk.
- Facilitating risk.
- Reputation risk.

3.5.1   EQUALITY RISK

Business leadership must recognize the concepts, theories and issues related to Equality, Diversity and Discrimination (EDD) topics when leading the organization. The concept of equality is concerned with ensuring that people are not discriminated unfairly, but are instead given the same and equal opportunities. The concept of diversity involves the valuing and respecting of difference, whether this difference (for example, race, disability, gender, ethnic background, national origin, etc.) is visible or not. There is a need to recognize that people are not all the same and that they have different but equally valuable life experience, knowledge and skills to offer. Morden (2011) analyzes the issues and dilemmas associated with the EDD agenda from leadership, governance, management, opportunity and performance-oriented perspectives. These analyses must support the business performance and risk management opportunities.

Morden (2013) has conceptualized "equality status" into three alternative forms: Equality-positive, Equality-neutral and Equality-negative.

Equality-positive, proactive and prioritized – a status in which equality, diversity, opportunity and discrimination (EDOD) provision is significantly in advance of the minimum required standards of performance and compliance. EDOD issues are the subject of systematic strategy formulation and performance management, and are characterized by a proper understanding of the moral, ethical, and practical benefits of mainstreaming equality, diversity and opportunity issues into the establishment of strategic, business, operational and social purpose. The benefits of such an equality status may include reputational gains, the award of government licenses and contracts, and the avoidance of generic and unnecessary Costs of Poor Quality (COPQ). An equality-positive status is likely to be associated with well-informed and proactive corporate governance and leadership vision.

Equality-neutral: a status in which EDOD provision is perceived to meet all necessary current standards of performance, but is driven by a focus that is restricted to the need for compliance with the law; and for evidence of that compliance.

In this sense, equality and diversity issues could be seen as being "bolted on" to the mainstream activity of the entity or the organization. The management of equality issues might then be delegated to some kind of legal, equality, or diversity function, or instead be made the responsibility of a Personnel or Human Resource Management department. Whether such delegation is associated with a functional authority to require compliance from line managers will be a matter for decision by those involved in corporate governance or senior leadership. Equality-neutrality may be proactive or reactive in nature, focusing mainly on EDOD risk and the potential costs of non-compliance as forms of COPQ.

Equality-negative: in which, for whatever reason, EDOD performance and compliance (if any) falls below the required standard, or is prone to blind spots, and is in consequence potentially subject to any of a range of EDOD risks and COPQ. These could include compensation payments and legal costs, loss of government or public sector contracts, reputational damage, the dismissal of responsible executives, and the potential for external intervention and investigation. Equality-negativity might be associated with a disinterested or dismissive attitude towards EDOD issues and EDOD risk at the level of corporate governance and enterprise leadership. An equality-negative status might instead be associated with an ignorant, incapable, incompetent or corrupt corporate governance and leadership process. There are various other inequality approaches which are resulting in organization/institution success including the following:

- *Gender inequality in global and political economy* – In a global ongoing economic crisis, any growth resource should be fully utilized to pull out of the crisis. Nevertheless, despite advanced domestic legislation and extended international regulation, women's labor is a resource of growth still not fully utilized globally. Different reasons explain this fact. Often, domestic decision-makers and international organizations are held responsible for it. Less attention is paid to the effect on labor conditions globally, and particularly utilization of women's services. There are two hidden players, multinational enterprises (MNEs) and non-governmental organizations (NGOs) are supporting women's rights behind the curtains (Munin, 2013). Munin explores the political economy behind a triangle of powers: women and NGOs representing them, governments and international economic organizations, and MNEs, analyzing political economy instruments and strategies used by NGOs and MNEs to promote their respective relevant interests in their relations with regulators, and assessing their effectiveness in achieving this goal. The study suggests the current deficiencies of global and domestic efforts in this respect may reflect a compromise that both groups of interests can live with, but the global economic crisis may provide a momentum to pull out of this mutual comfort zone.
- *Income inequality in a political environment* – In a democratic political structure, citizens' income is based on the demand and supply of their talents. Government generally sets some guidelines, but individuals control their income. Therefore, there is a huge income inequality

in the US Woellert and Chen (2014) have studied the income structure in China and they found that the income inequality in China has surpassed the US and the widest in the world, while China is not a democratic country. A common measure of income inequality almost doubled in China between 1980 and 2010 and now points to a "severe" disparity, according to researchers at the University of Michigan. The finding conforms to what many Chinese people already say they believe – in a 2012 survey, they ranked inequality as the nation's top social challenge, above corruption and unemployment, the report showed.

- *Business success in partnership within ethnic group* – Peterson and Roquebert (2001) conducted a semi-structured interview with 24 of the most successful Cuban-born business founders in Dade County (Miami) Florida. This provided the context for understanding the development of the larger Cuban-owned businesses in Dade County. The interview results indicate the sources of power upon which the entrepreneurs were able to draw, particularly their motivation and ability to use various forms of "Latin connections" with respect to suppliers, employees and markets. The development of this enclave supporting entrepreneurial initiatives has implications for the potential for entrepreneurship in various communities.

- *The financial implications of institutional rankings* – College costs continue to increase faster than per capita income. Institutions are relying more on endowment funds to meet their needs. Michael (2005) conducted a study where Pearson product moment correlation coefficient was used to investigate the relationship between endowment funds and variables associated with the ranking as determined by the *U.S. News* and *World Report*. Michael's study found that endowment was positively associated with almost all the variables used for ranking top national doctoral universities with the largest endowment amounts. When endowment per student was used, the association became even stronger with these ranking variables. Endowment was weakly associated with almost all the variables used for ranking top national doctoral universities with the lowest endowment amounts. Relationship of endowment and ranking variables were stronger at medical research schools, business schools and weaker at engineering schools. The administrators at the higher learning institutions must realize that these variables are cost-inducing factors that cannot be fully satisfied. Unbridled pursuit of ranking variables will increase cost without commensurate increase in educational quality. Hence, leaders must decide what rankings their resources allow and what position within the ranks is acceptable to them. Ranking agencies interested in quality should realize that money plays a significant role in how an institution is ranked. Therefore, institutions should be grouped according to the available resources before comparative analysis of ranking variables is made.

- *The tension between equity and excellence* – This is fundamental in science policy and this tension might appear to be resolved through the use of merit-based evaluation as a criterion for research funding. This is not the case. Merit-based decision-making alone is insufficient because of inequality aversion, a fundamental tendency of people to avoid extremely unequal distributions. The distribution of performance in science is extremely unequal, and no decision-maker with the power to establish a distribution of public money would dare to match the level of inequality in research performance. Hicks and Katz (2011) argue the inequality issue in research funding that decision-makers who increase concentration of resources because they accept that research resources should be distributed according to merit probably implement less inequality than would be justified by differences in research performance. Hicks and Katz show that the consequences are likely to be suppression of incentives for the very best scientists. The consequences for the performance of a national research system may be substantial and the decision-makers are unaware of the issue, as they operate with distributional assumptions of normality that guide the everyday intuitions.

3.5.2   OPERATIONAL RISK

Operational risk management (ORM) in twenty-first century is much broader than losses, insurance and claims. Its goal is to manage any facet of risk that threatens a firm's ability to achieve its strategic objectives. Any operational risk solution must be fully integrated at the enterprise-level, so the process can be repeated with best practices across the enterprise. For example, Dell Computer moved the product ordering system online where they can process millions of orders without any order-processing error.

Continuous improvement is the key for the successful execution of an ORM strategy, which lies in the organization's ability to establish a common platform for mitigating risk exposures discovered from both reactive (incident-based) and proactive (assessment-based) processes. Integration of these typically disparate processes and systems provide leaders with information that raises the awareness of and improves responsiveness to resolving management system weaknesses. These weaknesses expose the business to operational risks, compliance issues, and some other costly consequences.

There are excellent observations about the organization's risk management; and without management sponsorship, risk management will not become embedded in the "way of doing business," and may therefore be seen as interference, or an optional add-on, to managing the business. The aim must be to develop risk management in an organization to a point where, perhaps controversially, risk management becomes so embedded in the way or working that it is no longer discussed as a separate subject (Tattam, 2011). Tattam also provides a context for risk management in terms of regulation and guidance through a critique of the Basel II regulatory framework, and basing the characteristics of risk management processes around ISO 31000.

Burton and Pennotti (2003) have used the concept of enterprise map to help the senior business leaders of a networking products company merge what they had described as "islands of quality" into an integrated quality system, complete with an operational "dashboard" for measuring and managing process performance. They have also used it to help the leaders of a network services company identify the operational implications of a new strategy and translate them into specific modifications of the business processes that were required to execute it. The effort also helped them set aside functional roles that had begun to hamper their performance and enabled them to address the strategic change as an integrated leadership team.

Value chain and supply chain are some of the most critical elements in the operational risk. Juha-Pekka (2007) has developed a planning process to make value chain stakeholders agree on the best way to manage their value chain. The developed process states that sales inventory and operations planning (SIOP) is aimed at getting consensus between various factors including procurement, manufacturing and logistics. The process also states that SIOP, which used to focus on matching demand and supply, already makes organizational alignment between plans and goals.

The concepts of supply chain management have been around for quite a while and have already shown their possible positive impact on the performance of a business. In recent years the stakes of this game have changed. It is no longer considered being a field of innovative competitive advantage over the competition, but a necessity to stay profitable and competitive. Most businesses have realized that only close collaboration with all involved partners can produce the kind of speed and reaction time to customer demands that are needed in today's business world.

There are two broad categories of risk affecting supply chain design and management: (1) risks arising from the problems of coordinating supply and demand, and (2) risks arising from disruptions to normal activities. The second category of risks, which may arise from natural disasters, from strikes and economic disruptions, and from acts of purposeful agents, including terrorists. Kleindorfer and Saad (2005) have designed a conceptual framework that reflects the joint activities of risk assessment and risk mitigation that are fundamental to disruption risk management in supply chains. They have also considered some empirical results from a rich data set covering the period 1995–2000 on accidents in the US chemical industry. Based on these results and other literature, they have discussed the implications for the design of management systems intended to cope with supply chain disruption risks.

To achieve excellence in the daily operations in the electronically connected world a business has to master both, e-business and value chain management. The advent of electronic data interchange and later of e-business processes introduced infinite possibility for businesses to really manage the whole value chain (Taninecz, 2000; Talurri et al., 2007). The key elements of e-business are:

a) sharing of information;
b) cooperation; and
c) conducting of transactions.

E-business can obviously boost the performance of a value chain as the transactions and internal processes of the value chain are simplified by the use of modern information technology. The savings regarding cost and time offered by e-business procedures should easily be translated into cost reduction and increased competitive advantage. Therefore, companies have to adjust their way of conducting business to meet global business environment by the implementation of an e-business infrastructure. Long (2008) has concluded in her research that value chain management is a prerequisite for e-commerce as a part of e-business. Only companies that have mastered their production in cooperation with their supply network will be able to offer the flexibility and speed necessary for e-business. Companies and value chains that are not responsive enough or lack the efficiency will lose the battle for e-business. As much as the speed and the connectivity of e-business have enhanced the value chain managements and as much as it has increased the pressure to perform and optimize value chain management.

Many companies see the chance to increase their profitability by utilizing these tools but overlook the limitations of the concept. The results can be clearly positive if the company pays attention to those limitations regarding the underlying products and services and carrying out of the actual online auction. This includes applying the concept only for suitable products that can easily be specified and the supplier can easily be switched. Long (2008) has also identified that there are significant concerns about the compatibility of value chain management and some forms of online reverse auctions. As long as long-term commitment and stability of the chain in some form is not considered in the process, the overall impacts for a company that has successfully implemented value chain management will be negative, even though the financial performance of the purchasing department will increase on the short run. A company without an efficient value chain management processes will take the wrong approach to future competitiveness and financial and operational soundness. When all these concerns are addressed and the procedure is used in accordance to the partnership with the pool of qualified supplier, the use of an online reverse auction can save time in regard to negotiation of the price and other operational measures.

3.5.3 POLITICAL RISK

In a globally competitive business world, many companies rely on the high risk/reward ratio of operating in unstable areas. Those companies are willing to engage in emerging or developing countries can often be exposed to a politically volatile environment over which they have little control. Political risk, therefore, is one of the most hazardous challenges that an international business can face. McKellar (2010) has provided a business-centric introduction to political risk that will familiarize international business leaders with the concept and accelerate the learning curve towards proficient and coherent political risk management. He explores a variety of issues including the key political risks that companies have faced in the recent past and current trends in the evolution of the political risk landscape. Political risk is generally reflected through business prosperity. Business prosperity stays great when the political risk is low and the following are some of the examples from different nations around the world would reflect the same.

Switzerland is an excellent example which is at the heart of Europe. It is famous for its precision engineering, pharmaceuticals, excellent financial reliability, and unsurpassed standard of living. Switzerland is currently enjoying the best of both worlds: close trade ties to major European markets, but without the drawbacks of the common currency. The mountainous country of some 8 million people has remained neutral amid war-torn neighbors for over a century. Gross domestic product per capita was US$81,100 in 2010, according to the International Monetary Fund (IMF) – two-thirds higher than that of the United States. But Switzerland was not always so wealthy. "Switzerland reinvented itself; it used to be a market where people brought production in because of the low costs. But Switzerland shifted from being a farming country to a production country," said Elmar Wiederin, chairman of the Boston Consulting Group in Switzerland. That success has required innovation and attention to quality.

Switzerland has long been famous for its chocolate, watches, skiing, and secretive bankers, but today's Switzerland generates a greater proportion of its wealth from making things than do either the United States or the United Kingdom as per the Foreign Policy (2012). Of the 10 largest Swiss companies by 2011 revenue, according to Fortune magazine, four are manufacturers, three are financial corporations, and three are in the trade, retail, or mining business. These top 10 companies include household names like Nestlé, Novartis and Roche. According to many economists, the main cause of Swiss prosperity lies in mechanical and electrical manufacturers known collectively as the MEM, which employs 11 percent of the workforce while generating 35 percent of exports. Best known companies are such as ABB in energy equipment and Schindler in elevators, but most of the 13,000 MEM companies are small and mid-sized and many of them are world class. "The MEM industry is the backbone of our economy," said Hans Hess, president of the Swissmem trade association.

The most important assets for MEM companies in Switzerland are innovation, research, and education.

However, this vital sector is facing a challenge with the strength of the Swiss franc, which has soared as investors flee other troubled currencies. "The strength of the Swiss franc has led and will lead to the deindustrialization of Switzerland," said Thomas Ladner, who chairs Zurich's exclusive Zum Rennweg business club.

Several companies in the MEM sector have decided to move elsewhere – a dangerous trend. Switzerland can survive in the long run if it captures the value-added in top industries such as pharmaceuticals and biotech, where costs are less important compared to the innovation factor.

The *Australian* nursing profession has made significant advances in the clinical, research, and political arenas in the twenty-first century (McMurray, 2010). Capitalizing on these advances is a critical step in empowering the professions and a sound investment in the health of the nation. There remains a need to energize and empower the professions, to see that the efforts of nursing profession be recognized as an enterprise that has value and a sense of worth because of Australian citizens well-being, quality of life and social justice. The contributions made by nurses and midwives need to be articulated in the policy arena, focused in professional decision-making and elaborated in Australian research agendas. Nursing professional organizations provide opportunities for solidarity, and the leverage people need to effect change at the bedside, the community and the whole of society. Renewed commitment to primary health care at the global, national and community level provides a timely rallying call to the professions to refine the way nurses articulate their position in health care, re-commit to culturally appropriate, socially just actions and embolden their professional goals to inspire the next generations of nurses for a more equitable future.

Luo and Tung (2007) have presented a springboard perspective to describe the internationalization of emerging market multinational enterprises (EM MNEs). EM MNEs use international expansion as a springboard to acquire strategic resources and reduce their institutional and market constraints at home. In so doing, they overcome their latecomer disadvantage in the global stage via a series of aggressive, risk-taking measures by aggressively acquiring or buying critical assets from mature MNEs to compensate for their competitive weaknesses. Luo and Tung have accurately described the peculiar strategies and activities undertaken by these firms in pursuit of international expansion as well as internal and external forces that might compel or facilitate their propulsion into the global scene. This study also explain the risks and remedies associated with this international "spring boarding" strategy and highlight major issues meriting further investigation.

Kerner and Lawrence (2014) are presenting the case that the political risk associated with foreign direct investment (FDI) is primarily a function of investment in fixed capital, and not a homogeneous feature of FDI. As such, heuristic tests of a political institution's ability to mitigate political risk should focus directly on investments in fixed capital and not on more highly aggregated measures of multinational corporation (MNC) activity, such as FDI flow and stock data that are affected by the accumulation of liquid assets in foreign affiliates. They have also found that the bilateral investment treaties with the United States correlate positively with investments in fixed capital and have little, if any, correlation with other measures of MNC activity.

The internationalization of Chinese enterprises is a subject that is receiving increasing attention in international business research. Quer et al. (2012) have analyzed the influence of political risk and cultural distance on the location patterns of large Chinese companies. Their results show some characteristics that differ from the conventional wisdom. A high political risk in the host country does not discourage Chinese multinationals. However, from a more conventional point of view, the presence of overseas Chinese in the host country is positively associated with Chinese outward foreign direct investment (FDI). In addition, firm size and the volume of Chinese exports to the host country have a positive influence.

3.5.4 CUSTOMS RISK

The twenty-first century is bringing a huge growth in world trade, so large containerships and information technology have triggered profound changes in international trade. A few years back, Customs officers at the border were meticulously checking goods and documents before releasing a shipment to the trader. A business could be confident that a shipment that had cleared Customs complied with all applicable regulations.

Currently, to reduce congestion and give the trade quick access to their goods, Customs have introduced risk management principles and a large number of shipments clear Customs automatically. Controls have moved from the border to the trader's premises and it is during site visits that Customs officers check the business compliance records. Moving from frontier checks to audit based controls has transferred a high level of responsibility and risk to trading businesses. It is now the duty of the trader to identify and report any error or irregularity and to keep an impeccable audit trail from initial quotation to receipt of payment. For the business, failing to provide satisfactory compliance records will result in delayed shipments and serious disruption in the supply chain. This will in turn impact on financial performance indicators such as days of inventory, days' sales outstanding, expected revenue and cash flow. The business will also have to endure in-depth Customs audits during which Customs officers will inspect each step of the audit trail disrupting day-to-day business operation. Errors uncovered during these audits will yield heavy financial penalties and a Customs debt. Ultimately, Customs risk will impact on shareholders' value. Customs and finance reporting should receive the same level of attention. However, if all companies check carefully their tax returns, only a few check their import or export declarations with the same scrutiny. Managing Customs risk is often seen as a cost center but it is also a source of competitive advantage.

A sound Customs management can reduce or remove Customs duties, generate savings and generally improve cash flow using the many Customs procedures available to the compliant trader. Truel (2010) has discussed about the Customs risk management.

There are some basic import/export procedures and paperwork involved in every country, but it is important to know what is applicable to an individual industry. For example:

- Goods depositing and storing at designated areas where duties and taxes are not applicable.
- International trade – some governments sign free trade agreements and schemes of preferences with other countries to help businesses pay less import tariffs or custom duties.
- Laws and regulations – business leaders should understand which type of legislations they would need to comply in the import/export situation in the respective countries as well as ways to handle disputes. Businesses need to comply with both civil and criminal laws. Business leader may want to engage a lawyer to provide legal advice and assistance for every aspect of their business. There are ways to handle disputes other than taking it to court. Consider all elements of dispute and options before deciding on the best option.
- Taxes – all businesses need to pay income tax as long as their income was derived or remitted into that country. There are other taxes businesses may need to pay (e.g. withholding, goods and services, property, etc.) depending on the type of business.
- Business excellence – it is fundamental requirement in a globally competitive market. Business leaders have to utilize quality management principles and tools systematically to lead and improve their business performance.

3.5.5 ETHICAL RISK

In the beginning of twenty-first century business environment has seen corporate scandals and the bankruptcy of financial institutions which forced the public to believe that one of the responsibilities of governments, regulators and corporate leaders is to do business in compliance with basic ethical values. It is now acknowledged that there has been a general decline in ethical standards in the business world, perhaps due in part to a celebrity culture that overvalues wealth and shallow notions of "success." Ethics used to be discussed only by philosophers and academics, but it is now apparent to business leaders that companies wishing to survive into the future have to develop effective protection against exposure to "ethical risk." Patetta Rotta (2010) provides a complete view of the subject and practical guidance to inform their daily business decisions. He explains the human behavior that gives rise to fraud and corruption in terms of a "fraud triangle theory" according to which unethical behaviors happen when three risk components – psychological pressure, opportunity and rationalization – are present. "Pressure" is linked to the unfortunate superstar culture, while "opportunity" can be reduced through application of adequate control mechanisms and corporate governance models. "Rationalization" has to do with the ability of an honest individual to justify a dishonest action in their own eyes. Ethics bears directly on this component and an ethical approach can prevent such self-justification.

In the US, the consensus regarding the need for ethical business practice has been codified in The Revised Sentencing Guidelines. Meeting the demand of the guidelines demands ethical leadership. Barenbeim (2006) presented an example of ethical leadership of the highest order; consider the case of Jawaharlal Nehru. In 1937, Nehru had just been elected to a second consecutive term as President of the Indian National Parliament. In a severe attack published in the *Modern Review*, one anonymous writer said that Nehru has all the makings of a dictator in him. He must be checked. The author of this vitriolic article was none other than Nehru himself. Nehru understood that a leader is most ethical and effective when his or her power is limited. From this great example of leadership Barenbeim draws three lessons:

1. ethical leaders do not hide from debate;
2. ethical leaders are active participants; and
3. actively testing institutional sustainability comes first.

Commonly used ethical approaches are the adoption of appropriate company cultures and corporate governance models, the selection and retention of ethically sound staff and implementation of fair incentive systems along with the roles within an organization of the Audit Committee and the Compliance Function. Additionally, businesses should offer a range of tools, such as codes of conduct, compliance programs, whistle blowing procedures and risk management processes.

As students go through their college education they should be provided some education in ethics. Gunderman (2011) says that many of the most important lessons in the education of physicians are not well conveyed by lectures, books and electronic media. These lessons touch on such topics as work ethic, goal setting, patient interaction, consultation, and coping with uncertainty and failure. Whether the medical educators are aware of it or not, each medical educator manifests characteristic patterns of conduct in these areas, and these habits exert a formative influence on medical students, residents and other learners. It is a mistake to conceptualize learning as the mere memorization of facts. It also involves the adoption of attitudes and patterned approaches to daily work, and this adoption often takes place at a subconscious level.

"The doctrine that capitalism works simply through greed met its denouement in the Great Crash of 2008. An alternative view is re-emerging, that morality is irreducible to individual preferences and that it plays an essential role in cementing social relations, even in a capitalist economy," as per Professor Geoffrey M. Hodgson, University of Hertfordshire, UK.

There are various *ethical models* in the literature including the following:

- *Transformative Leadership*: The ongoing cynicism about leaders and organizations calls for a new standard of ethical leadership that Caldwell et al. (2012) have labeled "transformative leadership." This new leadership model integrates ethically based features of these researchers and combines their key normative and instrumental elements in the leadership model. Transformative leadership honors the governance obligations of leaders by demonstrating a commitment to the welfare of all stakeholders and by seeking to optimize long-term wealth creation. They have also identified that key elements of the researchers perspectives that make up transformative leadership, suggest leaders who exemplify each perspective, describe the ethical foundations and message of each perspective, and offer 10 propositions that scholars and practitioners can use to test the dimensions of this new transformative leadership model.
- *Morality and Ethical Risk*: Most modern moral theories are impartial in character. They perceive the demands of morality as standing in opposition to partial concerns and acting as constraints

upon them. Mendus (2008) argues that everybody's partial concerns in general, and their love and concern for others in particular, are not ultimately at odds with the demands of morality, impartially understood, but are the necessary preconditions of their being motivated by impartial morality. If everybody cares about morality then each individual must first care about people and things other than morality. If individuals are to be educated morally then they must first be educated in the emotions.

- *Morality and Ethics*: There is a gap between what we think and what we think about ethics. This gap appears when elements of individual's ethical reflection and their moral theories contradict each other. It also appears when something that is important in individual's ethical reflection is sidelined in their moral theories. The gap appears in both ways with the ethical idea *glory*. Chappell (2011) has studied this idea is a case study of how far actual ethical reflection diverges from moral theory. This divergence tells against moral theory, and in favor of less constricted and more flexible modes of ethical reflection.

Ethics plays a critical role in every area whether it is in business, governmental or in academia category; and some of those are discussed here.

Ethics and Environment: Environmental issues are business issues and that is why they seem to be playing, increasingly, a more significant role within organizations. It is the global and national regulations that are enticing businesses to take into account the environmental impacts of all their processes, products and services. Hence, there has recently been much focus, at both the operational and strategic levels, on environmental auditing and environmental systems standards.

The concepts and goals should formulate the umbrella that provides the overall environmental long-term picture. The processes of measurement, whether qualitative or quantitative as well as those that control the progress of sustainable development, should be directed towards an enduring industrial society. As non-financial performance yardsticks have become a vital tool in management decision-making and strategic planning, environmental dimensions should be incorporated into the measurement systems. Greenberg and Unger (1992) have analyzed the nature of environmental processes and identified eight measurable and key inputs: people, equipment, methods, materials, physical setting, internal support and administrative functions, external groups and, finally, feedback. Similarly (Wells et al., 1992) recognize three generic environmental success measures which are those related to environmental results, process improvement and customer satisfaction. They argue that the latter two can be as important as the first and the latter are especially relevant as they link the environment to issues of competitive advantage.

A number of forces are now driving organizations to measure their environmental performance (James and Bennett, 1994). These include demonstrating progress towards targets, ensuring better data for decision-making as well as supplying information to regulators and all major stakeholders. Their detailed model is in the form of a continuous loop, consisting of eight sequential steps for effective environmental performance appraisal:

1. Define the environmental context and objectives.
2. Identify potential measures.
3. Select appropriate measures.
4. Set targets.
5. Implement measures.
6. Monitor and communicate results.
7. Act on results.
8. Review.

Similarly (Mosley, 1996) suggests that the idea of such a performance cycle can be perceived as a dialogue and a focal point across the organizational divide, between the specialist measurers and the functional managers. Stainer and Stainer (1997) study revealed that industrial competitiveness and protection of the environment are inextricably linked. Business excellence and environmental excellence should go together. There must be a reconciliation of environmental and economic concerns as the former should be perceived as the "natural" economy. What is required is for organizations to thoroughly examine their business ethics and corporate cultures. They should proceed in a strategic direction that fully considers the green scenario, with the environment as the silent partner. In an ever-expanding global economy, they must build up trust with all their stakeholders as this trust is based on its moral behavior and its reputation for integrity. The highest standards of societal and professional ethics should be demonstrated in order to become a world-class competitor. The level of ethical behavior should extend from beyond what is legally required to what is morally right. Enlightened organizations are beginning to realize that they must take charge of their own environmental concerns.

Ethics and University Research: There are at least two fundamental ethical responsibilities of university researchers as they gather their information to seek the truth and serve society. The American Association of University Professors (AAUP) produced a cautionary report as a proactive response to the 9/11 attack and their executive summary reinforced the organization's main premise: "that freedom of inquiry and the open exchange of ideas are crucial to the nation's security, and that the nation's security and, ultimately, its well-being are damaged by practices that discourage or impair freedom," AAUP (2003). MacKay and Munro (2012) are presenting their case that "information warfare (IW)" will likely become common as both private and public organizations are increasingly sensitive to their informational environment as a source of both opportunity and possible conflict. There are several researchers who have defined the concept of IW (Schwartau, 1996; Denning, 1998; Waltz, 1998; Hutchinson, 2002), but the same information is also referred as "information operations (IO)" which includes both peace-time and war-time operations.

The word in information warfare (IW) is "information," which is conceived as both a threat and an opportunity and may be manipulated to achieve competitive advantage over others. Berkowitz (1997) recognized the need to explore the relationship between the military and civilian society in preparing for information warfare, while protecting democratic values – namely, freedom of expression and personal privacy – but taking the measures necessary to defend against an IW threat. Nonetheless, the issues still remain while both technology and information continue to proliferate in a world that is rapidly globalized.

Fisher and Shorter (2013) argued that the military and other governmental agencies with a vested interest in national defense uphold fundamentally different values from academia and that these oppose the open and public dissemination of knowledge where it may negatively impact national security. Political discourse is polarized between those who believe secrets should stay secret and those who believe all information should be made publicly available regardless of the fallout produced. Alarmingly, there also appears to be some public consensus that putting the US intelligence community, military and intelligence informant's in harm's way due to the WikiLeaks is being frowned upon by both sides of the political spectrum (democrats and republicans alike).

Some research programs may be designated "sensitive" according to the US State Department's Mantis list. (Where "Mantis" is a State Department system which was developed to monitor international student visas for study in export controlled technologies, such as nuclear engineering, electronic guidance systems, or munitions. This list also includes nuclear technology, navigation and guidance control, chemical and biotechnology engineering, remote imaging and reconnaissance, information security, lasers and directed energy systems, and robotics.) The problem with this is that many research areas are included that many universities may consider as public domain material. At least one American university, Massachusetts Institute of Technology (MIT), has already rejected several federal proposals or contracts on research that fell into the "sensitive" category because of the requirement that required access to the project and its results be limited to US citizens (Greenwood and Riordan, 2001).

Fisher and Shorter (2013) concluded in their research that the changing role of information and an increasing recognition of its strategic importance have raised new issues in relation to its ownership and dissemination. The debate on these issues is likely to be conducted in the context of national security and lead, increasingly, to a restriction of the dissemination of research results. Universities will need to be able to define a different context for this argument to combat this ideological gap between academic freedom and national security interests, particularly given the billions of federal research dollars at risk. A report issued by the National Research Council (2007) reiterated the need for "maintaining the open exchange of scientific information" and suggested that the federal government establish a standing entity, preferably a Science and Security Commission, that would review policies guiding the exchange of information and the participation of international scientists and students in research.

3.5.6 TECHNOLOGICAL RISK

Technology permeates the operations of an entire enterprise and therefore technology risk cannot be compartmentalized as a process that focuses on a particular business/area. Technology enables key processes that an enterprise uses to develop, deliver, and manage its products, services and support operations. Understanding the role that technology plays in enabling core business operations establishes the framework for understanding where relevant technology risks lie. Once business leaders understand the role that technology plays in supporting their various business functions then the leadership would be in a better position to determine the relative importance of these functions and prioritize the systems, applications, and data involved. Technology risks are present throughout the enterprise and must be addressed as a whole. Identifying vulnerabilities and threats provides the business leadership with a view of the risks faced by the enterprise given the enabling role of information technology. Once these risks have been identified, an appropriate technology risk management strategy can be developed and implemented.

An integrated internal control and risk management program enables an organization to sustain the value that has been created. It also ensures compliance with Sarbanes–Oxley, which mandates the establishment of a control and risk management framework. Risk management should be a continuous process of impact analysis and risk identification and should include risk mitigation strategies – for example, disaster recovery and business continuity.

To survive and thrive in today's highly competitive business environment, companies need more adaptive and agile information technology (IT) solutions, which inevitably translate into higher levels of technology and operational risk. An IT governance program defines the IT structure, measures, and monitoring framework needed to effectively identify and manage risk. Weill and Ross (2004) have studied 250 enterprises worldwide that have demonstrated superior governance. They conclude that an effective IT governance structure is the single most important predictor of whether an organization will derive value from IT. Furthermore, they establish that companies that have followed specific strategies and demonstrated above-average governance have had 20 percent higher profits than companies that have followed the same strategies but had poor governance. Other studies reinforce Weill's and Ross' findings.

Robinson (2005) describes the role in IT governance of functions such as value creation (distilling company's mission and strategic direction into business needs for IT applications), value delivery (formal project management methodology and system development life cycle), value preservation (integrated control and risk management program), resource management, performance management (capability maturity model, Balanced Scorecard, Six Sigma), and oversight. His research findings are that when governance is effective, IT becomes a valued asset, inseparable from the business and regarded as an asset, not a cost.

3.5.7 PRODUCT RISK

Globalized industrial revolution is not only creating domestic but also international competition among enterprises. This creates a significant product risk as product is utilized in different countries and risk varies from product to product. Two specific product scenarios are discussed.

- Comparing products coming out from the emerging countries and Italy in the US.
- Developing an enterprise while staying in academics.

Comparing products coming out from the emerging countries and Italy in the US: Businesses in established industrialized nations are experiencing difficult times, and they are all facing complex challenges. One of these challenges is clearly connected to the changes that have characterized the last over three decades of global competition. The international market is not the same as it was during the 1980s. New manufacturing firms have successfully entered the global market, radically changing the structure and locations of contemporary industry. Due to growing competition coming from emerging countries, European and North American businesses have to define strategies to accelerate the upgrading of their products and entry into new market segments. It is also clear that these actions are even more urgent than in the past given the ongoing international recession, in a context where a fall in international demand has made global competition stronger than ever before.

Literature search shows that in most cases the pressure on industrialized countries started in low- and medium-technology sectors, where the entry of emerging countries began. However, in many sectors, the rapid industrial upgrading of countries such as China, India or Brazil suggests that the process will quickly evolve. Today it would be difficult to argue that medium- and high-technology sectors are immune from competition from the new economic powers (Nolan, 2001, 2003; Prasad, 2004; Spatafora et al., 2004; Kaplinsky, 2006; Di Tommaso et al., 2012).

Italy is in a different position compare to other industrialized countries due to the specific industrial structure. Specifically, the Italian industrial system is heavily based on so-called low-tech/ traditional sectors (Faini and Sapir, 2005; Di Tommaso and Rubini, 2009; Barbieri et al., 2009). This has exposed Italy to more competition from emerging countries, which are able to sell these traditional products on international markets at lower prices. Hence, the sustainability of Italian specialization remains one of the most debated issues among Italian economists and non-Italian observers (De Nardis and Traù, 1999; Toniolo and Visco, 2004; Lissovolik, 2008; Bennett et al., 2008).

Di Tommaso and Rubini (2012) developed a study which is based on the comparison between Italian and a selected group of emerging countries' (Brazil, China, India, Malaysia, Mexico, Thailand and Vietnam) exports of fashion-related goods to the American market by means of a new index, called the RUPD (revealed unit price differential). The index is based on the comparison between the average export prices of Italian and of the selected emerging countries' fashion goods (at a five-digit level). The RUPD "reveals" ex post how much more a consumer has been shown to be willing to pay for a specific good in comparison to another good sold on the same market, belonging to the same category and produced in another country (or group of countries). If the

RUPD is calculated using sufficiently disaggregated data (at least at the four- or five-digit level) they can hypothesize that such an index can actually reflect how different consumers perceive a product in comparison with another one, implicitly considering it as non-homogeneous and non-substitutable. The analysis of RUPDs between Italy and the selected emerging countries shows that most Italian fashion goods are sold on the American market at much higher prices. The relative weight of sectors with higher RUPD has been rising over the years, with a growing number of products showing an increasing unit price differential between Italian products and those from emerging countries.

Developing an enterprise while staying in academics: This is a very special situation where an individual is trying to develop his business as well as maintaining his faculty position in a public university. Public university's research information is copyrighted by the university and is defined as public information, therefore, this faculty member has to be very careful in keeping his business information separate from the university research information. He has to make sure that he is not creating the conflict of interest situation.

Banes (2013) started a niche biotech company in 1985 called Flexcell® to distribute an enabling technology, mechanobiology devices, to the field. He was the first University of North Carolina faculty member to start a company and stay with it as he pursued his career in academics. That was an unpopular route at that time, but a path he was driven to navigate. Those interests, merged with his training, led to the design and manufacture of mechanobiology devices such as the Flexercell® Strain Unit and the BioFlex® flexible bottom culture plates to study fundamental responses of cells to strain. Principles in these devices were also incorporated into bioreactors for tissue engineering, which are standard in the marketplace today. Banes identified the major roadblocks that were overcome to help build the field of mechanobiology and created a small biotechnology company. Through example, he is discussing to achieve milestones including, the DRIVE it takes to get there ["DRIVE": Determination (Confidence), Research and Development (R&D) and Risk-Taking, Innovation (Imagination) and Intellectual Property, achieving Victory, and Enterprise].

3.5.8 COMPETITIVE RISK

People are the most critical elements in an enterprise. Individuals have differences in risk-taking approaches and the concept of competitive risk between the individuals or the organizations is typically following the same approach.

Risk-sensitivity theory predicts that organisms will engage in riskier behavior whenever they are unlikely to achieve their goals through "safe," low-risk means. For example, birds are more likely to forage in predator-prone patches when starving than when satiated (Caraco et al., 1980; Stephens, 1981; Stephens and Krebs, 1986). These risky strategies may often fail, but this failure is no worse than what would have likely happened to disadvantaged individuals who take no risks. A loss is a loss, dead is dead, and it does not matter to natural selection whether it occurs in adolescence or in a celibate centenarian. A large body of evidence suggests that both non-human and human animals make decisions consistent with risk-sensitivity theory (Stephens and Krebs, 1986; Kacelnik and Bateson, 1996; Kacelnik and Bateson, 1997; Mishra and Fiddick, 2012).

Intelligence is important for social competition: all else being equal, both men and women are more likely to hire, befriend, and mate with intelligent people (Li et al., 2002; Prokosch et al., 2009), and intelligence is associated with greater academic performance, career potential, creativity and job performance (Kuncel et al., 2004). Intelligence is even associated with better health and longevity (Gottfredson and Deary, 2004). Risk-taking is adaptive when one is unlikely to succeed in social competition through safe means: taking risks may represent one's only hope of achieving some success. Mishra et al. (2014) predict that people exposed to cues indicating that they are competitively disadvantaged relative to others with regard to intelligence will take more risks. Furthermore, they predict that ameliorating these cues of competitive disadvantage will return risk-taking to normal levels, given that unnecessary risk-taking is costly.

The link between power and risk-taking is contingent on the nature of power held by someone (Maner et al., 2007) and Jordan et al. (2012). They have also found that the unstable powerful and the stable powerless engaged in greater risk-taking compared to the stable powerful and the unstable powerless. In all of these studies, those who engaged in higher risk-taking were in some condition of need, which should motivate risk-taking according to risk-sensitivity theory. Hence, power and competitive disadvantage may represent two different pathways leading to elevated risk-taking. Another potential pathway to elevated risk-taking is honest signaling: those who have certain positive qualities may engage in greater risk-taking because they personally experience lower downside costs with larger upside opportunities (Bliege et al., 2001).

Domain specificity of risk-taking is typically understood using the risk-return framework, e.g. (Weber and Milliman, 1997). This framework posits that individuals vary in their perceptions of the costs and benefits of risks in different domains, e.g., financial vs. recreational; Weber et al. (2002) and thus exhibit domain-specific patterns of risk-taking (Hanoch et al., 2006). Domain-general risk-taking can also be explained through linked perceptions in different domains without invoking embodied capital as a mediator. For example, intelligence is widely perceived to be associated with economic outcomes (Ceci and Williams, 1997). Perceived competitive disadvantage in intelligence may therefore lead to elevated risk-taking in the perceptually linked economic domain.

Building a systemized approach to addressing competitive risk can enhance customer experience and improve business efficiency. For example, banks should adopt an analytics-based system to help restore the trust of customers and regulators, and ensure an efficiently run banking system that benefits everybody (customers, banks and regulators). Combating competitive risk is an undeniable challenge, but the tools to meet it are available. While expert opinion is essential when designing the policies and processes that address both business opportunities and competitive risk responsibilities, it is data-driven analytics that can provide the clearer, deeper insight that will tell the bank leadership where the next competitive risk exposure is coming from. A fully operationalized, analytics-driven framework will help harness and manage their competitive risk exposure and turn it into one of their greatest competitive advantages.

3.5.9   FACILITATING RISK

Facilitation is the opportunity process to improve the value of products, processes and services; and there is risk associated with the process depending on how well the facilitating process was conducted. There are different ways of classifying facilitation. For example, classify facilitation as incremental, modular, architectural, and radical depending on the degree of product/architectural knowledge required to facilitate. Facilitation may be technical or non-technical in nature including organizational and marketing activities. Facilitation differs in every sector, for example, patterns of facilitation in product design differing from those in services. Facilitation risk includes services, business processes, models, marketing and enabling technologies that present a broad vision of facilitation and its importance not only to manufacturing but also for services. Hence, to develop a better understanding of facilitation risk in context, it is worthwhile exploring some of the facilitation activities in some of the areas including construction, software and team learning.

Environmental sustainability has been the dominant driver during the twenty-first century and will continue to be so for the foreseeable future, as energy, water and other natural resources become increasingly stretched. The next level of driver list includes the growing shortage of labor and skills facing the industry. First among the resultant challenges is the need to improve the business environment of construction. There has been a long-held view that the construction industry is hampered by an adversarial contractual nature where each party seeks to mitigate their own costs and risks by passing them on down the supply chain. Developments in public procurement and partnering have been in response to this, as have other contractual forms such as public/private partnerships. Nevertheless, the problems persist in large sectors of the industry worldwide and it is in finding new ways to collaborate and integrate supply chains for better performance and more equitable pain and gain share that the challenges manifest themselves.

As a significant economic variable, the measurement of facilitation has attracted a lot of attention. However, measuring facilitation is not an easy task due to the complexities inherent in the whole process. Most facilitations require a multitude of organizations that are responsible for the co-production of these activities as is the case for the most knowledge-intensive and complex technologies. Facilitation should be seen as an evolutionary, nonlinear, and interactive process, requiring intensive communication and collaboration between different partners. However, facilitation measurement has tended to focus on products and related production systems that are based on measuring inputs to facilitation (e.g. education expenditures, and capital investment) and intermediate outputs (workforce size and experience, and innovative products).

Management of construction facilitation is complicated by the discontinuous nature of project-based production in which, often, there are broken learning and feedback loops. Project-based firms need to manage technological innovation and uncertainty across organizational boundaries, within networks of interdependent suppliers, customers and regulatory bodies, but in tight time-spans and with little feedback on what works well. On the other hand, project-based firms are always facilitating at the local level; they must because their work is always unique and always achieving something new.

Globalization of software work has become common in today's market. As part of cost-reduction strategies, many product-focused software companies started shipping their product development to insourcing and outsourcing offshore locations. Unfortunately, moving software products from one site to another is not always a good business strategy for either the organization or the product. Smith and Wohlin (2011) findings suggest that certain product, personnel and process characteristics can facilitate the execution of an offshore insourcing transfer. They conducted research with partnership with Ericsson Company and shared a list of critical factors alleviating transfer difficulties and seven strategies facilitating transition of software work across sites.

Raes et al. (2013) investigate how and when teams engage in team learning behaviors (TLB). More specifically, they look into how different leadership styles facilitate TLB by influencing the social conditions that proceed them. Four hundred ninety-eight health-care workers from 28 nursery teams filled out a questionnaire measuring the concepts leadership style, TLB, social cohesion and team psychological safety. Analysis was performed using structural equation modeling. The results of this cross-sectional study show that transformational leadership predicts TLB better then laissez-faire leadership, because transformational leadership is primarily related to team psychological safety and only secondarily to social cohesion while for laissez-faire leadership it works the other way around. Transformational leadership matters because it facilitates psychological safety in the team.

3.5.10   REPUTATION RISK

Reputation is the reason why people and organizations do business with customers. Its influence is not confined to customers only but also to investors and strategic partners. It can significantly affect corporate relationship with regulatory agencies, professional organizations, the media and the local community. It is a key component of any organization's license to do business. For example, the most valuable asset for a physician is their reputation. Risk to reputation needs to be managed in the same way that other elements of a physician's practice are assessed as the potential for their reputation to be damaged is increasing all the time. The intrusiveness of today's reporting, the techniques of modern news gathering and the speed with which inaccurate and unfair allegations can be published to a global audience mean that a reputation that may have taken years to build can be destroyed in the time it takes to open an email or read a headline. Hence, risk, reputation and revenue are inextricably linked. Protecting one's good name is essential to physician whose livelihoods depend on their personal and professional standing. The risk to reputation is increasing all the time, but an awareness of the scale and extent of that risk will usually be enough to take control of such a situation before it controls the individuals. Therefore, reputation can be the result of many years of investment – not only financial investment in advertising, public relations and marketing, but also intangible investment in quality, innovation, customer care, stakeholder relations and corporate standards.

Reputation is one of a group of intangible assets whose value in most organizations has soared in recent years. Even though the statistics are a few years old, they are are still valid. According to Davies (2002), in the industrial age, physical assets – buildings, machinery, stock – typically accounted for 75 percent of an organization's worth. Today, intangible assets account for the lion's share of value – between 75 percent and 95 percent – with physical assets making up the meagre difference. In addition, many of the other intangible assets are employees, culture, strategic relationships and the "license to operate." The two not mentioned, intellectual property and "know-how" are in turn largely dependent on the organization's ability to recruit, retain and motivate talent – which, again, is dependent on its internal and external reputation.

Reputation can be lost in many ways, but business leaders' tendency has been to concentrate on reputation loss following major disasters. For example:

- Coca-Cola Foods recalled its "Cool Cuffs" in 1989. In cooperation with the Consumer Product Safety Commission (CPSC), Coca-Cola Foods voluntarily recalled a promotional item called "Cool Cuff" which was distributed in conjunction with Hi-C fruit drinks. The premium was being recalled because it contains small parts that do not comply with CPSC regulations. "Cool Cuffs" were a brightly colored version of a wristband used worldwide in hospitals, water parks, amusement parks, concert arenas and summer campgrounds. The CPSC was concerned that the plastic locking device which holds the bracelet in place could be removed and become a choking hazard for small children.

- Perrier recalled its water in US after benzene was found in bottles in 1990. The company that made bottled mineral water chic was voluntarily recalled its entire inventory of Perrier from store shelves throughout the United States after tests showed the presence of the chemical benzene in a small sample of bottles. The impurity was discovered in North Carolina by county officials who so prized the purity of Perrier that they used it as a standard in tests of other water supplies.

- Exxon Valdez oil spill in Prince William Sound, Alaska in 1989. When Exxon Valdez, an oil tanker bound for Long Beach, California, struck Prince William Sound's Bligh Reef at 12:04 a.m. local time, Library-Thinkquest (1989) and spilled 260,000 to 750,000 barrels (41,000 to 119,000 m³) of crude oil over the next few days (Bluemink, 2010). The Valdez spill was the largest ever in US waters until the 2010 Deepwater Horizon oil spill, in terms of volume released, Hazardous Materials Response and Assessment Division (1992). However, Prince William Sound's remote location, assessable only by helicopter, plane, or boat, made government and industry response effort difficult and severely taxed existing plans for response.

- British Petroleum's (BP) Deepwater Horizon oil spill in 2010 in the Gulf of Mexico near Mississippi River Delta. The Gulf of Mexico oil spill, and the Macondo blowout began on April 20, 2010 in the Gulf of Mexico on the BP-operated Macondo Prospect. It claimed 11 lives (*Daily Telegraph*, 2010; Jervis and Levin, 2010; Robertson and Krauss, 2010) and is considered the largest accidental marine oil spill in the history of the petroleum industry, an estimated 8 to 31 percent larger in volume than the previously largest, the Ixtoc 1 oil spill. Following the explosion and sinking of the Deepwater Horizon oil rig, a sea-floor oil gusher flowed for 87 days, until it was capped on July 15, 2010 (Robertson and Krauss, 2010; Al Jazeera, 2010). The US government estimated the total discharge at 4.9 million barrels (210 million US gal; 780,000 m³), On Scene Coordination Report (2011). After several failed efforts to contain the flow, the well was declared sealed on September 19, 2010 (Weber, 2010). Some reports indicate the well site continues to leak (Kistner, 2011; Jamil, 2012).

In such rapidly occurring events, with the glare of media attention shining, the quality of the organization's crisis response is critical. However, reputation can also be lost gradually, as a result of an aggregation of minor stories about poor service, dubious ethical practices, etc. Organizations whose reputation capital is depleted by such stories will be far less able to maintain public confidence when one or more major disasters occur.

Davies (2002) is suggesting a simple strategy for managing the reputation:
- Understanding it in depth. For reputation to be cost-effectively managed, the Pareto principle that the organization gets 80 percent of the result for 20 percent of the effort holds good. However, like all Pareto applications, it only works if the business leadership knows where to apply the 20 percent.
- Minimizing the chances of the events or allegations that would seriously damage the organization's reputation.
- Having the ability to respond rapidly and effectively to both the early warnings of reputation damaging circumstances and to a reputation crisis.
- Circumstances and to a reputation crisis.

Whenever challenged about the management of their reputation risk, most organizations take false comfort from the fact that they have a public relations or publicity department. Reputation risk management is seen as being synonymous with "media management," and this type of phrase itself gives false comfort as managing the media is a virtually impossible task, but in any event the media aspects of reputation risk management are but the tip of a very large iceberg.

Davies (2002) has developed a best practice plan which can be summarized as follows:

- It is very important to understand the corporate reputation.
- Align stakeholders' expectations with corporate growth strategy.
- Meet board's expectations and the promises that the organization makes to customers and business world.
- Do not ignore the complaints from customers, employees, stakeholders, media and others.
- Collect, analyze and utilize information from complaints and dissatisfaction.
- Reputation crises calls for skills, experience and a lot of preparation, therefore, preparation is a very critical element.
- Employees training and rehearsals are very important.
- Update the reputation plan as business requirements are changing.

3.6   Characteristic Forces and Quantifying Risk

There are various characteristic forces in creating and quantifying risk and also there are some key elements in these forces including:

1. *More – and More Complicated – Risk*: when some risks interact with other events and conditions to cause great damage to businesses. For example:
   - Hazard risks: Threat of fire, tornado, hurricane, flood, etc. Hurricane in combination with heavy rain may flood the area, which can easily destroy both residential and commercial properties. In a very dry and windy environment, fire may destroy several homes in a residential area before fire can be contained.
   - Financial risks of foreign exchange rates due to globalization: Firm's costs and margin will fluctuate more frequently as exchange rate varies in the global market.
   - Increase in operational and strategic risk due to failure in control mechanism: When financial institutions did not follow the control guidelines in approving the home mortgage loans which created the twenty-first century banking crises. It impacted significantly the business dynamics of financial institutions.
   - If any, some or all of the following elements are not utilized correctly then the business risk would get even worsen:
   - the advancement in technology;
   - the accelerating pace of business;
   - business globalization and competition;
   - increasing financial sophistication;
   - uncertainty of irrational terrorist activity.
2. *External Pressure*: Most of the external institutions/organizations are creating external pressure that the company's leadership should take greater responsibility; and some of those external organizations are:
   - regulators;
   - corporate governance oversight bodies;
   - rating agencies;
   - institutional investors;
   - stock exchange.

   In publicly traded companies, the shareholders are pressuring the business leadership for stable and predictable earnings.
3. *Portfolio Risk*: It is extremely complex and challenging risk. There is a growing effort to quantify portfolio risk, but it is much more difficult due to individual risks and interactions between individual risks. Some of the examples are:
   - collective risk of financial instruments and the individual security;
   - entire organization and key risk decisions facing that organization.
4. *Quantification*: It is critical to quantify risk and due to advancements in technology even infrequent and unpredictable risks (historically difficult to quantify) can be quantified. For example:
   - Hurricane modeling, the key elements are structural engineering, technological expertise and insurance. Generally these are probabilistic models and some other examples are earthquake and man-made disasters (terrorist attacks). Key requirements to support these models are to constantly collect and analyze data, evaluate management standards and financial analysis. These requirements provide level of confidence and allow the financial institutions and the regulatory agencies to take actions to operate within established parameters.

5. *Boundary less Benchmarking*: Businesses should share their ERM practices and tools with other organizations except of course their competition:
   - Investors make initial investments and then make subsequent investments as they see growth in business.
   - Individual investors have their individual level of understanding and risk-taking capability, therefore, investment level will vary from individual to individual.
6. *Risk as Opportunity*: The old concept of risk management was defensive posture that was to minimize or avoid risk. The new concept of risk is considered as opportunity (value-creating potential of risk). There are various reasons for the new concept including the following:
   - Time brings experience/expertise in organizations to have better understanding and familiarity with risk related issues.
   - Due to the availability of better and more information as well as tools, organizations are becoming more capable of managing risk.
   - There are opportunities to evaluate for better trade-off between risk and return or costs and benefits.
   - Organizations are more aggressive in decision-making process.
   - Organizations are also recognizing that risk is unavoidable, and in fact, informed risk-taking is a means to competitive advantage.

3.7 Risk Management Guidelines

The ultimate responsibility of risk management stays with the executive business leadership and the board of directors, but the executive business leadership needs to develop a risk management guideline which must include who is going to oversight the defined risk category. Some examples are presented in Table 3.1.

Table 3.1   Examples of risk management guideline

Risk Category	Operations Risk	Financial Risk	Information Technology Risk	Business Reputation Risk
Risk Owner(s)	COO	CFO	CTO	CEO
Risk Metrics	Daily operations metrics at each manufacturing site	Policies for periodic performance and security	Daily performance metrics for security, back-up and recovery	Approved specific Policy metrics with date
Monitoring Metrics	Throughput Delivery	Periodic monitoring against established performance	Daily monitoring against established performance standards	Corporate communications
Policy Action Plan	Plan in place for each checking point	Security plans in place and periodically testing	Contingency and back-up plans and periodically testing	Approved and Updated plan with date
First Level Leadership Oversight	Risk Management Team-Audit	Financial Committee Internal as well as external Audit	Operating Committee Internal Audit	Senior Executive Leadership
Highest Level – Leadership	Risk Committee	Audit Committee Internal and External	Multifunctional Audit Committee	Full Board

4

Enterprise Transformation (ET)

Today's large and complex enterprises are facing technical challenges of increasing global competitiveness in meeting or exceeding customer needs, reducing product costs and improving overall effectiveness. They invest billions of dollars every year in business improvements that are often not successful. They have to define the intellectual building blocks that shape how enterprises can fundamentally transform as the world around them shifts in response to changes, economic conditions and global competition. Understanding the elements involved in executing the business process improvements is not enough; success depends on developing and executing business growth strategies while managing risk at the enterprise-level change. Successful enterprise transformations involve a holistic approach that integrates view points and multiple stakeholders, processes and disciplines (Valerdi and Nightingale, 2011). Therefore, transformation is an essential driving force for today's enterprises for their sustained competitive growth and development. The business vision, specific to each enterprise, gives rise to variety of goals including simplification, cost reduction, better customer service, improved processes, etc. To realize each of these goals, it almost becomes imperative that an enterprise utilizes transformation as a core concept. An enterprise's transformation objectives provide the anchor for consistent decision-making and execution of the processes (Kumar et al., 2012). Rouse and Baba (2006) very strongly believe that fundamental enterprise changes begin by looking at the challenges from technical, behavioral and social perspectives. Research in enterprise transformation must yield both understanding of fundamental change and the methods and tools that can make change possible. They also believe that this will come from taking multiple perspectives on the problems of change – what drives it, what enables it, and what elements facilitate and hinder its success. Rouse (2005) identifies four main drivers of transformation:

1. New market and/or technology opportunities.
2. Anticipated failure due to market and/or threats.
3. Other players' (for example, competitors) transformation initiatives.
4. Crises resulting from declining market performance (revenue and profitability), cash flow problems, etc.

Enterprise systems' research and its applications are influencing the transformation of various traditional product organizations including aerospace, automotive, electronics and heavy equipment, but also increasingly in-service enterprises such as financial institutions, government agencies, hospitals, and safety and security services. As technological developments are taking place, improved/newer products and services are developed and offered in the market to meet or exceed customer needs. To support (offer, deliver and service) these products and services as well as resources (people, equipment, technology, etc.) transformation would be required. Therefore, a constantly transforming enterprise is always better equipped to handle the demands of customer needs and supply the satisfactory products. The approach to transformation is dependent on organizational culture, maturity, available resources and also the organization's appetite for change. Transformation is of higher importance to small enterprises which survive mostly by providing customer services to products produced by larger enterprises. A small enterprise has to ensure that it is constantly updated about the technological breakthroughs that have been established by larger enterprises so that they can make consistent progress in the ever-competitive market.

There are various definitions of enterprise transformation in the literature including the following:

- Enterprise transformation is a dynamic process that many organizations go through, and it may occur naturally as an organization develops and grows, or it may be induced should the organization feel the need for change that has not occurred naturally (Garvin, 1998).
- Enterprise transformation is about making fundamental changes in how business is conducted in order to help cope with a shift in market environment (Kotter, 2007).
- Enterprise transformation is driven by experienced and/or anticipated value deficiencies relative to needs and/or expectations due to:
  - Experienced or expected losses of value, for example, declining enterprise revenues and/ or margin.
  - Experienced or expected failures to meet projected or promised upside gains of value, for example, failures to achieve anticipated enterprise growth.
  - Desired to achieve new levels of value, for example, through exploitation of market and/ or technological opportunities (Rouse, 2005, 2006).
- Business Transformation is a wholesale shift in the way parts – or all – of a business operates. Typically, business transformation is led by a strategic vision set out at the most senior levels of leadership and the result is a process of change which aims to review, optimize and re-engineer business structure, processes and technology to serve those strategic goals. Business transformation objectives are broadly defined in terms of cost reduction, revenue and profit growth or improved customer satisfaction (source unknown).
- Corporate business model transformation is a change in the perceived logic of how value is created by the corporation, when it comes to the value-creating links among the corporation's portfolio of businesses, from one point of time to another (Aspara et al., 2013).

Zhongyuan et al. (2011) predict that companies will transform their enterprise by some combination of predicting better, learning faster and acting faster, as long as the market is sufficiently predictable to reasonably expect that transformation will improve the market value the company can provide. If this expectation is unreasonable, then companies will sit tight and preserve resources until the market becomes more fathomable. Companies make transformation decisions in response to the dynamic situations in which they find themselves. These decisions are affected by both what the company knows (or perceives) and the company's abilities to predict, learn, and act. Indeed, decisions to transform abilities to predict, learn and act reflect desires to fundamentally change the company's overall ability to create market value. In this way, transformation decisions can enhance a company's abilities to address the ongoing and anticipated transformations needed for success in dynamic markets.

Aspara et al. (2013) believe that corporate business model is not totally idiosyncratic to its top business leaders' thoughts (despite partly deciding as a logic in their minds) is that their beliefs about the firm's businesses and their value-creating links are often shared by other stakeholders in the industries/communities in which the firm operates. For example, if two of a corporation's businesses serve the same customers and provide them with mutually complementary offerings, the business leaders' perception of the situation are likely to be shared to a great extent by both the corporation's customers and its competitors. This reflects the common place notion in leadership research and related disciplines that a firm's internal corporate or organizational identity (i.e., the leadership and employees' perceptions of the corporation and its businesses) usually corresponds or should correspond to the firm's external organizational image or reputation (Gioia et al., 2000; Brown et al., 2006; Cornelissen et al., 2007). In other words, there are shared – "inter-organizational" – cognitions about the corporation's businesses which are held by the firm's business leaders and its stakeholders, and which may also play special roles in leadership's decisions about corporate business model transformation.

Aspara et al. (2013) have identified three specific types of inter-organizational cognitions which may require some special attention in developing and executing the transformation process:

1. *Whole corporate business model:* There is the issue of the overall legitimacy of the whole corporate business model. For example, corporate business leaders are concerned about the legitimacy of their current corporate business model – relative to that of any potential new corporate business model – in the eyes of their various stakeholders (e.g., internally among employees and middle managers), while a possible new model configuration might be seen as commending more support from others (e.g., investors and governmental agencies). Thus, corporate leadership faces the task of balancing such dynamics in choosing (or not) to transform their corporate business model. Prior research on inter-organizational cognitions has studied a similar issue under the level of "industry recipes" (Spender, 1990; Porac et al., 2002; Porac and Thomas, 2002). The concept refers to the overall business logic – ways of operating and competing – that are considered legitimate and appropriate in any given industry (i.e., by its participants and stakeholders).

2. *Reputational ranking:* There is the issue related to reputational ranking of the firm's current and potential new businesses. Reputational ranking essentially refer to how firms' reputations, or performance statuses, are evaluated in inter-organizational communities vis-à-vis competition – in simple-terms, how well a firm is perceived to be performing in its community of competitors (Grinyer and Spender, 1979). Each industry in which a firm operates will usually have its own reputational ranking orders, so a multi-business firm may have different ranks in the various industries in which it operates. Thus a firm does not hold one identity that is similar in all the industries where it operates, but rather has multiple coexisting identities (Pratt and Foreman, 2000; Balmer and Greyser, 2002), and differing reputational rankings in each. A firm can also have non-industry-specific reputational rankings in such broader communities as society at large, or financial markets in general. These situations create critical questions for the business leadership – which specific reputational ranking corporate aim to exploit and/or improve by their corporate business model transformation – and how well will it consider the concerns of business leadership (Fombrun, 1996; Chen, 2005; Rhee and Valdez, 2009).

3. *Boundary beliefs:* While reputational rankings indicate the reputation of a firm or its business unit(s) in organizational communities, boundary beliefs can be thought as those elements that allow a firm or a business to be seen as a legitimate member of those communities in the first place (Porac et al., 2002). Most often, the firm's or its unit's products and customers are the de facto boundary elements that determine its identity as belongs to a particular industry community (e.g., as a consumer electronics company, home appliances company, etc.). For example, a multi-unit corporation like Sony, the corporation and its businesses may have multiple boundary elements that can be both shared and distinct, making the corporation or its businesses belong to multiple industries or communities in the minds of its top business leaders and stakeholders. Therefore, when it comes to business model transformation, the

essential question comes in mind, which boundary elements do corporate leaders want to retain, and which to renew? Retaining some elements and renewing others allows leadership to reduce the contours of the corporation and its businesses.

Aspara et al. (2013) conducted the case study of Nokia's corporate business model transformation and the study suggests that corporate executives can make their decisions about changing the composition of their corporation's businesses and the value-creating links between them based in part, on their recognition of inter-organizational cognitions. In Nokia's case, the cognitions that drove or influenced their strategies transformation choices included: new, emerging corporate recipes deemed more legitimate among key stakeholders that were internalized and taken into account at a time of corporate crisis; the current reputational ranking of the corporation's businesses in their respective industries; beliefs about shared current boundary elements between businesses (i.e., currently complementary products and customers); and the elements of same existing unit's business models to which they attributed failure.

Enterprise transformation (ET) may create change, not just routine change but fundamental change that substantially alter an organizational relationship with one or more key groups, e.g., customers, employees, suppliers and investors (Rouse, 2005). Transformation can involve new value propositions in terms of products and/or services, how these offerings are delivered and supported, and/or how the enterprise is organized to provide these offerings. Transformation can also be involved where old value propositions are primarily changed to new ways. The objectives of ET also provide the anchor for consistent decision-making and process execution. The ET process supports the relationship between small- and large-enterprises, and their partnership in the supply chain management.

Enterprise transformation should be a continuous process, essential to any organization in executing its enterprise growth strategy along with mitigating risk and achieving its vision. It is an ongoing requirement since growth strategy, risk and vision will always need adapting and refining as changing economic influences impact. Enterprise agility, or the ability to achieve the enterprise transformation, is therefore a true measure of both leadership and corporate success.

Customer demand in the market is defined as customer needs which are a function of several variables including economic situation. Therefore, the customers, suppliers and the manufacturers and their resources are linked in this economic system. Enterprise transformation takes place as new products come in the market, but the pace of transformation depends on economic situation. Transformation within any organization would depend on work assignments, their processes and costs, and their throughput. Some of the other elements that would impact transformation are business leadership (Kouzes and Posner, 1987; George, 2003), individual and team competencies (Katzenbach and Smith, 1993; King and Kosminsky, 2006), values and culture (Davenport, 1999), and rewards and recognition system (Weiss and Hartle, 1997).

Therefore, the following sections are presented in this chapter:

4.1   Enterprise Assessment Process
4.2   Elements of Enterprise Transformation, why and how it happens
4.3   Mobility and Social Networks in Enterprise Transformation
    4.3.1   Social Alliances and Transformation
4.4   Financial Transformation Initiatives
    4.4.1   How to Implement Financial Transformation Process
    4.4.2   How to Make Financial Transformation Work
    4.4.3   How to Handle Negative Thinkers
4.5   Workforce Transformation
    4.5.1   Workforce Transformation through WIRED

4.1   Enterprise Assessment Process

Van de Ven and Ferry (1980) developed an organizational assessment process model which is based on the results of the Organizational Assessment (OA). The OA process model offers a comprehensive approach to organizational assessment. It recognizes the role of the following elements:

*   understanding motivation and planning for the assessment;
*   feedback mechanism, which allows for concurrent implementation of phases;
*   timely adjustment of activities depending on outcomes of subsequent phases.

However, the OA model does not specifically recognizes the impact that organizational behavior may have on the assessment process, which may not ensure assessment effectiveness.

Nightingale et al. (2008) suggest an integrated analytical framework for guiding transformation – Enterprise Strategic Analysis and Transformation (ESAT) – it is aimed at diagnosis and improvement of overall enterprise performance, based on qualitative and quantitative analysis of the enterprise's current state and leading to creation of a future state vision, actionable transformation plan and infrastructure for support of the transformation implementation. The assessment of the enterprise is carried out during the analysis of the enterprise's current state. The assessment helps to identify strengths and weaknesses in current performance and indicate future performance and envision a desirable future state. It also provides input into future strategy and/or implementation plans.

Despite the benefits that the organizational assessment has to offer, many organizations fail to derive benefits, for a variety of reasons (Abdimomunova and Valerdi, 2010):

*   Organizational culture and behaviors during the assessment process impact the assessment results.
*   The assessment process model, or the way it was implemented in practice, may be unsatisfactory.
*   Characteristics of the assessment tool itself made the assessment difficult to implement.

They found that the assessment process spans beyond performing the assessment itself. In order for the assessment to provide the expected benefits, the organization first of all must create an environment that ensures consistent understanding of the role of the assessment in the enterprise transformation process and promotes open and frequent discussion about the current state and future goals. The assessment process must be carefully planned to ensure that it runs effectively and efficiently and that the assessment results are accurate and reliable. The assessment results must be analyzed and turned into specific recommendations and action plans. During the organization's assessment process, the assessment process itself must be evaluated and adjusted, if necessary, for the next cycle of assessment.

Abdimomunova and Valerdi (2010) are recommending an assessment process model, which includes mechanisms to change behavior of the organization through pre-assessment phases. It allows adjusting the assessment process itself based on the results and experience of participants so that it better suits needs and practices of the organization. The desired assessment process may be an interim goal that evolves as the organizational behavior improves. A healthy, effective organization will continue to expand its goals for its behavior and processes. The conceptual flow chart of the model is presented in Figure 4.1, which presents the dynamic alignment between organizational behavior and assessment process.

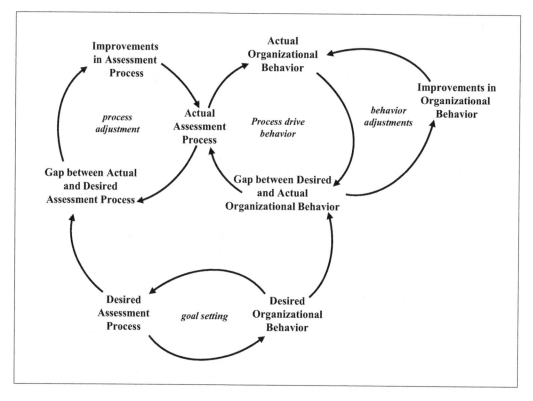

Figure 4.1   **Dynamic alignment between organizational behavior and assessment process**

4.2   Elements of Enterprise Transformation, Why and How It Happens

The elements of any enterprise system can broadly be divided into external and internal elements, and all these elements are linked directly and/or indirectly with the enterprise. Rouse's (2005) conceptual structure is presented in Figure 4.2. Customer demand is affected by economy, which affects the market that, in turn, affect enterprises. Of course, it is not that simple hierarchical economic relationship that can directly affect enterprises. There are various other elements such as laws, regulations and taxes. It is interesting to realize that the nature and extent of transformation are context-dependent. Transformation should also be looked at within the enterprise. There are

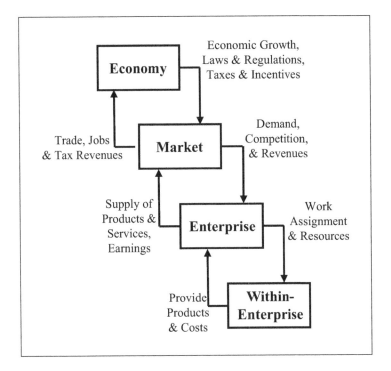

Figure 4.2   Structural relationship of enterprise transformation

various work assignments carried on through work processes yield work products. This includes all the other elements including costs, values and culture, and employees/team competencies.

Similar concepts can also be applied to public sector enterprises. The term "market" can be replaced with "constituency." The financial metrics should be replaced with elements such as diseases cured, reducing/eliminating neighborhood crimes, etc. Some transformation examples are presented later in this chapter.

The enterprise leadership analyzes their internal strengths, competencies and weaknesses in relation to external opportunities and threats. Therefore, the possibilities for transformation are defined through the relationship between the enterprise and the opportunities and threats. The enterprise transformation must recognize the inputs, such as resources (people, technology and investments), which affect the internal processes as well as the product output. Another element to recognize is "state" of the enterprise. It is very critical to the theory of enterprise transformation. The state of the enterprise provides the values that enable assessing where the enterprise is and projecting where it is going to be. Hauser and Clausing (1988) suggest an enterprise-oriented version of the House of Quality, Kaplan and Norton (1996a) are suggesting Balanced Scorecard, while Rouse (2001) believes that financial variables are usually insufficient to project the future of an enterprise.

Some of the key elements of the output derived from the evolving state of the enterprise are number of units sold and revenue received. Profitability can be determined knowing the costs of providing offerings. Sold units would relate, at least in part, to meeting or exceeding customer satisfaction as determined by product and service functionality.

From the enterprise transformation perspective, state variables such as revenue, costs, quality and price determine value (Rouse, 2005). These variables are themselves determined by work processes and the architectural relationship among processes. Therefore, the value of projected outputs influences how input resources are attracted and allocated as well as competencies are developed to support the output. Many fundamental changes address value from the perspective of customers and, to a lesser extent, suppliers and employees. Peter Drucker (2001) said that the purpose of a business is to create a customer. While a business is losing its market share and subsequently decreasing stock market valuation can be viewed as end effects in themselves, they may also be seen as symptoms of declining value of products and services as perceived by customers. Definitely, a broader view of value is needed (Slywotzky, 1996; Slywotzky and Morrison, 1997).

Historical, current or projected value deficiencies drive enterprise transformation initiatives. Deficiencies are defined relative to both current enterprise states and expected states. Projections may be based on extrapolation of historical enterprise states. They may also be based on perceived opportunities to pursue expanded markets, new markets, technologies, etc. Therefore, deficiencies may be perceived for both reactive and proactive reasons.

According to Rouse (2005), enterprise transformation is driven by perceived value deficiencies relative to needs and/or expectations due to:

- experienced or expected downside losses of value; for example, declining enterprise revenues and/or profits;
- experienced or expected failures to meet projected or promised upside gains of value; for example, failures to achieve anticipated enterprise growth; and
- desires to achieve new levels of value; for example, via exploitation of market and/or technological opportunities.

Transformation initiatives involve addressing what activities enterprise has already undertaken and how these activities are accomplished and how the remaining activities are going to be accomplished. The work of the enterprise transformation activities ultimately affects the state of the enterprise, which is reflected, in part, in the enterprise's financial statements. Other important elements of the enterprise state might include brand image, market advantage, employee and customer satisfaction, and so on.

Oliff (2012) summarizes the enterprise transformation, which begins with a corporate strategy founded on the drive to create value with customers as well as recognize building new business structures with distinctive competencies. It relies on the development of stretch cultures to sustain any meaningful improvements. Building distinctive competencies begins when business leaders start viewing internal resources as value generators and bundles of cross-functional corporate-wide abilities. Developing stretch culture begins only after the business leaders recognize the difference between performance and potential at every level within the enterprise, beginning with the individual employee. Enterprise transformation assumes large-scale (relative to the size of a business) interdependent changes in the strategy, structures and leadership/human systems of the business. Personal transformation relies on significant changes in the business objectives, focus and discipline. Enterprise transformation rarely occurs without sustained personal transformation. It begins and ends with business leader.

4.3 Mobility and Social Networks in Enterprise Transformation

Today's most enterprises face a common set of challenges when integrating their mobile employees into their enterprise-wide collaboration networks. Mobility and social collaboration networks are transforming in almost every industry sector and they have a profound impact on customers and employees (Mann, 2012). Social networking and mobility solutions come together to the point where social collaboration networks primarily focus on building online communities of people and mobility becomes the most preferred delivery channel not just to improve the return on investment, but also to expand global reach and improve the operational efficiency of the enterprise employees.

Mobile enablement means the rendering of an existing web application on a mobile channel, whereas mobile social network-enablement means embedding on-demand social networking and collaboration capabilities into the application to increase its utility. In a twenty-first century environment, there is a variety of businesses that either leverage a mobility platform to host social networks or they would create scalable mobile applications available in social networking platform. Therefore, it has become imperative to make a clear distinction between mobile enablement and mobile social network-enablement. Mann (2012) is identifying that social networking and collaboration solutions are growing across business portfolios, driven by the need to increase productivity and improve decision-making, with increased short-term and real-time access through mobile channels and such adoption helps to improve internal employee interaction, customer collaboration, network building and information sharing.

Social computing and networking has created a significant evolution in the way people collaborate and interact through the Internet. Social computing represents the collection of technologies that collect, process, compute and visualize social information. This emerged new social structure is creating an array of loosely integrated social elements. Enterprise-wide collaboration is not only a business objective, but it has also become a requirement for enterprises to remain competitive and provide decision-making information in a timely manner. Organizations face a variety of challenges in enabling of social collaboration including the following:

- customer needs;
- marketing strategy;
- lack of correct and/or on-time information;
- customer service;
- resources availability.

Social networks play several roles. First, of course, they constitute how work gets done in terms of who does what, who knows what, who knows who, and so on. They can also facilitate or impede change. Social networks can facilitate change by embracing and rapidly diffusing change as has been seen recently for email and smart phones. Social networks can also impede change, acting in ways analogous to an enterprise immune system (Rouse, 1998). One way to impede change is to deny that it is needed. This delays recognition of market signals that the value of an enterprise's offerings is declining. Another impedance is reluctance to change work processes. Competencies that provided competitive advantage in the past may be preserved, perhaps receiving sustained investment, despite their decreased relevance to competing in the future.

Enterprises need a strong mobility platform to gain the benefits from enterprise mobility. The enterprise mobility will not only open up new channels for collaboration but also provides the means for accessing the critical customer information – anytime and anywhere. Based on Mann's (2012) experience, a sharp distinction has to be drawn between technology-focused mobile strategy, which refers to helping employees in selecting the correct devices, platform and applications, and a business-focused strategy for mobility, which analyzes how mobility will affect various stakeholders. He has experienced a significant improvement in revenue and cost reduction through the enterprise mobility and value proposition.

Social network and mobility deployment would not only help to improve the effectiveness of on-the-move employees, but also result in creating a dynamic ecosystem of online services, environment and applications. Social networks are providing a unique connecting link to engage communities, initiate communication and developing innovative ideas. Social business collaboration allows enterprises to exchange thoughts and ideas in a fashion that is integrated with business processes and promises to become a strong business tool. Therefore, the greatest benefit will come from combining the collaborative power of social networks with the mobility strategy.

Some reading references on mobility and social networks:

Barnes, S.J. 2003. Enterprise mobility: Concepts and examples. *International Journal of Mobile Communications*, 1(4): 341–59.

Basole, R.C. 2008. Enterprise mobility: Researching a new paradigm. *Information Knowledge Systems Management*, 7: 1–7.

Golbeck, J. and Rothstein, M. 2008. Linking Social Networks on the Web with FOAF: A Semantic Web Case Study. Proceedings of the Twenty-Third Conference on Artificial Intelligence (AAAI'08), July 13–17, Chicago, Illinois. Proceedings published by The AAAI Press, Menlo Park, CA in book and CD format. Abstract is available at: http://www.aaai.org/Library/AAAI/aaai08contents.php

Hendrix, P. 2012. Mobilizing the Enterprise with off-the-Shelf Apps and Custom Mobile Solutions. Whitepaper Sponsored by SAP. August 2012.

Simoudis, E. 2014. Mobilizing Enterprise Applications. Available at: http://www.enterpriseirregulars.com/71554/mobilizing-enterprise-applications/

4.3.1   SOCIAL ALLIANCES AND TRANSFORMATION

Human development and the reduction of poverty remain as significant challenges of society (World Economic Forum [WEF], 2004). Alongside governments, national and international initiatives independently and/or collaboratively engage in efforts to improve the welfare and living standards of disadvantaged populations. Service delivery through non-governmental channels is increasing (Austin, 2000; Googins and Rochlin, 2000; Nelson and Zadek, 2000; Wymer and Samu, 2003; Berger et al., 2004; Millar et al., 2004) and a wide variety of programs are undertaken to contribute to social transformation at economic, cultural and political spheres (Alvord et al., 2004). A new model where collaboration between the private, government, and civil sectors play a central role in achieving sustainable communities is evolving (Googins and Rochlin, 2000).

There is a long history about business community's concern for society. Moral and internal drivers, the Industrial Revolution, and the emergence and the decline of the welfare state affected the way corporations engaged socially over time (Brown et al., 2010). In a similar manner, corporate social engagement shifted from philanthropy to cross-sector collaboration (CSC) and is increasingly used strategically as a form of social investment (Baron, 2001; Epstein, 2002; Porter and Kramer, 2002).

Through strategic use of CSC, business enterprises aim at supporting core business activities and contributing to the firm's effectiveness in accomplishing its mission (Burke and Logsdon, 1996). Strategic CSC programs may result in greater customer loyalty, new products and/or productivity gains, enhanced reputation and image as well as increased sustainability (Pivato et al., 2008; McElhaney, 2009). There have been attempts to demonstrate empirical support for the commercial value of CSC; its impact on profitability, however, is controversial. Some findings suggest that corporate social responsibility and financial performance are generally positively related across a wide variety of industry contexts (Orlitzky et al., 2003; Smith, 2007) and that CSC initiatives can lead to long-term profitability (McPeak and Tooley, 2008). However, there are also studies which report a neutral or a negative relationship between CSC and financial performance (Vance, 1975; Alexander and Buchholz, 1978; Abbott and Monsen, 1979).

Normative pressures stem from organizations which develop norms about organizational structures, processes and practices, such as professional, industrial and businessmen's associations, non-governmental organizations (NGO) and universities. As a response to normative pressures from supranational organizations such as United Nations (UN) and Organization for Economic Cooperation and Development (OECD), companies began to participate increasingly in schemes like Corporate Codes of Conduct (Falkner, 2003; Mattli, 2003; Gulbrandsen, 2004), accept Guidelines for Multinational Enterprises (OECD, 2004), disclose social responsibility activities in their annual reports, Ertuna and Tükel (2010) and engage in efforts to solve social problems alone or though cross-sector collaborations (WEF, 2006).

No party can tackle on its own multidimensional social problems bring in the need for collaboration between businesses and social enterprises. In an effort to build an infrastructure to deal with poverty for example, the role of aid relief and subsidies was challenged and wealth creation through private and social sector collaboration was suggested as an alternative (Prahalad, 2005a). In response to growing social problems, cross-sector collaborations in the form of social alliances as well as firm/NGO partnerships aiming the poor as consumers or producers have increased significantly in number recently (Elkington et al., 2000; Wymer and Samu, 2003; Berger et al., 2004) and have drawn the attention of academicians from various disciplines (Selsky and Parker, 2005).

Sakarya et al. (2012) analyzed 6 social alliance cases, covering 12 organizations (6 business enterprises and 6 social enterprises) through multiple sources of evidence including several secondary data sources and in-depth interviews with key informants from each partner. Their observations suggest that both social and business enterprises have the common alliance-level objectives for forming the social alliance: "joint value creation" and "community capacity building." At the partner level, however, businesses aim at "stakeholder appreciation" whereas social enterprises seek for "fund raising" opportunities.

4.4   Financial Transformation Initiatives

The ever-increasing expectations of shareholders in a globally competitive market are creating a growing demand for greater corporate accountability and improved guiding procedures in today's business environment. There is no room for financially mismanaged corporations like Enron and WorldCom. Even though the chief executive officer (CEO) is the key leader in the corporate structure, there is another player now beginning to assume unprecedented responsibility: the chief financial officer (CFO) (Kumar, 2010a). The CFO is quickly becoming the person upon whom many boards now depend for answers.

The CEO is the business leader and leads the business strategy, while the CFO is the key leader in implementing the strategy. The CFO also plays a critical role in restoring public trust and serving as an important bridge between the CEO and the board on governing issues. The new CFO's goals are not easy and he/she has to manage several contradicting activities concurrently (Kumar, 2010a). Some of the key responsibilities of any CFO are to:

- Protect the company's bottom line.
- Enable the profitable growth and shareholders value creation.
- Maintain/re-establish corporate trust and business integrity.
- Improve the efficiency, effectiveness and quality of financial operations.

Protect the company's bottom line: Currently, most businesses are focused on top line growth in revenue and profitability. As global economic competition increases and the rate of growth in profitability decreases, many corporate executives today face major challenges. This global competition forces them to reduce costs and to protect their bottom line growth. This places the CFO and their finance team on the center stage, and today's competitive and dynamic markets require businesses to engage in intelligent cost reduction. These cost reductions must not hurt their existing growth potential, intangible assets, for example, people, intellectual capital, customer and business partnership relations, and should not place their future at risk. These activities force corporate executives, business leaders, and controllers to require extended information about current performance and future risks, and new business opportunities. This is way beyond the traditional profit and loss (P&L) statement and balance sheet deliveries. CFOs must now react to a new environment and provide new analytic tools that deliver not only accurate and timely information on current financial performance, but also on its drivers across the entire business. One of their key objectives is to provide as accurate a forecast as possible, not just of financial performance but also of the underlying business drivers. Combining these forecasts would provide the foundation for dynamic performance management to business leaders.

Enable the profitable growth and shareholders value creation: Internal growth requires a significant cost reduction in the business. CFOs have to help business leaders to understand the economics of their businesses to create profits and value. For example, CFOs have to help their business leaders to understand customer needs from an economic perspective and to select the appropriate level of products/services. Continuous improvement is one of the critical activities for resource and cost efficiency. CFOs have to establish and implement the procedures and systems to make that happen. These created values must be properly communicated to the financial community, both internal and external, so that it can be recognized and reflected in the company's share price. Merger and acquisition (M&A) is another way to create shareholder value. When assets are exchanged at full market price, no added value is created. Still there are situations where M&A and financial dealings create value, but these dealings require accuracy and discipline in the evaluation and integration phase. However, for most companies, shareholder value comes from internally generated growth and/or resources, and costs and capital efficiencies. CFOs are involved very heavily both in M&A activities as well as in internal growth, and play a leading role in strategy planning and execution, in long-term efficiency and productivity leadership.

Maintain/re-establish corporate trust and business integrity: Investor trust in corporations has declined recently due to some corporate scandals – Enron, WorldCom, etc. The CFO and the financial activities in the corporation now play the leading role in restoring corporate trust and business integrity. Some of the key activities are:

* financial integration and accountability;
* meeting new corporate rules and guidelines.

Improve the efficiency, effectiveness and quality of financial operations: Many businesses utilize these approaches in the twenty-first century and recognize the significant weaknesses in their financial operations. Most CFOs are interested to know:

* how to predict future financial performance and liquidity.
* how to reduce processing and service costs.
* how to change over to efficient and integrated financial systems from old and obsolete systems.
* how to reduce account receivables, bank accounts and support reduced business cycle time.

Innovative CFOs are increasing focus on finance transformation strategies to enable their corporations to succeed in the global competitive marketplace. These CFOs are not emphasizing mundane transactional processing and account analysis tasks, but rather supporting value-creation strategies which should eventually revolutionize enterprise performance and positively influence corporate outlook. The answers to the following questions will support the new financial strategy:

- How to implement financial transformation process?
- How to make finance transformation work?
- How to handle negative thinkers?
- How to minimize risk management? Discussion is presented in Chapter 3 – ERM.

4.4.1   HOW TO IMPLEMENT FINANCIAL TRANSFORMATION PROCESS

A program that involves gradual change over a period of time is known as an evolutionary. When several tactical or operational projects are combined into a program this too is an evolutionary program. A strategic project that is enterprise-wide, led by the CFO and generally takes three to five years is defined as financial transformation (Kumar, 2010a). The key properties of a financial transformation are:

- a broad scope;
- multiple objectives;
- substantial impact on the enterprise.

For example, replacing several service centers with one centralized service center, outsourcing basic manufacturing of parts and components and maintaining core competency, and replacing several legacy information systems into one system. These types of initiatives can impact several business units and financial processes, if not the whole enterprise.

Rabinowitz (2006) recommends that the financial transformation process uses 12 steps:

1. The CFO is the executive champion.
2. A visionary phase is completed at the beginning of the program.
3. The transformation is continually marketed to the company.
4. Change in management and communication are critical components of the program.
5. Escalated issues are effectively resolved.
6. Flexibility is built into the program.
7. The company engages outside resources to complement its capabilities.
8. Consultant experience is leveraged to help expedite decision-making.
9. Activities are completed in parallel whenever possible.
10. The relationship between program components and delivery are understood.
11. Existing process and technology standards are used when possible.
12. Financial data are understood and controlled.

The CFO is the executive champion: The CFO must lead the transformation and try to maintain program momentum. Without CFO's support, the transformation program may not be able to overcome organizational resistance and may eventually fail.

A visionary phase is completed at the beginning of the program: The visioning phase allows all stakeholders to develop a common understanding of the outcome and objectives of the transformation. The visionary phase can also help the CFO identify resources which may not support the change and these resources should be convinced to adopt the company's vision or, probably, forced to leave the company.

The transformation is continually marketed to the company: The transformation process may create some disruption and discomfort in the company, so the stakeholders should be reminded of the need for the transformation and the benefits it can create. There are several avenues for this type of communication – leadership presentations, email updates, mailing hard copy updates, or other communication methods.

Change in management and communication are critical components of the program: There is a high probability that the financial transformation will impact workforce, processes and technology both inside the financial functions and across other areas in the company. The amount of changes including organizational and cultural occurring at any given time should be managed carefully as the transformation process goes on.

Escalated issues are effectively resolved: During financial, or any other, transformation, there will be issues that will need to be escalated to program leadership and even to the executive leadership team. Resolution of these issues will have a direct impact on the effectiveness of the program. Leadership must not have the attitude of "just get it done" and avoid blaming others for the issues that may arise. Instead, leadership should strive to fully understand the issue and then identify the appropriate resources to solve it.

Flexibility is built into the program: There is a high probability in these types of programs that changes and corrections will continually be made to plans, design, processes, applications and other activities. The program team should anticipate and plan for unknowns that may occur later in the program. This could mean adding additional resources for activities that are not fully understood or implementing a technology which was not easily scaled in the beginning.

The company engages outside resources to complement its capabilities: If a company does not have an internal resource to manage program like this, the company should consider bringing in a business collaborator to help navigate the activities involved in the transformation. A similar concept applies in technology areas; if the company does not have a highly experienced person to select technology then an outside resource should be utilized in the decision-making process.

Consultant experience is leveraged to help expedite decision-making: Take advantage of the consultant's knowledge and experience when making project decisions. Let the consultants identify leading practices, strategies and solutions that have been effective in similar situations. This type of approach can save time and the company will achieve its transformation objectives quickly.

Activities are completed in parallel whenever possible. Rapid financial transformation requires that many of the activities be completed in parallel. As Rabinowitz (2006) observed, after the first four activities, the rest of the activities should be in parallel. This can require a significant amount of ongoing planning and communication to work effectively. It is critical in an activity's parallelization to determine inter-team dependencies and deliverables during the planning phase of the project.

The relationship between program components and delivery are understood: Team members and other participants should also understand how program components are related to one another and how their completion and/or delivery can be staged to suit the overall program schedule most effectively. For example, data entry systems can be deployed at the beginning of the month and a reporting system at the end of the month when the reports are needed.

Existing process and technology standards are used when possible: The program team should concentrate on making the important changes that are required to transform the company, existing processes and standards should be used whenever they meet the transformed company's business needs. For example, if the existing customer relationship management system meets the needs of the transformed company, there is no need to perform an exhaustive evaluation for the system.

Financial data are understood and controlled: There are certain portions of data required to measure, monitor and manage the company. Identify this type of data and manage it during the transformation, to avoid any significant interruption in the business decision-making process.

According to Daum's (2003) benchmark study, the finance organization's cost is 0.43–1.05 percent of revenue in a corporation, and the cost of world-class finance organizations is at the lower end (0.43 percent of revenue). This creates a tough benchmark for many CFOs.

4.4.2 HOW TO MAKE FINANCE TRANSFORMATION WORK

Most finance operations are not ready to fulfill their new task of finance transformation for their companies. To assure corporate governance, continuously reduce costs related to financial activities and provide high-quality services at the same time. These operations are not specifically in a position to support the business in a proactive way that supports future business needs and to immediately implement required processes and system accordingly. Current operations have significant weaknesses in their existing organizational, process and systems design that require too many resources in the daily operations, so these resources are not available to support the transformation.

Every project starts with better concepts. CFOs first have to come up with more intelligent processes and organizational concepts for finance and then they have to find ways to depart from where they are today to realize quick cost savings that free up resources needed for the next step. It is not necessary to spend lots of money on technology. Best-in-class companies generally do not spend more on technology than average companies to achieve cost efficiency and high-quality financial services. The keys to the financial transformation for an intelligent business are financial and information technology (IT) concepts where business/finance concepts have to be the starting point and not technology.

According to Drucker (1999), a new information revolution "I" is underway (where "I" is from IT) and it is not a revolution in technology, machinery, techniques, software or speed. It is a revolution in concepts. For the last 50 years, information technology has centered on "data" – their collection, storage, transmission and presentation. It has focused on the "T" in "IT." The new information revolutions focus on the "I" and are asking, "What is the meaning of information and its purpose?"

4.4.3 HOW TO HANDLE NEGATIVE THINKERS

According to Hackett (1997), generally the opinions for any good idea are distributed as follows:

- 70 percent of people buy into good ideas;

- 10 percent never buy in and will fight against the idea;
- 20 percent hold the opinion of the last person they talked with.

To accomplish a major change program business leader needs 85 to 90 percent of the organization to accept the change. To accomplish this, the leader has to keep those who hate their ideas away from those who support their ideas. Business leaders must spend a lot of time selling change.

Most people think of a change program as a technical implementation, and most programs do not fail for technical reasons – they fail for personal reasons. There are individuals who do not like change or were not consulted for their input early enough in the decision process, and there are some people who are simply cranky individuals.

Business leaders must confront the negative thinkers head-on if they want to implement change, and think and act upon the following:

- Understand their concerns first.
- Sit and talk with them.
- Explain business leadership vision or proposal.
- Find the common ground, then isolate the differences and talk through them.
- Determine if the differences are true or simply differences in semantics.
- If the differences are semantics, adapt to the negative thinkers words and give in.
- If there are true differences, listen carefully and try to accommodate the negative thinkers. It is possible that the business leaders are missing something that they find very important.
- Talk to the individuals again one week after business leaders' initial discussion, and give it another try after two weeks have passed. Business leaders probably will have won them over by that time.
- Communicate constantly with the 70 percent who have agreed with business leaders change program. They will put pressure on the negative thinkers as well as try to reduce their count.
- Senior leaders must support the business leaders and their chief responsibility is selling change, not implementing the technical aspects of the program.

If business leaders cannot prove to someone that they are proposing a correct idea, they must assume that they are wrong. They are either not taking into account something others find important, or are doing a poor job of articulating their idea.

4.5 Workforce Transformation

High-performance organizations rely on high-performance people. The American workforce is constantly being called on to perform myriad duties and functions both at home and abroad. Mission responsibilities are continuing to grow and at the same time the nature of work is also becoming more complex. Further, many of the most experienced performers are eligible to retire. The primary challenge is a reduction in the workforce over the coming five to eight years, which could create a knowledge deficit in key and critical programs.

For the next 10 or more years, every health-care provider will struggle to provide optimal patient care against staffing shortages. To complicate the matter, the aging population will bring an increase in patient volumes that will challenge health-care facilities across the nation. Every health-care organization must have a plan to support long-term growth while providing patients with the best care possible and yet still give employees an environment that fosters job satisfaction. Neglecting to take action could result in reliance upon staffing (overtime, call-back, agency, etc.), spiraling labor costs, unhappy patients and other unacceptable consequences. However, a successful transformation effort can result in dramatically increased workforce efficiencies and effectiveness plus significantly improved employee and patient satisfaction. Other challenges relate to the need to develop strong relationship with foreign countries through empowering local workforces – again a reality that leading companies can exploit to achieve competitive advantage.

In every organization, the workforce plays a critical role and strategic plans are only as effective as the people that execute them. In today's globally competitive market, every business has to do more with limited resources and the workforce is one of the critical constraints. Businesses need to align employees with business mission and objectives, equipping them with the skills and tools they need and developing the environment in which results drive actions efficiently to capitalize on scarce people and financial assets.

As business leadership goes through the process of vision, mission and strategic planning which leads to financial analysis, laws and regulations, and internal and external customer satisfaction/dissatisfaction can still challenge the business's ability to efficiently leverage its people capital to improve organizational performance. Every organization can effectively leverage their people capital to:

- Align the workforce structure with their organization's purpose, mission, goals and objectives, positioning resources for efficient and effective operational execution.
- Execute transition strategies in workforce plans through targeted approaches such as recruiting/hiring, training, performance management and succession planning.
- Prioritize and programmatically deploy people capital management initiatives, empowering the workforce to create value and achieve professional development and business goals.
- Position human resource (HR) functionality strategically within the business organization.
- Streamline traditional HR business processes and optimize service delivery models to increase efficiency, reduce costs and improve HR's ability to support employee empowerment.

Human resource executives are on the move, and they are shifting their focus from the front line to the bottom line. They are also playing the critical role of strategist and steward to businesses that are facing the difficult task of people-related challenges such as intense pressure for growth and increased regulatory scrutiny among them.

To succeed in this globally competitive market, the HR department must turn its inward focus outward. They are recognizing the workforce trends, shaping and executing business strategy, identifying and addressing people-related risks and regulations and transforming the workforce through improving performance and productivity. An HR department can earn its place among the top value drivers in the organization. The following are some of the examples of workforce transformation:

- Workforce transformation through WIRED (Workforce Innovation in Regional Economic Development).
- Workforce transformation in food and nutrition services.

4.5.1 WORKFORCE TRANSFORMATION THROUGH WIRED

The US Department of Labor realized that government help is required in this globally competitive market to transform the US workforce, and asked state authorities to develop their proposals in this area and submit them to the US Department of Labor for financial support. Over 100 proposals from across the US were submitted to the Department of Labor and only 13 regions were awarded the federal grant of $15 million for three years for each region (Kumar, 2010a).

Piedmont Triad Partnership (PTP) is one of the seven regions in the state of North Carolina. PTP developed their proposal and submitted it to the US Department of Labor, focusing on six strategies (Table 4.1) to support the region's transition to a twenty-first century economy. These strategies will create a new regional paradigm which will enhance the Piedmont Triad Region's global economic competitiveness. PTP demonstrated the need and desire to expand their economic development base and to provide the latest technology advantage to companies within the PTP region: they were selected as one of the first WIRED organizations in the US. A sample summary of the announcement letter is presented in Table 4.2. PTP's compilation summary of the idea behind the WIRED award for the region's public and these facts are presented in Table 4.3.

Table 4.1   Piedmont Triad region's proposed strategies

1. Develop a regional organization to transform the Piedmont Triad into a national and global hotspot.
A Piedmont Triad Regional Outreach Center will be created and staffed under the umbrella of the Piedmont triad Partnership (PTP) to manage both the traditional programs of work of the PTP and the WIRED initiative.
2. Cultivate economic clusters that can support high-wage, high-skill jobs.
Building on the work of the Piedmont Triad Vision Plan and other target cluster studies, roundtables will be organized to support nine industry clusters: health care (including biotechnology), logistics and distribution, wholesale trade, food processing, finance and insurance, creative enterprises/the arts, chemicals and plastics, motor vehicle transportation, and legacy industries (textiles, apparel and furniture). Members will be drawn from industry (large employers, small business, and entrepreneurs), education at every level, economic development, workforce development, and other relevant organizations. The roundtables will be charged with identifying the workforce and other needs of these growth industries.
3. Enlist the region's educational resources to support high-wage, high-skill jobs and develop the workforce to meet employer demands.
The primary emphasis of the WIRED demonstration project is the development of Cluster Hubs in each of the region's nine community colleges to support targeted workforce training. The establishment of the Cluster Hubs will include the development and updating of Model Employee training manuals for key occupations in each cluster. In addition, the WIRED staff will enlist educational partners to form the Pre-K-12 School-to-Work and the Higher Education Innovations Council.
4. Outreach to rural counties and underserved populations.
Resources will be dedicated to rural outreach initiatives identified in the proposal, and to initiatives described in the proposal meant to reach underserved populations. The intent is to ensure that rural and minority populations receive the benefits of transformational economic development strategies implemented through the WIRED initiative and are represented in their development.
5. Create a Regional Leadership Development Center.
The PTP will partner with the Center for Creative Leadership to create a Regional Leadership Development Center, which will promote regional thinking among community leaders.
6. Develop an outreach strategy that promotes awareness of the WIRED initiative and creates an image of the Piedmont Triad as an innovative region.
The PTP will convene meetings, develop a website, and create a multi-faceted outreach campaign to (i) promote awareness of the WIRED initiative and related regional activities, (ii) emphasize the importance and value of education, and (iii) present the Piedmont Triad as a creative and innovative region.

Source: Piedmont Triad Partnership Publication. March 20, 2006. Greensboro, NC.

Table 4.2   A summary of the WIRED announcement letter

U.S. Department of Labor Secretary Elaine Chao sent a letter to the nation's Governors in November 2005 announcing a new initiative called Workforce Innovation in Regional Economic Development, or WIRED.

The Department of Labor initiative would fund a limited number of regions in the nation where educational institutions, companies, governments, and workforce and economic development organizations could partner regionally to create innovative national demonstration projects to transform and rebuild their regional economies.

The Piedmont Triad Partnership was alerted in February 2006 that it had been awarded a three-year, $15 million grant to help the region transition from its traditional economy based on textiles, apparels, furniture and tobacco to a new economy based on nine growing industry clusters.

The Piedmont Triad is one of 13 regions to be awarded the grant from across the nation out of over 100 proposals submitted. Other regions receiving the grant are: Coastal Maine, Northeast Pennsylvania, Upstate New York, Central Michigan, Western Michigan, Florida Panhandle, Western Alabama/Eastern Mississippi, North Central Indiana, Greater Kansas City, Denver Metro Region, Central and Eastern Montana, and the California Coast.

The Piedmont Triad Partnership will use the grant to implement a new "total systems" economic development strategy that focuses on supporting high-wages, high-skill occupations that are projected to grow in the region. The nine industry clusters that will be supported through this grant are: health care (including biotechnology); logistics; wholesale trade; finance and insurance; food processing; creative enterprises/the arts; transportation equipment; chemicals and plastics; and legacy industries (including textiles, apparel, and furniture).

The grant money will, among other things, support community college workforce development programs, support a K-12 initiative to prepare elementary and secondary students for jobs in these key sectors, create a regional Leadership Development Center at the Center for creative Leadership and support an outreach program intended to emphasize the value of an education. Roundtables including industry, education and workforce leaders will be established to identify workforce needs, infrastructure needs and research and development needs in these key industries.

Source: Piedmont Triad Partnership Publication. March 20, 2006. Greensboro, NC.

Table 4.3   Piedmont Triad Partnership's compiled facts behind the WIRED award

- The Piedmont Triad Region was chosen by the U.S. Department of Labor as one of 13 regions nationwide to receive a three-year, $15 million Workforce Innovation in Regional Economic Development (WIRED) grant to assist in transforming its regional economy.
- The WIRED program reflects Washington's belief that the nation can best compete in the global economy by focusing assets on regions and regional competitiveness, and by thinking regionally, when it comes to economic and workforce development.
- The Piedmont Triad's grant application stresses the transitional nature of the region's economy from textiles, furniture and tobacco to a modern economy focused on logistics, transportation, advanced manufacturing and health care, among other high-skilled sectors. The grant is intended to support this transition.
- The money will be spent to develop services and programs identified as necessary to prepare the local workforce for jobs in the new economy, and to determine how educational institutions can support innovation in our target industry clusters.

Table 4.3   Continued

- The grant program will be structured around a series of "roundtables" in the nine targeted industry clusters. The roundtables will meet regularly over the life of the grant to, among other things, identify the skills workers will be required to have to find employment in the Region's growth clusters.
- The roundtables will include industry leaders and entrepreneurs, educators from K-12 through post-graduate, economic developers, workforce development professionals, Chamber of Commerce executives, and others. Criteria will be established for selecting members to insure effectiveness and inclusiveness.
- Community colleges are a particular focus of the WIRED grant, which provides money for community colleges to hire personnel and to develop programs and infrastructure to meet the needs of the new economy workforce.
- The grant further provides for a regional leadership program to be developed by the Center for Creative Leadership, which will teach key Piedmont Triad leaders in business, government, civic affairs and education to think and plan with a more regional outlook.
- The WIRED proposal includes a strategy to extend the benefits of the Region's economic transformation to rural counties and minority populations.
- Money from the grant will also be used for a regional outreach program to include billboard and cable television advertising that will emphasize the importance of education and the importance of a regional approach to rebuilding the Piedmont Triad economy.

Source: Piedmont Triad Partnership Publication. March 20, 2006. Greensboro, NC.

The US Department of Labor has published their transformation guideline which consists of a five-step process as presented in Table 4.4. This clearly shows that the process works and there is a great support program from the US government.

Table 4.4   Five steps of economic and workforce transformation through WIRED

1.   Identify the Regional Economy
Transformation starts by identifying the surrounding communities and counties that share a regional economy. Political boundaries and even borders have become virtually irrelevant in the global economy. The systems and structures that feed and support the economy must now react accordingly. Regional economies are not static, and for this region, economic transformation cannot be a linear process. The boundaries should continually be reassessed to account for added growth and assets.
2.   Form Core Leadership Group
Once a regional identity and assets are defined, a core leadership group representing the major assets of the region must be formed to lead the effort. This includes employers, economic and workforce development professionals, state and local governments, foundations and also education entities such as K–12 education systems, community colleges and research and development laboratories, and the additional diverse partners consist of: • Senior level commitments from stakeholders; • Shared financial and resource contribution; • Collaborative responsibility for strengths, weaknesses, opportunities and threats (SWOT) analysis, asset mapping and critical self-assessment; and • Collective access to products, tools, resources and expertise.

Table 4.4   Continued

3.   SWOT Analysis
The core leadership group must measure the strengths, weaknesses, opportunities and threats in a region before developing a comprehensive regional economic strategy. The analysis should thoroughly consider a region's attributes including existing assets, natural resources, current business climate and demographics, such as educational attainment levels of workers in the region. Regions should also look to evaluate existing infrastructures (physical, virtual, governmental and educational) and cultural nuances (collaboration, innovation and entrepreneurship) that will be critical to success.
These elements for evaluation must be measured against benchmarks such as graduation rates; SAT and ACT scores; Census, NSF and BLS data; quality of High Education (media ranking and endowments; and also look at investments made in educational institutions that nurture talent).
4.   Devise Strategies
Strategies for regional economic and workforce development must be Specific, Measurable, Achievable, Realistic and with a Timeline (SMART). Additionally, strategy must account for:
• Region's infrastructure (including roads, building, and technology);   • Region's investment (availability of risk capital); and   • Region's available capital.
In developing strategies that spur transformation, regions should focus on:
• Building innovation (through R&D and intellectual property formation);   • Bringing innovation to market;   • Identifying new industries;   • Developing new initiatives for capital creation.
5.   Leverage Resources and Implement
After a strategy is in place, the region must leverage resources from private, non-profit and government sources in support of those common goals. These resources are used to:
• Bolster small businesses;   • Promote sustainable entrepreneurship; and   • Fund job training programs at education centers like community colleges.

Source: See http://www.doleta.gov/wired/tools/5steps.cfm.

4.5.2 WORKFORCE TRANSFORMATION IN FOOD AND NUTRITION SERVICES

Gates et al. (2000) have presented the case study to show how the food and nutrition workforce can be transformed. Recent health-care system changes have required the food and nutrition service workforce to learn new job skills and to work with significantly less supervision. At Bay Crest Center for Geriatric care (892 beds), the Food and Nutrition and the Education and Organizational Development departments have collaborated to budget for, plan and implement an educational program to transform a traditional workforce into an effective self-managing team. The workforce actively participated in a needs assessment process to identify the skills and behaviors requiring change. Clear behavioral objectives were developed. Training sessions involved realistic video modeling, role-playing and discussion. Crucial to the success of the training were overcoming negative attitudes and promoting positive anticipation. Indicators such as an incident audit sheet were developed to evaluate program effectiveness. After taking part in the educational program, staff members were more willing to identify and solve problems requiring intervention and were better able to discuss change and suggest options. Problem-solving work teams focus on the issues rather than on accusing others or becoming defensive. This training process is ongoing and requires continual coaching and application. If follow-up training sessions are deferred, benefits may soon be lost.

There are numerous ways to describe the workforce teams: for example empowered and re-empowered teams, self-managed teams and quality circles. The Bay Crest Center scenario is best described as sharing with frontline employees four organizational elements:

1. Information about the organization's performance.
2. Rewards based on the organization's performance.
3. Knowledge that enables employees to understand and contribute to organizational performance.
4. Power to make decisions that influence organization direction and performance.

Need assessment: The Director of Education and Organizational Development and the Director of Food and Nutrition Services met to define the organizational development needs and to explore the possible options. In addition, these two directors held a meeting with the vice president of Information and Support Services to ensure that their plan was in agreement with the center's strategic direction. Staff demographics and their effect on learning were considered. The staff consisted both of men and women with various levels of education, length of service, and English language skills. After all the input from staff and management was considered, the following educational goals were developed:

- enhanced staff problem-solving skills;
- improved communication among team members and with management;
- improved team effectiveness;
- enhanced conflict management and allowing staff to work more independently;
- improved team ability to deal with change;
- improved staff receptiveness to management's coaching in specific behaviors.

Implementation: Many team members had mixed feelings about the training. Several had experienced difficulties in their formal education and had some apprehensions about a classroom setting. Adult learners need to feel that their experience is respected and that the learning is meaningful to real-life problems. The implementation plan therefore had to create a positive environment for this learning experience; setting the stage for a positive experience was critical to the success of the program. This was accomplished through practicing good adult learning principles.

Workplace needs were also addressed. Participants were encouraged to identify resources (budget items) that would enhance their ability to perform as individuals and as a team. The resources included items and even processes that promised to make a positive impact on both internal and external customers. This information was generated in the education sessions with the participants' agreement and the information was also communicated to management. Depending on participants' needs, the training program included the following topics:

- Introduction to the basic principles of effective relationships.
- Effective listening skills.
- Resolving issues with others.
- Being a team player.
- Giving and receiving constructive feedback.

- Problem-solving.
- Positive response to negative situations.
- Dealing with changes.

Several changes were also made to employees' job duties. For example, employees were allowed to:

- Fill out maintenance requisitions directly, to ensure that equipment repairs occurred in a timely manner.
- Order minor equipment directly.
- Solve problems due to unexpected work schedule changes (e.g., a fire drill).
- Participate with management to plan procedural changes.
- Assist other staff when required without the need for a supervisor to change job duties officially.
- Provide positive and constructive feedback to follow workers.
- Listen to fellow workers with the understanding that there are other sides to issues.

Outcome and assessment: These indicators were developed to evaluate the program's effectiveness including incident audit sheets, management review discussions, monthly cleaning records, staff attendance reports, and pre- and post-training questionnaires.

Since the start of this program, the majority of the food service workforce demonstrates an ability to solve problems. In addition, the staff readily identifies and reports problems requiring external intervention and the team focuses on the issue, rather than on accusing others or being defensive. A general analysis of the incident audit sheet data showed that approximately 7 to 18 significant issues occurred each month before most of the service workforce completed the educational program. Now (after the educational program), there are one to three issues each month. Moreover, team members are better able to discuss change and suggest options. For example, the workforce contacts the maintenance department directly for equipment repairs, and also follows up to ensure the repair has been completed in a timely manner. The incentive for participating in the program is that employees enhance their skills and develop their credentials independently. Once the majority of the staff has been given the opportunity to participate in the program, participation will become the requirement for advanced job postings. In addition, the program gives employees an additional qualification, should they apply for position outside Bay Crest Center.

4.6   Environmental Transformation

Most industrialized countries have gone through two major transformations where the first produced the capitalist group and the second one created the working class. The capitalist group is interested in economic growth, while the organized working class can harmonize with their respective country's emerging interest in legitimating the political economy through curbing capitalism's inequality. Environmental conservation could now emerge as a core in each country's interest, growing out of these established economic and legitimating imperatives (Kumar, 2010a).

Globalization and the Environment: Politicians are stressing the need to eliminate the environmental regulations to make national industries more competitive in global economy. At the same time, the representatives of large international corporations and multilateral economic institutions are not referring to globalization when demanding liberalization, privatization and the lifting of protective measures. During 1990s, a wide variety of environmental non-governmental organizations, trade unions, developing countries and others were able to come together under loosely defined umbrella of "sustainable development"; however, they were unable to identify a common target for their concern – the environment.

A key question in the twenty-first century is "Why are environmentalists hostile toward globalization?" As Castells (2000) noted, global networks and flows are viewed as the "true architectures of the new global economy." The concept of globalization is well accepted by politicians, public, researchers and businesses from the early 1990s. It reflects a common-sense view of the interdependent transformations experienced by many people around the world. During most of the twentieth century, activists' main strategy for combating social and environmental problems was to extend and strengthen the national regulatory capacity. Now, globalization, along with deregulation and privatization, is infringing upon that very capacity.

Held et al. (1999) believe that there are three perspectives on globalization:

- hyperglobalists;
- skeptics;
- a more neutral school of analysts focusing on transformation.

Skeptics believe that effective environmental regulation is structurally difficult to attain within the framework of global capitalism. According to these analysts, economic globalization will lead to the same kind of disasters that are felt in industrial capitalism, but on a global scale. The natural school analysts focus on transformation and depart from such a pessimistic view, while also acknowledging the negative consequences of globalization and especially the consequences of global capitalism. The believers' transformation is observing the ability of capitalism to overcome internal contradictions and even produce positive change.

Dryzek et al. (2002) have shown that environmental conservation could now emerge as a state interest, growing out of these established economic and legitimating imperatives. This examination is grounded in a comparative historical study of four countries: the US, Norway, Germany and the UK, each of which exemplifies a particular kind of interest representation. They have also shown that the US was an environmental pioneer around 1970 and then was eclipsed by Norway, and now Germany leads the way in addressing environmental concerns. For a person who believes in environmental transformation, it is not so much the celebration of globalization or the condemnation of global capitalism but rather the transformation processes which come with globalization. Yet, in analyzing globalization-related transformation with respect to the "environmental sphere," most transformation believers still emphasize the destructive character of global capitalism, rather than acknowledging positive changes toward environmental reforms.

Sonnenfeld and Mol (2002) have examined three important innovations:

- supranational environmental institutions;
- market-based environmental reform;
- the role of a global civil society.

Supranational environmental institutions: During 1970s and 1980s, political scientists and international relations specialists paid increasing attention to the construction of multilateral environmental agreements. More recently, the focus has shifted to the experience of supranational economic and political institutions as vehicles of environmental reform in a globalizing world. Most new, supranational environmental institutions are equivalent to the national arrangements which inspired them. The basic idea is that since environmental problems have spread from a local to a national level, and from national to supranational levels, political institutions and arrangements to deal with them should be up-scaled accordingly to be effective. This approach has three issues:

- Dynamics of environmental deterioration and reform are different in twenty-first century than in 1970s and 1980s. Now they are related to processes of globalization and local factors.
- Supranational political institutions are relevant in different ways to different countries. Countries vary significantly in terms of economic development, political and economic integration in the world, national political institutions and environmental reform capacity.
- Global environmental politics, regardless of the level, now involves new participants along with traditional political agents and institutions.

Twenty-first century environmental politics and institutions are changing significantly at the national and supranational levels in almost every country. Such changes can be understood only in the context of the globalization process, new and different roles for each nation, increasing the power of economic interests and civil society partners, and institutionalization of the environment in economic and political domains.

Market-based environmental reform: As per the most contested provisions of ecological modernization theory and related perspectives has been the notion that economic partners and market dynamics have constructive roles to play on the stage of environmental reform. Such reforms are coming through the interplay of economic markets and partners on one hand, and organized citizen-consumers and political institutions on the other. Such partnerships allow environmental considerations, requirements and interests to become increasingly institutionalized in the economic domain. Market-oriented environmental reforms have taken place mainly at the national level in the advanced industrial nations. Now the question is that in the era of globalization, "Will they develop further and how might they be different?"

The role of a global civil society: It seems that those who are first to emphasize the universality of environmental norms and principles, the growing power of the global environmental movement, and the pressure on global capitalism through civil society, are removed even further from the actual practice of what has become known as a "global civil society." This includes top leaders like the former USA Vice President Al Gore. He stressed the major role of a globalizing civil society, closely linked to revolutions in information technology in achieving environmental reforms.

4.7   Safety and Security Transformation

Human security is the topic of discussion in the twenty-first century which includes common security, corporate security, national security, global security and comprehensive security. All these types of security words encourage policy-makers (business leaders, politicians and others) and scholars to think about international security as something more than the military defense of state interests and territory. Human security is a people-centered approach to foreign policy which recognizes that lasting stability and security cannot be achieved until people are protected from violent threats to their safety and rights (Kumar, 2010a).

Among the most vocal promoters of human security are the governments of Canada and Norway, which have the leadership in establishing a "human security network" of states and non-governmental organizations (NGOs) that endorse the concept (Human Security Network, 2000). The other states in the network are Austria, Chile, Greece, Ireland, Jordan, Mali, the Netherlands, Slovenia, Switzerland, and Thailand. Therefore, the key question is, "What is human security?"

The first major statement about human security appeared in the Human Development Report from the United Nations Development Program (UNDP) (1994). The concept of security, the report argues, has far too long been interpreted narrowly:

as security of territory from external aggression, or as protection of national interests in policy or as global security from the threat of nuclear holocaust ... Forgotten were the legitimate concerns of ordinary people who sought security in their daily lives.

This statement is clear and forceful, but following this statement the subsequent information about "human security" lacks precision. Human security can be said to have two main aspects:

* safety from such chronic threats as hunger, disease and repression;
* protection from sudden hurtful disruptions in the pattern of daily life at places such as in homes, in jobs or in communication.

The scope of this definition is very broad; virtually any kind of discomfort (irregular or unexpected) could conceivably constitute a threat to one's human security.

This definition of human security is so expansive and vague that a redefinition of the concept is required with narrower and more precise terms. King and Murray (2000) offer a definition of human security that is intended to include only "essential" elements that they consider as "important enough for human beings to fight over or to put their lives or property at great risk." Using this standard, they identify five elements as indicators: well-being-poverty, health, education, political freedom and democracy. These elements they consider to be an overall measure of human security for individuals and groups.

Human security has been described as several different things: a political campaign, violent conflict, a new conceptualization of security, a guide for policy-makers and academic researchers. The concept of human security has successfully united a diverse coalition of states, international agencies, and non-governmental organizations.

Workplace safety and security: Government agencies who oversee workplace safety are beginning to incorporate security issues into comprehensive safety plans in response to the growing recognition of violence in the workplace. Peak-Asa and Howard (1999) have presented the collected statistics of the California Division of Occupational Safety and Health for the period from January 1993 through January 1997. The inspections were examined by initiating source, industry, type of event and citations issued, and compared with distributions of known victimizations. The factors predicting whether a citation was issued were determined through logistic models. Over 200 inspections were conducted in 11 industries, with retail and health-care establishments inspected most frequently. Employee complaints initiated 50.6 percent of events and accident reports initiated 40.1 percent. One-third of inspections were initiated because of a fatal event, and 27.4 percent were initiated in response to a physical assault. Citations for security hazards were issued to 23.6 percent of businesses. Inspections were initiated by employee complaints, in response to customer-related security issues, and those involving non-fatal assaults were the most frequently cited reasons for inspection. The California Division of Occupational Safety and Health conducted security inspections in a large range of industries and for diverse issues, even though no specific security codes exist.

Terrorist attacks and public opinion: Davis and Silver (2004) conducted a survey research on political tolerance and democratic rights shortly after the September 11, 2001 attack on America to investigate people's willingness to trade civil liberties for greater personal safety and security. They found that the greater people's sense of threat, the lower their support for civil liberties. This effect interacts, however, with trust in government. The lower people's trust in government, the less willing they are to trade off civil liberties for security, regardless of their level of threat. African Americans are much less willing to trade civil liberties for security than whites or Latinos, even with other factors taken into account. This may reflect their long-standing commitment to the struggle for civil rights. Liberals are less willing to trade off civil liberties than moderates or conservatives, but liberals converge toward the position taken by conservatives when their sense of the threat of terrorism is high. This is not a forecast, but the results indicate that Americans' commitments to democratic values is highly contingent on other concerns and that the context of a large-scale threat to national or personal security can induce a substantial willingness to give up rights.

Human safety and highway driving: Houston (1999) has conducted a highway safety study to evaluate the impact of the 65 mph (miles per hour) speed limit of traffic safety. He used the data for the years 1981 to 1995 for all the 50 states in the US and conducted a pooled time series analysis. Roads were divided into four categories:

- rural interstate highways;
- rural non-interstate roads;
- all roads except for rural interstate highways;
- all other roads.

He reported that the 65 mph speed limit increased fatality rates on rural interstate highways but was correlated with a reduction in state fatality rates on the three other categories of roads. Although raising the maximum speed limit to 65 mph on only rural interstate highways has not compromised traffic safety to the extent many thought it would, this same effect may not be found with more recent state changes to speed limit laws. States have continued to raise the maximum speed limit on rural interstate highways to 70 mph and above. In addition, maximum speed limits on other highway types have begun to rise to 60 mph and above. Further research should focus attention on the safety consequences of these more recent changes in state traffic policy.

Past efforts at designing and implementing high assurance systems for government safety and security have centered on the concept of massive and uniform security responsible for a system-wide security policy. This approach leads to inflexible, overly complex operating systems which are too large to evaluate at the highest assurance levels. Alves-Foss et al. (2004) suggest a new multilayered approach to the design and verification of embedded trustworthy systems that is currently being used in the implementation of real-time, embedded applications. The framework supports multiple levels of safety and multiple levels of security, based on the principles of creating separate layers of responsibility and control with each layer responsible for enforcing its own security policy.

4.8 ET Case Studies

The discussed ET theory has been applied to four case studies: Heavy equipment manufacturer (John Deere's agricultural tractor manufacturing business), Jet engine manufacturing (Pratt & Whitney's engine manufacturing business), Software and IT system's consulting (IBM's business) and Small supporting businesses to major manufacturers in automobiles' power steering system. These studies are covering some 40 years of time span (from early 1970s to 2014); while each business transformation within an industry took 7–11 years. The scope of these transformations varied by industry (e.g., transformation at John Deere was a total business transformation while at Pratt & Whitney was mainly manufacturing transformation). As businesses innovate products; and technology improves processes (manufacturing and services) then these businesses need transformation. Therefore, these transformations are not just one-time processes. Businesses have to go through these kinds of transformations as they innovate products/services as well as changes in their process technology to stay competitive in the global market.

4.8.1   JOHN DEERE TRACTOR DIVISION – BUSINESS TRANSFORMATION CASE STUDY

This was John Deere's tractor division which was manufacturing tractors from 85 HP through 375 HP to primarily supporting the farming businesses in North America and was located in Waterloo, Iowa. This case study discusses a period of approximately 10 years from early 1970s through the early 1980s, and the total business from product design and testing through manufacturing and distribution. The whole business was located at one site (also known as down-town site). Product demand was growing and at the same time manufacturing technology was advancing. Therefore, the total facility was continuously growing to meet the market demand as well as the processes were upgraded due to technological changes. John Deere's products and services were among the best available in the global market. Literally, customer's name (farmer) was written on every tractor on the final assembly and test line. To support the products and services, John Deere were continually innovating their manufacturing processes and upgrading their core competency to sustain their competitive advantage. Marketing was forecasting a continuous growth period for a long time (could be several years). John Deere's business leadership recognized that with the rate at which the business was growing as well as technology was advancing, it would be very difficult to meet or exceed market demand and deliver the product on time at competitive price and expected margin. Leadership came to the conclusion that the business transformation is needed to continue to compete in the market. The following is a high-level description of the planning and the execution of the transformation process.

Business leadership selected a group of experts from different areas of business along with some consulting organizations, and assigned the task to study the business operations and make recommendations to transform this tractor business to meet or exceed the future market requirements at competitive price and margin with on-time delivery. The recommended plan must accommodate the continuation of their current production schedule while implementing the recommended transformation. The whole business was located next to down-town and there was not enough space for the whole business to stay there while expanding to meet the market demand. The team studied the requirements based on given constraints and divided the whole business into the following areas:

*   product design engineering and test;
*   foundry to cast products such as engine blocks, transmission cases, front hanging weights, etc.;
*   engine manufacturing and test;
*   hydraulics components manufacturing, assembly and test;
*   sheet metal manufacturing, and tractor sub- and final assembly and test;
*   heat treatment area;
*   steel parts manufacturing;
*   casted manufacturing (machining); and
*   raw material storage.

The team utilized the concept of group technology (GT) in separating the product manufacturing areas by classifying into the part families. Key elements in GT analyzing process were material (e.g., cast iron, steel, aluminum and sheet metal), part geometry (e.g., rotational, non-rotational and sheet metal) and manufacturing processes (e.g., turning, grinding and forming), which supported in developing part families. The team also analyzed the capacity and space requirements for each area to meet the future requirements. The team started with a key quality constraint for all the above defined manufacturing areas that any manufactured product in one area must be acceptable as quality input product both internally within the company as well as outside the company without any inspection and/or testing. Leadership was not interested to move any of the above-listed businesses out of the Black Hawk County in Iowa. The above GT, space and capacity analysis as well as constraints helped the team to develop enough information about these business areas. The team reviewed the above-identified areas' information with business leaders and received the initial approval. The following was the specific analysis along with transformation recommendations for each identified business area:

Product design engineering and test: This business could easily be relocated offsite slowly in piece meal basis without interrupting the product delivery schedule. It was not required that this business had to be in the manufacturing facility. Therefore, team considered moving this business offsite and the vacated space could easily be used for meeting the office and manufacturing space requirements. Therefore, team recommended relocating this business first and another team managed the relocation project.

Foundry: This was an old cupola coal foundry during the analysis period and were producing steel castings. The state of Iowa passed very strict air pollution laws where John Deere had to convert the foundry from coal to electric. Electric foundry requires a lot of electricity to run the foundry. There was no guarantee from the electric company to meet the foundry energy requirements. John Deere had their own power generating facility on site to support the additional electricity requirements for manufacturing as well as providing steam for winter heating. Therefore, foundry had to stay there to meet the energy requirements as well as converted from coal to electric to meet the new air pollution regulations from the state of Iowa.

Engine manufacturing and test: Once engine is manufactured and tested it should be delivered anywhere for use (or as an input product) in the bigger product without any additional testing. This was one of the business leadership's requirements to maintain the product quality and optimize the cost. Manufacturing technology was advancing, so the manufacturing processes also needed upgrading. These products are generally manufactured on transfer line. Transfer line is a concept where manufacturing machines are installed in a row and the part is mounted on a fixture which travels from one machine to the next without changing the fixture. Therefore, these lines are generally shut down when these process improvements are implemented. So far only the product engineering and test business was moved out and the current site space was not large enough for the remaining businesses to grow. This business could be relocated to somewhere else (offsite), but could not be relocated in peace meal basis due to engine manufacturing transfer lines. Material handling was another issue, since the engine blocks were casted in the above-identified foundry, and these casted engine blocks were used for engine manufacturing. Engine manufacturing and test processes also need engineering support, therefore the recommended location was away from the current site, but between the new design engineering and test location and the existing foundry. While the company decided to relocate the engine manufacturing business to another site, they also decided to upgrade the needed manufacturing processes. Therefore, this was the next business recommended for relocation.

Hydraulics components manufacturing, assembly and test: These were small parts and components relative to other components such as transmission, engine, sound guard body, etc. These parts and the assembly processes were accommodated in an on-site building which was meeting future capacity requirements.

Sheet metal manufacturing, and tractor sub- and final assembly and test: These business areas were spread all over the down-town site. Coordination between sub-assemblies and the final assembly was a major issue. This was creating a huge inventory of sub-assemblies as well as affecting the on-time delivery of the final product (tractors) to dealers. It was difficult to implement newer material handling technologies in the final assembly area due to building space and ceiling height limitations. All the analyses indicated that the future schedule with on-time delivery would be very difficult (if not impossible) to achieve at the current site. Therefore, it was recommended to relocate to a new site within the same county to minimize the material handling cost and maintain on-time delivery of tractors.

So far three businesses were recommended to move out from the current site: product design engineering and test, engine manufacturing and test, and sheet metal manufacturing and tractor sub- and final assembly and test; and these businesses were in the process of moving out. Foundry business was upgraded from coal cupola to electric foundry at the current site to meet the state's air pollution requirements as well as a kind of guarantee to receive the electric energy to run the foundry (due to John Deere's own power generating facility). Hydraulics parts and components manufacturing was also consolidated in a building on site. The remaining businesses left on the current site were:

- heat treatment area;
- steel parts manufacturing;
- casted manufacturing (machining);
- raw material storage.

Again the capacity and space analysis was done to check whether the remaining business areas would meet or exceed market demand with on-time delivery, and the analysis validated that the future demands would be met for these businesses with process improvements at the current site.

Heat treatment area: This business area had mostly long continuous heat treating (e.g., annealing, carburizing, etc.) furnaces. This was a supporting business mainly to hydraulics and steel manufacturing as well as for the connecting rods from the engine manufacturing which were also normalized before machining at the engine manufacturing site. Since these furnaces are large and expensive, it was economical to normalize the connecting rods in this business area. Therefore, the heat treatment area was recommended to stay at the down-town site.

Three remaining business areas were steel parts manufacturing, cast-iron manufacturing (machining) and the raw material storage area. These areas were also recommended to stay at the current site. Steel parts manufacturing and casted manufacturing were separated using the GT concept. Steel manufacturing was mostly for gears, shafts, axle, etc. These are rotational parts, so the machining equipment requirements are very similar to these parts. Casted manufacturing (machining) was mostly for castings coming out from the foundry, e.g. transmission housing. Machining equipment requirements were a lot different as well as machining of these casting also create some dust in the area, which is not acceptable in the steel machining areas. Most of the raw material requirements for the down-town site were stored in the raw material storage area.

This transformation took 7–9 years, several hundred million dollars, and a large and dedicated resource of company employees and consultants. Without this transformation John Deere would not have met the market demand in that competitive market. The transformation had full leadership participation and support. Without their participation and support these transformations would never have succeeded and achieved their goals. Financial and resources participation information is confidential. Most of the competition like International Harvester, Messy Ferguson, Ford, and so on are either gone or sharing a very small percentage of the market share. This is one of the key intermediate steps in the process to achieve the enterprise excellence through growth strategy and mitigating/minimizing the enterprise risk while building sustainable competitive advantage.

4.8.2   PRATT & WHITNEY – MANUFACTURING TRANSFORMATION CASE STUDY

Pratt & Whitney (PW) is a division of United Technologies Corporation (UTC) and the division office is located in East Hartford, Connecticut. PW designs and manufactures large jet engines for both defense and commercial customers. This transformation case study discusses a period of five to seven years from early the 1980s, and primarily for the manufacturing side of the business. PW was one of the prime sources of engines for war planes during World War II (WWII) and there were several manufacturing sites during this period of conflict. The leadership of PW wanted to produce as many parts and components of an engine as possible at each site with the strategy that if any site gets bombarded then PW would still be able to produce engines to support the engine requirements for the WWII planes. The war was over in 1945, but PW continued to produce engines with the same strategy through late 1970s and early 1980s. This strategy was acceptable during WWII, but it was very expensive and inefficient during the peace-time economy of the late twentieth century. Even though there are only three large jet engine manufacturers – General Electric (GE), Pratt & Whitney (PW) and Rolls-Royce (RR) – in the non-communistic world, they all have very tough competition. They design, manufacture and service their products. All three companies are very innovative and they continually improve their core competency to support their products and services to sustain their competitive advantage.

President Regan (1981–88) increased the defense budget very significantly during his presidency, which increased business for all defense contractors including Pratt & Whitney, and some of that budgeted money was continued during President Bush's presidency (1989–92). Global demand for commercial planes was also increasing due to growth in the global economy. There were three big commercial jet plane manufacturers – Boeing (BA), McDonald Douglas (MD) and Airbus (A) – producing jet planes, including BA737, BA747, BA757, MD91, MD11, A320 and A340. PW had some old, as well as some new, engines including JT8D, JT9D, PW229 and PW4000 to support and compete in both defense and commercial markets.

During 1970s through to the early 1990s defense contracts were allowed to manufacture engine parts and components together with commercial engine parts and components, but were required to keep their engine design and the final assembly and test at separate physical locations (e.g., PW's commercial engine design was located in Connecticut and defense engine design was located in Florida; commercial engine's final assembly and test areas was established in Middletown while defense engine's final assembly and test area was in East Hartford). Most of PW's manufacturing business was located in Connecticut except a small portion which was located in two other states (Maine and Georgia).

Since both the defense and the commercial businesses were growing, the PW leadership recognized that PW would not be able to deliver products to meet or exceed customer demands had they continued the WWII type manufacturing strategy. Therefore, they decided to transform PW's manufacturing business. PW leadership selected a group of experts from their manufacturing/engineering departments, along with some consulting organizations, and assigned them the task to study the manufacturing business operations and make recommendations – how to transform the manufacturing business to meet or exceed the future market requirements at a competitive price and margin with on-time delivery. The recommended plan would have to accommodate the continuation of their production schedule while implementing the recommended transformation. The other business areas (e.g., finance, marketing, etc.) were recognized as supporting business areas with minimum modifications/changes as necessary, but were not included in the manufacturing business transformation project.

Since most of the manufacturing business was located in Connecticut it was decided to keep the business in there. The selected team studied the business and divided the whole manufacturing business into part families utilizing the concept of group technology (GT). The team also studied the production requirements based on given forecasts and constraints and divided the Connecticut engine manufacturing business into the following:

- drum rotor manufacturing;
- blades and vanes manufacturing, and stainless steel disk and hub manufacturing;
- sheet metal manufacturing;
- distribution center;
- two final engine assembly and test areas (defense and commercial as identified earlier).

Drum rotor manufacturing site: This is a key rotating component in jet engines. Disks and hubs are very large diameter key parts – somewhere from 20–25 inches to 40–50 inches, depending on the rated thrust of the engine as well as the disk location in the drum rotor. Forgings are used as an input material in the machining processes of these disks and hubs. These machining processes are an example of precision machining and may take hours of work in the manufacturing area. During 1970s through 1990s, advanced and precision machining was considered a part of PW's core competencies, therefore PW tried to keep those processes in-house. Only a small percentage (less than 20–25 percent) of these forgings were coming from the Georgia (PW) facility and the remaining forgings were from suppliers around the US. These forgings are made of titanium and nickel alloys, which are very hard materials for machining. These parts not only require advanced precision machining but also temperature and relative humidity tempered manufacturing facilities to meet the parts tolerance specifications. These disks and hubs are joined together either through vacuum welding or inertia welding processes to make the drums. Shavings from titanium and nickel alloy parts are very expensive, therefore could not mix with stainless steel parts' shavings. Stainless steel disks and hubs were used in older engines, hence stainless steel disks and hubs were recommended to be manufactured at different sites. The team analyzed the capacity and space requirements for parts manufacturing, component assembly and testing, and material handling for the defense/commercial drum rotor assembly to meet the future marketing demand, and thus the business was recommended for the Southington site in Connecticut.

Blades and vanes manufacturing, and stainless steel disk and hub manufacturing site: Blades and vanes are small parts which are also made of titanium and nickel alloys. They are also manufactured utilizing the advanced precision machining processes as well as the required temperature and relative humidity tempered manufacturing facility. Similar capacity and space analysis was done along with the material handling requirements and recommended for the North Haven, Connecticut site. It was also realized that stainless steel disks and hubs could also be manufactured there due to space availability, as well as shavings from blades and vanes were very small in relation to stainless steel shavings from disks and hubs.

Sheet metal manufacturing site: These were the remaining parts and components of the manufacturing business which do not require advanced precision machining or temperature and relative humidity tempered manufacturing facilities. However, it is nice to have a temperature and relative humidity controlled facility during summer months if possible. There was not enough space to keep the sheet metal parts in the Middletown facility, but there was enough space available in the East Hartford facility. Therefore, the sheet metal business was recommended for the East Hartford, Connecticut site. These parts and components are used in both the commercial and defense engines.

Distribution center site: The main responsibility of this center was to control the flow of parts and components to the final engine assembly and test sites (East Hartford and Middletown). They had to make sure that the correct parts and components inventory were provided to the final engine assembly area to meet the product delivery schedule. Business leadership did not want to see that several million dollars of engine was waiting for a few parts on the final assembly stand.

Two final engine assembly and test sites: To meet the defense contract constraints the two recommended sites were East Hartford (for defense engines) and Middletown (for commercial engines) in Connecticut. Engines from both sites were transported either by trucks and/or planes.

Later in 1990s these defense constraints were removed, therefore all engine design engineering (both for defense and commercial) was relocated in East Hartford, Connecticut, and all final engine assembly and testing (both for defense and commercial) was moved to Middletown, Connecticut.

Core competencies require continuous improvement as technology and customer needs are changing. Demands on organizations continue to change and today's core competencies may be tomorrow's table stakes. Organizations that provide standard services are in high demand; organizations that do not operate in a highly competitive environment or enjoy monopolies will usually not possess or need core competencies. Table stakes are more than sufficient for their success. As technological developments in manufacturing technology went through from the 1970s through the early 1990s, some of PW's core competencies in advanced precision machining became table stakes. Therefore, to stay efficient and cost effective, PW had to outsource a lot of machining (e.g., disks and hubs, blades and vanes, etc.) during mid-to-late 1990s to consolidate the manufacturing business and sustain the competitive advantage. This significantly reduced the in-house manufacturing, which resulted in closing several manufacturing facilities. This is an example where PW went through their initial transformation during the early-to-late 1980s and then the next transformation during the mid-to-late 1990s.

Therefore, transformation is not a one-time process. As businesses innovate products and processes (manufacturing and/or services), and achieve technological advances then businesses have to go through the transformation process to stay competitive in the global market.

4.8.3 IBM CORPORATION – BUSINESS TRANSFORMATION CASE STUDY

As technological developments are taking place, improved/newer products and services are developed and offered in the market to meet or exceed customer needs. Therefore, transformation would be required to support (e.g., product offering and delivery, and services) these products and services, and resources (e.g., people, equipment, technology, etc.). A constantly transforming enterprise is always better equipped to handle the demands of customer needs and supply the satisfactory products. Gerstner's (2002) approach to enterprise transformation was to turn IBM Corporation into a market-driven rather than internally focused, process-driven enterprise.

Transformation of IBM Corporation was started in 2003, going on currently and planned to be continued through 2015. This is an excellent example of a large corporation which is in the midst of their transformation.

IBM Corporation is going through their multiyear internal enterprise transformation and improving its ability to capitalize on talent, skills and market opportunities. The success of this transformation has been demonstrated by IBM's strong business results as presented in Table 4.5 (Standard and Poor's report and Wall Street), where, despite difficult economic times, the company has posted almost double-digit earnings growth every year. Their earnings per share have more than tripled between 2003 and 2013 from $4.34 per share to $16.28 per share. Linda Sanford, IBM's senior vice president of enterprise transformation, detailed in 2010 that an aggressive strategy would drive to even more growth over the next five years (2011–15). Sanford is committed to shave an additional $8 billion off of IBM's $78 billion in total expenses by 2015. A big reason for IBM's success has been the deployment of business analytics, cloud computing and process improvements that have driven billions of dollars in cost savings and productivity improvements. Besides delivering efficiencies across the business, the use of these technologies has been instrumental in supporting IBM's pursuit of growth markets around the world.

Table 4.5   IBM Corporation's financial statistics

Fiscal Year	EPS*, $ (US)	EPS* Growth Rate, %	Revenue, $ Billion (US)
2003	4.34		89.131
2004	4.94	13.8	96.293
2005	4.91	—	91.134
2006	6.06	23.4	91.424
2007	7.18	18.5	98.786
2008	8.93	24.4	103.630
2009	10.01	12.1	95.757
2010	11.52	15.1	99.871
2011	13.06	13.4	106.916
2012	14.37	10.0	104.507
2013	16.28	13.3	99.751
2014	15.59	−04.2	92.793

Note: * EPS: Earnings per share.

According to Darryl K. Taft, IBM has been on a journey to transform its business since 2003 and the following six principles are guiding IBM as it implements its latest, "smarter" phase of business transformation:

- *Start a Movement*: IBM engages its workforce through "jams" and social software. This exchange of ideas enabled the company to capture the imagination of its workforce and re-establish the core of its culture and brand for the twenty-first century. IBM WorldJam produced 35 ideas that led to more than $500 million in savings and a new structure to bring decision-making closer to the client.

    JAM Software offers powerful software for system administrators and professionals that helps to manage their everyday work more efficiently.
- *Establish Clear Transformation Governance*: IBM established key decision-making bodies to guide critical transformation and IT initiatives, taking a disciplined approach to determine what new initiatives to fund based on a review of business cases. Through active and integrated oversight,

the company achieved strong alignment of its strategy with transformation goals and put consistent metrics in place to measure the business value of transformation investments.

- *Transformation Requires a Data-Driven Discussion*: IBM is turning raw data into competitive insight across its business. For example, the IBM Resource Analytics Hub provides up-to-the-minute access to a repository of information on IBM's services workforce and current staffing requirements. The Hub has helped Global Business Services improve its measure of unassigned resources, or bench, from 8 percent to 3 percent. The productivity of IBM's consultants improved 18 percent from 2005 to 2009, enabling IBM to more aggressively pursue its growth objectives.
- *Radically Simplify Business Processes*: End-to-end process improvements have been pivotal to IBM's success at global integration of its operations. During the past several years, IBM has developed hundreds of professionals with business process skills in Lean Six Sigma and other methodologies. By standardizing and automating work across key global processes, IBM delivered $500 million in productivity improvements in 2009 and put itself in a strong position to support its growth initiatives worldwide.
- *Invest in Transformation Innovation*: IBM applies new technologies to accelerate its transformation and keep employees engaged in the effort. The company's intranet, the On Demand Workplace, has been transformed into one of the most robust social networking platforms in the industry. Social software – blogs, wikis, live chat, communities, even virtual worlds – are now an integral characteristic of IBM's corporate culture. IBM's leadership in collaborative innovation has helped keep it No. 1 in the number of new US patents for 17 consecutive years. The company has also been an enthusiastic adopter of cloud technology as a cost-effective platform for development, research, storage and other uses. The development/test cloud has accelerated the test environment set-up process from one week to 1 to 2 hours.
- *Embody Creative Leadership*: IBM has an ongoing focus on developing twenty-first century global leaders as an essential element in its transformation success. The company recently refreshed a core set of competencies for all IBM employees to provide guidance on skills development and set the inspirational direction for all employees. The overall goal: develop and sustain a workforce that is equipped to capture new revenue in growth markets.

4.8.4   SMALL BUSINESS TRANSFORMATION – AUTOMOBILE POWER STEERING SYSTEM'S REPAIR AND OVERHAUL BUSINESS CASE STUDY

The enterprise transformation concept applies to all sizes of enterprises (large or small) and this case study is about a small business. This business is repairing and overhauling automobile's power steering system.

Power Steering System: The term power steering is usually used to describe a system that provides mechanical steering assistance to the driver of a land vehicle, for example a car or truck. For many drivers, turning the steering wheel in a vehicle that does not have power steering requires more force (torque) than the driver of a vehicle having mechanical steering assistance and especially when the vehicle is moving at a very slow speed. Steering force is very sensitive to the weight of the vehicle as much as to its length, therefore this is most important for large vehicles. If a vehicle is equipped with a power steering system then the driver can turn the steering wheel with a slight retarding force and any normal driver can drive the vehicle even when the vehicle is parked. This is because the power steering system furnishes most of the energy required to turn the steering wheels of the car.

Therefore, the power steering system in automobile facilitates vehicle maneuvering, irrespective of the prevailing road or environmental conditions, with minimal effort, safely and accurately. The need for such a system was first felt during WWII when the military personnel found it very hard to turn the heavy artillery and tanks, and this concept gained popularity. The adoption of such a system eased the steering to such an extent that this concept was immediately followed into the commercial vehicle production, and the rest, as it is known, has been the revolution that led to the US becoming one of the biggest automotive hubs of the world.

Hydraulic Power Steering System: The power steering in the initial days consisted of rotary pumps and hydraulic cylinders with piston arrangements operated by valves, more commonly known as the hydraulic power steering (HPS) system and a schematic diagram is presented in Figure 4.3. The steering booster consists of a steer torque detector, controlled pressure distributor case, hydraulic booster pump, tank with a working liquid and connection hoses. The working liquid, also-called "hydraulic fluid" or "oil," is the medium by which pressure is transmitted. The working liquid travels from a tank to the pump inlet opening due to gravity. The liquid travels under pressure from the pump to the distributive gear. The distributive gear has an elastic element, a torsion bar or a spring, which causes the cross-section area of bypass holes (drain ports) to vary in proportion to the effort applied to the steering wheel. In a neutral position section of the bores passing a liquid in the right and left part of the hydro cylinder is equal to section of bores issuing a liquid from them in a tank. The pressures in the right and the left parts of the hydro cylinder are equal too. When the wheel is turned, because of forces of friction and other forces there is an effort deforming an elastic element, changing the section of bores of the distributive gear and, thereby, pressure in the right and left parts of the hydro cylinder.

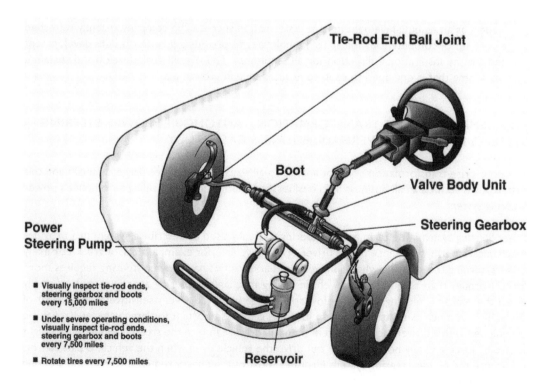

Figure 4.3   Schematic diagram of hydraulic power steering system

Since late 1980s, automobile manufacturers have started introducing the *electric power steering* (EPS) system in automobiles which has advantages over hydraulic power steering system and literature survey validates the concept. The core competency of HPS system serving businesses is in mechanical systems, while EPS system would require core competencies in electrical and electronic components, and computer technology, which these businesses generally do not have. Therefore, these businesses would have two options to stay competitive in repair and overhaul business: (1) as the HPS system business declines the business leaders would need to bring in some other mechanical products due to their core competency in the mechanical systems, or (2) they would have to develop their core competencies in electrical and electronic components, and computer technology to support the EPS system. This decision would be based on their business strategy. Project team (NCSU staff and graduate students) did not explore the other mechanical products possibilities due to timing and project funding (Kumar et al., 2012).

4.8.4.1 Small business enterprise transformation case study

There are numerous small enterprises that are repairing and overhauling the HPS system. These businesses will start shrinking in the future if they do not add any new business in their enterprises. One of the key elements which would help them to decide a new product is their core competency. Businesses with specific strength in areas such as marketing, product design and manufacturing can be said to have a core competency in those areas, which would support them to add other businesses. The core part of the term identifies that the individual has a strong basis from which to gain the additional competence to do a specific job or that a business has a strong basis from which to develop additional products/services. The core competency of these enterprises is in overhauling the HPS system and that is in fixing mechanical products. Therefore, the additional mechanical products would be in the areas such as some other mechanical systems in automobile, heavy equipment, earth moving equipment, etc.

Since the client requested a study of the EPS system, it was assumed that the business leadership had decided to stay in the power steering overhaul business, therefore sooner or later they would have to overhaul the EPS system. The EPS system requires an additional core competency in electrical and electronics components, and computer technology along with the mechanical components. Core competency is developed in-house with the help of qualified and competent employees and the cost of developing these competencies should be a part of business planning and financial model. Thus, how can these enterprises transform themselves into one that would handle EPS systems along with the current HPS system? These enterprises need to understand, plan and execute the following activities to stay in power steering repair and overhaul business:

a) Identify major components, their functionality and test; and also their repair and overhaul requirements.
b) Identify resource (people, equipment, technology, etc.) requirements to support transformation.
c) Marketing research would need various information including EPS introduction schedule, EPS system failure information by manufacturer and by model.
d) Development and analysis of a business model.
e) Development of the financial model: analyze the capital requirements, return on investment (ROI) and payback period analysis.
f) The execution of the transformation strategy to achieve the transformation goals.

The first three activities (a–c) would be common for all small enterprises; requirements for activities (d and e) would vary and also would depend on how their business leaders are going to set their goals; and activity f (the execution) is the most important activity for all types of businesses to achieve their goals.

Reverse engineering concepts were applied to study the functionality of each component and the functionality of the whole system. The EPS system was obtained from Honda, which was disassembled into its major components: *Torque sensor*, *Electric motor* and *rack and pinion mechanism*; and the team studied the functional relationship of these components (Kumar et al., 2012). The least expensive component was the torque sensor and the most expensive component was the rack and pinion box assembly. From a business point of view, the repair and overhaul business should check the rack and pinion assembly first. If this assembly is bad then it would not be worth overhauling the EPS system. It would be expensive to repair the EPS system, therefore it would be less expensive to replace the whole EPS system with another good EPS system. All cost elements of repair and overhaul should be included in D and E activities.

Every business leader has to plan his resource requirements – people, equipment and technology – to support transformation. These requirements would vary depending on various elements including current employees' interest in continuing education/training, geographic location, employees' compensation and job market. For example, people in HPS system's overhaul business are not required to have knowledge and experience in electrical and electronics products and computer technology, but it is required for overhauling the EPS system. Leadership would need to evaluate whether the current personnel would be happy to get educated and trained in these areas or whether they would have to hire new people who would have education, training and experience in these areas. Sometimes geographical locations of business may become a constraint. These highly trained people might not like to go to some particular locations if they find work in their preferred geographical locations.

Marketing research is critical for a business planning and transformation model. Unfortunately, few EPS system failure statistics were available. These statistics were collected by a third party and most of the collected information was through qualitative survey. These statistics were also grouped: for example, EPS system was grouped under electric and electronics. Product design was another factor which would impact the service requirements, and there is a high probability that the design will improve with time. Therefore, business leaders must be careful in utilizing the available statistics in business planning and transformation (Kumar et al. 2012).

The activities a–c would lead the development of activities d and e, and these are typical business and financial activities, which would vary based on the decisions made in activities a–c. Activity f is the most critical activity. Without execution, the transformation goals would not be achieved. The above discussion presents a high-level analysis to achieve transformation in a small business environment.

5

Strategy Execution and Measurement

Growth strategy development through transformation is the essential phase of enterprise excellence planning. Enterprise risk must also be incorporated while developing the growth strategy and without it, there would be no successful businesses. Or, rather, there would only be successful business, as being successful would be so easy that any start-up would have an idyllic path to quarterly revenue bonanzas. Risk is vital to the business world so that those organizations that are able to overcome their challenges can show the rest how it is done (Wade, 2010).

In order to achieve the enterprise excellence while sustaining competitive advantage, growth strategy has to be executed and the measurement system must validate that the strategy goals are achieved. Therefore, strategy execution and measurement are the main connecting links between aspiration and results to achieve the enterprise excellence. In today's rapidly changing and increasingly competitive world, achieving sustained success depends on having a solid strategy and aligning on organization's decisions, effort and resources to execute that strategy. Thus execution is the major job of a leader. Bottom line results of any growth strategy execution are measured in financial terms: growth in revenue and profitability, and reduction in business cycle time.

Effectiveness of strategy depends both on the formulation and execution. Excellence in execution would depend on the integration of strategy and operations in a cyclic manner. The first key process in the execution cycle is "align"; aligning the strategy with people, processes, technology, units, operations, policies/operating procedures, budgets and best practices. Once the strategic and operational plans are aligned, it would be efficient and error free with suitable level of automation of processes, plans, performance management systems, support systems, information systems/controls, analytics and knowledge base across the value network of the organization.

Therefore, execution is a systematic process where participants discuss rigorously the how and what, questioning, persistently following through and ensuring accountability. Some leaders believe that they may end up micromanaging. Actually, there is an enormous difference between leading an organization and managing it. Leaders who boast that they take a hands-off or put their faith in empowerment are not dealing with the issues of the day. They are not confronting the people responsible for poor performance or searching for problems to solve and then making sure that these problems get solved. These types of leaders are only doing half of their job.

Leaders who excel at execution literally make themselves participative to a certain extent in the execution process and even in some of the key details. They use their knowledge of the operation to constantly probe and question. They bring weakness to light and rally their people to correct them. The following sections presented in this chapter are some of the approaches to execute and measure strategy and reasons and/or issues for failing in strategy execution:

5.1   Strategy Execution Approaches
    5.1.1   Organizational Resources Alignment

5.1   Strategy Execution Approaches

There are various strategy execution approaches in the literature and some of those are discussed here:

- organizational resources alignment;
- organizational behavior;
- critical relationship of major domains;
- strategy execution keys;
- some specific researchers' strategy execution approaches.

5.1.1   ORGANIZATIONAL RESOURCES ALIGNMENT

Strategy without execution is like a race boat without enough horsepower in the engines: the boat looks great in water, but it does not impresses anyone who sees it in the race. A similar concept applies: some CEOs generally do not lose sleep over the design of strategy, but rather worry very about their company's inability to deliver the strategy's intended results.

If business leaders accelerate the alignment of strategy, organizational models and people, they increase the probability of maximizing the potential of their business and ultimately their business results (King and Kosminsky, 2006). This type of success requires that people with the right training and experience and motivation find their company to be in the environment that is conducive to flawless execution. This is not an easy process but it is aided greatly by the objective and robust analysis of any firm's people and culture, and can be developed through multidimensional employee assessment. Boomer (2007) identifies eight primary areas of alignment in most firms. Large, multiple-office firms have different challenges than local, one-office firms, but alignment is similar. Alignment within the firm is required in order to execute strategy. The majority of firms fail to execute because they do not focus resources on priorities – and in a majority of cases, employees have not been informed of the strategy. They are told to simply work hard and get in the required number of charge hours. The successful execution of strategy requires the alignment of the strategy, the firm, the employees and the management systems.

Based on Mankins and Steele's (2005) experience, on average, most strategies deliver only 63 percent of their potential financial performance. Their survey identified that the leading reason for performance loss as a failure to have the right resources, including people, in the right place at the right time. Other prominent difficulties are poor communications and action planning. Insight Formation, Inc. (2007) presented the results of a 10-year study which found that the ability to execute a strategy has a six times greater impact on value than the choice of strategy. They also found that 70 to 90 percent of businesses fall short when it comes to executing their strategies. Clearly success depends on these most critical variables: people and whether they have the organizational support structure, information, skills, equipment and tools, and motivation to execute the plan.

5.1.1.1   King and Kosminsky model

King and Kosminsky (2006) suggest that organizations have to have three types of "capital" at their disposal that can support strategy:

- competence capital;
- motivational capital;
- organizational capital.

If all three types of capitals are not in harmony, execution is compromised. The concept is presented in Figure 5.1 on the following page.

Competence Capital: The measure of the proper fit between a strategy's requirements and skills and experience of employees. If a business strategy requires new products, do employees have innovative capabilities to develop new products to meet or exceed customer needs and reduce production and service costs? If the business has been producing low-cost, high-volume-oriented strategy products for years then the business workforce probably has lost the creativity required for innovation.

Motivational Capital: The organization's ability to meet its employees' expectations, therefore, they are motivated and driven to perform at their best. Business leadership should nurture employees for their "right" behaviors. Organizations must provide a career path to employees according to their motives. Employees should be rewarded in ways that are meaningful to them and allowed to make decisions they believe are right.

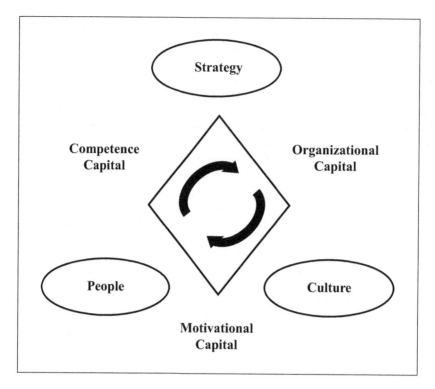

Figure 5.1   The foundation of effective strategy execution

Organizational Capital: Measures the fit between a company's strategy and the organizational model. Whatever the company recognizes must be aligned with the leaders' strategic drive or failure, must be analyzed. For example, if leadership wants to sell value-added services, performance appraisals need to include a measure of their sales pipeline and not just the number of visits or successes. If the business leaders do not provide incentives for those hard-to-pull opportunities, the sales people will focus on low-hanging fruits, not necessarily the ones business leaders want.

Getting every aspect of the company moving in the same direction to support the business leaders' strategy is both a science and an art. The resulting objective information generally enhances the "science" side of the equation. There are three basic elements of a company's organizational model:

- organizational structure;
- valued behavior;
- recognition and rewards system.

Organizational structure identifies the line of authority, reporting and coordination, real and perceived career paths and decision-making authority. It plays a significant role in strategy execution. For example, if business leader's strategic drive is innovation (learning), do people have the freedom to explore ideas? If business leader's strategy is to increase the market share (competitive), are people held accountable for aggressive goals?

Valued behavior is not defined specifically here. If the business strategic drive is to be an industry expert, are the employees reliable, precise and always on top of the latest skills? If the business strategy is to be the first mover (entrepreneurial) then does the business allow employees to take risks without fear of punishment for failure?

The recognition and rewards system reveals the true intensions of an organization. It demonstrates the tangible and intangible ways that employees' behaviors are reinforced. For example, a company with an "expert" strategic drive would need to give technical employees control of R&D spending and of their professional skills development. If this is not occurring or those employees do not perceive that it is occurring, the "expert" strategy will not provide great results.

5.1.1.2   The McKinsey 7S Framework

While some models of organizational effectiveness go in and out of fashion, one that has persisted is the McKinsey 7S Framework. Developed by Robert Waterman, Thomas Peters, and Julien Philips (Waterman et al. 1980) working as consultants at the McKinsey & Company consulting firm, the basic premise of the model is that there are seven internal aspects of an organization that need to be aligned if it is to be successful. The McKinsey 7S model involves seven interdependent factors which are categorized as either "hard" or "soft" elements (Table 5.1).

Table 5.1   Hard and soft elements of the McKinsey 7S framework

Hard Elements	Soft Elements
	Shared Values
Strategy	Skills
Structure	Style
System	Staff

"Hard" elements are easier to define or identify and leadership can directly influence them: these are strategy statements, organization charts and reporting lines, and formal processes and IT systems. "Soft" elements, on the other hand, can be more difficult to describe, and are less tangible and more influenced by culture. However, these soft elements are as important as the hard elements if the organization is going to be successful. The way the model is presented in Figure 5.2 (see next page) depicts the interdependency of the elements and indicates how a change in one affects all the others.

The characteristics of each element specifically is as follows:

- *Strategy*: the plan devised to maintain and build competitive advantage over the competition.
- *Structure*: the way the organization is structured and who reports to whom.
- *Systems*: the daily activities and procedures that staff members engage in to get the job done.
- *Shared values*: called "superordinate goals" when the model was first developed, these are the core values of the company that are evidenced in the corporate culture and the general work ethic.
- *Style*: the style of leadership adopted.
- *Staff*: the employees and their general capabilities.
- *Skills*: the actual skills and competencies of the employees working for the company.

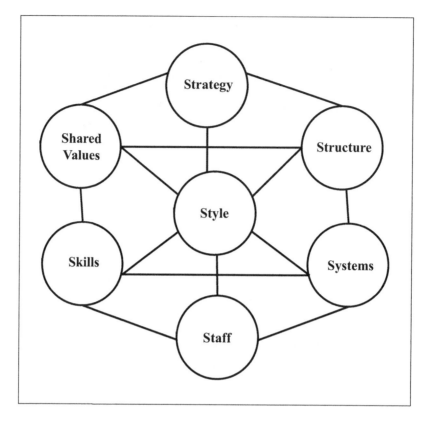

Figure 5.2 The McKinsey 7S Framework

Bhatti (2011) is stating that the model is used to analyze over 70 large organizations. The McKinsey 7S Framework was shaped as identifiable and easy to remember in the field of business. The 7S model can be used in a wide variety of situations where an alignment perspective is useful (Manktelow and Carlson, 1991) for example, to help the business leader to:

- improve the performance of a company;
- examine the likely effects of future changes within a company;
- align departments and processes during a merger or acquisition;
- determine how best to implement a proposed strategy.

The model is based on the theory that, for an organization to perform well, these seven elements need to be aligned and mutually reinforcing. Therefore, the model can be used to help identify what needs to be realigned to improve performance, or to maintain alignment (and performance) during other types of change. Manktelow and Carlson (1991) are suggesting some questions which business leaders would need to explore to help them to understand their situation in terms of the 7S framework. They would need to analyze their current situation, and then repeat the exercise for their proposed situation.

Strategy:
- What is our strategy?
- How do we intend to achieve our objectives?

- How do we deal with competitive pressure?
- How are changes in customer demands dealt with?
- How is strategy adjusted for environmental issues?

Structure:
- How is the company/team divided?
- What is the hierarchy?
- How do the various departments coordinate activities?
- How do the team members organize and align themselves?
- Is decision-making and controlling centralized or decentralized? Is this as it should be, given what we're doing?
- Where are the lines of communication? Explicit and implicit?

System:
- What are the main systems that run the organization? Consider financial and HR systems as well as communications and document storage.
- Where are the controls and how are they monitored and evaluated?
- What internal rules and processes does the team use to keep on track?

Shared Values:
- What are the core values?
- What is the corporate/team culture?
- How strong are the values?
- What are the fundamental values that the company/team was built on?

Style:
- How participative is the management/leadership style?
- How effective is that leadership?
- Do employees/team members tend to be competitive or cooperative?
- Are there real teams functioning within the organization or are they just nominal groups?

Staff:
- What positions or specializations are represented within the team?
- What positions need to be filled?
- Are there gaps in required competencies?

Skills:
- What are the strongest skills represented within the company/team?
- Are there any skills gaps?
- What is the company/team known for doing well?
- Do the current employees/team members have the ability to do the job?
- How are skills monitored and assessed?

5.1.1.3 The Higgins Eight S's model

As the business environment becomes more complex and more changeful, the need to reformulate strategy and/or to adjust elements of the existing strategy becomes more frequent. As a result senior executives find themselves confronted with the need to integrate a number of changes

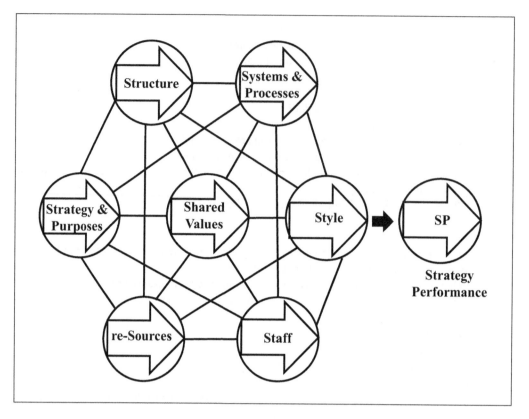

Figure 5.3   The Higgins Eight Ss model

in the execution of the new or revised strategy. This dissemination and integration of execution actions is especially difficult across cross-functional activities. Higgins (2005) has developed the Eight S's model (Figure 5.3), which is a revision of the original McKinsey 7S Framework developed in 1980. This is a heuristic model which enables senior business leaders to more effectively and efficiently lead the cross-functional execution of strategies. Higgins pins down that those executives who are successful spend a great deal of their time on strategy execution. They believe and realize that execution of strategy is as important and crucial as its formulation.

In Higgins' (2005) opinion much of strategy execution revolves around aligning key organizational functions/elements with the chosen strategy. However, with frequently occurring changes in the business environment, strategies are modified/updated more often as compared to the past, making the alignment process a bigger challenge. Senior business leaders must align the cross-functional organizational elements; structure, system and processes, leadership style, staff, resources and shared values with the new strategy so that the strategy opted can succeed. All these factors are identified in the Eight Ss model as presented in Figure 5.3 and are vital for successful strategy execution.

Higgins model is developed into two parts; the Seven Contextual Ss and strategy performance. The key of the model is that all the Contextual Seven Ss must be aligned to achieve best possible strategic performance. It is important to note that organization's arrows should be pointing in the same direction that is they should be aligned with one another.

Bhatti (2011) provides some understanding about the Eight Ss:

1. *Strategy and Purpose:* Strategies are formulated to achieve an organization's purpose. Strategic purpose includes strategic intent, vision, focus, mission, goals and strategic objectives. There are four types of strategies famed by Higgins; corporate, business, functional and process strategies. Change in strategic purpose leads to change in strategy.
2. *Structure:* Organizational structure consists of five parts; jobs, the authority to do jobs, the grouping of jobs in a logical fashion, the managers span of control and mechanism of coordination. Therefore, when executing a business strategy, decisions are to be made regarding how an organization is structured. Organization structure would have a critical impact on job assignment; for example, how the job will be completed, who has authority to do the job, how the jobs should be grouped into departments and divisions, etc.
3. *Systems and Processes:* Systems and processes enable the organization to execute daily activities, which may be about various elements including formal and informal procedures, planning systems, budgeting, resources allocation and information systems.
4. *Style:* This refers to leadership/management mode exhibited by the leaders/managers when relating to subordinates and other employees.
5. *Staff:* After defining company's strategic purpose, leadership must settle, as how many employees are needed and what are the required backgrounds and skills essential to achieve the strategic purpose. Some other activities are also included such as staff training, career management and employees promotion.
6. *Resources:* Business leadership must ensure that an organization has access to sufficient resources toward successfully strategy execution. Resources include people, money, technology and other management systems.
7. *Shared Values:* These are on the whole related to organizational culture. Therefore, shared values are the values shared by the members of the organization making it different and diverse from the other organizations.
8. *Strategic Performance:* This is a derivative of the other seven Ss. Strategic performance is possessed by an organization as a total, or for profit-based parts of the whole. Performance can be measured at any level. Financial performance measurements are critical barometers of strategy performance. There are some other measures as well.

The most significant change comes in the deletion of skills from the McKinsey's 7S Framework and the addition of resources in its place. Furthermore, Strategic Performance has been added to the model to help focus the strategy execution effort.

Skills replacement with resources: It is believed and very much an accepted fact that an organization cannot successfully execute strategies without resources. Without some additional resources such as finance, information technology and the time required of business leaders and others in the organization cannot effectively execute strategies (Higgins, 2005). Higgins also clearly states that he examined a number of enterprises and found that resources are highly essential for an enterprise when it comes to executing their strategies.

Addition of Strategic Performance: Strategic performance was added in the Higgins Eight S's model over the McKinsey's 7S Framework. This can be used in different ways, starting from objectives to measuring results. It provides the forces as what is required or what is to be achieved and closure once attaining the set objectives.

5.1.1.4   The Khadem's alignment model

If business leaders are continually searching for a better business strategy, they are on the right track, but if their current one is being poorly executed, it is more important to learn how to assure excellent execution (Khadem, 2008).

Khadem (2008) has discovered that the most effective way is through alignment and follow-up. Imagine that everyone in an organization from its executive team all the way down to the frontline workers is laser-focused on making the organization's strategy work. This is the state of alignment Khadem is talking about, where everyone understands the strategy, buys into it, knows how to make a real contribution, and strives to make a contribution to its realization. In the process of playing their parts, thousands of managers at all levels generate thousands of commitments to action that directly impact strategy. A systematic follow-up of these commitments is essential to making the organization's strategy successful.

If alignment and follow-up are crucial to success, why are so many organizations with competent, creative and determined resources lacking in these two elements? Sometimes their strength can become their weakness. Companies that lack alignment often have competent, creative and determined resources that do not agree with the strategy, do not share the vision, or do not buy into the culture of the organization as defined by the top executives. For example, at the culture clash of Daimler Benz-Chrysler and its devastating impact on its stock value or the recent tensions between Korean and American managers at Hyundai's US operations. According to the report in *Business Week*, "many of the American executives who do stay find parent Hyundai Motor's corporate culture to be suffocating." How committed will these American managers be to implementing the company strategy?

Therefore, what is total alignment (Khadem, 2008)?

Two people are aligned when they move in the same direction. They are integrated when they cooperate with one another. Total alignment encompasses both alignment and integration. Can they be aligned and not integrated? Yes. Two people move in the same direction but without cooperation. Can they be integrated and not aligned? That is also possible when people work together but get nowhere. Therefore, both alignment and integration are needed.

If a company intends to be aligned and integrated, it needs a center of focus or frame of reference for all jobholders in the organization. This frame of reference is, of course, the vision, values, and strategy of the organization. When Khadem (2008) talks about alignment, he means alignment with the vision, values and the strategy.

Competent, creative and determined people often do not buy into what they have not invented themselves. They have to be convinced of the value of what was invented elsewhere, and that is the first challenge in establishing total alignment. Business executives should take as much time as necessary to involve people in formulating vision, values, and strategy. The investment of time may pay back more than any other investment and may hold the key to the survival and prosperity of the business. Involvement produces ownership and understanding, the key to uniting divergent corporate cultures.

In reality, it is more important to be aligned with strategy than to be aligned with the vision. Every person in the organization, no matter what that individual does, can claim to be implementing the shared vision. There are many paths to achieving vision. The best path, by definition, is strategy. If people do not align with the best path, then the resources of the organization would be too stretched to enable it to achieve its vision in the shortest possible time. Therefore, people need to be aligned with vision, values and strategy not because they are forced but because they see themselves making a difference in turning the vision into reality.

Aligning with these three is by no means an easy task. It requires effective processes, a change of mindset and determined effort. Khadem (2008) is presenting his alignment and strategy execution approach through the following process:

- vision indicating tree;
- strategy indicator tree;
- alignment map;
- aligning accountability;
- aligning competency;
- aligning behaviors;
- aligning compensation;
- sustaining alignment.

Total alignment provides a system for strategy execution. Once this system is in place, it will be apparent very quickly how well current strategies are working. Then, when business leaders search for a better business strategy it will be because they need one, not because they cannot get their existing one to work.

5.1.2   ORGANIZATIONAL BEHAVIOR

There are several faces of organizational behavior, and leadership has to analyze these phases for successful strategy execution.

- *Strategy understanding*: do employees really understand the business strategy and what it means for their jobs? Do they buy into it and support it?
- *Customer focus*: do employees have an understanding of the customer-supplier relationship and the value proposition? Do they know how to deliver value to the customer?
- *Leadership behavior*: does business leadership communicate a passion and excitement for the future? Is there the necessary style, motivation and commitment from employees?
- *Performance management*: are the leadership performance metrics in line with the leadership's developed strategy? Are employees recognized, evaluated and rewarded according to these metrics?
- *Organizational culture*: do the attitudes, values and beliefs of employees match the organization's core values and core strategy?

These phases are not new as independent concepts, but together they form an interconnected and interdependent system that must be managed as a whole. Actions taken in one or more areas must be supported by actions in the other areas to be effective.

Herbiniak (2005) has identified four issues in strategy execution, all of which are people-related:

- Managers are trained to plan, not execute.
- Some top executives do not see themselves as responsible for implementation of the strategies they formulate.
- Strategy execution happens over a much longer time frame than strategy formulation.
- Strategy implementation involves more people than strategy formulation.

The execution of a strategy very often fails because leaders do not focus on the critical issue of aligning the people to the strategy and the processes. Too often, strategy is formulated in a vacuum and then centrally broadcast as a "done deal." The communication is either too vague or too detailed for anyone to understand what it really means. No effort is made to check for understanding or measure the effectiveness of communication in terms of buy-in translated into action.

If more people are involved in helping to shape the strategy and/or shape the execution plan, they will feel part of the process and are likely to support it. Also, the more knowledge leaders can get from the front line of the organization, the more effective their strategies and execution will be.

Insight Formation's (2007) approach for strategy execution depends on leadership efforts to improve alignment and devise a robust framework that addresses the following key enablers:

- *Communication*: leadership's top priority must be to communicate often and clearly and to employees. This will improve organizational effectiveness and productivity, and reduce frustration due to employees understanding of how best they can contribute to organizational goals.
- *Resources allocation*: strategy is about effectively allocating resources toward the priorities of the organization. A robust frame work must be in place to define and communicate the critical drivers of strategic success, the resources and investments that will be applied in alignment with the most valuable strategic priorities of the organization. The result is that resources – such as IT investment, training dollars, continuous improvement programs, innovation and product development – will support the strategy execution.
- *Organizational effectiveness orchestrated across multiple functions*: the traditional organizational structural silos of responsibility assignment and budget allocation should be eliminated to improve effective collaboration between various groups of the organization for effective performance. Mapping out strategy with cause and linkage conveys very clearly the organization-wide cooperation and collaboration required for efficient strategy execution. Link objectives with clearly related measures and initiatives; create the alignment required for effective strategic performance. Individual employees' objectives must be linked to the corporate mission.
- *Strategic performance measurement and management*: simply expanding the use of operational and financial measurement is not the answer for managing strategic performance. Sales analysis, financial modeling, real-time operational monitoring, and budget variance reporting are all useful performance measurement and management tools, but are not designed for strategic alignment and execution. Measures are powerful tools when used properly. Strategic alignment and measurement go together to optimize execution. Organizations that significantly improve their alignment are frequently able to move ahead of their competition.
- *Best principles for improving alignment and strategy execution*: numerous authors and consultants who have developed a vast array of methodologies and techniques for addressing these issues, and organizations often move from one approach to another – each with different language and philosophy. Insight Formation (2007) points out that many of these practices evolved around the work of Robert Kaplan and David Norton, who developed and popularized the concept of the Balanced Scorecard. Many organizations who tried using a Balanced Scorecard found that it had little impact on their performance: others, however, found that the Balanced Scorecard Concept (BSC) approach enabled them to have breakthrough results. The BSC is discussed further in Section 5.3.

To achieve successful execution of strategy, an effective organizational diagnostic instrument should measure and monitor the alignment of employees to the strategy. Show employees how well their corporation, division or plant actively supports their strategy, and if required, uncover the reasons why they do not, and appropriate actions can then be taken.

5.1.3 CRITICAL RELATIONSHIP OF MAJOR DOMAINS

Simply understanding the difference between strategy development as thinking (analysis, planning, setting goals, etc.) and strategy implementation as doing (follow-through, top-to-bottom, operational, goal achieving, etc.) is not enough to execute the developed strategy. Currently, this type of thinking is considered a traditional planning effort and has proven either too expensive or time-consuming: many major top-down strategy initiatives have failed. Today's challenge is how to build execution into strategy (Chan and Mauborgne, 2005).

Organizations must recognize that all sections of the organization and people at all levels need to participate in the process of setting goals. Kaplan and Norton (2000) state that while many leaders accept the idea of making strategy as everyone's business, they often fall into the same old routines of hiring outside experts to formulate their strategy or forcing their strategies from the top down without gaining bottom-up input during the formulation process.

Surowiecki's (2004) latest research shows that the "many are smarter than the few" philosophy of management is gaining acceptance. Whether it is a simple problem (for example, measuring length, weight, etc.) or solving a complex problem (for example, how to grow business revenue and profit), collective judgment almost always outperforms the expert. Organizations can utilize the concept of collective judgment by consulting a broad group of employees in the planning process; this approach has the added benefits of creating support for change, which is essential for successful execution.

As the philosophy of strategy execution evolves and organizations seek to improve the link between strategy and execution (Donlon, 2007) has identified five major domains as critical elements for any organization. Their conceptual relationships is presented in Figure 5.4 (see the following page):

- Focus.
- Resources.
- Operations.
- People.
- Information.

Focus: Focus is about organizational commitment and alignment to the strategy. Alignment occurs in three major areas:

1. Forging a consensus among top leadership teams.
2. Creating a vertical line of sight between the corporate goals and those pursued by employees on the front lines.
3. Creating horizontal linkage between functional teams and external partners who must collaborate to achieve shared goals associated with key customer-oriented processes.

It is also important to implement measurements which help drive focus and commitment, and they must be linked to strategy. If business leaders do not measure it, they cannot manage it, therefore, if they do not manage it, do not measure it.

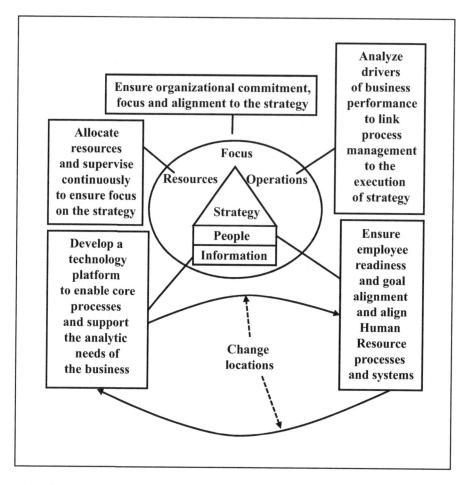

Figure 5.4 The conceptual relationship of organizational elements to build strategy execution capabilities

Resources: This domain involves allocating financial and other resources required to fund strategy and operations, and monitoring those resources continuously to ensure goal(s) achievement.

- Perform gap analysis (actual or expected performance gaps) and utilize scorecard measurement concept.
- Strategic initiatives are intervention projects and are treated as special expenditures which are easily distinguished from operational expenses and capital expenditures.

Operations: Includes analyzing the drivers of business performance and linking operational processes to the execution of strategy:

- The critical links between strategy and operations are key processes. Processes must be mapped to support strategic objectives and continuously monitored through a metrics system.
- The cause-and-effect relationship between process elements and operational leadership can determine the appropriate metrics to the process.

People: This domain is about ensuring employee readiness and personal goal alignment, and aligning human resource processes and systems to support the strategy:

- Just as strategy is executed through initiatives and operations are executed through processes, similarly the awareness and commitment, or lack of, among people in any organization can achieve or lose success.
- Since strategy is about commitment and change, and operations are about compliance with established processes, therefore, people need to be involved at both levels through continuous leadership communications, personal goal alignment and employee reward and recognition systems.

Information: This domain involves developing a technology platform to enable core processes and support the analytic needs of the enterprise:

- In today's knowledge economy, business strategy cannot be executed without technology. The growth of business intelligence applications such as scorecards and dashboards are a reflection of reality that information is the new critical element in strategy execution.
- Every enterprise depends on the leadership of the information technology (IT) organization to develop a platform and information architecture that supports timely decision-making at both the strategic and operational levels. This effort must start with a clear understanding of business requirements and must also adapt as business needs change over time.

5.1.4   STRATEGY EXECUTION KEYS

The strategy execution concept is also discussed in this section through discussing some specific approaches. There are numerous professional practicing authors in the literature including the following who are presenting their strategy execution experiences in a simple form called "Strategy execution keys." Their presentation is a high-level approach of presenting the strategy execution concept:

- Zagotta and Robinson's strategy execution approach of seven keys.
- Hart's strategy execution approach of four keys.
- Beaudan's strategy execution approach of five keys.

5.1.4.1   *Zagotta and Robinson's approach of seven keys*

Successful CEOs understand the need for a sound business strategy and invest significant time, effort, and money in strategy development. But the real value of strategy can only be recognized through execution. The new emphasis on execution reveals a simple truth: it does not matter how good the plan is if the business leader cannot make it happen. More important, many companies lack the tools for turning strategy into an execution process that guarantees accountability and yet is adaptable to change (Zagotta and Robinson, 2002). The seven keys to executing strategy successfully are:

- quantify the vision;
- communicate strategy through mantras;

- plan results, not activities;
- plan what leaders are not going to do;
- open strategy to the organization;
- automate status and progress management; and
- create a virtuous circle of execution and strategy.

Let me expand further:

1. *Quantify the vision*: Mention "vision" to CEOs and many will roll their eyes. The word too often prompts painful memories of endless meetings resulting in breathless statements about "becoming the industry leader" or "best-of-breed provider." The first key to developing an effective vision lies in quantifying the dream in a way that supports execution planning-in essence, taking the time to transform ambiguous corporate hopes and dreams into concrete, tangible targets.

2. *Communicate strategy through mantras*: Strategic plans can be complex. Nevertheless, business leader should be able to communicate their essence concisely, so that employees at all levels can live the strategy in their day-to-day activities. A mantra is a short, simple, meaningful phrase that answers the question: How is the company going to achieve the vision? For example, of Ford's ad slogan "quality is job one," adopted at a time when American automakers were struggling with issues of quality. By the time Lou Gerstner became CEO of IBM in 1993, Big Blue had suffered years of slowing growth and declining stock prices. One of his early actions was to introduce the simple but powerful mantra: "Win, Team, Execute." Gerstner's succinct mantras have become so deeply woven into the fabric of IBM that they are still used in performance reviews.

3. *Plan results, not activities*: Popular methodologies such as "Norton and Kaplan's Balanced Scorecard (BSC) urge companies to measure leading indicators as an 11 early alert" management tool. Such measurements are important, but they do not go far enough. For example, in a company, one of the indicator is customer satisfaction rating which may be one of the leading indicators leadership choose for the BSC – certainly an important metric. But it is usually not tied in a visible, specific way to the strategic initiative that company is applying resources against. Customer satisfaction drops; the alert on the BSC flashes red, and everyone panics. By that time, executive management is asking who is accountable and what is being done. Numbers simply do not tell the whole story because they do not provide a guide to the execution of leader's initiative. The drivers of the measures are not visible. Every time a measure goes south, executives must retrace their steps and determine what activities are off track or need to change.

4. *Plan what leaders are not going to do*: Strategic initiatives often fail because they are perceived as extra work to be accomplished on top of existing work. Indeed, one of the biggest barriers to successful execution is the common tendency to take on too much and then do everything "just OK." Business leaders know that they are taking on too much when they cannot rationalize the budget and human resources against the requirements of the initiative. Business leaders must decide what initiatives will no longer be pursued and communicate that message clearly. By specifying exactly what the new strategy replaces, the initiative becomes a positive and powerful force for change and transformation. This enables corporate leaders to focus resources and organizational attention. It also makes it clear to other leaders in the company not to pursue pet projects that blur focus and do not contribute to the desired results.

5. *Open strategy to the organization*: Once, companies and organizations kept knowledge in the hands of a select few. Knowledge was power, power was control, and control seemed to

be a key to success. Today, successful strategy execution reverses this idea. Knowledge is crucial for agile decision-making, and decision-making happens every day at every point in the company. By getting strategy out of the binders and into the hands of employees, CEOs generate better alignment because decisions are made in allegiance with strategy.

6. *Automate status and progress management*: Roughly 65 percent of executives' time is spent giving and getting status reports. Without an efficient mechanism to report status, valuable meeting time is spent reviewing activities instead of making critical decisions. Face-to-face meetings aren't necessary for reviewing status anyway, but they are crucial when it comes to hammering out decisions about strategic execution. If they spend less time hearing about where they are, CEOs can spend more time deciding about where they are going and how they're going to get there.

7. *Create a virtuous circle of execution and strategy*: Successful strategy execution is a living, dynamic process. Strategy itself begins life as a set of agreements about markets, products, revenues, growth, and the like. The rest is execution. And unless there is an ongoing process for evaluating execution, making decisions about it, and closing the loop with the original strategy, the initiative dies. That's why it's important to distinguish between strategic planning – those high-level agreements – and strategy management-an ongoing process for reviewing and maintaining strategic progress.

The importance of an ongoing process for evaluating execution cannot be overemphasized. Consider how even a single, timely adjustment in execution can pay big dividends: case study from Zagotta and Robinson (2002). A $200 million professional services company was pursuing a growth strategy designed to increase firm revenues significantly. In adopting the strategy, they also instituted a decision-making process consisting of a monthly strategy meeting among the core team of CEO, COO and CFO. In these meetings, the executives examined external research, internal progress against their strategic plan, and financial results. External research showed dramatically increased competition in the company's market space. Internal progress – measured by lead-generation, sales calls and deals closed – showed that the company's 22 offices around the world were all aggressively pursuing business. Nevertheless, revenue milestones were not being achieved, and if the company continued on its present course, it would fall short of its goals. Instead of concluding, long after the fact, that times were tough because of increased competition and that the growth strategy was unrealistic, the executives looked more closely at strategy execution. They found that offices focused on building business with existing customers were achieving growth targets (and generating higher profits) more often than offices that focused more on pursuing new customers. By quickly refocusing all offices on increasing "share of customer," the firm was soon hitting revenue and profit milestones.

5.1.4.2 *Hart's strategy execution approach of four keys*

Just as the most dangerous part of a jet flight is going from cruise altitude to landing, making the transition from a lofty vision and innovative strategy to ground-level implementation requires great focus and flawless execution (Hart, 2005). Having perspective and strategy is important; however, when business leaders examine business plans that miss the mark, they find that the problem is rarely with the vision or strategy but rather with implementation and execution. Hart's work experience working with senior executive teams on implementing sound strategies has found that four key elements must be in place:

1. Assessing and developing the knowledge and competency of the senior leaders. Assess the

strengths and competencies of the senior management team and identify potential gaps that could impact implementation. Senior leaders can learn what gaps in skills or knowledge exist through formal assessments conducted by an experienced third party to encourage candor and objectivity. Leaders must know their strengths and shortcomings and address the gaps, either by recruiting new members or developing the requisite skills or knowledge.

2. The senior leadership team must be fully aligned with the intent and direction of the strategic initiative. Although candor and cooperation among senior leaders are crucial, functional heads often pursue their own objectives to the detriment of the strategic initiative. The implementation of key initiatives requires the full alignment and shared accountability of senior leaders. Unless senior leaders embrace the strategic objective and commit to its implementation, the odds for success are low.

3. The culture must support the initiative and adhere to the Essential Values Set. Certain values are so vital that are generally referred to as the Essential Values Set. Culture is largely determined by the values shared by its members. This Essential Values Set is a universal set of principles that govern how the organization defines acceptable behavior.

4. The reward and recognition system must be aligned with the outcomes of the strategy. The cash compensation plan, along with other rewards, needs to be aligned with the cross-functional goals of the strategic initiative. Leaders should be rewarded for accomplishments in their areas of responsibility and for their support of cross-organizational initiatives.

Hart (2005) is characterizing high-performance teams by six healthy values:

1. *Performance value*: This "make it happen" value focuses on setting challenging expectations and achieving results with accountability. With a healthy performance value, people seek innovative ways to overcome obstacles, encourage teamwork, and accept prudent risk-taking.

2. *Collaborative value*: Collaboration is built upon principles of trust, sharing, open and direct communication, and a belief in the positive intent of team members. Collaboration promotes teamwork, mutual support, and decisions made for the greater good.

3. *Change value*: The successful execution of key initiatives requires innovation, openness, and positive support for new ideas. Leaders operating from a healthy change mindset act as coaches, as opposed to judges or critics of new ideas. They encourage innovation, risk and growth, as opposed to dismissing new ideas or diverse points of view.

4. *Customer value*: The customers' experience is a barometer of overall health. This value can also be defined as how well the organization focuses on a greater purpose – something beyond itself. The best leaders are focused on better serving internal and external customers. Positive and productive initiatives are framed in the context of a customer-value perspective.

5. *Integrity value*: Integrity refers to the consistency between the senior leadership's words and their actions. Integrity is crucial for effective strategy execution. Integrity goes beyond simple compliance. At its core, integrity goes to consistency between word and deed to walking the talk.

6. *Health value*: Senior leadership teams that execute well share a healthy climate characterized by openness, trust, mutual respect, optimism and hopefulness. This health value enables leaders to generate positive energy, assume the best motives and intentions in others, be more present and listen to one another for different points of view.

These six values position senior leaders as positive role models. If there is mistrust, internal competition, or negative assumptions of motives among senior leaders, the implementation of the strategy will be impaired.

CASE STUDY

Hart (2005) is presenting a case study of a telephone company where he applied the four keys approach, which he has developed from his long strategy execution experience. The new CEO of a cellular telephone company and his executive team grappled with many challenges – one being to determine a strategy for competing in markets dominated by better-financed competitors. The senior leaders concluded that excellence in customer service was the key. They believed that if they could endear themselves to their customers, they could reduce the erosion of their customer base and free up resources to attract new customers. Reducing turnover by improving its service could result in $400 million in additional annual profits.

Here is how this firm used the Four Elements of Execution to achieve this goal:

1. Assessing and developing the knowledge mid-competency of the senior leaders. They assessed the strengths and capabilities of staff to ensure that those charged with leading the initiative had the requisite skills. Their analysis revealed some gaps in knowledge that would be difficult to develop internally. So, they recruited several new executives with these capabilities.

2. Senior feeders must be fully aligned with the intent mid-direction of the strategic initiative. The success of the initiative hinged on everyone becoming committed to improved customer service. Knowing that employees would be looking to them, senior managers resolved their differences behind closed doors. While dissent and alternative points of view were welcomed in staff meetings, a unified front was required after the meetings.

3. The culture must support the initiative and live the essential values. Presenting a positive and unified front reinforced the desire to better serve the customer. Although the leaders came from different business units, they put aside their individual needs and collaborated to identify innovative methods for serving the customer. Their ability to coach others and maintain focus on the customers' experience contributed to the success. Senior leaders held each other accountable to "walk the talk." They faced many setbacks and obstacles but maintained a healthy climate with an optimistic view of the future and cast a positive shadow.

4. The reward and recognition system must be aligned with outcomes of the strategy. Senior leaders realigned their executive compensation reward and recognition system to support the collaborative measures necessary to implement the strategic plan.

After two years, the company moved from seventh place to first in the JD Powers ranking of Cellular Customer Service and Loyalty. Customer turnover levels were 67 percent lower than national competitors. This resulted in hundreds of millions of dollars in additional profits.

5.1.4.3   Beaudan's strategy execution approach of five keys

Beaudan (2010) has developed a creative strategy execution formula with five key ingredients. Simply mastering these five ingredients, leaders will learn how to construct a creative strategy execution formula that differentiates their organization and vastly increases their ability to achieve extraordinary results against the odds. The five ingredients are unique strategy, candid dialogue, clear roles and responsibilities, bold action and visible leadership. Senior leaders would need to unleash creative execution in their organization, and they would also need to 1) evaluate their strategy; 2) encourage bold thinking; and 3) lead from the front.

1. A Unique Strategy understood and accepted by everyone. The first ingredient of creative execution – indeed of all execution – is a unique, compelling strategy.
2. Candid Dialogue. The openness with which the business leaders have to deal with their peers and superiors must be a hallmark of their personality.

3. Clear Roles and Accountabilities. Once they shared their strategy with their superiors and peers, the strategy must be documented and published for all, so that it must be clear who is responsible for what.
4. Bold Action. Business leaders must demonstrate their willingness to take bold actions wherever and whenever necessary.
5. Visible Leadership. Only by being visible during the actual activities that occur throughout execution can leaders unleash people's creative powers.

Beaudan (2010) is demonstrating through the following examples that the positive results are possible when the strategy is executed correctly:

• Over 70 percent of Boeing's highly touted 787 Dreamliner, a carbon-composite aircraft that took its maiden flight in December 2009, is designed and manufactured in China, Russia and India. Not only are Chinese workers bending sheet metal for the Dreamliner, but Chinese and Indian designers are putting together the specifications for the aircraft.
• Likewise, in 2008, European aircraft maker Airbus opened its first plant outside Europe in China – where it now employs 600 workers to assemble the popular A320 airplane. And so China is no longer just buying Boeing and Airbus's planes – which is what it did in the 1980s and 1990s – it is actually learning how to design, manufacture and assemble the planes. This significant shift will likely see China form its own aircraft industry in the near future.

5.1.5 RESEARCHERS' APPROACHES FOR STRATEGY EXECUTION

There are numerous scholars in the literature (Bossidy and Charan, 2002b; Morrill et al., 2003; Harpst, 2008; O'Connor, 2012; Hug, 2013; Miller, 2014) who are presenting their strategy execution research and experiences in the literature. Bossidy and Charan's (2002b) is selected to discuss in this section. They have identified three key points in executing a strategy:

• Execution is a discipline and integral to strategy.
• Execution is the major job of the business leader.
• Execution must be a core element of an organization's culture.

5.1.5.1 Execution is a discipline

Execution is fundamental to strategy and has to shape the strategy. No valuable strategy can be planned without considering the organization's ability to execute it. Execution is a systematic process of rigorously discussing how and what, questioning, persistently follow through and try to make sure that everybody has accountability. Execution is a systematic way of exposing reality and acting on it.

5.1.5.2 Execution is the job of the business leader

Leadership thinks strategically and tries to inspire its people with vision, while managers do the detailed work. Who would not want to have all the fun and glory while keeping their hands clean? This work style is a dream and one that creates great damage to the business. Organizations can execute strategy only if the leader's heart and soul are fully participating in the business. The leader is not only required to think big and work with investors and law makers but also has to be engaged personally and deeply in the business.

The leader is the only person who can set the tone of dialogue in the organization. Dialogue is the core of culture and the fundamental unit of work. Bossidy and Charan (2002b) expect every manager to handle at least the following three issues:

- highest integrity;
- customer comes first;
- three processes for people, strategy and operation.

5.1.5.3 Execution has to be the organization's culture

Execution has to be a part of the reward system and a critical element of normal behavior that everyone practices. One way to get a handle on execution is to think of it as akin to the Six Sigma process for continual improvement. Leaders who execute mainly look for deviations from desired and actual outcome in everything from people solution for promotion to profit margins. Execution has to be a part of the organization's culture and must drive the behavior of all leaders at all levels, but execution should begin with the senior leaders.

Leadership needs to work with aggressive desire. For example, sales and revenue must increase by X and Y percent respectively in the next six months in a flat market. Leaders should also recognize whether goals are realistic or not and should ask questions like:

- Where will the sale increase come from?
- What product will generate the growth?
- Who will buy them and what pitch sales group is going to develop for these customers?
- What will their competitors' reaction be?
- What will their milestones be? If a milestone has to be achieved before first quarter and is running late, how can the plan be modified?

Therefore, as a leader/manager, they have to discuss a variety of issues such as:

- a wide array of facts and ideas;
- the permutations and combinations of these ideas which can be a very large number;
- what risk to take and where;
- to go through these details and selecting those that count;
- assign to the right people and be sure to synchronize their work.

Leadership without the discipline of execution is incomplete and ineffective. The following are some additional points where execution makes the difference:

- Many leaders do not realize what needs to be done to convert a vision into specific tasks, because their high-level thinking is too broad.
- They do not follow through and get things done.
- They get bored when go through details.
- They do not crystallize thought or anticipate roadblocks.
- They do not know how to pick the people in their organization who can execute.
- Their lack of engagement deprives them of the sound judgment about people that comes through practice.

- Not recognizing the problem/issue and incorrectly fixing the root cause of the problem does not support the strategy execution.
- Stretch goals can be useful in forcing people to break old rules and do things better. They are worse than useless if they are totally unrealistic or if the people who have to meet them are not given the chance to debate them beforehand and take the ownership of them.

Bossidy and Charan (2002b) have identified three elements as building blocks for strategy execution and three processes of execution:

- Leader's seven essential behaviors:
  - Know your people and your business.
  - Insist on realism.
  - Set clear goals and priorities.
  - Follow through.
  - Reward the doers.
  - Expand people's capabilities.
  - Know yourself.
- Creating the framework for cultural change.
- The job leaders should find a way to do rather than deleting it, and having the right people in the right place.

Three processes of execution for working with people and operations:

- the people process;
- the strategy process;
- the operations process.

Bossidy and Charan (2002b) have also presented analysis of several case studies and have tried to identify the root cause of their strategy failure. In all cases root cause was not properly executing their strategy. Analysis of one of these case studies is presented below.

Sample Case Study with Analysis

The chief executive officer (CEO) developed a great strategy with the help of his team, the brightest in the industry. He empowered them and gave them the freedom to do what they needed to do. Everybody knew what had to be done and their responsibilities. They worked together with high energy but failed.

The fiscal year came to an end and they missed the goals. The company has had to lower their earnings estimates several times during the past fiscal year. They have lost their credibility with Wall Street. The CEO does not know what to do and he is not sure where the bottom is.

As this case was analyzed, the CEO made several acquisitions and created great relationships with Wall Street. He has a great marketing and deal-making skills, so initially the company's common stock went up with expectations that the company would grow both in revenue and profitability. The CEO set the goals and the CEO handed the numbers down to the operating people, leaving the details of implementation to those who report directly to him. The only report he was looking at was quarterly numbers. From the standard on conventional management analysis, the CEO did all the right things. By the standard of execution, he did almost nothing correctly.

One of the major issues was that production facilities could not produce enough of the products to meet market needs. Managers were 12 months behind in implementing the process improvement activities that put the production schedule also 12 months behind. Because the CEO never tried to understand the execution details, he did not know what was going on in the production facilities. He never asked why the production managers did not make the schedule to meet the market needs. An execution-savvy leader would have asked that right away and would then have focused on the root causes. For example, he could ask those who report to him directly; "Is the process improvement on schedule?" The important question is do the people in the chain of command know the reasons and what are they doing about it?

The CEO believed that it was the production director's job to ask such questions and leadership's job is to make sure that these types of questions were asked. Even though the CEO picked the right people for the right job, none of them had experience in execution. For example, the production director was a highly intelligent finance person and came from a consulting firm with no execution experience. The plant managers reporting to him did not respect him. The vice president of operations was not stable on any job and was moved every two years to a new job.

How could this CEO have behaved differently if he had the concept of execution? The following are some thoughts for the reader's analysis:

1. He could have involved all the people responsible for the strategic plan's outcome – all those people participating, including the key production people in shaping the plan. These people could have set the goals based on the organization's capabilities for delivering results.
2. The CEO could have asked his people about the "how" of execution. This "how" means specifically, "Were they going to achieve their projected goals on the timely basis, inventory turns and reduction, and quality and cost goals?" If any answer was missing or unsatisfactory, the team had to get that answer before the plan was launched.
3. The CEO must have set the milestone activities for the progress of the plan with strict accountability for the people in charge.

5.2 Elements Impact on Strategy Execution

There are numerous elements that have implications on strategy execution including accounting, relationship, challenges, performance, leadership excellence, pricing, value alignment and budget. Some of those are discussed here.

ACCOUNTING

Without strong leadership in a professional firm, constructive change is not possible. Strategy is formulated at the top of the firm, but executed from the bottom up. Most employees in accounting firms are undermanaged simply because management skills are not valued, and people have not been trained to manage. Accountants need effective management, just like other professionals. Management training programs have become a popular and effective means to meet this need (Boomer, 2007).

RELATIONSHIP

Was 2012 presidential election won with a superior campaign design or with memorable speeches? Whether the arena is politics, sports or business, the question is arousing hope or desire. Which is more important: to have a great strategy or a great execution? If business leaders go through the literature of the 1980s and 1990s, they will find that well-known strategy consulting firms such as Boston Consulting Group, McKinsey and others, were practicing strategy development and helping hundreds of clients to improve their performance. More recently the desire for strategy development only has gradually decreased and strategy execution along with strategy development has become a more common phenomena. Bossidy and Charan (2002b) have introduced the concept of execution with strategy development. The execution of strategy is as important as strategy development.

In the case of proven business, it is about performing at or above defined standards (metrics). Many established and large corporations are able to achieve success because they hold their leadership accountable to meeting or exceeding the set standards: this is different in an un-established business. It is about finding/developing the best possible strategy and executing it; and in the process, discovering what standards are possible. One of the approaches to develop strategy is that business leaders develop their strategy and constantly improve through questioning. As they develop a product and a pricing model, quickly collect information about which features customers valued, which features they did not, what they were willing to pay for and what they were not. Business can be profitable in today's market if leaders understand that when it comes to innovation and execution, it is not about filling the market with a product, but constantly improving to meet or exceed customer needs.

CHALLENGES

If any organization meets the following challenges, the strategy execution goes smoothly (IBM, 2009):

- Make sure that every employee understands the strategy, and how what they do contributes to success.
- Ensure organizational alignment and focus by cascading and interlocking the objectives and targets.
- Visualize the status of objectives and respond to exceptions through intuitive status maps.
- Speedily response to threats or opportunities by providing accurate status and integrated collaboration tools.
- Receive real-time monitoring of internal and external dependencies or changes.
- Use intuitive navigation through scorecards and dashboards with drill down and roll-up capabilities to monitor progress and risk.

Bottom line benefits include improved productivity in meeting objectives, timely visibility to potential performance gaps, and speed in responding to gaps.

PERFORMANCE

Analyze a government service that provide professional services where every function, every operation, and even every executive, manager and employee perform in complete alignment with the government strategy for delivering value to the public. Or picture a defense equipment manufacturer that is totally synchronized and behaves, operates and functions at the optimum level to execute the firm's business strategy.

Companies like this, or very nearly like it, exist. They are the leaders in their industries. In consumer products, there are well-known brand names that have consistently grown and profited. There are thousands of consumer product firms in the world, and these leaders are somewhat rare. Similarly, there are variety of R&D laboratories, but that of the army is reinforced operationally by leadership that has spent its career at that facility, as well as technologists who further the major missions by supporting that facility and the national policy of relevant missions.

The problem is not that companies who perform at lesser levels do not want to join the leadership rank – most do. The problem is how to do it. Company leadership teams create strategy and take actions to be sure everyone understands the strategy. Often, at year-end, achievements fail to meet goals. The problem is execution – not strategy. This is commonplace. The heart of the problem is that company leadership has only their personal judgment and experience to help them analyze what went wrong. Sometimes they isolate and fix the real problem but often, their corrective efforts are misdirected or ineffective.

LEADERSHIP EXCELLENCE

There are various scholars identifying that leadership excellence is one of the most critical elements in strategy execution (e.g., Harpst, 2008; Haudan, 2009; Ruhmann, 2011). If the company is taking an important journey, it helps to have a map that charts the course. Strategy tends to serve as this map, describing how the company plans to achieve its goals and realize its dreams. Strategy execution has the greatest impact on success and leadership excellence is one of the most critical required elements to execute the strategy. Therefore, generally two elements are missing in strategy execution: (1) to be engaged, people want to solve their strategic puzzles; and (2) they must be linked in a process that spells out the roles of leaders, managers, and individual contributors in executing that strategy (Haudan, 2009).

Typically leaders are responsible to create the strategic plan. Given the way managers and employees typically work together, those most responsible for execution are rarely clear about how what they do impacts the strategic direction, thus hindering execution. Many leaders use traditional annual performance appraisals, which managers and employees alike find difficult and often fail to complete in a timely manner, if at all. With leadership excellence, the focus is on the manager, employee, and how employees contribute to long-term goals (Ruhmann, 2011).

PRICING

Pricing is now a dramatically different area than it has been historically. New software tools give companies a new way of setting, optimizing, and enforcing pricing changes within the organization. With the best tools, an integrated view of customers, their past purchases, benchmarked pricing by segment and size of purchase, relationship data and comparison of trends over time – all are available to provide decision support to field sales representatives, sales managers, marketers and general managers. While as a group these tools are still generally immature, and the companies building them often at early stages of development, the payback from successful implementation is frequently so high that it's an obvious target for potentially rapid profit improvement (Davidson and Simonetto, 2005).

Surprisingly, surveys suggest that in spite of the large upside available at low risk, few companies are pursuing systematic revenue enhancement through pricing execution. While many companies are currently experimenting with price optimization models, AMR Research survey (2005) suggests that only three percent of the firms it surveyed are attempting pricing execution management. Many CEOs may wake up in the morning thinking about prices and revenues, most corporate leaders clearly do not yet contemplate the need for an overall pricing strategy supported by new software tools.

A survey of 153 pricing management projects by AMR Research and internal Deloitte data found that successful pricing projects result in high rates of return. Typical reported annual outcomes (AMR Research 2005) include:

- Average benefit: $3-45 million increased annual revenues.
- Increased revenues: 1–2 percent.
- Increased gross margin: 10–15 percent.
- Increased contribution margin: 20–50 percent.
- Project paybacks: 3 to 10 times or more.

Improved pricing strategy and execution can also have capital market benefits. The benefits of improved pricing execution are likely to be high in rapidly changing industries, such as high-tech segments where new business models appear frequently (Takhan, 2005) or old models get re-invented, and customers have a large variety of purchase options.

5.2.1 WHY PRICING TENDS TO BE AD HOC

Pricing variability tends to be the rule in many companies with complex multi-product businesses. So-called "pocket prices" – the list price, net of discounts, dealer promotions and allowances – often vary widely. At one major company, a review of its largest deals over a multi-year period found discounts that ranged into the 90 percent range. The firm's senior leadership was surprised at what had been approved by their internal sales management team through an ad hoc pricing process (Davidson and Simonetto, 2005).

This is not as unusual as it sounds because pricing is a moving target, particularly in project-oriented markets where partnering occurs, or in highly competitive markets such as personal computers, where the value of inventories can depreciate very fast. In personal computers and many other industries, customers have different volume and contract histories, different expectations about pricing and different relationships with suppliers, all leading to different price negotiation outcomes.

List prices are only the starting point in the pricing execution process. The ongoing marketing and sales activities of the organization often revolve around the discounts, promotions, channel discounts, rebates and myriad other ways that get invented to motivate stocking and purchase. These discounts have been described as the "pricing waterfall" (Marn and Rosiello, 1992; Simonetto et al., 2004). Pricing can easily be categorized into four groups based on existing and new businesses:

1. Setting pricing strategy for an existing business.
2. Managing pricing for an existing business model.
3. Setting pricing strategy for a new business model.
4. Managing pricing for a new business model.

If CEOs and other leaders make it a priority, companies can find surprisingly large opportunities by focusing upon pricing execution and the difference between the pricing set and the pricing received or "pocket pricing," (Marn and Rosiello, 1992; Simonetto et al., 2004).

5.2.2 WHAT SHOULD THE CEO DO?

Different pricing models support different kinds of strategic objectives. While it is hard to generalize about every company and industry, Davidson and Simonetto (2005) are suggesting the following approach:

- Educate the senior management team on the opportunity that pricing management represents. Signal that turf wars are not an acceptable response to the pricing execution initiative.
- Make pricing a priority in the organization and provide visible CEO sponsorship.
- Set-up a Program Management Office to select, test and implement a pricing execution management program. Such an office should have as its mission the task of introducing and making successful the software, processes, training and monitoring for improved pricing processes, and capabilities. A key task for the project office will be to select the right software, demonstrate early success and build upon such early successes.
- Establish complementary business intelligence support to simplify the process of designing, testing and refining targeted pricing promotions.
- Establish a business-intelligence Center of Excellence to facilitate the use and improvement of pricing data in the organization.
- Have the organization develop capabilities that will support one-to-one marketing, pricing and sales.

Pricing execution offers both growing and mature companies a lower-risk approach to revenue, margin, profit, and shareholder-value growth than innovation and acquisitions. And where companies are creating innovative business models and making acquisitions, improved measurement combined with better pricing execution can help the organization generate better financial outcomes from these generally more uncertain initiatives.

5.2.3 VALUE ALIGNMENT

Value Alignment (VA) diagnostics changes the concept of strategy execution (Dunbar, 2007). With VA, any business leader in virtually any industry can review entire operations rapidly and identify how elements are operating (or not) in alignment with the firm's value delivery strategy. This provides the business leader the power to get all the required elements on the same track and heading in the same direction. With all elements of the firm operating in support of the strategy for delivering value to customers, the leadership team can focus on improving performance and actually achieving consistent, long-term revenue and profit growth.

VA is new – very new. Two professors (Valerie Kijewski and Norma C. Powell) from the University of Massachusetts have developed it and validation testing was completed in June 2007. VA builds on three value delivery strategies:

- Product.

- Solution.
- Cost.

Optimum performance is achieved when a firm delivers unmatched value in one of these three while meeting threshold standards in the other two. Take these value strategy definitions and identify operational characteristics for each. These operational characteristics or discriminators are used to construct data collection and analysis tools. These tools can be used to review a firm's operations and identify elements that are or are not operating in alignment with the firm's strategy. VA is the starting point for improving performance. It diagnosis the situation and not the prescription for cure. For many business leaders, knowledge of the problems quickly leads to effective corrective actions. More complex or subtle problems may require deeper investigation to identify the effective corrective action.

There are three steps in implementing VA:

- Leadership.
- Executive.
- Management.

These steps start at the top, but the understanding if the firm's leaders must share the same strategic view. The next two steps (two and three) move sequentially to lower levels, deepening the analysis, and finding indicators of alignment or lack of alignment and spreading the alignment concepts. At the end of the process, all three levels of management are focused on these elements most in need of alignment correction and share a common definition of that needed to bring the organization into full alignment with the value strategy.

While every company, product offering, market, management team and strategic situation is unique, executives indicated many common practices in managing performance and executing business strategy that, when applied, deliver top performance. Top performers achieve strong results through their own combination of the following practices:

- Defining their value aspirations in the competition for investors' capital and customers' attention.
- Setting performance targets for achieving this value that descends to all levels of the organization.
- Managing business performance to meet these targets using metrics of both financial and operating goals.
- Linking employees' rewards, incentive, career development, and performance evaluations to their success or failure in delivering these results.

Finance executives say that a shared view of how a company generates value sets the stage for effective strategy development. No single concept of value dominates the top performers, but the concept of how the company generates value is an important organizing principle for crafting strategy and managing performance. Typically leading finance teams carry this value mindset to the rest of the organization as supporters, partners and leaders of business planning.

5.2.4 BUDGET

In most organizations, the traditional annual budget is the mechanism that governs the allocation of resources to support both strategy and operations. The budget, however, is not usually well suited for the type of resource allocation that supports successful strategy execution. The typical budget process is a painful, distracting, month-long exercise that consumes a tremendous amount of resources and quickly becomes outdated and irrelevant for decision-making. Because most organizations do not explicitly link their operational plans to strategy, the financial plan, operations and strategy often remain disconnected. Once the budget is approved, managers spend the next year's budget while attempting to analyze and explain results compared to a set of flawed and misunderstood targets contained within the budget.

Veth (2006) discusses how driver-based planning is built upon casual models and provides a mechanism to overcome many of these limitations. Driver-based planning uses operational driver models to predict future financial results. These models are essentially equations that represent the mathematical relationships between key operational drivers or business activities and financial outcomes. These models are created by determining the cause-and-effect relationships between drivers, business activities, resource requirements and financial outcomes. While each relationship has always been the basis for budgeting, but they are typically not represented in a formal, systematic and transparent way.

Norton and Peck (2006) have presented an example (Figure 5.5) of a driver-based casual model of a corporate call center. The marketing group of this company produces a series of advertisements (a driver) that results in a volume of inbound inquiry (an activity). To answer these calls, phone agents must be staffed accordingly (resource requirements), which generates call center workforce expenses (financial outcomes). This is the major difference for modeling and projecting the financial plan for the call center's workforce expenses. In contrast to the casual model, the traditional budget provides only a financial expense estimate while the detail assumptions behind the projected workforce expense remain invisible.

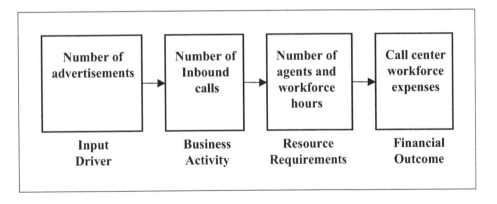

Figure 5.5   Driver-based causal model for a corporate call center

Traditional and Driver models are presented in Table 5.2. If business leaders compare the output of a traditional budget with the explicit assumptions and casual relationships of a driver model, the former workforce expenses for call center operations appear as one number. None of the assumptions underlying the final expense figure are visible or tracked systematically. Consequently, they are not available for review, discussion or subsequent analysis. In contrast, the driver model on the right consists of a series of equations that derive the final expense figure and expose the business assumptions behind the numbers.

Table 5.2   Traditional budget versus driver model

Traditional Budget		Driver Model – Call Center Workforce Expense	
	Plan	*Drivers and Values*	
Gross Sale	$8,200,000	Inbound calls per month	250,000
Less Discounts and Rebates	$400,000	Working days per month	20
		Calls per agent per day	75
Net Sale	$7,800,000	Peak absence factor	20%
Cost of Goods Sold (COGS)		Cost per agent per month	$2,600
Product Cost	$5,030,000	*Modeling and Results*	
Call Center	$520,000	Capacity per agent per month	
Operation-Workforce		= (Calls per day) × (Working days per month)	
Other	$50,000	= 75 × 20 = 1,500	
Gross Margin	$2,200,000	Number of agents required	
R&D	$200,000	= (Calls capacity per agent) × (1+Factor)	
Selling	$200,000	= (250,000/1,500) × (1.2) = 200	
General & Administration	$300,000	Monthly Workforce Expense	
Strategic Investment	$500,000	= (# of agents) × (Cost per agent)	
		= 200 × $2,600	
Operating Margin	$1,000,000	= $520,000	

Using a driver-based model as the starting point for operational planning and financial forecasting provides numerous benefits. The act of developing a driver-based model actually helps to establish a common language for talking about and analyzing the business. Leaders are forced to achieve consensus on which drivers are important, how financial-statement line items are derived from these drivers and the scope of their individual accountabilities. With the underlying assumptions visible, managers cannot hide behind the numbers.

Strategy execution is all about the "operational" level understanding of strategy, but it is not straightforward and takes as much self-examination as it does external analysis. Robert Kaplan (2007) suggested five key principles that leadership should assess when developing a strategy execution plan:

1. Deliver exceptional leadership.
2. Communicate the mapping.
3. Demonstrate organizational alignment.
4. Provide the inspiration.
5. Strategy as a continuous process.

Delivering exceptional leadership: Corporate change in a leadership void is a recipe for disaster. Organizational leaders must be visible and consistently available to align the organization to a new or even existing strategy.

Communicating the mapping: The mapping of strategy to operational terms needs to be pervasive and communicated consistently and constantly. Message must become the part of corporate culture and core values.

Demonstrating organizational alignment: A fundamental question is, "What happens if the result of business leader's strategy map is the realization that one or more of their initiatives are off-strategy?" This makes the situation ever more complicated if the initiative has significant momentum or has had a significant capital investment. As typical consultant answer is that it depends. However, the "answer" depends more on the resolution of leadership to stay on strategy and to assure organizational alignment and less on the tangible elements.

Providing the inspiration: It is critical for business leaders to provide motivation/inspiration to their team. Kaplan uses the word "motivation" and Healy (in his blog) uses the word "inspiration." Motivation is limited to reward and inspiration is linked to deeper purpose which may provoke greater engagement for a longer period.

Strategy as a continuous process: Strategy development needs to be embraced. It is very similar to game plan. The same game plan does not necessarily apply to every game a team play. The team must have the ability to adapt to changing environments, different competitors, etc. Leadership must recognize the issues such as change management, cultural change and global workforce.

5.3 The Balanced Scorecard Concept

The Balanced Scorecard Concept (BSC) was created by Robert S. Kaplan and David P. Norton in 1992 with a simple premise that measurement motivates and the BSC locates strategy in the middle of management processes, allowing organizations to implement strategies rapidly and reliably.

As identified earlier, there are various factors that make it difficult to implement the strategy today. As domestic competition in some industries and global competition in most continues to accelerate, with frequently changing technology and the workforce is more diverse and mobile than ever before, these elements have made the strategy implementation even more difficult than in the past.

The industrial age has been replaced with the knowledge age with transformational effects on the workplace and the economy. The shift from tangible assets such as plant and equipment and other properties to intangible assets such as intellectual property, people and brands are hard to understate in today's economy. Much of the market evaluation in today's economy is based on intangible assets. For example, Apple's physical assets are minor compared to their brand and intellectual properties.

While the business world continues to evolve, management systems have not kept up. Most management systems and the measurement systems were designed to meet the needs of a stable and incrementally changing world, but they do not meet the need of today's dynamic economy. Businesses are good at measuring tangible assets, for example, business leaders can depreciate a piece of equipment for eight years and the book value may be closely related to the market value, but they cannot keep-up with intangible assets. For example, where do they find the brand equity line?

The BSC will help the business leaders to measure the strategy and the intangible assets in the intangible dominated globally competitive market. It is very important for every business to develop their strategy and measure the execution impact on business. Some of the intangible assets are skills and knowledge of workforce, business core competency, the information technology available inside and outside the business, and the competitive environment that encourages innovation and products/services development. All of these assets support the development of value for the business, but the question for leadership is which one and how? Obtaining the answer of these questions is the essence of defining the strategy outcomes which will help the leaders in identifying the assets and activities required to achieve the strategy.

Some of the key intangible assets identified in the BSC are:

- *Indirect asset value*: examples include technology and knowledge. These assets generally do not have frequent impact on tangible results like revenue and profit. For example, some of those assets are workforce education and training.
- *Level of asset value*: the value of each intangible varies with time and application, for example, strategy development versus tactical planning. It also varies from a product versus service providing business.
- *Potential of tangible asset*: raw material value is based on the value of the end product for the customer. For example, a hammer is used by a construction contractor in the home building versus a physician is using one in the surgery room. Such tangible asset's potential value does not become real until it is transferred into tangible end product to customer.
- *Grouping intangible assets*: rarely intangible assets provide tangible values individually. These assets have to be grouped to create value. For example, new advertising strategy might require new information, a new software system and may be new employees' incentive program to make the advertising successful.

The BSC is based on simple expectations:

- The created value should be consistent with the mission and supporting the organization goals.
- Defined strategy should be using unique organizational approach to create value.

Strategy-focused organizations are generally able to break free of the traditional measurement and management systems and build management system-based strategy. They are able to succeed where so many others fail because they understand the concept of cause-and-effect linkages of the strategy. They have a better understanding of leading indicators of strategic change and generally able to motivate their organizations to focus on the strategy.

Breakthrough results do not happen by accidents. They are the results of a clear strategy, execution and leadership. To drive change, leadership must develop a case for change and a vision and strategy for where they want to drive the organization. They must create accountability and ensure that the entire leadership team is aligned. They must define the "road map" toward becoming a strategy-focused organization, as presented in Figure 5.6. This type of organization is eventually linked to shareholder value.

A strategy-focused organization using the BSC can take the corporate strategy and translate it into terms that the organization can understand and act upon (Figure 5.7). This process helps the organization to determine key objectives, measures, targets and initiatives to drive the strategy. The enterprise excellence planning and structural relationship concept is presented in Chapter 1. Once a Balanced Scorecard is developed at the corporate level, it can also be created at the operating and support levels. This allows each area of the company to understand how they contribute to the strategy.

While strategy may be formulated at the top executive level, it has to be executed at all levels in the organization. Communication and education are, therefore, most critical to executing strategy. Aligning incentives and personal objectives are also critical for success.

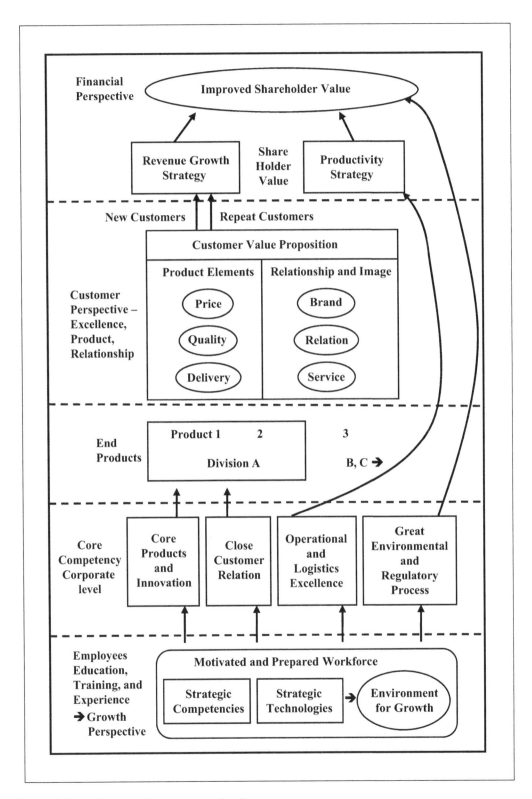

Figure 5.6   **Strategy-focused organization**

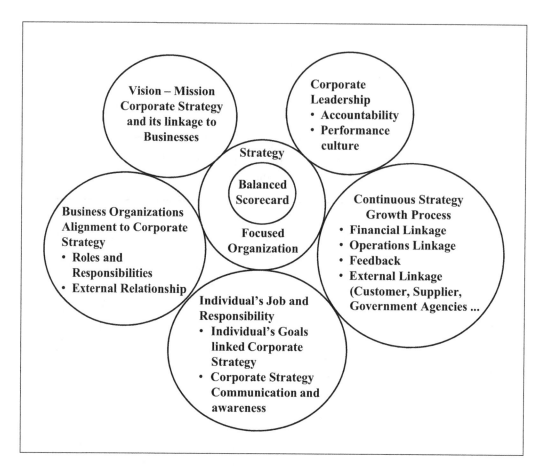

Figure 5.7   Strategic linkages in growth strategy

5.4   Measurement of the Executed Strategy

Properly executed growth strategy leads to more business, but how many enterprises effectively measure their efforts? Not as many as one would think. Most enterprises struggle to measure the impact of their growth strategy to see if it spurs growth. Often, this is because they are not sure what to be measuring and what should be the expectations for success. Almost anything can be measured, although not all metrics will provide the necessary information. Therefore, it is important to search the literature before setting up a measuring system.

Kaplan and Norton (1992) introduced the concept of Balanced Scorecard (BS). They began with the premise that an exclusive reliance on financial measures in the leadership system. At the same time, these financial indicators are lagging indicators that are reporting on the outcomes from the past activities. Porter (1992) and AICPA (1994) reported that exclusive reliance on financial indicators could promote behavior that sacrifices long-term value creation for short-term performance. The BSC approach retained measures of financial performance that are based on lagging outcome indicators, but also supplemented those measures with the lead indicators, of future financial performance.

The limitations of managing solely on the financial measures have been known since the late twentieth century. Non-financial measurements were added on ad hoc basis as more like a checklist of measures for business leaders to keep track of and improve the comprehensive system. Kaplan and Norton (1993), linked the measurement system with the strategy as well as with the cause-and-effect that described the hypotheses of the strategy, Kaplan and Norton (1996a). The tighter connection between the measurement system and the strategy elevated the role for non-financial measures from an operational checklist to a comprehensive system for strategy execution, Kaplan and Norton (1996b).

The industrial-age competitive advantages of the nineteenth century and much of the twentieth century businesses were achieved through their investment and management of tangible assets such as facility, equipment and inventory (Chandler, 1990). In tangible assets dominated economy, financial measurements were adequate to support the growth strategy. Income statements could capture the expenses associated with the use of these tangible assets to produce revenues and profits, but by the end of the twentieth century, intangible assets became the major source for competitive advantage. In 1982, tangible assets book values represented 62 percent of industrial organizations' market values; in 1992, the ratio dropped to 38 percent (Blair, 1995). By the end of the twentieth century, the book value of tangible assets accounted for less than 20 percent of companies' market values (Webber, 2000, quoting research by Baruch Lev).

Commonly identified intangible assets are innovative products and services, supplier/manufacturer/customer relationship, responsive and high-quality processes, knowledge and skills of the workforce, the information technology that supports the workforce and links the business to its suppliers and customers, supports the continuous improvement and problem-solving activities, and maintains the organizational environment that encourages innovation. All of these assets support the product/service throughput, but businesses were unable to adequately measure their intangible assets. Incomplete or insufficient information from management publications indicated that many companies could not implement their new strategies in this environment (Charan and Colvin, 1999). They could not manage what they could not explain or measure. Tangible assets are still critical in financial statements, but strategies for creating value have been shifted from managing tangible assets to knowledge-based strategies that create and deploy an organization's intangible assets.

Kaplan and Norton (2001) developed the Balanced Scorecard model for organizing strategic objectives into four perspectives: financial, customer, internal business processes, and learning and growth. They developed the framework for describing and implementing strategy. They also believe that their model would be useful along with the traditional framework for income statement, balance sheet and statement of cash flows for financial planning and reporting. Kaplan and Norton (2004) have created a new tool – the "strategy map" – that enables companies to describe the links between intangible assets and value creation. They argue that the most critical aspect of strategy – implementing it in a way that ensures sustained value creation – depends on managing four key internal processes: operations, customer relationships, innovation, and regulatory and social processes. Kaplan and Norton (2008) initiatives are linked to strategy maps and Balanced Scorecards. They are also integrating operational tools such as process dashboards, rolling forecasts, and activity-based costing in their strategy execution. All of these perspectives are analyzed and discussed in the enterprise excellence model developed in this book along with some additional specifics including the following:

- Financial perspective is in the key financial statements such as P&L Statement, Balance Sheet, Cash flow and Financial Ratios.

- Internal perspective includes variety of topics including enterprise transformation, mobility and social networks, social alliances and people leadership.
- Learning and growth perspective: core competency provides competitive advantage which supports the development of growth strategy. Customer perspective is one of the major elements in core competency where customer needs and wants must be supported through the core competency. The concept is not only to retains the customers, but also creates customer growth through delivering quality product/service, on time and at competitive prices to meet or exceed customer needs.
- Enterprise growth strategy and the risk management plan must be developed concurrently; and developed strategic plan would not achieve their goals without execution. In today's rapidly changing and increasingly competitive world, achieving sustained success depends on having a solid strategy including risk planning and aligning on organization's decisions, effort and resources to execute that strategy.

Most of the intangible assets impact the business cycle time and the value analysis of these assets is presented below:

Value analysis of intangible assets: In today's economy, businesses have more intangible assets than tangible assets and it is not possible to place these assets in company's balance sheet. Several elements would prevent valuation of intangible assets on balance sheet:

- The value achieved from intangible assets is indirect. For example, information technology (IT) seldom has a direct impact on revenue and profit. Improvements in IT affect financial outcomes through chains of cause-and-effect relationships involving a few intermediate steps. Consider the linkages in the service management area:
  - Investments in IT lead to improvements in service quality;
  - Better service quality leads to higher customer satisfaction;
  - Higher customer satisfaction leads to increased customer loyalty;
  - Increased customer loyalty generates increased revenues and margins; and
  - This will also reduce the *business cycle time*.
  (*Business cycle time:* is defined as the time period between the clock starts – when the customer order is recorded in the system, the product/service is delivered to the customer and the clock stops once the customer makes the payment.)

The above-described relationship is complex for intangible assets and it is difficult, if not impossible, to calculate the financial value on these assets, much less to measure period-to-period changes in their financial values.

- The value of intangible assets depends critically on organizational structure and the business strategy. These values are almost impossible to separate from the organizational processes that transform intangibles into customer and financial outcomes. Generally, intangible assets must be bundled with other intangible and tangible assets to create value. For example, a growth strategy could require new knowledge about customers, new training for marketing employees, new database, new information systems, and a new organization structure. Investing in just one of these capabilities, or in all of them, but any one of these intangibles could cause the growth strategy to fail. The value does not reside in any individual intangible asset. It arises from creating the entire set of assets along with the strategy that links them together. The value-creation process is complex, and their resultant impact will be visible in reducing the business cycle time.

- Some suggest that businesses should follow the same cost-based convention for their intangible assets — capitalize and subsequently amortize the expenditure on conducting research and development, purchasing and developing databases, employees training and development, etc. that creates market growth. But such costs are not good approximations of the realizable value created through investing in these intangible assets. Intangible assets can create value for businesses, but does not imply that they have separable market values. Many internal business processes are linked, such as design of product/service, and production to delivery and service, are required to transform the potential value of intangible assets into products and services that have tangible value.

The above presented points clearly conclude that intangibles are linked and very difficult to measure financially, but they impact the business cycle time. Therefore, *business cycle time* is another measure along with the financial measures that should be used in the strategy execution measurements.

5.5 Strategy Derailment and Failure

A good strategy is not enough; there are several other factors that may derail strategy. The University of Michigan conducted a recent study to the factors that may derail strategy (Welbourne, 2005). These factors will help leaders to improve their strategy execution. The statistics presented in Table 5.3 below are based on a sample of over 4,000 short surveys with the goal to creating a dialogue around the leaders and helping these leaders to continually learn and bring value to their organizations.

Technology did not receive high score as a "derailing" element, but for any Chief Information Officer (CIO), the company's past, culture and leadership team are in the top factors that get in the way of strategy execution. Along with the other leaders in the business, the CIO's office has a role to play in making sure their teams do not get in the way of execution.

Firms offer many different value-creation strategies to achieve marketplace success. Some of those are:

- Some companies might have differentiating product/service with others like Lexus.

Table 5.3 Strategy execution survey statistics

Percent of leaders who agreed that these issues were problems in executing strategy:

- 35% Company's past and habits
- 39% Economic climate or budget
- 23% Company culture
- 20% Way the employees work together
- 18% Senior leadership team
- 14% Customers
- 13% CEO/President or lack of confidence
- 11% Technology
- 9% Middle management
- 7% Reputation, Human Resources Management of employees

- Some companies might be offering outstanding customer service like Nordstrom.
- Some companies might be positioning themselves as the low-price leader like Southwest Airline and Wal-Mart.
- Some companies might be leveraging individualized customer service like Dell computer.

This concept is presented in Chapters 1 and 2. Company's business strategy defines their firm's intent and articulating a good strategy is only the beginning. Its execution determines whether the firm can turn good intentions into revenue and profit growth. Glatstein (2007) suggests four primary reasons for strategies do not reach to full potential:

1. *The strategy fails to recognize the limitations of the existing organization*: marketplace strategy makes great demands on the organization's capabilities and resources. While some organizations can certainly transform their capabilities over time, but there is a limit to how far and how fast it can transform. Recognizing these capabilities before crafting a new direction is essential to these firms' success.
2. *Employees do not know how the strategy applies to their daily work*: most firms do not communicate strategy broadly or effectively to their employees. For example, if a company's strategy is to offer the lowest cost products, what does that really mean? What does it mean to their sales associates who are directly meeting customers, to their customer service representative at the service center and their marketing leadership in corporate office? If company employees do not know how the go-to-market strategy affects their daily work, they are not likely to implement it properly.
3. *The organization's business systems or processes cannot support the strategy*: it is difficult to implement a new strategy without changing the way the organization works. It is critical to ask the question, does the workflow across the various departments of the business and divisions support their marketplace strategy? Can business systems and tools meet the demands of the strategic vision? Executing a new strategy with old capabilities is a recipe for disaster.
4. *Performance metrics and rewards are not aligned with the strategy*: is the organization leadership communicating that it wants to be a service leader, but also rewards its customer service representative for keeping calls short? Or are the organization leaders creating measurement tools that make employees feel good about their performance, but do not really measure the company's key success factors. Metrics and rewards must tie as a package to employee behaviors and this concept will support the company's strategic vision.

Reilly (2007) points out that only 3 percent of company executives are very successful at executing corporate strategies, while the majority (approximately 62 percent) admit that their organizations are moderately successful or worse at strategy execution. The American Management Association (AMA) also found that executives and managers are trained to plan strategies, but believe they often fall short in execution due to a lack of skills and the existence of a process to facilitate implementation of plans.

Significant efforts are invested in Chapters 1–5 to present and discuss the enterprise excellence process through execution and measurement. Chapter 1 – development of the enterprise excellence model, Chapters 2 and 3 – concurrent development of the enterprise growth strategy and risk management, Chapter 4 – any needed enterprise transformation before the strategy execution and measurement, which is Chapter 5. Alignment concept is presented in Chapter 5, and the alignment practices is one of the most commonly used strategy execution methods. Some of the alignment approaches are:

- aligning strategy with corporate vision and mission statements;
- aligning corporate goals with strategy;
- aligning business units' goals with corporate goals;
- aligning business units with corporate strategy.

Higher-performing organizations are considerably more likely than other organizations to use certain alignment strategies. Specifically, higher performers are more likely to align organizational goals with strategy and to align incentive rewards and recognition with strategy.

Leadership practices also influence strategy execution and the concept is presented in Chapter 5. Organizations need to build "execution-focused leadership capabilities" and should use the concept of succession planning to develop leaders who are good at strategy execution. However, higher-performing organizations use the practices to a higher degree than their lower-performing counterparts.

An AMA survey discovered that organizations have the same CEO for over five years are better at strategy execution than organizations with less seasoned leaders. It appears that stable leadership is linked to strategy execution. This is an important finding at a time when CEOs' "change rates" are record high. Another interpretation of the same data could be that leaders who are good at execution are more likely to retain the top job over long periods of time.

Of course, every organization has different execution challenges. However, if the organization masters certain basics such as clarity, leadership, alignment, adoptability and resources can go a long way toward enabling businesses to turn their best strategic plans into organizational successes.

5.6   Enterprise Excellence Model Summary: Chapters 1–5

Enterprise excellence (EE) process is discussed in Chapters 1 through 5 in this book and as stated in the first chapter, "The Enterprise Excellence (EE) philosophy is a holistic approach for leading an enterprise to total excellence by focusing on the needs of the customer ..." and how to achieve the EE; and key elements to achieve the EE:

- complete customer satisfaction;
- minimum cycle time;
- minimum resources consumed;
- sustainable competitive advantage.

Therefore, the EE model was developed in the first chapter as presented in Figure 1.3. In order to completely satisfy customer, businesses must meet or exceed customer needs, and at the same time businesses will improve their revenue and profitability while minimizing the resources consumed. Business cycle time clock starts once the customer order is booked in the system and the clock does not stop until the product is delivered to the customer and the payment is received from the customer. This is defined as business cycle time. Once businesses reduce their cycle time, they are going to improve their cash flow. If a business can achieve all of this at a sustainable basis then the business is achieving their enterprise excellence, or achieving the EE through the following:

- supporting the markets and products growth;
- acquiring new or expand business;
- improving margin;
- increasing revenue and profitability;

- reducing business cycle time.

The developed EE model (Figure 1.3) would guide the businesses to achieve the EE as they follow the model. Therefore, the key elements in the model are listed below with the assigned chapter for details:

- Enterprise Growth Strategy (EGS): covered in Chapter 2.
- Enterprise Risk Management (ERM): covered in Chapter 3.
- Enterprise Transformation (ET): covered in Chapter 4.
- Enterprise Execution and Measurement: covered in Chapter 5.

Business executives have to develop EGS and ERM simultaneously to create a balance between growth strategy and risk management to achieve their EE.

5.6.1   ENTERPRISE GROWTH STRATEGY – CHAPTER 2

There are several questions business executives have to answer during the growth strategy development process such as:

- What must enterprise do to grow?
- What product, market, and/or service do they need to grow?

And the key sub-elements to support the EGS are:

- Business Vision and Mission.
- Innovative Growth Ideas.
- Market Growth Strategy.
- Core Competency.

Visioning is a practical process of business leadership whose responsibilities and authorities stems from the facilitation of strategic conversations among stakeholders and the reflexive engagement of business leaders (Finkelstein et al., 2008). Visioning works best when grounded in the knowledge and understanding of existing leadership teams. Visioning also works because it stimulates reflexivity, opening up the conversational space needed to challenge existing assumptions and introduce fresh possibilities.

A *mission* statement is a statement of the purpose of a company, organization or person, its reason for existing. The mission statement should guide the actions of the organization, spell out its overall goal, provide a path, and guide decision-making. It provides "the framework or context within which the company's strategies are formulated." It's like a goal for what the company wants to do for the world (Hill and Jones, 2008).

An enterprise that offers higher-quality, lower- or competitive-price products (goods and/or services) over a sustained period of time is an "*innovative enterprise.*" The objective of the business enterprise is to offer competitive products that customers want or need at prices that they are willing or able to pay. Therefore, the innovative enterprise is the one that generates the higher-quality, lower- or competitive-price products that provide better than the industry average profit margins, as well as give households with employment incomes and with enough consumer choice on product markets.

Innovation is defined as the act which endows resources with a new capacity to create wealth (Drucker, 1985). While Lieberman and Montgomery (1988) suggest that innovative firms enter the market first will be able to develop a stronger base for building competitive advantage. Therefore, innovation is the basis of wealth creation, and by implication the future success of firms is driven through innovation.

All businesses are under increasing pressure to deliver effective solutions with fewer resources that will produce results over shorter time frames. The *market growth strategy* team can help business executives, and their support team members facing today's challenges through providing processes, guidance, solution and tools that will support the planning, designing, and implementing the market growth strategy. The risk element increases as businesses move further away from known markets and existing products. Thus, new products and new markets typically create greater risk of penetration than the existing products in present markets.

Core competencies can represent a set of tacit and collective knowledge which is developed through learning processes and which provides the enterprise with particular strengths and superior value relative to other enterprises. They are source of innovation, customer benefits and sustainable competitive advantage (Lei et al., 1996). Espinoza et al. (2011) offer insights regarding the core leadership competencies in leading the workforce. They state that millennials are making its significance in the organizational agenda wherein US Bureau of Labor Statistics reveals that millennials constitute almost 25 percent of the workforce in the US. Espinoza et al. (2011) also mentioned that an efficient business leaders should start with the millennials' experience and suspend their own bias. A proactive reaction to perceived millennial orientations and millennial intrinsic values are core competencies that effective business leaders need to master and cites several required leadership competencies which include motivating, directing, and engaging.

5.6.2 ENTERPRISE RISK MANAGEMENT – CHAPTER 3

Business leaders expose the enterprises to risk because they believe that they can exploit these risks to their advantage and generate value to the enterprises. This may be one of the reasons why firms embark into emerging markets that have significant political and economic risk and into technologies especially during the latter part of twentieth century and in the twenty-first century where ground rules and information are changing very rapidly. History validates the concept where auto companies like Ford and General Motors in the 1930s and 1940s, computer hardware companies like IBM in the 1950s and 1960s and Dell in 1990s, software companies like Microsoft and Intel in the 1980s and 1990s and now companies like Google and Facebook in the twenty-first century. These companies have achieved their success by seeking the risk and not avoiding it.

Risk, for lack of a better word, is good. Without it, there would be no successful businesses. Or, rather, there would only be successful business, as being successful would be so easy that any start-up would have an idyllic path to quarterly revenue bonanzas. Risk is vital to the business world so that those organizations that are able to overcome their challenges can show the rest how it is done (Wade, 2010).

According to the Corporate Treasurers Council of the Association for Financial Professionals (AFP 2006), there is an increasing focus on risk management at the highest levels within organizations and it has been used as the catalyst for broad financial transformation initiatives. Jeff Glenzer, Executive Director of the Corporate Treasurers Council of the AFP, said: "There is an increasing dialogue and accountability at the executive management and board levels for enterprise risk management, and treasury's role has grown in the process." There is a growing movement toward enterprise risk management (ERM) in organizations. The statistics are as follows:

- 25 percent are currently managing an ERM program.
- 30 percent are planning to launch an ERM initiative within the next two years.

Approximately three-quarters of organizations conduct risk management with the objective of reducing the variability of earnings and/or cash flow.

Enterprise Risk Management (ERM) is an emerging model at companies and organizations where the management of risks is integrated and coordinated across the organization as a whole. ERM takes a holistic approach to risk management – moving from a fragmented methodology to integrated and broadly focused. ERM expands the process to include not just risks associated with unintended losses, but also financial, strategic, operational, and other risks.

The executive leadership also has the responsibility to clearly use, and share and communicate risk information in a common risk language throughout the organization (CAS, 2003; COSO, 2004; Aabo et al., 2005; Beasley and Frigo, 2007; Shenkir and Walker, 2007; Frigo, 2008; IIF, 2009; Rochette, 2009; ISO, 2009a and 2009b; Frigo and Anderson, 2009; Lai and Samad, 2010; Abrahim et al., 2013; Deloitte, 2012; IRM, 2012; Zurich and HBRAS, 2012). Organizations must provide continuing education opportunities to employees (Lam, 2001; Lam and Associates, 2008).

A general argument gaining momentum in the literature is that the implementation of an ERM system will improve firm performance (Barton et al., 2002; Lam, 2003; Stulz, 1996 and 2003; COSO, 2004; Nocco and Stulz, 2006). Even in the health-care industry, the company's (CAREMARK International Inc.) board of directors recognized that ERM is the process by which the board of directors and the business executives can define the firm's strategies and objectives so as to strike an optimal balance between growth and return goals and related risks (Bainbridge, 2009). It encompasses determining an appetite for risk consistent with the interests of the firm's equity owners and identifying, preparing for, and responding to, risks.

Various enterprise related risk topics are discussed such as why ERM is important, how ERM can be achieved through strategic risk management (SRM) and holistic risk management (HRM), and integrated risk management (IRM). Some other risk areas have also been discussed including equality risk, political risk, Customs risk, ethical risk and product risk. Literature search and the above-listed topics clearly validate that the enterprise risk must be investigated, analyzed and then develop a management strategy along with the enterprise growth strategy. A few supporting topics have been discussed including characteristic forces and quantifying risk, and some risk management guidelines have also been provided.

5.6.3   ENTERPRISE TRANSFORMATION – CHAPTER 4

There is always some direct and/or indirect impact of improving/breakthroughs knowledge in science and technology on every product, service and process. For example, innovation of new products and better processing equipment due to advancement in science and technology, people would need learning and training in these science and technology areas to be more productive. Therefore, some transformation activities are always required before executing the developed strategy.

Business executives would need to evaluate their challenges from technical, behavioral and social perspectives. Enterprise transformation must yield both understanding of fundamental change and the methods and tools that can make change possible. Business executives would also need to ask multiple questions on the problem of change – what drives it, what enables it, and what elements facilitate and hinder its success. Rouse (2005) identifies four main drivers of transformation:

1. New market and/or technology opportunities.
2. Anticipated failure due to market and/or threats.
3. Other players' (for example, competitors) transformation initiatives.
4. Crises resulting from declining market performance (revenue and profitability), cash flow problems, etc.

Transformation is a kind of prerequisite before strategy execution. Transformation boundaries are very flexible and would vary from business to business. Therefore, a constantly transforming enterprise is always better equipped to handle the demands of customer needs and supply the satisfactory products. The approach to transformation is dependent on organizational culture, maturity, available resources and also the organization's appetite for change. Transformation is of higher importance to small enterprises which survive mostly by providing customer services to products produced by larger enterprises. A small enterprise has to ensure that it is constantly updated about the technological breakthroughs that have been established by larger enterprises so that they can make consistent progress in the ever-competitive market.

Aspara et al. (2013) have identified three specific types of inter-organizational cognitions which may require some special attention in developing and executing the transformation process: Whole corporate business model, Reputational ranking and boundary beliefs. Aspara et al. (2013) conducted the case study of Nokia's corporate business model transformation and discussing some results.

Key steps of enterprise transformation are discussed in Chapter 4 (e.g., enterprise assessment process, elements of enterprise transformation – why and how it happens, mobility and social networks in enterprise transformation, and social alliances and transformation). Some specific areas transformation requirements are discussed (e.g., financial transformation, workforce transformation, and safety and security transformation). Four transformation case studies are also presented and these all are different types. Three transformation case studies are about large corporation: corporation, division of a corporation and the operations portion of a division; and the fourth transformation case study is about a small business.

5.6.4   STRATEGY EXECUTION AND MEASUREMENT – CHAPTER 5

The developed strategy must be executed to achieve the strategy goals. These goals must be measured to check whether the defined goals are attained or not. If the goals are achieved then it is considered that the enterprise is achieving its excellence. Chapter 5 is discussing how the developed strategy must be executed and what elements should be measured during and after executing the strategy.

Several topics are discussed about strategy execution, but it is critical to align resources (e.g., people, culture, skill, etc.), organizational behavior (e.g., customer focus, leadership behavior, performance management, etc.) and strategy relation to major domains (e.g., focus, operation, information, etc.). Strategy execution must be disciplined, led by the business leader and must be the organization's culture. Key measurement elements are discussed in this chapter (Chapter 5) and these elements are sustained growth in revenue and profitability, and reduction in business cycle time. This summarizes the enterprise excellence approach discussed in this book.

6

Enterprise Excellence Case Studies

From growth strategy development through transformation are the essential phases of enterprise excellence planning while enterprise risk analysis and planning must be concurrent to the growth strategy development. Without enterprise risk management, there would be no successful enterprise excellence planning. Or, rather, there would only be successful business, as being successful would be so easy that any start-up would have an idyllic path to quarterly revenue bonanzas. Risk is vital to the business world so that those organizations that are able to overcome their challenges can show the rest how it is done (Wade, 2010).

In order to achieve the enterprise excellence, growth strategy has to be executed and the measurement system must validate that the strategy goals are achieved. Therefore, strategy execution and measurement are the main connecting links between aspiration and results to achieve the enterprise excellence. In today's rapidly changing and increasingly competitive world, achieving sustained success depends on having a solid strategy and aligning on organization's decisions, effort and resources to execute that strategy. Thus execution is the major job of a leader. Bottom line results of any growth strategy execution are measured in financial terms: growth in revenue and profitability, and reduction in business cycle time. Whenever there is a discussion about an enterprise achieving its excellence, the elements listed in Figure 1.3 (discussed in Chapters 2–5) should be evaluated asking the following questions (Kumar, 2014):

- What was the business vision and mission in the last several years and how it was evolved with time and market needs? This period could be 5–20 years depending on the business type, for example, in aerospace industry could easily be 15–20 years.
- How product innovations and core competencies supported the enterprise growth strategy while managing the enterprise risk in achieving and sustaining the enterprise excellence?

Every product will have a life cycle with an infant period, growth period and then the maturity/decline period (Figure 1.1). This product curve is also known as "S" curve. Tarde (1903) defined the "S" process as the innovation-decision process. Once innovation occurs then the innovations generally spread from the innovator to other individuals and groups in the organization. The S-curve maps growth of revenue or productivity against time. In the early stage of a particular innovation, growth is relatively slow as the new product establishes itself. At some point customers begin to demand and the product growth increases more rapidly. New incremental innovations or changes to the product allow growth to continue. Towards the end of its life cycle growth slows and may even begin to decline. In the later stages, no amount of new investment in that product will yield a normal rate of return.

Aerospace products case studies are discussed in this chapter and demonstrate how these enterprises achieve their excellence and build sustainable competitive advantage:

- Two commercial airplanes manufacturing companies: Boeing and Airbus.
- Three aerospace manufacturing companies: United Technologies Corporation (UTC), General Electric Company (GE) and Rolls-Royce Holdings, Plc. (RR).

Therefore, the following sections are presented in this chapter:

6.1 Case Study of Two Commercial Airplane Businesses

Business cases of two aerospace companies (Boeing and Airbus) are presented in relation to some of the elements of the enterprise excellence (Figure 1.3) and their impact in achieving the excellence and sustaining the competitive advantage. Two questions to evaluate the EE model elements are written in general format in the beginning of this chapter, but now these questions have to be rewritten specifically for these companies which are going to be discussed in relation to their business strategies (Kumar, 2014).

- What was the business vision and mission during 1950s and 1960s (specifically for the Boeing, since Airbus was not established until 1970) and how was it evolved with time and market needs during the latter part of the twentieth century and now in the twenty-first century?
- How did commercial airplane products' innovation and core competencies in these two companies support the enterprise growth strategy while managing the enterprise risk in achieving the excellence and sustaining the competitive advantage?

Before discussing the two companies (Airbus and Boeing), it is important to provide their brief background. Both the companies are in aerospace industry where Airbus is primarily in commercial aircraft business while Boeing is not only in commercial aircraft business but also in defense and space programs.

Airbus S.A.S. Company Profile
Airbus S.A.S. (commonly known as Airbus) was established in 1970 by a consortium of French and German companies. The Spanish company CASA joined the consortium in 1971, while British Aerospace became a full partner of the consortium in the late 1970s. Airbus is a subsidiary of European Aeronautic Defense and Space Company (EADS) and is one of the largest commercial

aircraft manufacturers in the world. It is headquartered in Blagnac Cedex, France. Airbus manufactures and sells A300/A310, A320, A330/A340, A350 and A380 family aircrafts.
Source: Airbus S.A.S Company Profile, Market line. See www.marketline.com.

Boeing Company Profile
The Boeing Company is the world's leading aerospace company. Boeing manufactures commercial and military aircrafts, electronic and defense systems, missiles, rocket engines, satellite launch vehicles and advanced information and communication systems. The company operates in 145 countries. It is headquartered in Chicago, Illinois. The commercial airplanes division of Boeing manufactures and sells 737, 747, 767, 777 and 787 family aircrafts.
Source: Boeing Company Profile, Market line. See www.marketline.com.

6.1.1 PRODUCTS OF LATE TWENTIETH CENTURY THROUGH THE EARLY TWENTY-FIRST CENTURY

Boeing was the dominant player in the industry before 1970. Since then, Airbus has dynamically entered the market and has managed to compete with Boeing in the commercial aircraft industry. The two rivals have been going head to head in the last several years and more specifically, in total, in the last 16 years (1999–2014), and it looks like that this competitive relationship is not going to change for several years in the future.

The Boeing 747 which was innovated during 1950s and 1960s is a wide-body and four-engine commercial airliner and cargo transport aircraft manufactured by Boeing's Commercial Airplane division. It is among the world's most recognizable aircraft and was the first wide-body ever produced. The 747-400 passenger version can accommodate 416 passengers in a typical three-class layout, 524 passengers in a typical two-class layout, or 660 passengers in a high density one-class configuration (Wikipedia, 2012a). It was first flown commercially in 1970 (Wikipedia, 2010).

McDonnell Douglas followed the Boeing's lead to mitigate their enterprise risk and produced MD-11 commercial aircraft in 1986. MD-11 is a three-engine medium-to-long range, wide-body jet liner, which originally was manufactured by the McDonnell Douglas, but later Boeing bought the company and continued to manufacture the jet liner at Boeing's Commercial Airplanes division. The following analysis of the Boeing activities demonstrates how the company was achieving and sustaining the enterprise excellence:

- To support the market, Boeing innovated and manufactured the product: Boeing 747 jet liner.
- Boeing wanted to mitigate their enterprise risk especially from their competitor's products. One of the strategic risk management approaches Boeing utilized was to buy the competitor's company. Therefore, not only to maintain but also to expand the market share. Boeing purchased the McDonnell Douglas Company and continued to manufacture the MD-11 jet liner to sustain the enterprise excellence. Strategic risk management (SRM) provided the following benefits to Boeing:
  - proved as an excellent tool for thinking systematically about the future and identified opportunities;
  - strategic risks were converted into opportunities;
  - provided better opportunities to utilize capital and reduce its cost;
  - also helped to mitigate/control/eliminate risk, which protected company's reputation;
  - building sustainable competitive advantage.
- By doing so, Boeing improved their margin and gained market share; which

- Provided increased revenue and profitability and less competition, which hopefully should have also reduced their business cycle time.

These points are discussed in Chapters 1–3, which validates the enterprise excellence model while building sustainable competitive advantage.

These jet liners take some 20 years from market research and innovative ideas through designing and manufacturing and then offering the product in the market, which also requires billions of US dollars. This is a very complicated and lengthy process. The innovative idea of 1950s ended up in providing the Boeing 747 for commercial flights in 1970s. Now continue the discussion along the time line. During 1970s, world faced oil embargo from the OPEC (Organization of the Petroleum Exporting Countries) which created a significant energy issue. Four-engine jet liners were one of the major sources of energy consumption in the commercial flights, therefore airlines were looking for more energy-efficient jet liners.

Boeing analyzed and strategically planned the integrated risk management (IRM) approach. Nottingham (1996) defines IRM: "Integrated risk management calls for a framework that allows the organization to identify, anticipate and effectively respond to the multiple events that may affect its ability to fulfill strategies and achieve objective." Boeing was inventing two-engine airplanes to meet the energy requirements, which had to fly over the Atlantic and the Pacific oceans, but two-engine airplanes had never flown before. The newly designed and manufactured airplanes must also be approved by the Federal Aviation Administration (FAA). This shows how Boeing was trying to mitigate their enterprise risk through the IRM.

Boeing leadership utilized their all critical elements of enterprise excellence including business vision and mission, innovative growth ideas, business core competency and market demand along with managing the enterprise risk elements and developed and manufactured Boeing 777 jet liner in 1995. The Boeing 777 is a long-range wide-body twin-engine jet liner developed and manufactured by Boeing's Commercial Airplanes division. It is the world's largest twinjet and has a typical seating capacity for 314 to 451 passengers, with a range of 5,235 to 9,380 nautical miles (9,695 to 17,370 km). Innovative ideas and core competency helps in creating core product(s) which ends-up producing commercial products. Boeing has developed several versions of Boeing 777 in the last 20 years as listed in Table 6.1.

Table 6.1   Boeing 777 models

Boeing Model	Year Introduced in the Market
777-200	1995
777-200 ER (Extended Range)	1997
777-300	1998
777-300 ER (Extended Range)	2004
777-200 LR (Long Range)	2006
777F (Freighter)	2009

If apply the same EE discussion for the 777 models as previously did, the results would be that Boeing did continue to achieve the enterprise excellence and sustaining the competitive advantage as they did for the Boeing 747. The Boeing products 747 and 777 are also satisfying the concept of product *life cycle* curve "S" as presented in Figure 1.1.

Airbus has also developed similar product series called A330 Family: the A330-200, A330-300, A330-200F, ACJ330 and A330 – which cover all market segments with one twin-engine aircraft type. The combination of low operating costs, high efficiency, flexibility and optimized performance. The above discussion of enterprise excellence while sustaining competitive advantage is also applicable to A330 Family.

The airplane's biggest operating cost is fuel and energy conservation is always an issue for all the airlines. Boeing continued to work through innovation to develop material, which is stronger and harder than aluminum, but also lighter than aluminum. With that as a breakthrough in Boeing's research, Boeing came-up with a new product (airplane), which is more fuel-efficient and lighter and stronger than the Boeing 777.

The next generation of twin-engine jet liners is Boeing's 787 (also known as Dreamliner) and A350 from the Airbus. Similar discussion can also be applied to Boeing's 787 and the Airbus A350. These two products have created a fierce competition between Boeing and Airbus. The following statistics validates the status of fierce competition as well as support their continued drive to sustain the enterprise excellence.

The Boeing 787 Dreamliner is a long-range, mid-size wide-body, twin-engine jet liner developed by Boeing Commercial Airplanes. Its seating capacity varies from 210 to 330 passengers. Boeing states that it is the company's most fuel-efficient airliner and the world's first major airliner to use composite materials as the primary material in the construction of its airframe (Norris et al., 2005). The Boeing 787 has been designed to be 20 percent more fuel-efficient than the Boeing 767 it is to replace (Craft, 2011; Schofield, 2012). The Boeing 787 was first introduced in the commercial flight (All Nippon Airways) on October 26, 2011 (Wikipedia, 2013b). By October 2013, the Boeing 787 program had logged 982 orders from 58 customers, with International Lease Finance Corporation (ILFC) having the largest number on order, Boeing 787 (2013).

The Airbus A350 XWB is a family of long-range, twin-engine wide-body jet liners developed by European aircraft manufacturer Airbus. The A350 is the first Airbus with both fuselage and wing structures are primarily made of carbon fiber-reinforced polymer (Wikipedia, 2009). It can carry 250 to 350 passengers in a typical three-class seating layout, or maximum seating of 440 to 550 passengers, depending on variant. The launch customer for the A350 is Qatar Airways, which ordered 80 aircraft of all three variants (Wikipedia, 2013a). The jet liner is scheduled to enter airline service in mid-2014, (Perry, 2012). As of October 2013, Airbus has received orders for 725 aircraft from 37 different customers around the globe (Wikipedia, 2013a). The prototype A350 first flew on June 14, 2013 at Toulouse-Balgnac Airport, France.[1]

There is a tough competition between Airbus and Boeing in the large jet airliner market since the 1990s. This resulted from a series of mergers within the global aerospace industry, with Airbus beginning as a European consortium while the American Boeing bought its former arch-rival, McDonnell Douglas in a 1997 merger. Other manufacturers, such as Lockheed Martin and Convair in the United States and British Aerospace, Dornier and Fokker in Europe, were no longer in a position to compete effectively and withdrew from the market. During the 1990s both companies researched the scope for a new model of very large aircraft, compared to the current largest passenger carrying aircraft then in use, Boeing's 747. Boeing decided the project would not be commercially viable (Wikipedia, 2011b) with Airbus launching it's full-length double-deck aircraft A380 a decade later. The latest modification of Boeing's largest wide-body airliner 747 is Boeing 747-8. Therefore, Boeing's 747-8 and the A380 are placed in direct competition on long-haul routes. Both Boeing 747-8 and Airbus A380 are four-engine jet liners. Fuel economy is one of the most critical issues for airliners in this globally competitive market. The following is a short list of claims from both the companies (Boeing and Airbus).

---

1   See http://www.a350xwbfirstflight.com/

Boeing claims the 747-8I to be over 10 percent lighter per seat and have 11 percent less fuel consumption per passenger, with a trip-cost reduction of 21 percent and a seat-mile cost reduction of more than 6 percent, compared to the A380. The 747-8F's (Freight liner) empty weight is expected to be 80 British tons (88 US tons) lighter and 24 percent lower fuel burnt per ton with 21 percent lower trip costs and 23 percent lower ton-mile costs than the A380F (Wikipedia, 2011a).

Equally, Airbus claims the A380 to have 8 percent less fuel consumption per passenger than the 747-8I and emphasizes the longer range of the A380 while using up to 17 percent shorter runways (Wikipedia, 2012b). The A380-800 also has cabin 478 square meters (5,145.1 sq. ft.) of floor space, 49 percent more than the 747-8. Other commentators noted the lack of engine noise, with the A380 being 50 percent quieter than a 747-400 on takeoff (Saporito, 2010).

Boeing 747 stayed in production for more than 30 years and Boeing has delivered 1475 jet liners through October 31, 2013 and 627 jet liners are still in operation (October 31, 2013) (Wikipedia, 2013e). Boeing is trying to offer a deal to buy back 747-400 and replace with 747–8 at the negotiated price. As of October 2014, confirmed orders for the 747-8 totaled 119, comprising 68 of the freighter version, and 51 of the passenger version (Wikipedia, 2014a). Airbus is also not receiving enough orders for A380 from around the world. Mostly Middle East airlines (e.g. Emirates) are ordering the jet liner. Mostly European and the US airlines are not interested in either Boeing 747-8 or A380. There are 317 firm orders by 18 customers for the passenger version of the Airbus A380-800, of which 152 have been delivered to 13 of those customers as of December 2014[update] (Airbus, 2014). There were originally 27 orders for the freighter version, the A380F, but when this program was "frozen" following production delays, 20 A380F orders were cancelled and the remaining seven were converted to A380-800s (Wikipedia, 2015a). According to the product "S" chart (Figure 1.1) these products are falling at the maturity/decline state of their life cycle even though the manufacturers are spending a great amount of their resources, but they are facing very tough time to sell the product. This again validates the concept of "S" curve.

The new Boeing 777X Series is now in development stage. Boeing expects to bring production in 2017, and start deliveries in 2020. This is a refreshed version of the 777, with a longer, composite wing and a new GE engine. The 777X family includes two jets: the 777-8X and 777-9X. The 8X will offer a range of over 9,300 nautical miles and have room for 350 passengers. The bigger 9X will have a range of over 8,200 nautical miles and have room for 400 on board. Competition does not have any matching product to 777-9X jet liner. Boeing says the 8X will compete with the Airbus A350-1000, while the 9X "is in a class by itself." In Dubai Air show of November 2013, Boeing sold 259 jet liners of family 777X to European and Middle East airlines in one day (Davies, 2013). The discussion of the above information in relation to the enterprise excellence model: Boeing has demonstrated an excellent vision with a defined mission for the market needs; they innovatively are utilizing their resources in developing the enterprise growth product (777X family); they have the core competency to support the innovative product; they are mitigating their enterprise risk throughout the process (planned production in 2017 and start of delivery in 2020) and they are executing their growth strategy to gain the market share (through offering the product in air show in Dubai, November 2013), and increasing their revenue and profitability (through advanced sale of their product). They are also clearly following the "S" curve as presented in Figure 1.1.

It is interesting to note that neither company is ready to walk away from the wide-body, four-engine jet liner and both the companies are offering their products: Boeing's 747-8 and A380 from Airbus. Individuals have differences in risk-taking approaches and the concept of competitive risk between the individuals or the organizations is typically following the same approach. Risk-sensitivity theory predicts that organisms will engage in riskier behavior whenever they are unlikely to achieve their goals through "safe," low-risk means. For example, birds are more likely to forage in predator-prone patches when starving than when satiated (Caraco et al., 1980; Stephens, 1981;

Stephens and Krebs, 1986). These risky strategies may often fail, but this failure is no worse than what would have likely happened to disadvantaged individuals who take no risks. A loss is a loss, dead is dead, and it does not matter to natural selection whether it occurs in adolescence or in a celibate centenarian. A large body of evidence suggests that both non-human and human animals make decisions consistent with risk-sensitivity theory (Stephens and Krebs, 1986; Kacelnik and Bateson, 1996 and 1997; Mishra and Fiddick, 2012).

There is a sound reasoning behind it: 627 (Boeing's 747-400) jet liners are still operational. Leadership of both the companies could be arguing that some percentage of this large number (627) plus some new prospective customers would still be interested in this wide-body, four-engine jet liners. Even the small percentage of operational 627 jet liners would be a significant number of jet liners, therefore, the business leaders of neither company are ready to walk away from the prospective customers. Boeing is trying to mitigate their enterprise risk through the purchase program of older 747-400 and replacing it with new 747-8 at the negotiated price.

Business scenarios of two businesses (Boeing and Airbus) have been discussed covering over 60 years of time period from 1950s through early decades of twenty-first century. Both the companies have their great vision and mission; they have been developing series of innovative products to meet or exceed the market needs, which are also following the life cycle "S" curve; they have been developing their core competency as market and product demands are changing throughout the discussion period; each company is innovatively managing their enterprise risk, and executing their growth strategies in achieving and sustaining the enterprise excellence as well as increasing their revenue and profitability.

6.1.2   MEASUREMENT OF THE AIRPLANE MANUFACTURING COMPANIES EXECUTED STRATEGIES

Strategies of two commercial airplane manufacturers (Boeing and Airbus) are discussed. Boeing's product innovation discussion started from 1950s, but Airbus did not come into market until 1970s. Several products development from both the companies for the past 60 years has been discussed and clearly both the companies are participating in this very competitive global market. As discussed in Chapter 5, the enterprises must execute their strategies to achieve the goals. Therefore, this section will evaluate how well these enterprises have executed their strategies. Three measuring elements are growth in revenue and profitability, and reduction in business cycle time.

6.1.2.1   *Financial information of the airplane manufacturing companies*

High-level financial information about the revenue and profit (also known as net income) is obtained through the quarterly and/or annual financial statements. Investigation revealed that the financial statements of Airbus are not available for public. Only some piece meal information about the balance sheets is available which would not provide data about revenue and profitability. Boeing's last 21 fiscal years (1994–2014) of financial statements are available and the revenue and profitability information is provided in Table 6.2 on the next page. Revenue information could be separated into three categories: Commercial Aircraft, Defense and Space and Others. Total Net Earnings (Profitability) is after taxes and is not separated into three categories as the revenues are separated in their financial statements. Financial data clearly show that the commercial aircraft's revenue went up from US$16.9 billion in FY 1994 to US$59.99 billion in 21 years (in FY 2014) which represents the total growth for the period of 355 percent or the compounded average

Table 6.2   High-level financial data of Boeing Company

Fiscal Year (Ends December 31)	Revenue from Commercial Aircraft	Revenue from Defense and Space	Other Revenue Sources	Total Revenue	Net Total Earnings (after Taxes)	Percent Increase in Commercial Aircraft revenue over previous year	Percent increase in Net Total Earnings over previous year
1994	16,851	5,073	183	22,107	856	Previous year (1993) data not available	Previous year (1993) data not available
1995	13,933	5,582	160	19,675	393	−17	v54
1996	19,916	14,934	603	35,453	1,818	43	363
1997	26,929	18,125	746	45,800	(178)	35	Loss
1998	35,545	19,879	730	56,154	1,120	32	Gain
1999	38,283	18,956	754	57,993	2,309	8	106
2000	30,672	19,912	737	51,321	2,128	−20	−8
2001	34,530	22,483	1,185	58,198	2,827	13	33
2002	27,961	24,583	1,525	54,069	492	−19	−83
2003	21,803	26,622	2,060	50,485	698	−22	42
2004	20,827	30,160	1,470	52,457	1,872	−4	168
2005	22,424	30,483	1,938	54,845	2,572	8	37
2006	28,152	32,082	1,296	61,530	2,215	26	−14
2007	33,303	32,000	1,084	66,387	4,074	18	84
2008	27,980	31,727	1,202	60,909	2,672	−16	−34
2009	33,924	33,535	822	68,281	1,335	21	−50
2010	31,712	31,820	774	64,306	3,307	−7	148
2011	36,135	31,944	656	68,735	4,018	14	21
2012	48,783	32,379	536	81,698	3,900	35	−3
2013	52,981	33,197	445	86,623	4,585	9	18
2014	59,990	30,881	(109)	90,762	5,446	13	19

Note: All revenue and earnings data in are in US$ in millions.
Other revenue resources: Sales of services; notes receivable; sales type leases; and customer and commercial finance.
Information source: Boeing Company's archived financial data.

annual growth of 6.15 percent. The total net earnings (which include all Boeing products) have also grown from US$856 million in FY 1994 to US$5,446 million in FY 2014 which represents the total growth of 636 percent. Therefore, the commercial aircraft products validate the growth strategy and the enterprise excellence model.

6.1.2.2 Business cycle time of the airplane manufacturing companies

Business cycle time is defined in Chapter 5. Intangible assets are the most critical elements in reducing the business cycle time. To start with, customer's order is entered in the ERP system through sales and marketing. The ERP system does the production planning based on the material availability, production processes and equipment's availability and also checks the customer's requested delivery date. At the same time, supply chain process is also very important element in the business cycle time. Supply chain process links suppliers, manufacturer and the customer. Suppliers generally have an access in the ERP system to check the inventory status; so they can deliver the material when the inventory reaches at the minimum ordering level. Suppliers are also paid electronically once they deliver the material and their supply is accepted in the ERP system. Engineering designs are generally maintained in a separate system, but are linked to the ERP system; so that the other business areas such as manufacturing, sales and marketing, and financial would have the product information available to them. ERP system is also used in financial planning and budgeting. Similarly, there are numerous intangible assets including, Internet, innovative products and services, supplier/manufacturer/customer relationship, responsive and high-quality processes, knowledge and skills of the workforce.

Most of the businesses these days have a good percentage of these intangible assets. The impact of intangible assets on business cycle tine is logically validated in Chapter 5 that these intangible assets support the reduction of business cycle time. In the case of Boeing and Airbus, most of this order booking information is not difficult to obtain, but the delivery information could be from mixed orders; the payment financial information is confidential and it is very difficult for others to have it. Therefore, it is assumed that both the companies are utilizing their intangible assets well to meet or exceed customer needs, which would definitely reduce their business cycle time.

6.1.3 CONCLUSION OF TWO ENTERPRISES CASE STUDY: THE AIRPLANE MANUFACTURING COMPANIES

The discussion of over 60 years of information from Boeing and Airbus is validating the EE model (Figure 1.3) in achieving their excellence and sustaining the competitive advantage through the enterprise growth strategy and also managing the enterprise risk with the following conclusions:

- To support the market and product growth, both the companies have been developing series of products to meet or exceed customer needs and supporting the concept of product life cycle curve "S" (Figure 1.1).
- Both the companies have either acquired other companies or developed consortium for expanding their businesses.
- Both the companies have been improving their margin through various elements of the enterprise growth strategy including vision and mission, innovative product growth ideas, core competency and market share.

- Both the companies have been utilizing the various elements of the enterprise risk management, for example, strategic risk management, integrated risk management and competitors risk management.
- Both the companies' executive leadership has been scrutinizing their risk management policies and procedures while continuing to offer new products and services to meet or exceed customer needs as well as achieving and sustaining their enterprise excellence.

These above-listed points clearly demonstrate that these companies have been following the EE model which is presented in Figure 1.3. The financial information presented in Table 6.2 is also concludes that revenue and profitability increases have been through the growth strategy while managing the enterprise risk. It is very difficult to find information about the business cycle time reduction, but both the companies are trying to reduce their business cycles time, which indirectly reflects in their cash flow.

6.2   Case Study of Three Aerospace Manufacturing Companies

Three commercial jet engines manufacturing companies are General Electric Company (GE), Rolls-Royce Holdings (RR) and United Technologies Corporation (UTC). This study is similar to the previous section (Section 6.1) study to continue the validation of the EE model. In this case study, the three aerospace companies, which are presented in relation to some of the elements of the enterprise excellence (Figure 1.3) and their impact in achieving the excellence and sustaining the competitive advantage. Previously listed two questions to evaluate the EE model elements are still valid and are rewritten specifically for these companies which are going to be discussed in relation to their business strategies (Kumar, 2014).

- What was the business vision and mission during 1970s and 1980s (specifically for GE and UTC, since RR came into picture later) and how was it evolved with time and market needs during the latter part of the twentieth century and now in the twenty-first century?
- How did commercial jet engine products' innovation and core competencies in these three companies support the enterprise growth strategy while managing the enterprise risk in achieving the excellence and sustaining the competitive advantage?

Before discussing these three companies (GE, RR and UTC), it is important to provide their brief overview. These three companies are globally in multi-product areas both in commercial and defense programs.

General Electric Company (GE) Profile

GE is an American multinational conglomerate corporation incorporated in New York and headquartered in Fairfield, Connecticut, and was founded in 1892. The company operates as an infrastructure and financial services company worldwide. The company's Power and Water segment offers gas, steam and aero derivative turbines, generators, combined cycle systems, controls, and related services; wind turbines and solar technology; and water treatment services and equipment. It's Oil and Gas segment provides surface and subsea drilling and production systems, equipment for floating production platforms, compressors, turbines, turbo expanders, reactors, industrial power generation and auxiliary equipment. The company's Energy Management segment offers electrical distribution and control products, lighting and power panels, switchgears and circuit breakers; engineering, inspection, mechanical, and emergency services; motors, drives and control technologies; and plant automation, hardware, software and embedded computing systems. Its Aviation segment offers jet engines, turboprop and turbo shaft engines, related replacement parts, and aerospace systems and equipment for military and commercial aircrafts; and maintenance, component repair and overhaul services. The company's Health-care segment provides medical imaging and information technologies, medical diagnostics and patient monitoring systems; and disease research, drug discovery, and remote diagnostic and repair services. Its Transportation segment offers freight and passenger locomotives, diesel engines for rail, marine and stationary power applications; railway signaling and communications systems; underground mining equipment; motorized drive systems; energy storage systems; and information technology solutions. Its Home and Business Solutions segment manufactures home appliances and lighting products. Its GE Capital segment offers commercial loans and leases, fleet management, financial programs, home loans, credit cards, personal loans and other financial services.[2]

Rolls-Royce Holdings plc (RR) Profile

RR is a British multinational public holding company that through its subsidiaries, designs, manufactures and distributes power systems, and is headquartered in City of Westminster, London, United Kingdom and was founded in 1971. The Company together with its subsidiaries, provides integrated power solutions for customers in civil and defense aerospace, marine and energy markets worldwide. It operates in five segments: Civil Aerospace, Defense Aerospace, Marine, Energy, and Power Systems. The Civil Aerospace segment develops, manufactures, markets and sells commercial aero engines, including civil large, small aircraft, and helicopter engines for various sectors of the airliner and corporate jet market, and provides aftermarket services consisting of a suite of managing services for its engines. The Defense Aerospace segment engages in the development, manufacture, marketing and sale of military aero engines for combat jets, helicopters, transporters, trainers, tactical aircraft, unmanned aerial vehicles, and distributed generation systems, as well as offers aftermarket services. The Marine segment is involved in the development, manufacture, marketing and sale of marine-power propulsion systems and aftermarket services. Its products include automation and control, bearings and seals, deck machinery solutions, power electric systems, engines, propulsions, reduction gears, ship design and systems, syncro-lift ship-lifts and transfer systems, and stabilization and maneuvering systems. This segment also integrates technologically complex systems for offshore oil and gas, merchant and naval surface, and submarine vessels. The Energy segment manufactures and sells power systems for the offshore oil and gas industry and electrical power generation, and aftermarket services. Its products include gas engines, gas turbine engines, gas compression, diesel engines, fuel cells, and automation and control systems. The Power Systems segment develops, manufactures, markets and sells reciprocating engines, propulsion systems, and distributed energy systems.[3]

United Technologies Corporation (UTC) Profile

UTC is an American multinational conglomerate headquartered in the United Technologies Building in Hartford, Connecticut and was founded in 1934. The company provides technology products and services to the building systems and aerospace industries worldwide. Its Otis segment designs, manufactures, sells, and installs a range of passenger and freight elevators, escalators and moving walkways; modernization products to upgrade elevators and escalators; and maintenance and repair services. The company's UTC Climate, Controls, and Security segment provides heating, ventilating, air conditioning, and refrigeration solutions, such as controls for residential, commercial, industrial and transportation applications. It also offers electronic security products, including intruder alarms, access control systems, and video surveillance systems; and monitoring, response and security personnel services, as well as designs and manufactures a range of fire safety products comprising specialty hazard detection and fixed suppression products,

---

2   Yahoo Finance. 2015. General Electric Company. February 3, 2015. Available at: http://finance.yahoo.com/q/pr?s=GE+Profile

3   Yahoo Finance. 2015. Rolls-Royce Holdings plc. February 3, 2015. Available at: http://finance.yahoo.com/q/pr?s=RR. L+Profile

portable fire extinguishers, fire detection and life safety systems, and other firefighting equipment. Its Pratt & Whitney (PW) segment supplies aircraft engines for commercial, military, business jet and general aviation markets, as well as provides fleet management services for commercial engines; spare parts; and maintenance, repair and overhaul services. The company's UTC Aerospace Systems segment supplies aerospace products, including electric power generation, management and distribution systems, flight control systems, engine control systems, intelligence, surveillance and reconnaissance systems, engine components, environmental control systems, fire protection and detection systems, propeller systems, aircraft nacelles, and interior, actuation, landing and electronic systems; and aftermarket services. Its Sikorsky segment manufactures military and commercial helicopters, as well as provides aftermarket helicopter and aircraft parts and services.[4]

6.2.1 BUSINESS STRATEGIES AND PRODUCTS DEVELOPMENT DURING LATE TWENTIETH CENTURY THROUGH THE EARLY TWENTY-FIRST CENTURY

In the current structural organization of Pratt & Whitney (PW) is also including two major joint ventures, the Engine Alliance with General Electric Company (GE) which manufactures engines for the Airbus A380, and the International Aero Engines Company with Rolls-Royce, MTU Aero Engines, and the Japanese Aero Engines Corporation which manufactures engines for the Airbus A320 and the McDonnell Douglas MD-90 aircraft (Wikipedia, 2013c).

Back in 1970s and early 1980s, PW was producing two very popular jet engines JT8D and JT9D for the commercial airplanes. The following is a short overview about these two engines:

JT8D engine
PW produced JT8D engine which was a low-pass (0.96 to 1) turbofan engine. It was introduced in February 1963 with the inaugural flight of Boeing 727. JT8D was a modification of the PW's J52 turbojet engine, which powered the US Navy A-6 Intruder attack aircraft (Wikipedia, 2013). There were eight models of the JT8D standard engine family, covering the thrust range from 12,250 to 17,400 pound-force (62 to 77 KN) and power Boeing's 727, 737-100/200 and DC-9 aircraft. More than 14,000 JT8D engines have been produced, totaling more than one-half billion hours of service with more than 350 operators making it the most popular of all low-bypass turbofan engines ever produced (Wikipedia, 2013d).

In response to environmental concerns which began in the 1970s, the company started developing a new version of the engine, the JT8D-200 series. Designed to be quieter, cleaner, more efficient, yet more powerful than earlier models, the -200 Series power-plant was re-engineered with a significantly higher bypass ratio (1.74 to 1) covering the 18,500 to 21,700 pound-force (82 to 97 KN) thrust range and powering the McDonnell Douglas MD-80 series. The JT8D-217 and -219 engine(s) were tested in 2001 and were deemed suitable replacements for the old TF33 engines on military and commercial aircraft as part of the Super 27 re-engineering program. The updated engines offer reduced (Stage-3) noise compliance standards without the need for hush kits, enhanced short field performance, steeper and faster climb rates with roughly a 10 percent reduction in fuel burn for extended range (Wikipedia, 2013d).

JT9D engine
PW's JT9D engine opened a new era in commercial aviation: the high-bypass-ratio engine to power wide-bodied aircraft (Pratt & Whitney, 2014). Since entering service on the Boeing 747 aircraft in 1970, the

---

4   Yahoo Finance. 2015. United Technologies Corporation. February 3, 2015. Available at: http://finance.yahoo.com/q?s=utx

JT9D engine has proven itself to be the workhorse for early 747, 767, A300, A310 and DC-10 aircraft models with more than 3,200 cumulative engines delivered.

The JT9D engine family consists of three distinct series. The JT9D-7 engine covers the 46,300- to 50,000-pound-thrust range, and the JT9D-7Q series has a 53,000 pound thrust rating. Later models, the -7R4 series, cover the 48,000- to 56,000-pound-thrust range. For JT9D-7R4 twinjet installations, the engines are approved for 180-minute ETOPS (Extended-range, Twin-engine Operations) (Pratt & Whitney, 2014).

As stated earlier (Section 6.1.1) that during 1970s, world faced oil embargo from the OPEC (Organization of the Petroleum Exporting Countries), which created a significant energy issue. Most of the oil forecasts during 1970s after oil embargo were stating that the remaining oil reserves in the ground were for 25–35 years, but later studies of 1980s and 1990s proved that the 1970s forecasts were incorrect.

By the way, the previous name of the United Technologies Corporation (UTC) was United Aircraft which changed to UTC in 1975. In 1974 after the oil embargo, Harry Gray joined the United Aircraft as a new CEO (Fernandez, 1983). This was a very tough time for the company. Both the commercial jet engines (JT8D and JT9D) were getting old with issues such as air pollution, noise and energy consumption. After oil embargo, fuel cost shot-up and was continue climbing, and nobody could see an end to it on the horizon. Both the engines needed a major overhaul to meet the environmental requirements as well as energy efficiency, and the estimated cost could be in billions of US dollars, resources and time. The way energy forecasts were in that time period (1970s), the overhauling of both the engines could be very risky strategy. The company also realized that people will still fly for long distances and the airlines would utilize large airplanes to carry these passengers. Therefore, overhauling of the large engine (JT9D) strategically was correct as well as the enterprise risk could also be mitigated. This strategy was requiring less capital and other resources while the remaining capital and resources could be utilized for the remaining business growth. Business diversification either through innovation and/or through merger and acquisition (M&A) is another critical element in business growth strategy to achieve the enterprise excellence while sustaining competitive advantage. Hence, the new CEO developed his strategy of diversification. He pursued a strategy of growth and diversification through overhauling the JT9D engine and acquiring developed businesses. This was also reflecting the company's intent to diversify into numerous high tech fields beyond aerospace (Fernandez, 1983).

The diversification was partially to balance civilian business against any overreliance on military business. UTC became a merger and acquisitions (M&A) focused organization. In 1976, UTC acquired Otis Elevator and in 1979, Carrier Refrigeration and Mostek were acquired (Fernandez, 1983). At one point the military portion of UTC's business, whose sensitivity to "excess profits" and boom/bust demand drove UTC to diversify away from it, actually carried the weight of losses incurred by the commercial M&A side of the business (Fernandez, 1983). Although M&A activity was not new to United Aircraft, the M&A activity of the 1970s and 1980s was higher-stakes and some argue that it was unfocused. Rather than aviation being the central theme of UTC businesses, high tech (of any type) was the new theme to mitigate the enterprise risk. Some Wall Street watchers questioned the true value of M&A at almost any price at that time (Fernandez, 1983). By the way, UTC sold Mostek in 1985 to a French electronics company Thomson (Wikipedia, 2014c).

SNECMA is a French company, which conducted research into the next generation of commercial jet engines, high-pass ratio turbofans in the 20,000 lbs. force (89 KN) thrust class, began in the 1960s (Norris, 1999). They had mostly built military engines until then, were the first company to seek entrance into the market by searching for a partner with commercial experience to design and build an engine in this class. They considered Pratt & Whitney, Rolls-Royce and General Electric Aviation as potential partners, but it was not until after two company executives, Gerhard Neumann from GE and René Ravaud from SNECMA, introduced themselves at the 1971 Paris Air Show that a decision was made. The two companies saw mutual benefit in the collaboration and met several more times, fleshing out the basics of the joint project (Norris, 1999).

Pratt & Whitney dominated the commercial market at that point in time (1970s). GE needed an engine in this market class, and SNECMA had previous experience of working with them, collaborating on the production of the CF6-50 turbofan for the Airbus A300 (Bilien and Matta, 1989). Pratt & Whitney had JT8D engine in this class and was considering for overhauling and upgrading to compete in the same class as the CFM56 as a sole venture, while Rolls-Royce dealt with financial issues that precluded them from starting new projects; this situation caused GE to gain the title of best partner for the program (Bilien and Matta, 1989). But later Pratt & Whitney could not upgrade their JT8D engine due to oil embargo, capital requirements and a major shift in corporate strategy of diversification as mentioned earlier.

The A320 family was developed to compete with the Boeing 737 classics (-300/-400/-500) and the McDonnell Douglas MD-80/90 series, and has since faced challenges from the Boeing 737 next generation (-600/-700/-800/-900) and the Boeing 717 during its two decades in service. As of 2010, the Boeing 737 and the A320 family are facing competition from Embraer's E-195 (to the A318) and the CSeries being developed by Bombardier to the A318/A319 (Maynard, 2008). Wikipedia (2015b) has developed a chart (Figure 6.1) showing that there is a very tough competition between Boeing's model 737 and the Airbus model A320. This chart is based on the deliveries from both the companies (Boeing and Airbus) from 1988 through December 2014. This competition is still valid today (2015) and looks like that it will continue for some time in the future. Chicago-based Boeing is fiercely competing with new models from European rival Airbus Group NV to capture its share of a world jetliner market estimated at $4.8 trillion over the next 20 years (Scott, 2014). "The three jetliner families will account for more than half of Boeing's commercial plane sales over 20 years," said Scott Fancher, senior vice president for airplane development. "What we have in work today really is the future of Boeing Commercial Airplanes," he said (Scott, 2014).

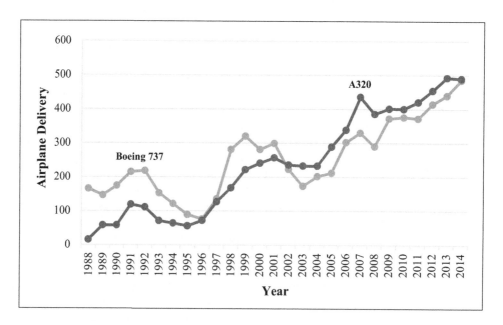

Figure 6.1   Yearly delivery of A320 and Boeing 737 airplanes

Just to look into some of the jet liners delivery statistics: Boeing's 737 aircraft just marked an aviation first: the 8,000th model has rolled off the assembly line, a round-number milestone for the best-selling airplane of all time (Bachman, 2014). Today, however, Airbus is a strong competitor in the market for medium-range, single-aisle aircraft with its A320 family, which made its debut in 1988 and topped 6,000 deliveries in March 2014 – an illustration of how much more quickly airplanes are turned out in recent decades than in the early days of the 737. Boeing builds 42 737s each month and says it will boost output to 47 in 2017 because of strong demand; Airbus is increasing A320 production from 42 to 46 per month by 2016 (Bachman, 2014). Planes ordering statistics is also very interesting: Boeing Co. launched its 737 family of jets in 1964, and since then the company has snagged 12,257 firm orders for the plane. Airbus launched its competitor single-aisle, narrow-body family, the A320, in March 1984 and claims 11,021 firm orders since the A320s launch (Ausick, 2014).

A320neo (new engine option)
Airbus has developed a new version of the A320, called A320neo, for new engine option, based on more efficient engines, at least partly in response to the threat posed by Bombardier Aerospace's development of the CSeries airliner, with which Bombardier hoped to compete directly with Boeing and Airbus for the first time (Wikipedia, 2015b). The choice for new engines include the CFM International LEAP-1A and the Pratt & Whitney PW1100G. Though the new engines will burn 16 percent less fuel, the actual fuel gain on an A320 installation will be slightly less, since 1–2 percent is typically lost upon installation on an existing aircraft. This means an additional range of 950 km (510 nautical miles), or two British tons (4,400 US lbs) of extra payload (Wikipedia, 2015b). After more than 20 years of gap (since JT8D engine went out of production), Pratt & Whitney announced in early June 2013 that PW1100G engine's first flight was successful. Airbus' CEO said to be "comfortable" with the projections of 20 percent lower maintenance cost for the Pratt & Whitney's PW1000G family, compared with engines powering the A320 (Wikipedia, 2015b). Airbus is targeting 2016 for the first delivery and plans to deliver 4,000 A320neo over 15 years. Virgin America became the launch customer with a firm order of 30 A320neo aircraft as a part of a 60 aircraft order on January 17, 2011. In January 2011 IndiGo reached a tentative agreement with Airbus to order 150 A320neo aircraft along with 30 more A320s (Wikipedia, 2015).

CFM International LEAP engine
The CFM International LEAP (formerly called LEAP-X) is a high-bypass turbofan engine. It is currently under development by CFM International, a 50:50 joint venture company between GE Aviation of the United States and SNECMA of France (Wikipedia, 2015c). The LEAP (Leading Edge Aviation Propulsion) incorporates technologies that CFM developed as part of the LEAP56 technology acquisition program, which CFM launched in 2005. The engine was officially launched as "LEAP-X" on July 13, 2008 (Wikipedia, 2015c).

Pratt & Whitney's PW1000G engine family
The Pratt & Whitney PW1000G is a high-bypass geared turbofan engine family, currently selected as the exclusive engine for the Bombardier Cseries, Mitsubishi Regional Jet (MRJ), Embraer's second generation E-Jets and as an option on the Irkut MC-21 and Airbus A320neo. The project was previously known as the Geared Turbofan (GTF), and originally the Advanced Technology Fan Integrator (ATFI) (Wikipedia, 2015d).

Pratt & Whitney first attempted to build a geared turbofan starting around 1998, known as the PW8000. This essentially was an upgrade of the existing Pratt & Whitney PW6000 that replaced the fan section with a gearing system and new single-stage fan. After several years of development the PW8000 essentially disappeared. Soon afterwards the ATFI project appeared, using a PW308 core but with a new gearbox and a single-stage fan. It had its first run on March 17, 2001 (Wikipedia, 2015d).

This led to the Geared Turbofan (GTF) program, which was based around a newly designed core jointly developed with MTU Aero Engines of Germany. The German company provides the high-speed low-pressure turbine and various stages of the high-pressure compressor (Wikipedia, 2015d).

In July 2008, the GTF was renamed the *PW1000G*, the first in a new line of "Pure Power" engines. Pratt & Whitney claims the PW1000G is 10 to 15 percent more fuel-efficient than current engines used on regional jets and single-aisle jets as well as being substantially quieter (Garvey, 2011). PW stopped the production of JT8D (mid-size engine) in 1980s and it took more than 20 years before PW announced the first successful flight of *PW1100G* engine in early June 2013, which is identified earlier. This brings back PW in competition with the joint partnership of GE and SNECMA.

Now continue with UTC's diversifying strategy and some of their major diversifications mile stones are listed below:

- During 1990s: UTC acquired Sundstrand Corporation in 1999, and merged it into UTC's Hamilton Standard unit to form Hamilton Sundstrand.
- During 2000s: UTC acquired several businesses and some of those are:
  - In 2003, UTC entered the fire and security business by purchasing Chubb Security.
  - In 2005, UTC further pursued its stake in the fire and security business by purchasing Kidde. Also in 2005, UTC acquired Boeing's Rocketdyne division, which was merged into the Pratt & Whitney business unit.
  - In November 2008, UTC's Carrier Corporation acquired NORESCO (UTC 10-K 2013; UTC 10-Q 2014Q1) which is one of the nation's largest energy service companies.
- During 2010s: UTC acquired a few businesses and one of the largest one is
  - In July 2012, UTC acquired Goodrich and merged it with Hamilton Sundstrand; the resulting organization is UTC Aerospace Systems.

General Electric Company's participation stayed with the partnership of French company SNECMA to meet the engine requirements for the Boeing 737 series and the Airbus A320 series including A320neo. Literature does not show that Rolls-Royce Holdings, Plc's engine was used either in the Boeing 737 series or the A320 series of Airbus. GE and RR are both large global conglomerate. Their total growth strategies discussion and their execution were beyond the scope of this case study.

6.2.2 MEASUREMENT OF THE AEROSPACE MANUFACTURING COMPANIES EXECUTED STRATEGIES

Strategies of three aerospace manufacturing companies (GE, RR and UTC) are discussed. GE's growth strategy and the enterprise risk management was limited to commercial jet engine for Boeing's 737 family and the family of A320s of Airbus. GE was very fortunate to have a partner (SNECMA) who primarily developed the engine, and at the same time GE had capital and other resources to bring the product in the commercial market. At the same PW's engine (JT8D) was becoming obsolete due to environmental issues (noise and air pollution requirements) and strategically UTC decided not to allocate capital and other resource requirements to overhaul and upgrade the engine.

When SNECMA was looking for a partner for their engine; GE, Rolls-Royce and PW all these three were the possible candidates. But at that time, PW was planning to overhaul and upgrade their own JT8D engine, so they were not interested, which later they decided not to do. RR had some financial issues, so decided not to be considered. GE was the only company left and the business leaders of GE and SNECMA got together and developed the partnership deal.

The critical elements that affected in UTC's growth strategy were: 1970s oil embargo, high tech products limited to aerospace and dependency on defense products which were creating significant variation in company's profit/loss statement. UTC leadership resolved these issues through:

- Diversification in growth strategy through merger and acquisition (M&A) and at the same time mitigating the enterprise risk.
- Continued to upgrade large commercial jet engine JT9D through innovation, core competency and strategically managed the enterprise risk.

Hence, this case study has analyzed and discussed UTC from 1970s through currently (early part of twenty-first century). Several M&A activities and products developments are identified for the company's growth strategy through execution for the past 30-plus years.

As discussed in Chapter 5 that the enterprises must execute their strategies to achieve the goals. Therefore, this section will evaluate how well these enterprises have executed their strategies. Three measuring elements are growth in revenue and profitability, and the reduction in business cycle time.

6.2.2.1   Financial information of the aerospace manufacturing companies

All these aerospace manufacturing companies (GE, RR and UTC) are global companies providing variety of products and services as listed in their overview. These companies (GE, RR and UTC) were not necessarily impacted at the same rate and time by deep recession of 2007–2009, which is visible in their financial information as presented in Tables 6.3, 6.4 and 6.5 respectively. Total strategies of all these companies were not within the scope of this case study. Therefore, it is important to analyze the financial information of these companies in relation to these facts.

General Electric Company's last 11 fiscal years (2004–2014) of financial statements are available, and their revenue and profitability information is provided in Table 6.3. GE's participation in this case study was to provide CFM 56 engine for Boeing's 737 family of airplanes and A320 family of airplanes of Airbus. GE has a French company SNECMA as partner in supplying these engines. As identified in the previous section (6.2.1) that a huge number of these planes (in thousands) have been delivered in the past 35-plus years. There are two engines in each plane and each engine sells for millions of US dollars that means billions of US dollars of revenue for GE and SNECMA. But GE is a very large company and their CFM56 engine business is a small part of the total business. GE and SNECMA are the sole engine providers with no competition since 1980s, therefore GE and SNECMA are doing great as far the CFM56 engine is concerned. Hence, CFM56 engine strategy execution is working very well. There new competition will come from Pratt & Whitney's PW1100G engine, which had its first successful flight in June 2013.

There should be a separate case study to analyze and discuss the total growth strategy of GE and that strategy analysis should be linked with the financial data presented in Table 6.3. Based on the presented revenue and profitability data (Table 6.3), GE was hit by deep recession in fiscal year (FY) 2009 where revenue reduced by 14 percent and profitability dropped by 37 percent year-to-year. GE's revenue has not been recovered to pre-deep recession level even in six years (FY 2014);

profitability has significantly improved, but also has not reached to pre-deep recession level. This would be a great project for the enterprise excellence case study.

Table 6.3   High-level financial data of General Electric Company

Fiscal Year (Ends December 31)	Total Revenue	Net Total Earnings (after Taxes)
2004	152,363	16,593
2005	147,702	16,353
2006	163,391	20,829
2007	173,621	22,154
2008	182,036	17,410
2009	156,730	10,994
2010	150,211	11,644
2011	147,413	14,151
2012	147,359	13,641
2013	146,045	13,057
2014	148,589	15,233

Note: All revenue and earnings data are in US$ in millions.
Information sources:

– General Electric Co., Annual Reports

– See http://www.stock-analysis-on.net/NYSE/Company/General-Electric-Co/Financial-Statement/Income-Statemen

– See http://income-statements.findthecompany.com/7065/General-Electric.

Rolls-Royce Holdings, Plc's last seven fiscal years (2007–2013) of financial statements are available, and their revenue and profitability information is provided in Table 6.4. RR did not participate in supplying engines to Boeing's 737 family of airplanes and A320 family of airplanes of Airbus. RR is also a global large corporation. RR's revenue and profitability information is very interesting. Their business suffered from deep recession in YR 2007, and affected both the revenue and the profit (after taxes income). Their revenue started improving since FY 2008 and showing a continuous

Table 6.4   High-level financial data of Rolls-Royce Holdings, Plc.

Fiscal Year (Ends December 31)	Total Revenue	Net Total Earnings (after Taxes)
2007	7,435	600
2008	9,082	(1,345)
2009	10,414	2,217
2010	11,085	543
2011	11,124	849
2012	12,161	2,335
2013	15,513	1,639

Note: All revenue and earnings data are in millions of British pounds.
Information sources for: Rolls-Royce Group plc Annual reports 2008–2013.

improvement all the way through FY 2013. RR's profitability is presenting a very unusual picture. FY 2007's profit went down with the revenue due to deep recession, which makes sense, but FY 2008's profit went in the negative territory. Some of the reasons could be to bring new products in the market and/or high marketing cost to improve revenue. Their profitability is fluctuating very significantly in FYs 2009–13. RR's financial data are presenting a case of very interesting study. Hence, this would be another global company case study for the enterprise excellence project.

United Technologies Corporation's last 11 fiscal years (2004–2014) of financial statements are available, and their revenue and profitability information is provided in Table 6.5. Originally UTC's division Pratt & Whitney supplied JT8D engine for Boeing's 737-100 and -200 airplanes during 1970s and 1980s. And now it is expected that Pratt & Whitney's PW1100G engine would compete for the next generation of airplanes A320noe of Airbus. UTC adopted the enterprise growth strategy of diversification through merger and acquisition (M&A) as well as upgrading only the large commercial jet engine "JT9D" during 1980s and the mid-size engine in the twenty-first century. This growth strategy was based on the constraints as identified earlier in Section 6.2.1 and a high-level listing of growth strategy execution is also discussed in the same section.

UTC's financial information (Table 6.5) shows that the company suffered deep recession during FY 2009 where revenue and profit both dipped to the lowest level. Data clearly show that the UTC's revenue went up from US$37.4 Billion in FY 2004 to US$65.1 billion in 11 years (in FY 2014) which represents the total growth for the period of 74 percent, or the compounded average annual growth rate of 5.71 percent. The total net earnings have also grown from US$2.67 billion in FY 2004 to US$6.22 billion in FY 2014 which represents the total growth of 130 percent, or the compounded average annual profit growth rate of 8.7 percent. UTC's growth strategy approach through diversification (M&A) and product growth through innovation while managing the enterprise risk is meeting or exceeding customer needs; and the financial information is

Table 6.5   High-level financial data of United Technologies Corporation

Fiscal Year (Ends December 31)	Total Revenue	Net Total Earnings (after Taxes)	Percent Increase in total revenue over previous year	Percent increase in Net Total Earnings over previous year
2004	37,445	2,673		
2005	42,725	3,069	14.1	14.0
2006	47,829	3.732	11.9	21.6
2007	54,759	4,224	14.5	13.2
2008	58,681	4,689	7.2	11.0
2009	52,425	3,829	-10.7	-18.3
2010	54,326	4,373	3.6	14.2
2011	55,754	4,979	2.6	13.9
2012	57,708	5,130	3.5	3.0
2013	62,626	5,721	8.5	11.5
2014	65,100	6,220	4.0	8.7

Note: All revenue and earnings data are in US$ in millions.

Information sources:

– United Technologies Corporation's Annual reports 2008 and 2010

– FactSet Research Systems. 2015. Annual Financials for United Technologies Corporation. FactSet Fundamentals. Available at: http://www.marketwatch.com/investigating/stock/UTX/financials

showing growth both in revenue and profitability. Therefore, UTC is achieving their excellence and sustaining the competitive advantage.

6.2.2.2 *Business cycle time of the aerospace manufacturing companies*

The discussion presented in Section 6.1.2.2 is fully applicable for UTC. These are all very large global corporations and they are utilizing their intangible assets very well to meet or exceed customer needs, which would definitely reduce their business cycle time.

6.2.3 CONCLUSION OF ENTERPRISES CASE STUDY: THE AEROSPACE MANUFACTURING COMPANIES

The discussion of 40 years of information from UTC is validating the EE model (Figure 1.3) in achieving the excellence and sustaining the competitive advantage through the enterprise growth strategy and also managing the enterprise risk with the following conclusions:

- To support the market and product growth, UTC has been developing series of products as well as going through M&A to meet or exceed customer needs and supporting the concept of product life cycle curve "S" (Figure 1.1).
- UTC has either acquired other companies or developed consortium for expanding their businesses.
- UTC has been improving their margin through various elements of the enterprise growth strategy including vision and mission, innovative product growth ideas, core competency and market share.
- UTC has been utilizing the various elements of the enterprise risk management, for example, strategic risk management, integrated risk management and competitors risk management.
- UTC's executive leadership has been scrutinizing and leading their risk management policies and procedures while continuing to offer new products and services to meet or exceed customer needs, achieving the excellence and sustaining the competitive advantage.

These above-listed points clearly demonstrate that UTC has been following the EE model which is presented in Figure 1.3. The financial information presented in Table 6.5 is also concluding that revenue and profitability increases have been through the growth strategy while managing the enterprise risk. It is very difficult to find information about the business cycle time reduction, but UTC is trying to reduce their business cycles time, which indirectly reflects in their cash flow.

APPENDIX

Glossary

Balance sheet is one of the key financial statements and generally prepared on a quarterly and annually basis. Some businesses may prepare as frequently as every month. This statement presents the financial condition (health) of the business at a specific point in time and the key elements are assets, liabilities and shareholders net equity.

Beta testing is to evaluate how the product would be performing in the real market, so before the product is introduced to the open market, perform some controlled tests and analyze the product performance results.

Business cycle time is defined as the time period between the clock starts – when the customer order is recorded in the system, the product/service is delivered to the customer and the clock stops once the customer makes the payment.

Business/enterprise excellence (BEE) models are derived from Total Quality Management (TQM) theory and practice and supporting America's Baldrige National Quality Award and the European Quality Award.

Business intelligence (BI) is also known as business management – which refers to applications and technologies which are used together to provide access to and analyze information about a firm's operations.

Cash cows are units with high market share in a slow-growing industry.

Cash flow (CF) is available cash for a specified period.

Catastrophic Risk Management is the process of envisioning and preparing for extreme events that could threaten the viability of the enterprise (SOA, 2006).

Commercialization step generally starts at the tail end of the technical implementation. Whatever is commercialized must be delivered on time and meet or exceed customer expectations based on the commercialization:

- Launch the product.
- Produce and place advertisements and other promotions.
- Fill the distribution pipeline with product.
- Critical path analysis is most useful at this stage.

Competence capital is the measure of the proper fit between a strategy's requirements and skills and experience of employees.

Competitive advantage is a position that an enterprise occupies in its competitive environment and it also represents the organization's capability to create superior value for its customers and superior profits for itself.

Continuous improvement (CI) process is based on several rules that may vary from company to company, but the underlying concepts are the same:

*   Be open-minded.
*   Maintain a positive attitude.
*   Reject excuses and seek solutions.
*   Ask questions – you can ask questions as many times and as often as you like, and there are no stupid questions.
*   Take action. Implement ideas immediately and do not seek perfection. Do what can be done now, with the available resources.
*   Keep the team together – team members may get tired, frustrated and dirty together.
*   Use team's knowledge – disregard rank. All team members are equal and everyone has something to contribute. The team's job is to make change happen.
*   Keep process simple.
*   Stress simple steps – continuous improvement process stresses linkages of simple steps that build on each other to reach the goal.

Core competency is the fundamental knowledge, ability, or a specific subject area or skill set.

Core values are essential for an organization and are composed of enduring tenets as well as a small set of general guiding principles.

Corporation pays the corporate income taxes and the shareholders pay income taxes on dividends and the capital received from the corporation.

Customer demand in the market is defined as customer needs which are a function of several variables including economic situation.

Diversity involves the valuing and respecting of difference, whether this difference (for example, race, disability, gender, ethnic background, national origin, etc.) is visible or not.

Dogs – more charitably called pets – are units with low market share in a mature, slow-growing industry.

Emerging market multinational enterprises (EM MNEs) as international companies originated from emerging markets and are engaged in outward foreign direct investment (FDI), where they exercise effective control and undertake value-adding activities in one or more foreign countries. Their definition excludes the following:

*   Import-export companies without outward FDI.
*   Investing mainly or exclusively in tax-haven countries, for example, Cayman and Virgin Islands.
*   State-owned enterprises completely pursuing political objectives designated by their respective home governments, for example, Indian Oil Corporation's acquisition of oil and gas resources in West Africa; or undertaking foreign aid investment programs to strengthen the political and diplomatic ties between home and host country governments, for example,

China's state-owned construction companies, which built bridges, stadiums, railroads and hospitals in Africa. These EM MNEs neither compete in global markets nor do they perform tasks to benefit enterprise gains.

Employee skills are the actual skills and competencies of the employees working for the company.

Enterprise growth strategy (EGS) is an integrated approach affecting every employee, every functional area and strategy within the organization. It relies on transformational change management. It is very different from implementing the firm's business strategies or executing process changes in isolation.

Enterprise resource planning (ERP) systems (also known as **enterprise systems (ESs)**) which were developed to meet the functional requirements of an organization. Traditionally, these systems integrated information from disparate sources such as customers, supply chain, human resources and financial accounting to make up the value chain of the enterprise enabling an organization to become significantly flexible and efficient.

Enterprise risk management (ERM) is a holistic approach to risk management – moving from a fragmented methodology to integrated and broadly focused. The ERM process includes not just risks associated with unintended losses but also financial, strategic, operational and other risks.

Enterprise transformation (ET) may create change, not just routine change but fundamental change that substantially alters an organizational relationship with one or more key groups, e.g., customers, employees, suppliers and investors.

Equality is ensuring that people are not discriminated against unfairly, but are instead given the same and equal opportunities.

Evolutionary program involves gradual change over a period.

Facilitation should be seen as an evolutionary, nonlinear and interactive process, requiring intensive communication and collaboration between different partners.

Facilitation risk is risk associated with the process depending on how well the facilitating process was conducted.

Financial transformation is a strategic project that is enterprise-wide, led by the CFO and generally takes three to five years.

Flow Line where material flow is unidirectional and several functional manufacturing types of equipment are installed to produce a family of components. The equipment layout in a flow line is in a U-shape. Generally efforts are made to add as much value as possible to material to finish the product in a flow line; rarely is 100 percent of a product completed in a flow line.

Focus is about organizational commitment and alignment to the strategy. The final strategy is focusing on a particular customer group, segment of the product line, or geographic market. Similar to differentiation, focus can take many forms. The low cost and differentiation strategies are aimed at achieving their objectives industry-wide, but the focus strategy is built around serving a particular target very well, and each functional policy is developed with this in mind.

Fuzzy front end is a distinct period in the new product development process. It is at the front end that the firm formulates a concept of the product to be developed and decides on whether or not to invest resources in the further development of an idea.

Group technology (GT) is a parts classification process based on material (e.g., cast iron, steel, aluminum and sheet metal), part geometry (e.g., rotational, non-rotational and sheet metal) and manufacturing processes (e.g., turning, grinding and forming).

Growth-share matrix (GSM) helps corporations to analyze their business units or product lines, which in turn helps the company to allocate resources and is also used as an analytical tool in brand marketing, product management, strategic management and portfolio analysis (originally created in the 1970s).

Income (P&L) statement measures a company's financial performance over a specific accounting period that indicates how revenue is transformed into net income.

Innovation is the development of new product/value/idea through solutions that meet or exceed existing and/or new customer requirements (needs) (various definitions in Chapter 2).

Innovation-decision process where every product will have a life cycle with an infant period, growth period and then the maturity/decline period. This product curve is also known as "S" curve. Tarde defined the "S" process as the innovation-decision process.

Innovation enablers are the internal elements necessary for the innovation spiral to work and organization leaders must be innovative and ready to take risk to achieve competitive advantage:

- leadership mindset and culture;
- people and skills;
- technology;
- infrastructure;
- organization and governance;
- risk management;
- measurement and KPIs (Key Performance Indicators);
- funding.

Innovative enterprise is the one that generates the higher-quality, lower- or competitive-price products that provide better than the industry average profit margins as well as give households with employment incomes and with enough consumer choice on product markets.

Innovation management matrix is represented through four quadrants where each quadrant represents an area of innovation, and in each quadrant requires finding novel solutions to important problems as well as the opportunity to create new products and services.

Integrated risk management (IRM) is that an event or action will adversely affect an organization's ability to achieve its business objectives and execute its strategies successfully.

International coach federation (ICF) is a coaching organization in which the coaching process is grouped into four clusters where the coaching elements fit together logically based on the common ways of looking at the competencies in each cluster.

Inventory (I) where money is invested in materials that the business is planning to sell.

Lean manufacturing (culture) is a systematic philosophy of production. Lean manufacturing philosophy questions factory physics basics, operational stability, continual improvement, and quality at the source. A lean manufacturing approach can dramatically improve the operation's performance and offer a new way of thinking, being and doing for the serious managers (leaders) (a way that will change the world).

Liability for foreignness (LOF) (also known as **border effects or frictions of distance**) where foreign firms in host country markets face costs over and above those faced by their incumbent competitors.

Market is the interface across the business which supports the flow of products, services, money and information.

Market growth is when demand for a particular product and/or service increases over time. Therefore, positive change in demand for products or services or both is defined as market growth.

Material requirements planning (MRP) is a computer-based system for managing the production material and schedule. This approach applies to discrete production in which many products are manufactured in periodic lots in several processing operations. A basic MRP system specifies the quantities and the order release times for the components. MRP system does not apply to continuous-flow-type production systems.

Mission statement should provide a clear and concise description of any firm's (or individual's) overall purpose.

Motivational capital is the organization's ability to meet its employees' expectations, therefore, they are motivated and driven to perform at their best.

Net profit (NP) it is a relationship between revenue and cost for a specified period. It may be before taxes and after taxes.

Operating Expense (OE) is the amount of money a business spends to convert the purchased material into throughput over a specified period of time.

Operation describes an activity out of a series of activities to produce a product.

Organizational capability is defined as the ability of an organization to perform a coordinated set of activities utilizing organizational resources, for the purpose of achieving a particular objective.

Organizational capital measures the fit between a company's strategy and the organizational model.

Organizational structure identifies the line of authority, reporting and coordination, real and perceived career paths and decision-making authority.

Outsourcing denotes the shift that occurs when a business entity takes work traditionally performed internally and contracts with an external provider for the provision of that work. Its intended purpose is to cut costs and improve quality through the use of experts in the area to perform those functions.

Primary market research involves the actual data collection for the defined usage patterns, liking and disliking of product features and so on, of target customers of their products.

Product-market growth matrix allows marketers to consider ways to grow the business via existing and/or new products in existing and/or new markets – there are four possible product/ market combinations, and the matrix helps businesses decide what course of action should be taken given current performance.

Purpose is an organization's fundamental reasons for existence: beyond making money, it is to represent the true motivation of employees to work for a company, but is not to be confused with business strategies or specific objectives.

Relative market share indicates likely cash generation, because the higher the share the more cash will be generated.

Return on assets (ROA) is a ratio between net profit and total assets for a specified period, and defined as (net profit) / (total assets).

Return on investment (ROI) is the benefit to the investor resulting from an investment of some resource.

Risk control is the process of identifying, monitoring, limiting, avoiding, offsetting and transferring risks (SOA, 2006).

Risk management is the identification, assessment and prioritization of risk followed by coordinated and economical application of resources to minimize, monitor and control the probability and/or impact of unfortunate events or to maximize the realization of opportunities (Hubbard, 2009).

Secondary market research takes place when marketing information is collected from a third source like periodicals, business magazines, etc.

Social-ecological enterprise (SEE) model stresses E3 (ethical, effective, efficient and transparent) strategy and governance as causal to enterprise performance of all sorts.

Social enterprise is used to refer to a set of organizations with primarily social purpose.

Stars are units with high market share in a fast-growing industry.

Strategic risk management (SRM) is a business discipline that drives deliberation and action regarding uncertainties and untapped opportunities that affect an organization's strategy and strategy execution.

Strategy is the plan devised to maintain and build competitive advantage over the competition.

Strategy execution keys – there are numerous professional practicing authors who are presenting their strategy execution experiences in a simple form called "Strategy execution keys."

Structure – the way the organization is structured and who reports to whom.

Supply chain is a system where vendor material is transformed into customer-demanded product and delivered to customers. The material from the vendor may go through a series of stages, such as manufacturing, transportation, distribution and so on. Also, the core business process is to create and deliver a product or service from development manufacturing or conversion – transportation – distribution to customer for consumption.

Sustainable competitive advantage (SCA) business processes are defined as SCA when it has value-creating processes that cannot be duplicated or imitated by competition while also maintaining a profit that exceed the average for its industry.

Table stakes are fundamental competencies which every organization requires to operate effectively, carry out their mission and sustain operations.

Task (activity) where one or more resources are assigned to a defined work with a given start and end dates. There are several tasks in a project.

Technical implementation once the product is proved to be acceptable in the controlled environment and looks profitable then the next step is technical implementation. The key steps of technical implementation are:

- new program initiation;
- program resource estimation;
- requirement publication;
- engineering operations planning;
- operations (manufacturing side) planning and scheduling;
- supplier collaboration;
- program review and monitoring;
- contingencies – what-if planning.

Total alignment – two people are aligned when they move in the same direction and they are integrated when they cooperate with one another; and total alignment encompasses both alignment and integration.

Transfer Line is a manufacturing process utilized for high-volume production products. Same product may be produced for several days or even weeks before any change in set-up for a different product. Material flows are unidirectional where raw material is fed at one end and the value-added product comes out from the other end.

Value is a measure of the extent to which an enterprise provides a market that the consumers in this market want. Value can also accrue from providing customers an offering they did not expect, e.g., Apple's iPhone.

Vision encapsulates the ideology or guiding philosophy of a business; expressing values, purpose and direction through a mission statement and set of corporate objectives (Collins and Porras, 1991). Vision has been conceived variously as a form of charismatic leadership, an approach to scenario planning, a set of organizational values, a logic underlying action, and a projected business image.

Airplanes Delivery Statistics: Airbus A320 and Boeing 737

The following is the last 27 years (1988 – 2014) of the Airbus A320 family of airplanes and the Boeing 737 family of airplanes delivery statistics. Airbus is sub-dividing their A320 family of airplanes into A318, A319, A320 and A321 models (Table A.1), but Boeing is providing their total delivery statistics and not sub-dividing into model delivery statistics (Table A.2).

Table A.1   Airbus's A320 family of airplanes delivery statistics

			Deliveries		
Year	A318	A319	A320	A321	Total
1988	—	—	16	—	16
1989	—	—	58	—	58
1990	—	—	58	—	58
1991	—	—	119	—	119
1992	—	—	111	—	111
1993	—	—	71	—	71
1994	—	—	48	16	64
1995	—	—	34	22	56
1996	—	18	38	16	72
1997	—	47	58	22	127
1998	—	53	80	35	168
1999	—	88	101	33	222
2000	—	112	101	28	241
2001	—	89	119	49	257
2002	—	85	116	35	236
2003	9	72	119	33	233
2004	10	87	101	35	233
2005	9	142	121	17	289
2006	8	137	164	30	339

Table A.1   Continued

		Deliveries			
Year	A318	A319	A320	A321	Total
2007	17	105	194	51	436
2008	13	98	209	66	386
2009	6	88	221	87	402
2010	2	51	297	51	401
2011	2	47	306	66	421
2012	2	38	332	83	455
2013	1	34	306	150	493
2014	—	34	306	150	490

Table A.2   Boeing's 737 family of airplanes delivery statistics

Year	Boeing 737 Deliveries	Year	Boeing 737 Deliveries
1988	165	2002	223
1989	146	2003	173
1990	174	2004	202
1991	215	2005	212
1992	218	2006	302
1993	152	2007	330
1994	121	2008	290
1995	89	2009	372
1996	76	2010	376
1997	135	2011	372
1998	281	2012	415
1999	320	2013	440
2000	281	2014	485
2001	299		

References

Aabo, T.J., Fraser, R.S., and Simkins, B.J. 2005. The rise and evolution of the chief risk officer: Enterprise risk management at Hydro One. *Journal of Applied Corporate Finance*, 17(3): 62–75.

Aabo, T., Hansen, M.A. and Pantzalis, C. 2012. Corporate foreign exchange speculation and Integrated risk management. *Managerial Finance*, 38(8): 729–51.

AAUP. 2003. Academic freedom and national security in a time of crisis. American Association of University Professors. Available at: http://www.aaup.org/report/academic-freedom-and-national-security-time-crisis/.

Abbott, W.F. and Monsen, J.R. 1979. On the measurement of corporate social responsibility. *Academy of Management Journal*, 22(3): 501–15.

Abdimomunova, L. and Valerdi, R. 2010. An organizational assessment process support of enterprise transformation. *Information Knowledge Systems Management*, 9: 175–95.

Abrahim, A., Henry, K., and Keith, J. 2012. ERM Culture Alignment to enhance competitive advantage. ERM Symposium, April 18–20, 2012, Washington, DC. Society of Actuaries. Available at: http://www.soa.org/Library/Monographs/Other-Monographs/2012/April/2012-Enterprise-Risk-Management-Symposium/.

Airbus. 2014. Orders and Deliveries. Airbus. December 31, 2014. Available at: http://centerforaviation.com/analysis/airbus-and-boeing-2014-the-rain-of-orders-and-deliveries-contunues-with-no-sign-of-slacking-202979.

Al Jazeera. 2010. BP begins testing new oil well cap. July 15, 2010. Available at: http://en.wikipedia/org/wiki/Deepwater_Horizon_Oil_Spill/.

Alexander, G.L. and Buchholz, R.A. 1978. Corporate social responsibility and stock market performance. *Academy of Management Journal*, 21(3): 479–86.

Allen, D., Kern, T., and Havenhand, M. 2002. ERP critical success factors: An exploration of the contextual factors in public sector institutions. The Proceedings of the 35th Hawaii International Conference on System Sciences, January 7–10, Big Island, Hawaii.

Al-Najjar, B. and Anfimiadou, A. 2012. Environmental policies and firm value. *Business Strategy and the Environment*, 21(1): 49–59.

Alves-Foss, J., Taylor, C., and Oman, P. 2004. A Multi-layered Approach to Security in High Assurance System. Proceedings of the 37th Annual Hawaii International System Sciences Conference, University of Hawaii Minoa, Hawaii. The CD/ROM distributed at the conference and sold afterwards by IEEE Computer Society Press.

Alvord, S.H., Brown, L.D., and Letts, C.W. 2004. Social entrepreneurship and social transformation: An exploratory study. *The Journal of Applied Behavioral Science*, 40(3): 260–93.

Ambrosini, V. and Bowman, C. 2009. What are dynamic capabilities and are they a useful construct in strategic management? *International Journal of Management Reviews*, 11(1): 29–50.

Ambrosini, V., Bowman, C., and Collier, N. 2009. Dynamic capabilities: An exploration of how firms renew their resource base. *British Journal of Management*, 20(s1): S9–S24.

American Institute of Certified Public Accountants (AICPA), Special Committee on Financial Reporting. 1994. *Improving Business Reporting – A Customer Focus: Meeting the Information Needs of Investors and Creditors.* New York: AICPA.

Amin, A. 2009. Extraordinary ordinary: Working in the social enterprise economy. *Social Enterprise Journal*, 5(1): 30–49.

AMR Research 2005. *The Customer Management Applications Report, 2004–2009*. Boston, Massachusetts, August 2005.

Andersson, T. and Svensson, R. 1994. Entry mode for direct investment determined by the composition of firm-specific skills. *Scandinavian Journal of Economics*, 94(4): 551–60.

Andreff, W. 2002. The new multinational corporations from transition countries. *Economic Systems*, 26(4): 371–9.

Ansoff, I. 1957. Strategies for diversification. *Harvard Business Review*, 35(5): 113–24.

Appold, S. 1995. Agglomeration, interorganizational networks, and competitive performance in the US metalworking sector. *Economic Geography*, 71(1): 27–54.

Aras, G. and Crowther, D. 2008. Governance and sustainability: An investigation into the relationship between corporate governance and corporate sustainability. *Management Decision*, 46(3): 433–48.

AS/NZS 3931. 1998. *Australia/New Zealand Standard: Risk Analysis of Technologica Systems – Application Guide*. Joint Publication – Standards Australia and Standards New Zealand.

Asmussen, C. 2009. Local, regional, or global? Quantifying MNE geographic scope. *Journal of International Business Studies*, 40(7): 1192–205.

Aspara, J., Lamberg, J.A., Laukia, A., and Tikkanen, H. 2013. Corporate business model transformation and inter-organizational cognition: The case of Nokia. *Long Range Planning*, 46: 459–74.

Association for Financial Professionals (AFP). 2006. *Organizations Focus on Risk Management*. Bethesda, MD: Association for Financial Professionals. Available at: http://www.afponline.org/pub/pr/pr_20060626_ctc.html/.

Atkinson, S., Schaefer, A., and Viney, H. 2000. Organizational structure and effective environmental management. *Business Strategy and the Environment*, 9(2): 108–21.

Ausick, P. 2014. World's most popular aircraft: Boeing 737 or Airbus A320? *Freelance Writer*, November 17, 2014. Available at: http://247wallst.com/aerospace-defense/2014/11/17/worlds-most-popular-aircraft-boeing -737-or-airbus-a320/.

Austin, J.E. 2000. Strategic collaboration between non-profits and business. *Non-profit and Voluntary Sector Quarterly*, 29(1): 69–97.

Australian Quality Council and Deloittes-Touche-Tohmatsu. 2000. *Achieving Business Excellence 2000: A Study of How Australian Organizations Approach Business Improvement*. Sydney: Australian Quality Council & Deloittes-Touche-Tohmatsu.

Avery, G.C. and Bergsteiner, H. 2011. Sustainable leadership practices for enhancing business resilience and performance. *Strategy & Leadership*, 39(3): 5–15.

Bachman, J. 2014. Boeing's 737 turns 8,000: The best-selling plane ever isn't slowing. *Freelance Writer*, April 16, 2014. Available at: http://www.bloomberg.com/bw/articles/2014-04-16/boeing-s-737-turns-8-000-the-best-selling-plane-ever-isn-t-slowing/.

Backman, M. and Butler, C. 2007. *Big in Asia: 30 Strategies for Business Success*. Basingstoke: Palgrave Macmillan.

Bainbridge, S.M. 2009. Caremark and enterprise risk management. *Journal of Corporate Law*, 34(4): 967–90.

Bakker, H.J.C., Babeliowsky, M.N.F., and Stevenaar, F.J.W. 2004. *The Next Leap: Achieving Growth through Global Networks, Partnerships and Cooperation*. London: Cyan Books.

Balasubramanian, S., Mathur, I., and Thakur, R. 2005. The impact of high-quality firm achievements on shareholder value: Focus on Malcolm Baldrige and J.D. Power and Associates awards. *Journal of the Academy of Marketing Science*, 33(4): 413–22.

Balmer, J.M.T. and Greyser, S.A. 2002. Managing the multiple identities of the corporation. *California Management Review*, 44(3): 72–86.

Bancroft, N.H., Sep, H., and Sprengel, A. 1998. *Implementing SAP R/3*, 2nd edn. Greenwich, CT: Manning Publications.

Banes, A.J. 2013. Out of academics: Education, entrepreneurship and enterprise. *Annals of Biomedical Engineering*, 41(9): 1926–38.

Barbieri, E., Di Tommaso, M.R., and Rubini, L. 2009. *Industria contemporanea: Governi, imprese e territori nella Cina Meridionale*. Rome: Carocci editore.

Barenbeim, R.E. 2006. Ethics. *Leadership Excellence*, 23(9): 19–20.

Barkema, H.G. and Vermeulen, F. 1998. International expansion through start-up or acquisition: A learning perspective. *Academy of Management Journal*, 41(1): 7–26.

Barnes, S.J. 2003. Enterprise mobility: Concepts and examples. *International Journal of Mobile Communications*, 1(4): 341–59.

Barney, J.B. 1991. Firm resources and sustained competitive advantage. *Journal of Management*, 17(1): 99–120.

Baron, D. 2001. Private politics, corporate social responsibility and integrated strategy. *Journal of Economics and Management Strategy*, 10: 7–45.

Bartlett, C.A. and Ghoshal, S. 1980. *Managing across Borders*. Boston, MA: Harvard Business School Press.

Barton, T.L., Shenkir, W.G., and Walker, P.L. 2002. *Making Enterprise Risk Management Pay Off: How Leading Companies Implement Risk Management*. Upper Saddle River, NJ: Prentice Hall.

Basole, R.C. 2008. Enterprise mobility: Researching a new paradigm. *Information Knowledge Systems Management*, 7: 1–7.

Beasley, M.S. and Frigo, M.L. 2007. Strategic risk management: Creating and protecting value. *Strategic Finance*, 88(11): 25–32.

Beasley, M.S., Branson, B.C. and Hancock, B.V. 2011. *Developing Key Risk Indicators to Strengthen Enterprise Risk Management*. COSO – The Committee of Sponsoring Organizations of the Treadway Commission. Available at: http://COSO.org/documents/COSOKRIPPaperFull-FINALforWebPostingDec110_000.pdf.

Beasley, M.S., Clune, R. and Hermanson, D.R. 2005. Enterprise risk management: An empirical analysis of factors associated with the extent of implementation. *Journal of Accounting and Public Policy*, 24(6): 521–31.

Beasley, M.S., Pagach, D. and Warr, R. 2008. The information conveyed in hiring announcements of senior executives overseeing enterprise-wide risk management processes. *Journal of Accounting, Auditing, and Finance*, 23(3): 311–32.

Beaudan, E. 2010. Creative Execution. *Ivey Business Journal Online*: N_A. March/April 2010.

Beaverstock, J. 2002. Transnational elites in global cities: British expatriates in Singapore's financial district. *Geoforum*, 33(4): 525–38.

Belderbos, R. and Heijltjes, M. 2005. The determinants of expatriate staffing by Japanese multinationals in Asia: Control, learning and vertical business groups. *Journal of International Business Studies*, 36(3): 341–54.

Bennett, H., Escolano, J., Fabrizio, S., Gutiérrez, E., Ivaschenko, I., Lissovolik, B., Moreno-Badia, M., Schule, W., and Tokarick, S. 2008. Competitiveness in southern euro area: France Greece, Italy, Portugal and Spain. IMF Working Paper, WP/08/112. Washington, DC: International Monetary Fund.

Bennis, W. and Nanus, B. 1985. *Leaders, the Strategies for Taking Charge*. New York: Perennial Library.

Berger, I.E., Cunningham, P.H. and Drumwright, M.E. 2004. Social alliances: Company/non-profit collaboration. *California Management Review*, 47(1): 58–90.

Berkowitz, B.D. 1997. War in the information age. In Arquilla, J. and Ronfeldt, D. (eds), *Athena's Camp: Preparing for Conflict*. Santa Monica, CA: RAND Corporation, 175–89.

Beugelsdijk, S., McCann, P., and Mudambi, R. 2010. Place, space and organization: Economic geography and the multinational enterprise. *Journal of Economic Geography*, 10(4): 485–93.

Bhagwati, J., Panagariya, A., and Srinivastan, T. 2004. The muddles over outsourcing. *Journal of Economic Perspectives*, 18(4): 93–114.

Bhatti, O.K. 2011. Strategic implementation: An alternative choice of 8S's. *Annals of Management Research*, 1(2): 52–9.

Bilien, J. and Matta, R. 1989. The CFM56 Venture. AIAA/AHS/ASEE Aircraft Design, Systems, and Operations Conference, July 31 – August 2, 1989, Seattle, Washington.

Bill Summary & Status – 111th Congress (2009–2010) – H.R. 4173 – All Information – THOMAS (Library of Congress). Washington, DC: Library of Congress.

Biloslavo, R. 2004. Web based mission statements in Slovenian enterprises. *Journal of East European Management Studies*, 9(3): 265–77.

Birkinshaw, J. and Mol, M. 2006. How management innovation happens. *MIT Sloan Management Review*, 47(4): 81–8.

Blair, M.B. 1995. *Ownership and Control: Rethinking Corporate Governance for the Twenty-First Century.* Washington, DC: Brookings Institution.

Bliege Bird, R., Smith, R.A. and Bird, D.W. 2001. The hunting handicap: Costly signaling in human foraging strategies. *Behavioral Ecology and Sociobiology*, 50(1): 9–19.

Bluemink, E. 2010. Size of Exxon spill remains disputed. *Anchorage Daily News*, June 10, 2010.

Boeing 787: Orders and Deliveries (updated monthly). 2013. *The Boeing Company.* Available at: http://www.boeing.com/commercial/.

Boomer, L.G. 2007. Strategy: Execution and alignment. *Accounting Today*, 21(9): 24.

Bossidy, L. and Charan, R. 2002a. *Execution: The Discipline of Getting Things Done.* London: Random House.

Bossidy, L. and Charan, R. 2002b. *The Discipline of Getting Things Done.* New York: Crown Business.

Bou-Llusar, J.C., Escrig-Tena, A.B., Roca-Puig, V., and Beltran-Martin, I. 2009. An empirical assessment of the EFQM excellence model: Evaluation as a TQM framework relative to the MBNQA model. *Journal of Operations Management*, 27(6): 1–22.

Bowman, E.H. 1980. A risk/return paradox for strategic management. *Sloan Management Review*, 21(3): 17–31.

Bowman, E.H. 1982. Risk Seeking by Troubled Firms. *Sloan Management Review*, 23(4): 33–42.

Bowman, C. and Ambrosini, V. 2003. How the resource-based and the dynamic capability views of the firm inform corporate-level strategy. *British Journal of Management*, 14: 289–304.

Bowonder, B, Dambal, A., Kumar, S., and Shirodkar, A. 2010. Innovation strategies for creating competitive advantage. *Research-Technology Management*, 53(3): 19–32.

Boyd, B., Henning, N., Reyna, E., Wang, D.E. and Welch, M.D. 2009. *Hybrid Organizations: New Business Models for Environmental Leadership.* Sheffield: Greenleaf Publishing.

Brenes, E.R., Mena, M., and Molina, G.E. 2008. Key success factors for strategy implementation in Latin America. *Journal of Business Research*, 61(6): 590–98.

Bridge, S., Murtagh, M., and O'Neil, K. 2009. *Understanding the Social Economy and the Third Sector.* Basingstoke: Palgrave.

Brooks, D.W. 2010. Creating a risk-aware culture. In Fraser, J. and Simkins, B.J. (eds), *Enterprise Risk Management: Today's Leading Research and Best Practices for Tomorrow's Executives.* Hoboken, NJ: John Wiley & Sons.

Brouthers, K.D. and Brouthers, L.E. 2000. Acquisition or greenfield start-up? Institutional culture and transaction cost influences. *Strategic Management Journal*, 21(1): 89–97.

Brown, D.L., Vetterlein, A., and Mahler, A. 2010. Theorizing transnational corporations as social actors: An analysis of corporate motivations. *Business and Politics*, 12(1): 1–37.

Brown, E., Derudder, B., Parnreiter, C., Pelupessy, W., Taylor, P., and Witlox, F. 2010. World city networks and global commodity chains: Towards a world-systems' integration. *Global Networks*, 10(1): 12–34.

Brown, T.J., Dacin, P.A., Pratt, M.G., and Whetten, D.A. 2006. Identity, intended image, construed image, and reputation: An interdisciplinary framework and suggested terminology. *Journal of the Academy of Marketing Science*, 34(2): 99–106.

Bruni, D.S. and Verona, G. 2009. Dynamic marketing capabilities in science-based firms: An exploratory investigation of the pharmaceutical industry. *British Journal of Management*, 20(s1): S101–S117.

Buckley, P.J. and Ghauri, P.N. 2004. Globalisation Economic geography and the strategy of multinational enterprises. *Journal of International Business Studies*, 35(2): 81–98.

Burke, L. and Logsdon, J.M. 1996. How corporate social responsibility pays off. *Long Range Planning*, 29(4): 495–502.

Burton, H.O. and Pennotti, M.C. 2003. The enterprise map: A system for implementing strategy and achieving operational excellence. *Engineering Management Journal*, 15(3): 15–20.

Cadbury, A. 1992. Cadbury committee's code of best practices. Available at: http://www.jbs.cam.ac.uk/cadbury/report/.

Cady, S.H., Wheeler, J.V., DeWoff, J., and Bordke, M. 2011. Mission, vision, and values: What do they say? *Organization Development Journal*, 29(1): 63–78.

Caldwell, C., Dixon, R.D., Floyd, L.A., Chaudoin, J., Post, J. and Cheokas, G. 2012. Transformative leadership: Achieving unparalleled excellence. *Journal of Business Ethics*, 109(2): 175–87.

Caraco, T., Martindale, S. and Whittam, T.S. 1980. An empirical demonstration of risk sensitive foraging preferences. *Animal Behavior*, 28: 820–30.

Carroll, T. and Webb, M. 2001. *The Risk Factor: How to Make Risk Management Work for You in Strategic Planning and Enterprise*. Harrogate: Take That Books.

CAS. 2003. Overview of Enterprise Risk Management. Enterprise Risk Management Committee. Casualty Actuarial Society. Available at: http://www.casact.org/erm/overview.pdf.

Castells, M. 2000. *Information Technology and Global Capitalism*. New York: The New Press.

Ceci, S.J. and Williams, W.M. 1997. Schooling, intelligence, and income. *American Psychologist*: 52(10): 1051–8.

Cendrowski, H. and Mair, W.C. 2009. *Enterprise Risk Management and COSO: A Guide for Directors, Executive and Practitioners*. Hoboken, NJ: John Wiley & Sons.

Chan, K.W. and Mauborgne, R. 2005. *Blue Ocean Strategy*. Boston, MA: Harvard Business School Press.

Chandler, A.D. 1990. *Scale and Scope: The Dynamics of Industrial Capitalism*. Cambridge, MA: Harvard University Press.

Chang, S.J. and Rosenzweig, P.M. 2001. The choice of entry mode in sequential foreign direct investment. *Strategic Management Journal*, 22(8): 747–76.

Chappell, T. 2011. Glory as an ethical idea. *Philosophical Investigations*, Special Issue: Ethics and Religion, 34(2): 105–34.

Charan, R. 2004. *Profit Growth is Everyone's Business: 10 Tools You Can Use Monday Morning*. New York: Crown Business.

Charan, R. 2009. *Owning Up: The 14 Questions Every Board Member Needs to Ask*. San Francisco, CA: John Wiley & Sons.

Charan, R. and Colvin, G. 1999. Why CEOs fail. *Fortune*, June 21, 1999.

Chell, E. 2007. Social enterprise and entrepreneurship: Towards a convergent theory of the entrepreneurial process. *International Small Business Journal*, 25(1): 5–26.

Chen, C.C., Law, C.C.H., and Yang, S.C. 2009. Managing ERP implementation failure: A project management perspective. *IEEE Transactions on Engineering Management*, 56(1): 157–70.

Chen, M.J., Smith, K.G., and Grimm, C.M. 1992. Action characteristics as predictors of competitive responses. *Management Science*, 38(3): 439–55.

Chen, S.F. and Zeng, M. 2004. Japanese investors' choice of acquisitions vs start-up in the US: The role of reputation barriers and advertising outlays. *International Journal of Research in Marketing*, 21(2): 123–36.

Cheng, C-Y., Pugh, T., Rothrock, L., and Prabhu, V. 2012. Enterprise transformation to enable university-industry collaboration: A case study in complexity and usability. *Service Science*, 4(1): 55–68.

Child, J. and Rodrigues, S.B. 2005. Chinese firms: A case for theoretical extension? *Management and Organization Review*, 1(3): 381–410.

Chittoor, R., Sarkar, M.B., Ray, S., and Aulakh, P. 2009. Third-world copycats to emerging multi-nationals: Institutional changes and organizational transformation in the Indian pharmaceutical industry. *Organization Science*, 20(1): 187–205.

Christenson, D. and Walker, D.H.T. 2004. Understanding the role of "vision" in project success. *Project Management Journal*, 35(3): 39–52.

Chun, R. 2005. Corporate reputation: Meaning and measurement. *International Journal of Management Reviews*, 7(2): 91–109.

Clarke, M. 1998. Can specialists be general managers? Developing paradoxical thinking in middle managers. *Journal of Management Development*, 17(3): 191–206.

Collins, J.C. 2001. *Good to Great: Why Some Companies Make the Leap … and Others Don't*. London: Random House.

Collins, J.C. and Porras, J.I. 1991. Organizational vision and visionary organizations. *California Management Review*, 34(1): 30–52.

Collins, J.C. and Porras, J.I. 1994. *Built to Last: Successful Habits of Visionary Companies.* New York: Harper Business.

Collins, J.C. and Porras, J.I. 1995. Building a visionary company. *California Management Review,* 37(2): 80–100.

Collins, J.C. and Porras, J.I. 1996. Building your company's vision. *Harvard Business Review,* 74(5): 65–77.

Colvin, G. 2009. *The Upside of the Downturn: 10 Management Strategies to Prevail in the Recession and Thrive in the Aftermath.* London: Nicholas Brealey Publishing.

Cornelissen, J.P., Haslam, S.A., and Balmer, J.M.T. 2007. Social identity, organizational identity and corporate identity: Towards an integrated understanding of processes. *British Journal of Management,* 18(s1): S1–S16.

COSO. 1992. *Internal Control – Integrated Framework: Executive Summary.* COSO – The Committee of Sponsoring Organizations of the Treadway Commission. Available at: http://www.coso.org/publications/executive_summary_integrated_framework.html/.

COSO. 2004. *Enterprise Risk Management – Integrated Framework: Executive Summary.* New York: AICPA. COSO – The Committee of Sponsoring Organizations of the Treadway Commission.

COSO. 2009. *Effective Enterprise Risk Oversight: The Role of the Board of Directors.* COSO – The Committee of Sponsoring Organizations of the Treadway Commission.

Crawford-Mathis, K., Darr, S., and Farmer, A. 2010. The village network (TM): Partnership and collaboration to abbreviate poverty in subsistence marketplaces. *Journal of Business Research,* 63(6): 639–42.

Croft, J. 2011. Powering the Dream: A typical paths to Boeing 787 EIS. *Flight International,* October 17, 2011.

Cumming, C.M. and Hirtle, B.J. 2001. The challenges of risk management in diversified financial companies. *FRBNY Economic Policy Review,* 7(1): 1–17.

Cummings, S. and Davies, J. 1994. Mission, vision, fusion. *Long Range Planning,* 27(6): 147–50.

Dahan, N.M., Doh, J.P., Oetzel, J., and Yaziji, M. 2010. Corporate-NGO collaboration: Co-creating new business models for developing markets. *Long Range Planning,* 43(2/3): 326–42.

Dahlgaard-Park, S.M. 2007. Our dreams of excellence: Learning from the past and architecturing the future, guest editorial. *Journal of Management History,* 13(4): 306.

Dahlgaard-Park, S.M. and Dahlgaard, J.J. 2007. Excellence: 25 years evolution. *Journal of Management History,* 13(4): 371–93.

Daily Telegraph. 2010. BP leak the world's worst accidental oil spill. *Daily Telegraph,* August 3, 2010. Available at: http://www.telegraph.co.uk/finance/newsbysector/energy/oilandgas/7924009/BP-leak-the-worlds-worst-accidental-oil-spill.html/.

Daum, J. 2003. *New Economy Analyst Report.* Available at: http://www.juergendaum.com/news/05_28_2003.htm/.

Davenport, T.H. 1998. Putting the enterprise into the enterprise system. *Harvard Business Review,* 76(4): 121–31.

Davenport, T.O. 1999. *Human Capital: What It is and Why People Invest It.* San Francisco, CA: Jossey-Bass.

Davidson, A. and Simonetto, M. 2005. Pricing strategy and execution: An overlooked way to increase revenues and profits. *Strategy & Leadership,* 33(6): 25–33.

Davies, A. 2013. Here's the Boeing 777X series that airlines are buying like crazy. November 18, 2013. Available at: http://www.businessinsider.com/.

Davies, D. 2002. Risk management – protecting reputation: Reputation risk management – the holistic approach. *Computer Law & Security Reviews,* 18(6): 414–20.

Davila, T., Epstein, M.J., and Shelton, R. 2006. *Making Innovation Work: How to Manage It, Measure It and Profit from It.* Upper Saddle River, NJ: Wharton School Publishing.

Davis, D.W. and Silver, B.D. 2004. *Civil Liberties vs. Security: Public Opinion in the Context of the Terrorist Attacks on America.* East Lansing, MI: Michigan State University Press.

De Nardis, S., Traù, F. 1999. Specializzazione settoriale e qualità dei prodotti: Misure sulla pressione competitiva dell'industria italiana. *Rivista italiana degli economisti,* 6(2): 177–212.

De Wall, A.A. 2013. Evergreens of excellence. *Journal of Management History,* 19(2): 241–78.

De Waal, A.A. and Frijns, M. 2009. Working on high performance in Asia: The case of Nabil Bank. *Measuring Business Excellence*, 13(3): 29–38.

Dellestrand, H. and Kappen, P. 2012. The effects of spatial and contextual factors on headquarters resource allocation to MNE subsidiaries. *Journal of International Business Studies*, 43(3): 219–43.

Deloitte. 2008. *Designing a Successful ERM function*. London: Deloitte Touche.

Deloitte. 2011. *Tech Trends 2011: The Natural Convergence of Business and IT*. London: Deloitte Touche Tohmatsu Limited.

Deloitte. 2012. *Cultivating a Risk Intelligent Culture: Understand, Measure, Strengthen, and Report*. London: Deloitte Touche.

DeLone, W.H. and McLean, E.R. 1992. Information systems success: The quest for the dependent variable. *Information Systems Research*, 3(1): 60–95.

Denning, D. 1998. *Information Warfare and Security*. Reading, MA: Addison-Wesley.

Di Tommaso, M.R. and Rubini, L. 2009. "Made in Italy" and "Made in China" in Europe and United States: Policy implications in crisis times. Paper presented at the XXXIII National Conference on Industrial Economics and Policy, 25–6, September, Ferrara.

Di Tommaso, M.R. and Rubini, L. 2012. Achieving excellence in exporting intangible-intensive goods: Measuring economic performances. *Measuring Business Excellence*, 16(3): 72–83.

Di Tommaso, M.R., Rubini, L., and Barbieri, E. 2012. *Southern China: Industry, Development and Industrial Policy*. London: Routledge.

Dive, B. 2004. *Education Management*. Auckland: New Zealand Management.

Doherty, N. 2000. *Integrated Risk Management*. New York: McGraw-Hill.

Donlon, B.S. 2007. Strategy execution: Five major domains critical to any organization. *DM Review Magazine*, February 2007. Available at: http://www.dmreview.com/article_sub.cfm?articleId=1075123/.

Drucker, P.F. 1985. The discipline of innovation. *Harvard Business Review*, 80(8): 95–102.

Drucker, P.F. 1988. The coming of the new organization. *Harvard Business Review*, 66(1): 45–53.

Drucker, P.F. 1999. *Management Challenges for the 21st Century*. New York: Harper Collins.

Drucker, P.F. 2001. *The Essential Drucker: In One Volume the Best of Sixty Years of Peter Drucker's Essential Writings on Management*. New York: Harper Business.

Dryzek, J.S., Hunold, C., Schlosberg, D., Downes, D., and Hernes, H.K. 2002. Environmental transformation of the State: The U.S.A., Norway, Germany and the UK. *Political Studies*, 50(1): 1–22.

Dumming, J.H. 1981. *International Production and the Multinational Enterprises*. London: Allen & Unwin.

Dumming, J.H. 1988. The electric paradigm of international production: A restatement and some possible extensions. *Journal of International Business Studies*, 19(1): 1–13.

Dumming, J.H. 2001. The electric paradigm on international production: Past, present and future. *International Journal of the Economies of Business*, 8(2): 173–90.

Dunbar, G.A. 2007. *VA: The High Performance Foundation for Strategy Execution*. Available at: http://www.garydunbar.com/features/va.html/.

Easterby-Smith, M., Lyles, M.A., and Peteraf, M.A. 2009. Dynamic capabilities: Current debates and future directions. *British Journal of Management*, 20(s1): S1–S8.

Edgeman, R. 2013. Sustainable enterprise: Towards a framework for holistic data-analysis. *Corporate Governance*, 13(5): 527–40.

Edgeman, R. and Eskildsen, J. 2012. The C4 model of people-centered innovation: Culture, consciousness, and customer-centric co-creation. *Journal of Innovation and Best Business Practice*, Article ID: 932564, DOI: 10.5151/2012.932564.

Edgeman, R. and Eskildsen, J. 2014. Modeling and assessing sustainable enterprise excellence. *Business Strategy and the Environment*, 23: 173–87.

EFQM. 2007. *The EFQM Framework for Risk Management*. European Foundation for Quality Management, Brussels. Available at: www.efqm.org/uploads.

Elkington, J. 1997. *Cannibals with Forks: The Triple Bottom Line of 21st Century Business*. Oxford: Capstone Publishing.

Elkington, J., Fennell, S., and Bendell, J. 2000. *Terms of Endearment: Business, NGOs and Sustainable Development*. Sheffield: Greenleaf Publishing.

Engelberger, J.F. 1982. Robotics in practice: Future capabilities. *Electronic Servicing & Technology Magazine*.

Enright, M. 2009. The location of activities of manufacturing multinationals in the Asia-Pacific. *Journal of International Business Studies*, 40(5): 818–39.

Epstein, E.M. 2002. The field of business ethics in the United States: Past, present and future. *Journal of General Management*, 28(2): 1–21.

Ernst & Young. 2010. *Risk Appetite: The Strategic Balancing Act*. London: Ernst & Young.

Ernst & Young. 2012. *Innovation for Growth: Innovation 2.0 – A Spiral Approach to Business Model Innovation*. London: Ernst & Young. Available at: http://emergingmarkets.ey.com/wp-content/uploads/downloads/2012/09/Innovation-Report-2012_DIGI.pdf.

Ertuna, B. and Tükel, A. 2010. Traditional versus international influences: CSR disclosures in Turkey. *European Journal of International Management*, 4(3): 283–9.

Eskildsen, J. and Edgeman, R. 2012. Continuous relevance and responsibility: Integration of sustainability and excellence via innovation. *Journal of Positive Management*, 3(1): 67–81.

Espinoza, C., Ukleja, M., and Rusch, C. 2011. Core competencies for leading today's workforce. *Leader to Leader*, 2011(59): 18–23.

Faini, R. and Sapir, A. 2005. Un modello obsoleto? Crescita e specializzazione dell'economia italiana. In Boeri, T., Faini, R., Ichino, A., Pisauro, G., and Scarpa, C. (eds), *Il Mulino*. Bologna: Oltre il decline.

Falkner, R. 2003. Private environmental governance and international relations: Exploring the links. *Global Environmental Politics*, 3(2): 72–87.

Farrel, J.M. and Hoon, A. April 2009. *What's Your Company Risk Culture?* Directorship of National Association of Corporate Directors.

Felin, T. and Foss, N.J. 2005. Strategic organization: A field in search of micro-foundations. *Strategic Organization*, 3(4): 441–55. Available at: http://soq.sagepub.com/contents/3/4/441.refs/.

Fernandez, R. 1983. *Excess Profits: The Rise of United Technologies*. Boston, MA: Addison-Wesley.

Fiegenbaum, A. and Thomas, H. 1988. Attitudes towards risk and the risk-return paradox: Prospect theory explanations. *Academy of Management Journal*, 31(1): 85–106.

Financial Reporting Council (FRC), 2005. *Internal Control: Guidance for Directors on the Combined Code* (The Turnbull Guidance). Available at: http://www.frc.org.uk/corporate/internalcontrol.cfm/.

Finkelstein, S., Harvey, C., and Lawton, T. 2008. Vision by design: A reflexive approach to enterprise regeneration. *Journal of Business Strategy*, 29(2): 4–13.

Fisher, K. and Shorter, J. 2013. Emerging ethical issues: Universities and information warfare. *Journal of Academic and Business Ethics*, 7: 1–9.

Fombrun, C. 1996. *Reputation: Realizing Value from the Corporate Image*. Boston, MA: Harvard Business School Press.

Foreign Policy. 2012. Switzerland: Excellent at the heart of Europe. *Foreign Policy*, 195:1.

Fousfuri, A. and Giarratana, M.S. 2009. Masters of war: Rivals' product innovation and new advertising in mature product markets. *Management Science*, 55(2): 181–91.

Fowler, S.J. and Hope, C. 2007. Incorporating sustainable business practices into company strategy. *Business Strategy and the Environment*, 16(1): 26–38.

Frankelius, P. 2009. Questioning two myths in innovation literature. *Journal of High Technology Management Research*, 20(1): 40–51.

Friedman, T.L. 2006. *The World is Flat: A Brief History of the Twenty-First Century*. New York: Farrar, Straus and Girous.

Friedmann, J. 1986. The world city hypothesis. *Development and Change*, 17(1): 69–83.

Frigo, M.L. 2008. When strategy and ERM meet. *Strategic Finance*, 1: 45–9.

Frigo, M.L. and Anderson, R.J. 2009. Strategic risk assessment: A first step for improving risk management and governance. *Strategic Finance*, 12: 24–33.

Frigo, M.L. and Anderson, R.J. 2011a. *Embracing Enterprise Risk Management*. Commissioned by COSO – Committee of Sponsoring Organizations of the Treadway Commission. Available at: http://www.COSO.org/documents/EmbracingERM-GettingStartedforWebPostingDec110_000.pdf.

Frigo, M.L. and Anderson, R.J. 2011b. What is strategic risk management? *Strategic Finance* (April 2011): 21, 22 and 61.

Galbraith, J.R. 2012. The future of organization design. *Journal of Organization Design*, 1(1): 3–6.

Galunic, D.C. and Eisenhardt, K.M. 2001. Architectural innovation and modular corporate forms. *Academy of Management Journal*, 44: 1229–49.

Garnsey, E. 1998. A theory of the early growth of the firm. *Industrial and Corporate Change*, 7(3): 523–56.

Garvey, W. 2011. Pratt gears up for PW1000G. *Aviation Week*, January 9, 2011. Available at: http://en.wikipedia.org/wiki/Pratt_%26_Whitney_PW1000G/.

Garvin, D.A. 1998. The processes of organization and management. *Sloan Management Review*, 39(4): 33–50.

Gates, D.M., Remmel, A., Adamson, B.J., and Hutt, L.J. 2000. A collaborative approach to workforce transformation: Food and nutrition services staff education. *Journal of Dietetic Practice and Research*, 6(1): 13–17.

Gemser, G. and Wijnberg, N.M. 2001. Effects of reputational sanctions on the competitive imitation of design innovations. *Organization Studies*, 22(4): 563–91.

George, B. 2003. *Authentic Leadership: Rediscovering the Secrets to Creating Lasting Value*. San Francisco, CA: Jossey-Bass.

Gerstner, Jr., L.V. 2002. *Who Says Elephants Can't Dance? Inside IBM's Historic Turnaround*. New York: Collins.

Gilbert, B.A., McDougall, P.P., and Audretsch, D.B. 2006. New venture growth: A review and extension. *Journal of Management*, 32(6): 926–50.

Gioia, D.C., Schulz, M., and Corley, K.C. 2000. Organizational identity, image, and adaptive instability. *Academy of Management Review*, 25(1): 63–81.

Glatstein, S. 2007. *Business Strategy Execution: Four Reasons Why Your Company's Strategy Isn't Working*. Gig Harbor, WA: Insurance Marketing Communication Association. Available at: tseibert@imcanet.com.

Goerzen, A. 2007. Alliance networks and firm performance: The impact of repeated partnerships. *Strategic Management Journal*, 28(5): 487–509.

Goerzen, A. and Beamish, P. 2003. Geographic scope and multinational enterprise performance. *Strategic Management Journal*, 24(13): 1289–306.

Goerzen, A. and Beamish, P. 2005. The effect of alliance network diversity on multinational enterprise performance. *Strategic Management Journal*, 26(4): 333–54.

Goerzen, A, Asmussen, C.G., and Nielsen, B.B. 2013. Global cities and multinational enterprise location strategy. *Journal of International Business Studies*, 44(5): 427–50.

Golbeck, J. and Rothstein, M. 2008. Linking Social Networks on the Web with FOAF: A Semantic Web Case Study. Proceedings of the Twenty-Third Conference on Artificial Intelligence (AAAI'08), July 13–17, Chicago, Illinois. Available at: http://www.aaai.org/Library/AAAI/aaai08contents.php/.

Googins, B.K. and Rochlin, S.A. 2000. Creating the partnership society: Understanding the rhetoric and reality of cross-sector partnerships. *Business and Society Review*, 105(1): 127–44.

Gordon, I. and McCann, P. 2000. Industrial clusters: Complexes, agglomeration and/or social networks? *Urban Studies*, 37(3): 513–32.

Gordon, L.A., Loeb, M.P. and Tseng, Chih-Yang. 2009. Enterprise risk management and firm performance: A contingency perspective. *Journal of Accounting and Public Policy*, 28(4): 301–27.

Gottfredson, L.S. and Deary, I.J. 2004. Intelligence predicts health and longevity, but why? *Current Directions in Psychological Science*, 13: 1–4.

Gottfredson, M. and Schaubert, S. 2008. *The Breakthrough Imperative: How the Best Managers Get Outstanding Results*. New York: HarperCollins.

Grant, R.M. 1991. The resource-based theory of competitive advantage: Implications of strategy formulation. *California Management Review* 33(3): 114–35.

Gray, B. 1985. Conditions facilitating inter-organizational collaboration. *Human Relations*, 38(10): 911–36.

Greenberg, R. and Unger, C. 1992. Improving the environmental process. *Total Quality Environmental Management*: 269–76.

Greenwood, M.R.C. and Riordan, D.G. 2001. Civic scientist/civic duty. *Science Communication*, 231: 28–40.

Grigg, N. and Mann, R. 2008. Promoting excellence: An international study into creating awareness of business excellence models. *The TQM Journal*, 20(3): 233–48.

Grinyer, P.H. and Spender, J.C. 1979. Recipes, crises, and adaptation in mature businesses. *International Studies of Management & Organization*, 9(3): 113–33.

Guenster, N., Bauer, R., Derwall, J., and Koedijk, K. 2010. The economic value of corporate eco-efficiency. *European Financial Management*, 17(4): 679–704.

Gulbrandsen, L. 2004. Overlapping public and private governance: Can forest certification fill the gaps in the global forest regime? *Global Environmental Politics*, 4(2): 75–99.

Gumus, S. and Apak, S. 2011. Strategies of international growth in enterprises and strategic alliances. In Ozsahin, M. (eds), The Proceeding of 7th International Strategic Management Conference, September 26, 2011.

Gunderman, R.B. 2011. *Achieving Excellence in Medical Education*, 2nd edn. London: Springer-Verlag.

Hackett, G. 1997. *How to Handle the Naysayers*. Hudson, OH: Hackett Group. Available at: http://www.aicpa.org/pubs/jofa/jan97/transfrm.htm/.

Hafeez, K., Zhang, Y., and Malak, N. 2002. Core competence for sustainable competitive advantage: A structural methodology for identifying core competence. *IEEE Transactions on Engineering Management*, 49(1): 28–35.

Hajer, M. 1995. *The Politics of Environmental Discourse: Ecological Modernization and the Policy Process*. Oxford: Oxford University Press.

Hales, C.P. 1999. Leading horses to water? The impact of decentralization on managerial behavior. *Journal of Management Studies*, 36(6): 831–51.

Hales, C.P. and Mustapha, N. 2000. Commonalities and variations in managerial work: A study of middle managers in Malaysia. *Asia Pacific Journal of Human Resources*, 38(1): 731–56.

Hales, C.P. and Tamangani, Z. 1996. An investigation of the relationship between organizational structure, managerial role expectations and managers' work activities. *Journal of Management Studies*, 33(6): 731–56.

Hamel, G. 1994. The concept of core competence. In Hamel, G. and Heene, A. (eds), *Competence-based Competition*. New York: John Wiley & Sons, 11–33.

Handy, C. 1989. *The Age of Unreason*. London: Business Books.

Hanoch, Y., Johnson, J. and Wilke, A. 2006. Domain-specificity in experimental measures and participant recruitment: An application to risk-taking behavior. *Psychological Science*, 17(4): 300–304.

Harpst, G. 2008. Strategy execution. *Leadership Excellence*, 25(9): 19.

Harrison, A. and McMillan, M. 2006. Dispelling some myths about offshoring. *Academy of Management Perspectives*, 20(4): 6–23.

Hart, J. 2005. Excellence in execution. *Leadership Excellence*, 22(12): 14.

Hart, S.L. and Dowell, G. 2011. A natural-resource-based view of the firm: Fifteen years later. *Journal of Management*, 37(5): 1464–79.

Hartigan, P. 2004. The challenge for social entrepreneurship. Schwab Foundation for Social Entrepreneurship Global Summit 2004, Brazil. Available at: http://www.Scribd.com/doc/8177320/Pamela-Hartigan-The-Challenge-for-Social-Enterprenership-2004#Scribd/.

Hastings, D.F. 1999. Lincoln Electric's harsh lessons from international expansion. *Harvard Business Review*, 77(3): 162–78.

Haudan, J. 2009. Strategy execution. *Leadership Excellence*, 26(8): 12–13.

Hauser, J.R. and Clausing, D. 1988. The house of quality. *Harvard Business Review*, 66: 63–73.

Hazardous Materials Response and Assessment Division. 1992. *Oil Spill Case Histories 1967–1991*. Report No. HMRAD 92–11 (PDF). Seattle: National Oceanic and Atmospheric Administration, 80.

Hedman, J. and Borell, A. 2002. The impact of enterprise resource planning systems on organizational effectiveness: An artifact evaluation. In Nah, F.F.-H. (ed.), *Enterprise Resource Planning Solutions and Management*. London and Hershey, PA: IRM Press.

Held, D., McGrew, A., Goldblatt, D., and Perraton, J. 1999. *Global Transformation*. Stanford, CA: Stanford University Press.

Helfat, C.E. and Peteraf, M.A. 2003. The dynamic resource-based view: Capability lifecycles. *Strategic Management Journal*, 24(10): 997–1010.

Helfat, C.E., Finkelstein, S., Mitchell, W., Peteraf, M.A., Singh, H., Teece, D.J., and Winter, S.G. 2007. *Dynamic Capabilities: Understanding Strategic Change in Organizations*. Oxford: Blackwell.

Henderson, B. 1970. *Growth-Share Matrix*. Boston, MA: Boston Consulting Group.

Henderson, R.M. and Clark, K.B. 1990. Architectural innovation: The reconfiguration of existing product technologies and the failure of established firms. *Administrative Science Quarterly*, 35(1): 9–30.

Hendrix, P. 2012. Mobilizing the Enterprise with off-the-Shelf Apps and Custom Mobile Solutions. White paper sponsored by SAP, August 2012.

Hennart, J.F. 1991. Control of multinational firms: The role of price and hierarchy. *Management International Review*, 31(Special Issue): 71–96.

Hennart, J.F. and Park, Y.R. 1993. Greenfield vs acquisition: The strategy of Japanese investors in the United States. *Management Science*, 39(9): 1054–70.

Hespenheide, E., Pundmann, S. and Corcoran, M. 2007. Risk intelligence: Internal auditing in a world of risk. *Internal Auditing*, 22(4): 3–8.

Hess, E.D. and Kazanjian, R.K. (eds) 2006. *The Search for Organic Growth*. Cambridge: Cambridge University Press.

Hicks, D. and Katz, J.S. 2011. Equity and excellence in research funding. *Minerva*, 49(2): 137–51.

Higgins, J. 2005. The eight "S"s of successful strategy execution. *Journal of Change Management*, 5(1): 3–13.

Hill, C. and Jones, G. 2008. *Strategic Management: An Integrated Approach*, 8th edn. Mason, OH: South-Western Educational Publishing.

Hillson, D. 2006. Integrated Risk Management as a Framework for Organizational Success. PMI Global Congress Proceedings, Seattle, Washington, 1–6. Available at: http://www.risk-doctor.com/pdf-files/adv13.pdf.

Hoffmann, E. 2012. *User Integration in Sustainable Product Development: Organisational Learning through Boundary-Spanning Processes*. Sheffield: Greenleaf Publishing.

Holland, C. and Light, B. 1999. A critical success factors model for ERP implementation. *IEEE Software*, 16(3): 30–36.

Hopkin, P. 2002. *Holistic Risk Management in Practice*. Livingston: Witherby & Co Ltd.

Hotho, J.J., Becker-Ritterspach, F., and Saka-Helmhout, A. 2012. Enriching absorptive capacity through social interaction. *British Journal of Management*, 23(3): 383–401.

Houston, D.J. 1999. Implications of the 65-mph speed limit for traffic safety. *Evaluation Review*, 23(3): 304–15.

Hoyt, R.E. and Liebenberg, A.P. 2011. The value of enterprise risk management. *Journal of Risk and Insurance*, 78(4): 795–822.

Hrebiniak, L.G. 2005. *Making Strategy Work: Leading Effective Execution and Change*. Upper Saddle River, NJ: Wharton School Publishing.

Hrebiniak, L.G. 2006. Obstacles to effective strategy implementation. *Organizational Dynamics*, 35(1): 12–31.

Hrebiniak, L.G. and Joyce, W.F. 1984. *Implementing Strategy: Collier*. London: Macmillan.

Hubbard, D.W. 2009. *The Failure of Risk Management: Why It's Broken and How to Fix It*. Hoboken, NJ: John Wiley & Sons.

Human Security Network. 2000. *Chairman's Summary*. Second Ministerial Meeting of the Human Security Network, May, Lucerne, Switzerland. Available at: http://www.dfaitmaeci.gc.ca/foreignp/humansecurity/chairman_summary-e.asp/.

Hutchinson, W. 2002. Concepts in information warfare. *Logistics Information Management*, 15(5): 410–13.

Huy, Q. 2013. An Emotional Approach to Strategy Execution. *INSEAD*: N_A. December 2013.

Hymer, S. 1976. *The International Operations of National Firms: A Study of Direct Foreign Investment*. Cambridge, MA: MIT Press.

IBM. 2009. *What is IBM Workplace for Business Strategy Execution 1.0?* Available at: http://www-1.ibm.com/support/docview.wss?rs=2333&context=SSESJN&dc=DB520&uid/.

Ifinedo, P. and Nahar, N. 2006. Prioritization of Enterprise Resource Planning (ERP) systems success measures: Viewpoints of two organizational stakeholder groups. Paper presented at the 2006 ACM Symposium on Applied Computing, April 23–27, Dijon, France, 1554–60.

IIF. 2009. *Risk Culture Reform in the Financial Services Industry: Strengthening Practices for a More Stable System*. The Institute of International Finance. Available at: iifreport_reformfinancialservicesindustry_1209.pdf.

Insight Formation, Inc. 2007. Strategy Execution and Alignment. Available at: http://www.insightformation.com/learn-more/strategy-execution-alignment.html/.

IRM. 2012. *Risk Culture under the Microscope Guidance for Board*. The Institute of Risk Management. Available at: http://www.theirm.org/media/885907/Risk_Culture_A5_WEB15_Oct_2012.pdf.

ISO. 2009a. *Guide 73*. International Organization for Standardization. Available at: http://www.iso.org/ISO/Catalogue_detail?CSnumber=44651/.

ISO. 2009b. *Risk Management: Principles and Guideline*. International Organization for Standardization. Available at: http://www.iso.org/ISO/Catalogue_detail?CSnumber=43170/.

Jacobs, J. 1984. *Cities and the Wealth of Nations*. New York: Random House.

Jamail, D. 2012. BP settles while Manondo "seeps." *Al Jazeera*, March 4, 2012. Available at: http://www.aljazeera.com/indepth/features/2012/03/201233133318459762.html/.

James, P. and Bennett, M. 1994. *Environmental-Related Performance Measurement in Business: From Emissions to Profit and Sustainability?* Berkhamsted: Ashridge Management Research Group.

Jankins, M. 2014. Innovate or imitate? The role of collective beliefs in competences in competing firms. *Long Range Planning*, 47(4): 173–85.

Jervis, R. and Levin, A. 2010. Obama, in Gulf, pledges to push on stopping leak. *USA Today*, Associated Press, May 27, 2010.

Jo, H. and Harjoto, M.A. 2011. Corporate governance and firm value: The impact of corporate social responsibility. *Journal of Business Ethics*, 103(3): 351–83.

Johanson, J. and Vahlne, J. 1977. The internationalization process of the firm: A model of knowledge development and increasing foreign market commitments. *Journal of International Business Studies*, 8(1): 23–32.

Johnson, S. 2007. SC Johnson builds business at the base of the pyramid. *Global Business and Organizational Excellence*, 26(6): 6–17.

Johnson, T., Richardson, K., and Turnbull, G. 2007. *Expanding Values: A Guide to Social Franchising in the Social Enterprise Sector*. Finland: SIPS Transnational Partnership.

Jordan, J., Sivanathan, N. and Galinsky, A.D. 2012. Something to lose and nothing to gain: The role of stress in the interactive effect of power and stability on risk-taking. *Administrative Science Quarterly*, 56: 530–58.

Juha-Pekka, M. 2007. Next Generation SIOP: Achieving operational excellence in an extended enterprise. *Supply Chain Europe*, 16(4): 26–9.

Kacelnik, A. and Bateson, M. 1996. Risky theories: The effects of variance on foraging decisions. *American Zoologist*, 36(4): 402–43.

Kacelnik, A. and Bateson, M. 1997. Risk-sensitivity: Crossroads for theories of decision-making. *Trends in Cognitive Sciences*, 1: 304–9.

Kanter, R.M. 1989. The new managerial work. *Harvard Business Review*, 67(6): 85–92.

Kaplan, R. 2007. It's all about strategy execution. Available at: http://www.jamehealy.com/it_s_all_about_strategy_execution/.

Kaplan, R.S. and Norton, D.P. 1992. The balanced scorecard: Measures that drive performance. *Harvard Business Review*: 71–9.

Kaplan, R.S. and Norton, D.P. 1993. Putting the balanced scorecard to work. *Harvard Business Review*: 2–15.

Kaplan, R.S. and Norton, D.P. 1996a. Using the balanced scorecard as a strategic management system. *Harvard Business Review*, 74(1): 75–85.

Kaplan, R.S. and Norton, D.P. 1996b. Linking the balanced Scorecard to strategy. *California Management Review* 39(1): 53–79.

Kaplan, R.S. and Norton, D.P. 2000. *The Strategy Focused Organization*. Boston, MA: Harvard Business School Press.

Kaplan, R.S. and Norton, D.P. 2001. Transforming the balanced scorecard from performance measurement to strategic management: Part I. *Accounting Horizons*, 15(1): 87–104.

Kaplan, R.S. and Norton, D.P. 2004. *Strategy Maps: Converting Intangible Assets into Tangible Outcomes*. Boston, MA: Harvard Business Publishing.

Kaplan, R.S. and Norton, D.P. 2008. *The Execution Premium: Linking Strategy to Operations for Competitive Advantage*. Cambridge, MA: Harvard Business Press.

Kaplan, R.S. and Norton, D.P. 2013. *The Execution Premium: Linking Strategy to Operations for Competitive Advantage*. Boston, MA: Harvard Business Press.

Kaplinsky, R. 2006. Asian drivers: Opportunities and threats. *IDS Bulletin*, 37(1): 107–14.

Katzenbach, J.R. and Smith, D.K. 1993. *The Wisdom of Teams: Creating High-performance Organizations*. Boston, MA: Harvard Business School Press.

Keeling, M. 2013. Mission statement: Rhetoric, realty, road map to success? *Knowledge Quest*, 42(10): 30–36.

Keil, T., Laamanen, T., and McGrath, R.G. 2013. Is a counter attack the best defense? Competitive dynamics through acquisitions. *Long Range Planning*, 46(3): 195–215.

Kerner, A. and Lawrence, J. 2014. What's the risk? Bilateral investment treaties, political risk and fixed capital accumulation. *British Journal of Political Science*, 44(1): 107–21.

Khadem, R. 2008. Alignment and follow-up: Steps to strategy execution. *Journal of Business Strategy*, 29(6): 29–35.

Khalifa, A.S. 2011. Three Fs for the mission statement: What's next? *Journal of Strategy and Management*, 4(1): 25–43.

Khan, A.M. 1989. Innovation and non-innovative small firms: Types and characteristics. *Management Science*, 35(5): 597–606.

Kim, J. and Wilemon, D. 2002. Sources and assessment of complexity in NPD Projects. *R&D Management*, 33(1): 16–30.

Kimmel, P.D., Weygandt, J.J., and Kieso, D.E. 2011. *Financial Accounting*, 6th edn. New York: John Wiley & Sons.

Kindleberger, C. 1969. *American Business Abroad: Six Lectures on Direct Investment*. New Haven, CT: Yale University Press.

King, G. and Murray, C. 2000. *Rethinking Human Security*. Cambridge, MA: Harvard University Press. Available at: http://gking.harvard.edu/files/hs.pdf.

King, K. and Kosminsky, F. 2006. *Maximize Strategy Execution by Aligning Organisational Resources*. Korn/Ferry International. Available at: http://www.kornferrt.com.

Kistner, R. 2011. The macondo monkey on BP's back. *Huffington Post*, September 30, 2011.

Klein, J.A. and Hiscocks, P.G. 1994. Competence-based competition: A practical toolkit. In Hamel, G. and Heene, A. (eds), *Competence-based Competition*. New York: John Wiley & Sons, 183–212.

Kleindorfer, P.R. and Saad, G.H. 2005. Managing disruption risk in supply chain. *Production and Operations Management*, 14(1): 53–68.

Kline, S.J. 1985. *Research, Innovation and Production: Models and Reality*. Report INN-1, Mechanical Engineering Department, Stanford University, California.

Koen, P. Ajamian, G. Burkart, R. Clamen, A. Davidson, J. D'Amore, R. Elkins, C. Herald, K. Incorvia, M. Johnson, A. Karol, R. Seibert, R. Slavejkov, A. and Wagner, K. 2001. Providing clarity and a common language to the "fuzzy front end." *Research Technology Management*, 44(2): 46–55.

Kogut, B. and Zander, U. 1996. What firms do? Coordination, identity, and learning. *Organization Science*, 7(5): 502–18.

Komashie, A., Mousavi, A., and Gore, J. 2007. Quality management in healthcare and industry: A comparative review and emerging themes. *Journal of Management History*, 13(4): 359–70.

Korsgaard, S. and Anderson, A.R. 2011. Enacting entrepreneurship as social value creation. *International Small Business Journal*, 29(20): 135–51.

Kotler, P. 2002. *A Framework for Marketing Management*, 2nd edn. Englewood Cliffs, NJ: Prentice Hall.

Kotter, J.P. 2007. Leading change: Why transformation efforts fail. *Harvard Business Review*, 85(1): 96–103.

Kouzes, J.M. and Posner, B.Z. 1987. *The Leadership Challenges: How to Get Extraordinary Things Done in Organizations*. San Francisco, CA: Jossey-Bass.

KPMG. 2008. *Understanding and Articulating Risk Appetite*. London: KPMG.

Kraatz, M.S. and Zajac, E.J. 2001. How organizational resources affect strategic change and performance in turbulent environments: Theory and evidence. *Organization Science*, 12(5): 632–57.

Krugman, P. 1991. *Geography and Trade*. Cambridge, MA: MIT Press.

Kumar, D. 2009. Notes on Enterprise Excellence Certificate (EEC) Program. (Unpublished). North Carolina State University.

Kumar, D. 2010a. *Enterprise Growth Strategy: Vision, Planning and Execution*. Farnham: Gower.

Kumar, D. 2010b. Role of enterprise excellence initiative. *International Journal of Business and Management*, 5(8): 3–12.

Kumar, D. 2014. Enterprise excellence through growth strategy and risk management. *British Journal of Economics, Management & Trade*, 4(5): 804–21.

Kumar, D., Menon, S.K., and Rachakonda, S. 2012. Transformation Case in a Small Enterprise. IIE Annual Conference & Expo 2012, May 19–23. Conference Proceedings CD/ROM were distributed in the conference and can be purchased through IIE.

Kuncel, N.R., Hezlett, S.A. and Ones, D.S. 2004. Academic performance, career potential, creativity, and job performance: Can one construct predict them all? *Journal of Personality and Social Psychology*, 86: 148–61.

Lafley, A.G. and Martin, R.L. 2013. *Playing to Win: How Strategy Really Works*. Boston, MA: Harvard Business School Publishing.

Lai, F.W. and Samad, F.A. 2010. Enterprise Risk Management Framework and the Empirical Determinants of Its Implementation. International Conference on Business and Economic Research. Available at: http://www.ipedr.com/vol1/73-G10003.pdf.

Lam, J. 2001. The CRO is here to stay. *Risk Management*, 48(4): 16–20.

Lam, J. 2003. *Enterprise Risk Management: From Incentives to Controls*, 1st edn. New York: John Wiley & Sons.

Lam, J. and Associates. 2008. Emerging best practices in developing key risk indicators and ERM reporting. Executive White Paper sponsored by Cognos.

Laszlo, C. and Zhexembayeva, N. 2011. *Embedded Sustainability: The Next Big Competitive Advantage*. Sheffield: Greenleaf Publishing.

LaVelle, R., Lesser, E., Shockley, R., Hopkins, M.S., and Kruschwitz, N. 2011. Big data, analytics, and the path from insights to value. *MIT Sloan Management Review*, 52(2): 21–31.

Lawrence, R.Q. 2005. ERM. Embracing a Total Risk Model. *Financial Executives International*, 21(1): 32.

Lazonick, W. 2014. Innovative enterprise and shareholder value. *Law and Financial Market Review*, 8(1): 52–64.

Lei, D., Hitt, M.A., and Bettis, R. 1996. Dynamic core competences through meta-learning and strategic control. *Journal of Management*, 22(4): 549–69.

Leonard-Barton, D. 1992. Core capabilities and core rigidities: A paradox in managing product development. *Strategic Management Journal*, 13(5): 111–25.

Li, J. 1995. Foreign entry and survival: Effects on strategic choices on performance in international markets. *Strategic Management Journal*, 16(5): 333–51.

Li, N.P., Bailey, J.M., Kenrick, D.T., and Linsenmeier, J.A.W. 2002. The necessities and luxuries of mate preferences: Testing the tradeoffs. *Journal of Personality and Social Psychology*, 82: 947–55.

Library-Thinkquest. Available at: http://library.thinkquest.org/10867/spill/timeline.shtml/.

Lichtenthaler, U. 2009. Absorptive capacity, environmental turbulence, and the complementarity of organizational learning processes. *Academy of Management Journal*, 52(4): 822–46.

Lieberman, M.B. and Montgomery, D.B. 1988. First mover advantages. *Strategic Management Journal*, 9: 41–58.

Light, P.C. 2005. *The Four Pillars of High Performance: How Robust Organizations Achieve Extraordinary Results*. New York: McGraw-Hill.

Lippman, S.A. and Rumelt, R.P. 1982. Uncertain imitability: An analysis of interfirm differences in efficiency under competition. *Bell Journal of Economics*, 13(2): 418–38.

Lipton, M., Neff, D.A., Brownstein, A.R. et al. 2010. Risk Management and the Board of Directors. Law firm of Wachtell, Lipton, Rosen and Katz. 51 West 52nd Street, New York, NY 10019-6150. Available at: RiskMan agementAndBoardOfDirectors-Law Firm-Wachtell-Lipton-etal-Dec2010.pdf.

Lissovolik, B. 2008. Trends in Italy's non-price competitiveness. Working Paper WP/08/124. Washington, DC: International Monetary Fund.

Litalien, B.C. 2006. Era of the social franchise: Where franchising and nonprofits come together. *Franchising World*, 38(6): 77–88.

Lockett, A., Thompson, S., and Morgenstern, U. 2009. The development of the resource-based view of the firm: A critical appraisal. *International Journal of Management Reviews*, 11(1): 9–28.

London, T., Rondinelli, D.A., and O'Neill, H. 2006. Strange bedfellows: Alliances between corporations and non-profits. In Shanker, O. and Reuer, J.J. (eds), *Handbook of Strategic Alliances*. Thousand Oaks, CA: SAGE.

Long, L. 2008. Value chain management in online reverse auction: Towards strategic and operational excellence. *Academy of Information & Management Science Journal*, 11(1): 13–28.

Lorenzen, M. and Mudambi, R. 2013. Clusters, connectivity, and catch-up: Bollywood and Bangalore in the global economy. *Journal of Economic Geography*, 13(3): 501–34.

Lubin, D. and Esty, D. 2010. The sustainability imperative. *Harvard Business Review*, 88(5): 42–50.

Luo, Y. and Tung, R.L. 2007. International expansion of emerging market enterprises: A springboard perspective. *Journal of International Business Studies*, 38(4): 481–98.

Ma, X., Tong, T., and Fitza, M. 2012. How much does subnational region matter to foreign subsidiary performance? Evidence from Fortune Global 500 Corporations' investment in China. *Journal of International Business Studies*, 44(1): 66–87.

Maan, J. 2012. A connected enterprise: Transformation through mobility and social networks. *International Journal of Managing Information Technology*, 4(3): 89–96.

MacKay, B. and Munro, I. 2012. Information warfare and new organizational landscapes: An inquiry into the ExxonMobil–Greenpeace dispute over climate change. *Organization Studies*, 33(11): 1507–36.

Maclean, M., Harvey, C., and Gordon, J. 2012. Social innovation, social entrepreneurship and the practice of contemporary entrepreneurial philanthropy. *International Small Business Journal*. Online. April 29, 2012. DOI: 10: 1177/0266242612443376.

Makino, S. and Neupert, K. 2000. National culture, transaction costs, and the choice between joint venture and wholly owned subsidiary. *Journal of International Business Studies*, 31(4): 705–13.

Malone, T.W. 2003. Is empowerment just a fad? Control, decision making and IT. In Malone, T.W., Laubacher, R., and Scott Morton, M.S. (eds), *Inventing the Organizations of the 21st Century*. Cambridge, MA: The MIT Press.

Maner, J.K., Gailliot, M.T., Butz, D.A., and Peruche, B.M. 2007. Power, risk, and the status quo: Does power promote riskier or more conservative decision making? *Personality and Social Psychology Bulletin*, 33: 451–62.

Mankins, M.C. and Steele, R. 2005. *Turning Great Strategy into Great Performance*. Boston, MA: Harvard Business School Publishing.

Manktelow, J. and Carlson, A. 1991. The McKinsey 7S Framework. *Mind Tools*. Available at: http://www.mindtools. com/pages/article/newSTR_91.htm/.

Mansfield, R.S. 1966. Building competency models: Approaches for HR professionals. *Human Resource Management*, 35(1): 7–18.

Maranville, S. 1992. Entrepreneurship in the business curriculum. *Journal of Education for or Business*, 68(1): 27–31.

Mark, M., Katz, B., Rahman, S. and Warren, D. 2008. *Metro Policy: Shaping a New Federal Partnership for a Metropolitan Nation*. Metropolitan Policy Program Report. Washington, DC: Brookings Institution, 4–103.

Markides, C. and Geroski, P.A. 2005. *Fast Second: How Smart Companies Bypass Radical Innovation to Enter and Dominate New Markets*. San Francisco, CA: Jossey-Bass.

Marn, M. and Rosiello, R. 1992. Managing price, gaining profit. *Harvard Business Review* (September–October 1992): 84–94.

Marsden, T. 2010. Mobilizing the regional eco-economy: Evolving webs of agri-food and rural development in the UK. *Cambridge Journal of Regions, Economy and Society*, 3(2): 225–44.

Martin, R.L. 2010. The execution trap. *Harvard Business Review*, 88(7/8): 1–8.

Mata, J. and Portugal, P. 2004. Patterns of entry, post-entry growth and survival: A comparison between domestic and foreign owned firms. *Small Business Economics*, 22(3–4): 283–98.

Mathews, J.A., Hu, M.-C., and Wu, C.-Y. 2011. Fast-follower industrial dynamics: The case of Taiwan's emergent solar photovoltaic industry. *Industry and Innovation*, 18(2): 177–202.

Mathrani, S., Mathrani, A., and Viehland, D. 2013. Using enterprise systems to realize digital business strategies. *Journal of Enterprise Information Management*, 26(4): 363–86.

Mattli, W. 2003. Public and private governance in setting international standards. In Kahler, M. and Lake, D.A. (eds), *Governance in a Global Economy: Political Authority in Transition*. Princeton, NJ: Princeton University Press.

Maurer, I., Bartsch, V., and Ebers, M. 2011. The value of intra-organizational social capital: How it fosters knowledge transfer, innovation performance, and growth. *Organization Studies*, 32(2): 157–85.

Maynard, M. 2008. A new Bombardier jet draws only tepid demand. *New York Times*, July 14, 2008.

McCallum, J. 1995. National borders matter: Canada–US regional trade patterns. *American Economic Review*, 85(3): 615–23.

McCann, P. and Mudambi, R. 2005. Analytical differences in the economics of geography: The case of the multinational firm. *Environment and Planning*, 37(10): 1857–76.

McCloughan, P. and Stone, I. 1998. Life duration of foreign multinational subsidiaries: Evidence from UK northern manufacturing industry 1970–93. *International Journal of Industrial Organization*, 16(6): 719–47.

McDonough, W. and Braungart, M. 2002. Design for the triple top line: New tools for sustainable commerce. *Corporate Environmental Strategy*, 9(6): 251–8.

McElhaney, K. 2009. A strategic approach to corporate social responsibility. *Leader to Leader*, 52: 30–36.

McFarlan, F.W. 1984. Information technology changes the way you compete. *Harvard Business Review*, 62(3): 98–103.

McIntire, J.T. 2008. Discover and use your core competency. Three Sigma, Inc. Available at: http://www. threesigma.com/.

McKellar, R. 2010. *A Short Guide to Political Risk*. Farnham: Gower.

McMurray, A. 2010. Empowerment and enterprise: The political economy of nursing. *Collegian*, 17(3): 113–18.

McPeak, C. and Tooley, N. 2008. Do corporate social responsibility leaders perform better financially? *Journal of Global Business Issues*, 2(2): 1–6.

Melville, N.P. 2010. Information systems innovation for environmental sustainability. *MIS Quarterly*, 34(1): 1–21.

Mendus, S. 2008. Life's ethical symphony. *Journal of Philosophy of Education*, 42(2): 201–18.

Meulbroek, L.K. 2002. Integrated risk management for the firm: A senior manager's guide. *Journal of Applied Corporate Finance*, 14: 56–70.

Meyer, K. and Day, M. 2014. Building dynamic capabilities of adaptation and innovation: A study of micro-foundations in a transition economy. *Long Range Planning*, 47(4): 186–205.

Meyer, M.H., Anzani, M., and Walsh, G. 2005. Innovation and enterprise growth. *Research-Technology Management*, 48(4): 34–44.

Mezias, J. 2002. Identifying liabilities of foreignness and strategies to minimize their effects: The case of labor lawsuit judgments in the United States. *Strategic Management Journal*, 23(3): 229–44.

Miccolis, J. and Shah, S. 2000. *Enterprise Risk Management: An Analytic Approach*. New York: Tillinghast-Towers Perrin Monograph.

Michael, S.O. 2005. The cost of excellence: The financial implications of institutional rankings. *International Journal of Educational Management*, 19(5): 365–82.

Miguel, P.A.C. 2004. *A Report on Comparing Worldwide Quality and Business Excellence Awards. Part 1: Systems of Operations, Core Values and Assessment Criteria*. Gaithersburg, MD: National Institution of Standards and Technology (NIST).

Millar, C.J.M., Choi, C.J., and Chen, S. 2004. Global strategic partnerships between MNE's and NGO's: Drivers of change and ethical issues. *Business and Society Review*, 109(4): 395–414.

Miller, A. 2014. Without execution there is no strategy. *Industry Week*: N_A. September 18, 2014.

Miller, K.D. 1992. A framework for integrated risk management in international business. *Journal of International Business Studies*, 23(2): 311–31.

Miller, K.D. and Waller, H.G. 2003. Scenarios, real options and integrated risk management. *Long Range Planning*, 36(1): 93–107.

Mintzberg, H. 1973. *The Nature of Managerial Work*. New York: Harper & Row.

Mintzberg, H. 2009. *Managing*. Harrow: Financial Times/Prentice Hall.

Mishra, S. and Fiddick, L. 2012. Beyond gains and losses: The effect of need on risky choice in framed decisions. *Journal of Personality and Social Psychology*, 102: 1136–47.

Mishra, S., Barclay, P. and Lalumiere, M. 2014. Competitive disadvantage facilitates risk taking. *Evolution of Human Behavior*, 35(2): 126–32.

Mitchell, W., Shaver, J.M., and Yeung, B. 1994. Foreign entrant survival and foreign market share: Canadian companies' experience in United States medical sector markets. *Strategic Management Journal*, 15(7): 555–67.

Moeller, R. 2007. COSO *Enterprise Risk Management: Understanding the new Integrated ERM Framework*. Hoboken, NJ: John Wiley & Sons.

Moeller, R. 2009. *Brink's Modern Internal Auditing: A Common Body of Knowledge*. New York: Wiley & Sons.

Monda, B. and Giorgino, M. 2013. An Enterprise Risk Management Maturity Model. Munich Personal RePEc Archive (MPRA). January 2013. Available at: http://mpra.ub.uni-muenchen.de/45421/.

Morden, T. 2011. *A Short Guide to Equality Risk*. Farnham: Gower.

Morden, T. 2013. *Equality, Diversity and Opportunity Management: Costs, Strategies and Leadership*. Farnham: Gower.

Morgan, G. 1993. *Imaginization*. London: Sage.

Morphew, C.C. and Matthew H. 2006. Mission statements: A thematic analysis of rhetoric across institutional type. *Journal of Higher Education*, 77(3): 456–71.

Morrill, L. and Warudkar, H. 2003. From strategy to execution. *Intelligent Enterprise*, 6(18): 20–27.

Mosley, A. 1996. Overcoming the practical barriers to implementing performance measures which are linked to organizational goals. London: Paper presented at the Conference on Effective and Meaningful Performance Measurement. June 17–18, 1996. Conference Proceedings at IIR Ltd.

Mudambi, R. and Swift, T. 2011. Leveraging knowledge and competencies across space: The next frontier in international business. *Journal of International Management*, 17(3): 186–9.

Munin, N. 2013. NGOs, Multinational enterprises and gender equality in labor markets: A political economy of conflicting interests? *Journal of Multidisciplinary Research*, 5(1): 5–26.

Murphy, J. 2000. Ecological modernization. *Geoforum*, 31(1): 1–8.

Murray, R. 2009. *Danger and Opportunity: Crisis and the New Social Economy*. London: Nesta.

Nachum, L. and Zaheer, S. 2005. The persistence of distance? The impact of technology on MNE motivations for foreign investment. *Strategic Management Journal*, 26(8): 747–67.

Nath, K. 2008. *India's Century: The Age of Entrepreneurship in the World's Biggest Democracy*. New York: McGraw-Hill.

National Research Council. 2007. *Science and Security in a Post 9/11 World: A Report Based on Regional Discussions between the Science and Security Communities*. Washington, DC: The National Academies Press.

Nature. 2010. Business leaders' contribution. *Nature*, 473: 26–32. January 7. DOI: 10.1038/463026a.

Nelson, J. and Zadek, S. 2000. Partnership alchemy: New social partnerships in Europe. Copenhagen, The Copenhagen Center. Available at: http://www.csrweltweit.de/uploads/tx_jpdownloads/Copenhagen_Centre_partalch.pdf.

Nelson, R.R. and Winter, S.G. 1982. *An Evolutionary Theory of Economic Change*. Harvard, MA: Belknap Press.

Nidumolu, R., Prahalad, C.K., and Rangaswami, M.R. 2009. Why sustainability is now the key driver of innovation. *Harvard Business Review*, 87(9): 57–64.

Nightingale, D.J., Stanke, A., and Bryan, F.T. 2008. *Enterprise Strategic Analysis and Transformation (ESAT)*. Release 2.0. Cambridge, MA: Massachusetts Institute of Technology.

Noble, C.H. 1999. The eclectic roots of strategy implementation research. *Journal of Business Research*, 45(2): 119–34.

Nobre, F.G. 2011. Core competencies of the new industrial organization. *Journal of Manufacturing Technology Management*, 22(4): 422–43.

Nobre, F.S. and Steiner, S.J. 2002. Beyond the thresholds of manufacturing perspectives on management, technology and organizations. Proceedings of the IEEE International Engineering Management Conference, August 18–20, Cambridge, 788–93.

Nobre, F.S., Tobias, A.M., and Walker, D.S. 2008. The pursuit of cognition in manufacturing organization. *Journal of Manufacturing Systems*, 27(4): 145–57.

Nobre, F.S., Tobias, A.M., and Walker, D.S. 2009. *Organizational and Technological Implications of Cognitive Machines: Designing Future Information Management Systems*. Hershey, PA: IGI Global.

Nobrega, W. and Sinha, A. 2008. *Riding the Indian Tiger: Understanding India – the World's Fastest Growing Market*. Hoboken, NJ: John Wiley & Sons.

Nocco, B.W. and Stulz, R.M. 2006. Enterprise risk management: Theory and practice. *Journal of Applied Corporate Finance*, 18(4): 8–20.

Nolan, P. 2001. *China and the Global Business Revolution*. Houndsmill: Palgrave.

Nolan, P. 2003. Industrial policy in the early twenty-first century: The challenge of the global business revolution. In Chang, H.J. (ed), *Rethinking Development Economics*. London: Anthem Press.

Norris, G. 1999. CFM56: Engine of Change. *Flight International*, May 19–25, 1999. Available at: http://en.wikipedia.org/wiki/CFM_international_CFM56/.

Norris, G., Thomas, G., Wagner, M., and Forbes Smith, C. 2005. Boeing 787 Dreamliner – Flying Redefined. *Aerospace Technical Publications International*. Available at: http://simple.wikipedia.org/wiki/Boeing_787_Dreamliner/.

Norton, D. and Peck, P. 2006. Linking operations to strategy and budgeting, balanced scorecard report and balanced scorecard collaboration. *Harvard Business Review*, September–October: 16–20.

Nottingham, L. 1996. Integrated risk management. *Canadian Business Review*, 23(2): 26–8.

O'Connor, T. 2012. Strategy to execution. *Oilweek*, 63(7): 75–6.

O'Donnell, S.W. 2000. Managing foreign subsidiaries: Agents of headquarters, or an interdependent network? *Strategic Management Journal*, 21(5): 525–48.

O'Reilly, C.A. III and Pfeffer, J. 2000. *Hidden Value: How Great Companies Achieve Extraordinary Results with Ordinary People*. Boston, MA: Harvard Business School Press.

O'Rourke, M. 2012. Refocusing risk management. *Risk Management*, June 2, 2012.

OECD. 2004. *OECD Principles of Corporate Governance*. Paris: OECD.

Oliff, M.D. 2012. A quick guide to enterprise transformation. *Industrial Engineer*, 44(3): 40–41.

Olson, E.G. 2008. Creating an enterprise level "green" strategy. *Journal of Business Strategy*, 29(2): 22–30.

On Scene Coordination Report on Deepwater Horizon Oil Spill. 2011. PDF Report. September 2011. Available at: http://www.uscg.mil/foia/docs/dwh/fosc_dwh_report.pdf.

Orlitzky, M., Schmidt, F.L., and Rynes, S.L. 2003. Corporate social and financial performance: A meta-analysis. *Organization Studies*, 24(3): 403–41.

Owen, J. 2009. *The Death of Modern Management: How to Lead in the New World Order*. Chichester: John Wiley & Sons.

Paletta, D. and Lucchetti, A. 2010. Senate passes sweeping finance overhaul. *Wall Street Journal*, July 16. Available at: http://www.wsj.com/articles/SB10001424052748704682604575369030061839958/.

Patetta Rotta, C. 2010. *A Short Guide to Ethical Risk*. Farnham: Gower.

Peak-Asa, C. and Howard, J. 1999. Workplace-violence: Investigation by the California Division of Occupational Safety and Health, 1993–1996. *Journal of Occupational and Environmental Medicine*, 41(8):716–21.

Pearce, J. 2003. *Social Enterprise in Anytown*. London: Calouste Gulbenkian foundation.

Pennings, J.M., Barkema, H., and Douma, S. 1994. Organizational learning and diversification. *Academy of Management Journal*, 37(3): 608–40.

Pepper, D. 1996. *Modern Environmentalism: An Introduction*. London: Routledge.

Perez-Aleman, P. and Sandilands, M. 2008. Building value at the top and the bottom of the global supply chain: MNC-NGO partnerships. *California Management Review*, 51(1): 24–49.

Perry, D. 2012. Airbus advances towards first flight of A350 twinjet. *Flight Global*. Available at: http://www.flightglobal.com/news/articles/airbus-advances-towards-first-flight-of-a350-twinjet-377959/.

Peteraf, M.A. and Barney, J.B. 2003. Unraveling the resource-based tangle. *Managerial and Decision Economics*, 24(4): 309–23.

Peters, T. 1989. *Thriving on Chaos*. London: Pan.

Peters, T. and Waterman, R. 1982. *In Search of Excellence*. New York: Warner Books.

Peterson, M.F. and Roquebert, J. 2001. Cuban-American entrepreneurs: Chance, complexity and chaos. *Organization Studies*, 22: 31–57.

Pitelis, C.N. and Teece, D.J. 2009. The (new) nature and essence of the firm. *European Management Review*, 6: 5–15.

Pivato, S., Misani, N., and Tencati, A. 2008. The impact of corporate social responsibility on consumer trust: The case of organic food. *Business Ethics: A European Review*, 17(1): 3–12.

Podolny, J.M. 1993. A status-based model of market competition. *The American Journal of Sociology*, 98(4): 829–72.

Porac, J. and Thomas, H. 2002. Managing cognition and strategy: Issues, trends and future directions. In Pettigrew, A.M., Thomas, H., and Whittington, R. (eds), *Handbook of Strategy and Management*. London: SAGE.

Porac, J., Ventresca, M., Mishna, Y. 2002. Inter-organizational cognition and interpretation. In Baum, J.A.C. (ed.), *The Blackwell Companion to Organizations*. Malden, MA: Blackwell: 579–98.

Porras, J., Emery, S., and Thompson, M. 2007. *Success Built to Last*. Harlow, PA: Wharton School Publishing.

Porter, M.E. 1980. *Competitive Strategy*. New York: Free Press.

Porter, M.E. 1992. Capital disadvantage: America's failing capital investment system. *Harvard Business Review*, 70(5): 65–82.

Porter, M.E. 1998. *Competitive Advantage: Creating and Sustaining Superior Performance*. New York: The Free Press.

Porter, M.E. 2001. Regions and the new economics of competition. In Scott, A. (ed.), *Global City-Regions: Trends, Theory, Policy*. Oxford: Oxford University Press, 139–52.

Porter, M.E. and Kramer, M.E. 2002. The competitive advantage of corporate philanthropy. *Harvard Business Review*, 80(12): 56–68.

Pouder, R. and St John, C. 1996. Hot spots and blind spots: Geographic clusters of firms and innovation. *Academy of Management Review*, 21(4): 1192–225.

Powell, T.C., Lovallo, D., and Caringal, C. 2006. Causal ambiguity, management perception, and firm performance. *Academy of Management Review*, 31(1): 175–96.

Prahalad, C.K. 2005a. Aid is not the answer. *The Wall Street Journal* (Eastern Edition), August 31, A.8.

Prahalad, C.K. 2005b. *The Fortune at the Bottom of the Pyramid*. Upper Saddle River, NJ: Wharton School Publishing/Pearson Education.

Prahalad, C.K. and Hamel, G. 1990. The core competence of the corporation. *Harvard Business Review*, 68(3): 79–81.

Prasad, E. 2004. China's growth and integration into the world economy: Prospects and challenges. Occasional Paper No. 232. Washington, DC: International Monetary Fund.

Pratt, M.C. and Foreman, P.O. 2000. Classifying managerial responses to multiple organizational identities. *Academy of Management Review*, 25(1): 18–42.

Pratt & Whitney. 2014. Products – Commercial Engines – JT9D Engine. Pratt & Whitney website, February 7, 2014. Available at: http://www.pw.utc.com/Commercial_Engines/.

Prevosto, V. 2008. Holistic Risk Management and Quantification. *ISO Review: News and Analysis for Insurance Executives*. Available at: http://www.verisk.com/ISO-home/ISO-Review-february-2009.html/.

Prokosch, M.D., Coss, R.G., Scheib, J.E., and S.A. Blozis. 2009. Intelligence and mate choice: Intelligent men are always appealing. *Evolution and Human Behavior*, 30: 11–20.

Public Company Accounting Oversight Board (PCAOB). 2007. An audit of internal control over financial reporting that is integrated with an audit of financial statements. Audit Statement No. 5. Sarbanes–Oxley Act of 2002. Available at: http://fl1.findlaw.com/news.findlaw.com/hdocs/docs/gwbush/sarbanesoxley072302.pdf

Pullan, P. and Murray-Webster, R. 2011. *A Short Guide to Facilitating Risk Management*. Farnham: Gower.

Quer, D., Claver, E., and Rienda, L. 2012. Political risk, cultural distance, and outward foreign direct investment: Empirical evidence from large Chinese firms. *Asia Pacific Journal of Management*, 29(4): 1089–104.

Quinn, R.E., O'Neill, R.M., and St. Clair, L. 2000. *Pressing Problems in Modern Organizations (That Keep Us Up at Night)*. New York: Amacom.

Rabinowitz, J. 2006. *Twelve Steps for Leading Rapid Financial Transformation*. New York: Deloitte & Touche.

Raes, E., Decuyper, S., Lismont, B., Bossche, P.V., Kyndt, E., Demeyere, S., and Dochy, F. 2013. Facilitating team learning through transformational leadership. *Instructional Science*, 41(2): 287–305.

Ragowsky, A. and Gefen, D. 2008. What makes the competitive contribution of ERP strategic. *ACM Digital Library, SIGMIS Database*, 39(2): 33–49.

Ramamurti, R. and Singh, J.V. (eds) 2009. *Emerging Multinationals in Emerging Markets*. Cambridge: Cambridge University Press.

Rashid, A.T. and Rahman, M. 2009. Making profit to solve development problems: The case of Telenor AS and the Village Phone Programme in Bangladesh. *Journal of Marketing Management*, 25(9–10): 1049–60.

Reed, R. and DeFillippi, R.J. 1990. Causal ambiguity, barriers to imitation, and sustainable competitive advantage. *Academy of Management Review*, 15(1): 88–102.

Reilly, E.T. 2007. *New Global Survey*. American Management Association. Available at: http://www.amanet.org/research/.

Reinmoeller, P. and van Baardwijk, N. 2005. The link between diversity and resilience. *MIT Sloan Management Review*, 46(4): 61–5.

Rhee, M. and Valdez, M.E. 2009. Contextual factors surrounding reputational damage with potential implications for reputation repair. *Academy of Management Review*, 34(1): 146–68.

Riefler, P., Diamantopoulos, A., and Siguaw, J. 2011. Cosmopolitan consumers as a target group for segmentation. *Journal of International Business Studies*, 43(3): 285–305.

Rittenberg, L. and Martens, F. 2012. Understanding and Communicating Risk Appetite. COSO – The Committee of Sponsoring Organizations of the Treadway Commission. Available at: http://www.COSO. org/documents/ERM-Understainding%20%20Communicating%20Risk%20Appetite-WEB_Final_r9.pdf.

Robertson, C. and Krauss, C. 2010. Gulf spill is the largest of its kind, scientists say. *New York Times*. August 2, 2010. Available at: http://www.NYTimes.com/2010/08/03/us/03spill.html?_r=0/.

Robinson, N. 2005. IT excellence starts with governance. *Journal of Investment Compliance*, 6(3): 45–9.

Rochette, M. 2009. From risk management to ERM. *Journal of Risk Management in Financial Institutions*, 2(4): 394–408.

Rouse, W.B. 1998. *Don't Jump to Solutions: Thirteen Delusions that Undermine Strategic Thinking*. San Francisco, CA: Jossey-Bass.

Rouse, W.B. 2001. *Essential Challenges of Strategic Management*. New York: John Wiley & Sons.

Rouse, W.B. 2005. A theory of enterprise transformation. *Systems Engineering*, 8(4): 279–95.

Rouse, W.B. 2006. *Enterprise Transformation: Understanding and Enabling Fundamental Change*. New York: John Wiley & Sons.

Rouse, W.B. and Baba, M.L. 2006. Enterprise transformation. *Communications of the ACM*, 49(7): 2006.

Rouse, W.B. and Basole, R.C. 2010. Understanding complex product and service delivery systems. In Maglio, P. (ed.), *Handbook of Service Science*. London: Springer: 461–80.

Rowan, L., Papineschi, J., Taylor, S. et al. 2009. *Third Sector: Investment for Growth*. Banbury: WRAP/Realliance.

Ruhmann, J.S. 2011. Strategy execution. *Leadership Excellence*, 28(8): 3.

SAI Global. 2007. About SAI Global. Available at: www.sai-global.com/ABOUTUS.

Saito, A. 2003. Global city formation in a capitalist developmental state: Tokyo and the waterfront sub-centre project. *Urban Studies*, 40(2): 283–308.

Sakarya, S., Bodur, M., Yildirim-Oktem, O., and Selekler-Goksen, N. 2012. Social alliances: Business and social enterprise collaboration for social transformation. *Journal of Business Research*, 65(12): 1710–20.

Sanchez, P., Ricart, J.E., and Rodriguez, M.A. 2007. Meeting unmet needs at the base of the pyramid: Mobile health care for India's poor. In Quelch, J.A., Rangan, V.K., Herrero, G., and Barton, B. (eds), *Business Solutions for the Global Poor: Creating Social and Economic Value*. San Francisco, CA: Jossey-Bass.

Sanchez, R, Heene, A., and Thomas, H. 1996. *Dynamics of Competence-based Competition: Theory and Practice in the New Strategic Management*. Oxford: Pergamon.

Saporito, B. 2010. Can the A380 bring the party back to the skies? *TIME Magazine*, September 19, 2010. Available at: http://en.wikipedia.org/wiki/Competition_between_Airbus_and_Boeing/.

Sassen, S. 1991. *The Global City: New York, London, Tokyo*. Princeton, NJ: Princeton University Press.

Sassen, S. 1994. *Cities in a World Economy*. Thousand Oaks, CA: Pine Forge/SAGE.

Sassen, S. 2001. Global cities and global city-regions: A comparison. In Scott, A. (ed.), *Global City-Regions: Trends, Theory, Policy*. Oxford: Oxford University Press, 78–95.

Sassen, S. 2002. Global cities and diasporic networks: Microsites in global civil society. In Anheier, H., Glasius, M., and Kaldor, M. (eds), *Global Civil Society*. Oxford: Oxford University Press, 217–40

Sassen, S. 2012. *Cities in a World Economy*. Los Angeles, CA: SAGE.

Satell, G. 2013a. *Before You Innovate, Ask the Right Questions*. HRB Blog Network. Available at: http://blogs.hbr.org/cs/2013/02/before_you_innovate_ask_the_ri.html/.

Satell, G. 2013b. What is innovation? April 2013. Available at: http://www.innovationexcellence.com/blog/2013/04/14/what-is-innovation-2/.

Schaltegger, S. 1996. *Corporate Environmental Accounting*. Chichester: John Wiley & Sons.

Schneider, G.P., Sheikh, A., and Simione, K.A. 2012. Holistic risk management: An expanded role for internal auditors. *Academy of Accounting and Financial Studies Journal*, 16(1): 25–33.

Schofield, A. 2012. ANA Says 787 exceeding fuel efficiency target. *Aviation Week* (subscription article), June 12, 2012. Available at: http://aviationweek.com/search/results/June%2012%2c%202010%20Schofield%20articles/.

Schoonover, S.C., Schoonover, H., Nemerov, D., and Ehly, C. 2000. Competency-based HR applications: Results of a comprehensive survey. Falmouth, MA. Arthur Andersen, Schoonover and SHRM.

Schumpeter, J. 2009. Taking flight. *The Economist*, September 19, 78.

Schumpeter, J.A. 1934. *The Theory of Economic Development*. Cambridge, MA: Harvard University Press.

Schuster, C.P. and Copeland, M.J. 2006. *Global Business Practices: Adapting for Success*. Mason, OH: Thomson/South-Western.

Scott, A. 2014. New Boeing jets hold key to more than half of future sales. *Freelance Writer*, May 1, 2014. Available at: http://www.reuters.com/article/2014/05/01/US-boeing-development-idUSBREA4002T20140501/.

Scott, A., Agnew, J., Soja, E., and Storper, M. 2001. Global city-regions. In Scott, A. (ed.), *Global City-Regions: Trends, Theory, Policy*. Oxford: Oxford University Press, 11–30.

Scott-Cato, M. and Hillier, J. 2010. How could we study climate-related social innovation? Applying Deleuzian philosophy to transition towns. *Environmental Politics*, 19(6): 869–87.

Sedlacek, V.O. 2008. Holistic risk management for perpetual portfolios: Keeping an eye on what's important. *Commonfund Securities, Inc.* January 2008. Available at: https://www.commonfund.org/InvestorResources/Publications/White%20Papers/Holistic%20Risk%20Management%20for%20Perpetual%20Portfolios.pdf

Seelos, C. and Mair, J. 2007. Profitable business models and market creation in the context of deep poverty: A strategic view. *The Academy of Management Perspectives*, 21(4): 49–63.

Selsky, J.W. and Parker, B. 2005. Cross-sector partnerships to address social issues: Challenges to theory and practice. *Journal of Management*, 31(6): 849–73.

Sepulveda, L. 2009. Outsider, missing link or panacea? Some reflections about the place of social enterprise (with) in and in relation to the Third Sector. TSRC Working Paper 15, Birmingham, England, Third Sector Research Center. © 2010.

Seyfang, G. and Smith, A. 2007. Grassroots innovations for sustainable development: Towards a new research and policy agenda. *Environmental Politics*, 16(4): 584–603.

Shane, S.A. 1996. Hybrid organizational arrangements and their implications for firm growth and survival: A study of new franchisors. *Academy of Management Journal*, 39(1): 216–34.

Sharir, M. and Lerner, M. 2006. Gauging the success of social ventures initiated by individual social entrepreneurs. *Journal of World Business*, 41(1): 6–20.

Sharma, S.K. and Gupta, J.N.D. 2003. Knowledge economy and intelligent enterprises. In Gupta, J.N.D. and Sharma, S.K. (eds), *Intelligent Enterprises of the 21st Century*. Hershey, PA: Idea Group Publishing.

Shaver, J.M. 1998. Accounting for endogeneity when assessing strategy performance: Does entry mode choice affect FDI survival? *Management Science*, 44(4): 571–85.

Shenkar, O. 2010. *Copycats: How Smart Companies Use Imitation to Gain a Strategic Edge*. Boston, MA: Harvard Business School Publishing.

Shenkir, W.G. and Walker, P.L. 2007. *Enterprise Risk Management: Tool and Techniques for Effective Implementation*. Institute of Management Accountants (IMA). Available at: http://www.imanet.org/.

Shepherd, D.A. and Patzelt, H. 2011. The new field of sustainable entrepreneurship: Studying entrepreneurial action linking "what is to be sustained" with "what is to be developed." *Entrepreneurship Theory & Practice*, 35(1): 137–63.

Shore, E.B. 1990. The road to enterprise excellence. Proceeding of the 5th Jerusalem Conference on Information Technology, October 22–5, 1990, Jerusalem, Israel, 600–601.

Simonetto, M., Davenport, C., and Olsen, R. 2004. Focus on pricing execution: Ways to improve profitability. *Chemical Market Reporter*, 266(11): N_A. October 4, 2004.

Simons, T. 2008. *The Integrity Dividend: Leading by the Power of Your Word*. San Francisco, CA: Jossey-Bass.

Simoudis, E. 2014. Mobilizing Enterprise Applications. Available at: http://www.enterpriseirregulars.com/71554/mobilizing-enterprise-applications/.

Singer, A.E. 2006. Business strategy and poverty alleviation. *Journal of Business Ethics*, 66(2/3): 225–31.

Singla, S. and Sagar, M. 2012. Integrated risk management in agriculture: An inductive research. *The Journal of Risk Finance*, 13(3): 199–214.

Sirkin, H.L., Hemerling, J.W., and Bhattacharya, A.K. 2008. *Globality: Competing with Everyone from Everywhere for Everything*. London: Headline Business Plus.

Sison, A.J. 2000. Integrated risk management and global business ethics. *Business Ethics: A European Review*, 9(4): 288–95.

Slangen, A. and Hennart, J.F. 2008. Do green fields outperform acquisitions or vice versa? An institutional perspective. *Journal of Management Studies*, 45(7): 1301–28.

Slywotzky, A.J. 1996. *Value Migration: How to Think Several Moves ahead of Competition*. Boston, MA: Harvard Business School Press.

Slywotzky, A.J. and Drzik, J. 2005 Countering the biggest risk of all. *Harvard Business Review*, 83(4): 78–91.

Slywotzky, A.J. and Morrison, D.J. 1997. *The Profit Zone: How Strategic Business Design Will Lead You to Tomorrow's Profits*. New York: Times Book.

Smith, A. 2005. The alternative technology movement: An analysis of its framing and negotiation of technology development. *Human Ecology Review*, 12(2): 106–19.

Smith, A., Stirling, A., and Berkhout, F. 2005. The governance of sustainable socio-technical transitions. *Research Policy*, 34(10): 1491–1510.

Smith, A.D. 2007. Making the case for competitive advantage of corporate social responsibility. *Business Strategy Series*, 8(3): 186–95.

Smith, D. and Wohlin, C. 2011. Strategies facilitating software product transfers. *Software IEEE*, 28(5): 60–66.

Smith, P.G. and Reinertsen, D.G. 1998. *Developing Product in Half the Time*, 2nd edn. New York: John Wiley and Sons.

Society of Actuaries. 2006. *Enterprise Risk Management Specialty Guide*. The ERM Working Group of the Society of Actuaries Risk Management.

Someren, N., Robinson, J., and Gibson, C. 2012. Holistic risk management: Perspective from IT professionals. An Economic Intelligence Unit Research Program Commissioned by IBM. IBM Global Technology Services – Research Report. April 2012. Available at: Holistic_risk_management-IT Professional Prospective-IBM-April 2012.pdf.

Sonnenfeld, D.A. and Mol, A.P.J. 2002. Globalization and the transformation of environmental governance: An introduction. *American Behavioral Scientist*, 45(9): 1318–39.

Spatafora, N., Yang, Y., and Feyzioglu, T. 2004. *China's Emergence and Its Impact on the Global Economy*. Washington, DC: IMF World Economic Outlook, International Monetary Fund.

Spear, S.J. 2009. *Chasing the Rabbit: How Market Leaders Outdistance the Competition and How Great Companies Can Catch Up and Win*. London: McGraw-Hill.

Spencer, A.M. 1979. Investment strategy and growth in a new market. *The Bell Journal of Economics*, 10(1): 1–19.

Spencer, L.M. and Spencer, S.M. 1993. *Competence at Work: Model for Superior Performance*. New York: John Wiley & Sons.

Spender, J.C. 1990. *Industry Recipes*. Oxford: Basil Blackwell.

Stainer, A. and Stainer, L. 1997. Ethical dimensions of environmental management. *European Business Review*, 97(5): 224–30.

Standard & Poor. 2008. Enterprise risk management: Standard & Poor's to apply enterprise risk analysis to corporate ratings. Standard & Poor's press release. Standard & Poor, May 7, 2008. Available at: www.standardandpoors.com.

Starbuck, W.H. 2005. Four great conflicts of the twenty-first century. In Cooper, C.L. (ed.), *Leadership and Management in the 21st Century: Business Challenges of the Future*. Oxford: Oxford University Press.

Steinberg, R. 2011. Using the new COSO risk-management guidance. *Compliance Week*, 8(86): 36–7.

Stemler, S.E., Bebell, D., and Sonnabend, L.A. 2011. Using school mission statements for reflection and research. *Educational Administration Quarterly*, 47(2): 383–420.

Stephens, D.W. 1981. The logic of risk-sensitive foraging preferences. *Animal Behavior*, 29: 628–9.

Stephens, D.W. and Krebs, J.R. 1986. *Foraging Theory*. Princeton, NJ: Princeton University Press.

Stulz, R. 1996. Rethinking risk management. *Journal of Applied Corporate Finance*, 9(3): 8–24.

Stulz, R. 2003. *Rethinking Risk Management: The Revolution in Corporate Finance*, 4th edn. Malden, MA: Blackwell Publishing.

Sun, H. and Zhao, Y. 2010. The empirical relationship between quality management and the speed of new product development. *Total Quality Management & Business Excellence*, 21(4): 351–61.

Surowiecki, J. 2004. *The Wisdom of Crowds*. New York: Random House.

Takhan, V. 2005. Technology Pricing. Deloitte White Paper.

Talluri, S., Narasimhan, R., and Viswanathan, S. 2007. Information Technologies for procurement decisions: A decision support system for multi-attribute for e-reverse auctions. *International Journal of Production Research*, 45(11): 2615–28.

Tan, D. 2009. Foreign market entry strategies and post-entry growth: Acquisitions vs greenfield investments. *Journal of International Business Studies*, 40(6): 1046–63.

Taninecz, G. 2000. Value chain IT infrastructure. *Industry Week*, 249(8): 33–8.

Tappin, S. and Cave, A. 2008. *The Secrets of CEOs*. London: Nicholas Brealey Publishing.

Tarde, G. 1903. *The Laws of Imitation*. New York: H. Holt & Co.

Tattam, D. 2011. *A Short Guide to Operational Risk*. Farnham: Gower.

Tatum, M. 2014. What is Integrated Risk Management? *wiseGEEK*, February 12, 2014. Available at: wisegeek@wisegeek.com.

Teasdale, S. 2012. What's in a name? Making sense of social enterprise discourses. *Public Policy and Administration*, 27(2): 99–119.

Teece, D.J. 1986. Profiting from technological innovation: Implications for integration, collaboration, licensing and public policy. *Research Policy*, 15(6): 285–305.

Teece, D.J. 2007. Explicating dynamic capabilities: The nature and micro-foundations of (sustainable) enterprise performance. *Strategic Management Journal*, 28(13): 1319–50.

Teece, D.J. 2009. *Dynamic Capabilities and Strategic Management: Organizing for Innovation and Growth*. Oxford: Oxford University Press.

Teece, D.J. 2010. Business models, business strategy and innovation. *Long Range Planning*, 43(2/3): 172–94.

Teece, D.J. Pisano, G., and Shuen, A. 1997. Dynamic capabilities and strategic management. *Strategic Management Journal*, 18(7): 509–33.

Tengblad, S. 2006. Is there a "new managerial work"? A comparison with Henry Mintzberg's classic study 30 years later. *Journal of Management Studies*, 43(7): 1437–61.

Terjesen, S., Patel, P.C., and Covin, J.G. 2011. Alliance diversity, environmental context and the value of manufacturing capabilities among new high technology ventures. *Journal of Operations Management*, 29(1–2): 105–15.

The Harvard Law School Forum on Corporate Governance and Financial Regulation. 2010. *Dodd–Frank Act Becomes Law*. Cambridge, MA: Harvard Law School. July 21.

The Washington Independent. 2010. Obama to sign Dodd–Frank Financial Regulatory Reform Bill into law today. *The Washington Independent*, July 21, 2010.

The Whetstone Group. 2005. Available at: http://www.TheWhetstoneGroup.com/our_approach_to_growth-2005.htm/.

Thoenig, J.C. and Waldman, C. 2007. *The Marking Enterprise: Business Success and Societal Embedding*. Basingstoke: Insead Business Press/Palgrave Macmillan.

Thompson, S. 2012. *Enterprise Risk Management: A Holistic Approach to Managing Risk*. Aspen Risk Management Group. Available at: www.aspenmg.com.

Tidd, J., Bessant, J., and Pavitt, K. 2005. *Managing Innovation: Integrating Technological, Market and Organizational Change*, 3rd edn. Chichester: John Wiley & Sons.

Tihanyi, L., Griffith, D., and Russell, C. 2005. The effect of cultural distance on entry mode choice, international diversification, and MNE performance: A meta-analysis. *Journal of International Business Studies*, 36(3): 270–83.

Tolmie, P., Hughes, J., Rouncefield, M., and Sharrock, W. 2003. The "virtual" manager? Change and continuity in managerial work. Department of Sociology, Lancaster University, Lancaster, England. Available at: www.comp.lancs.ac.uk/sociology/papers/Tolmie-et-al-Virtual-Manager.pdf.

Tonello, M. 2012. *Strategic Risk Management: A Primer for Directors*. The Harvard Law School Forum on Corporate Governance and Financial Regulation, August 23, 2012.

Toniolo, G. and Visco, V. (eds). 2004. *Il declino economico dell'Italia*. Milan: Mondadori.

Tracey, P. and Jarvis, O. 2007. Toward a theory of social venture franchising. *Entrepreneurship: Theory & Practice*, 31(5): 667–85.

Trist, E.L. 1983. Referent organizations and the development of inter-organizational domains. *Human Relations*, 36(3): 247–68.

Truel, C. 2010. *A Short Guide to Customer Risk*. Farnham: Gower.

Tsang, E.W.K. 2002. Learning from overseas venturing experience: The case of Chinese family business. *Journal of Business Venturing*, 17(1): 21–40.

Tucker, R.B. 2001. Innovation: The core competency. *Strategy & Leadership*, 29(1): 11–14.

UNCTAD. 2013. *World Investment Report 2013*. Geneva: United Nations.

United Nations Development Programme (UNDP). 1994. *Human Development Report*. New York: Oxford University Press.

United Nations Office for Partnerships. 2009. *United Nations Office for Partnership Annual Report 2009*. Available at: http://www.un.org/partnerships/Docs/A_65_347.pdf.

UTC 10-K. 2013. United Technologies Corporation/De/2013 Annual Report Form (10-K). United States Securities and Exchange Commission. February 6, 2014.

UTC 10-Q. 2014. United Technologies Corporation/De/2014 Q1 Quarterly Report Form (10-Q). United States Securities and Exchange Commission. April 25, 2014.

Valerdi, R. and Nightingale, D. 2011. An introduction to the *Journal of Enterprise Transformation*. *Journal of Enterprise Transformation*, 1:1–6.

Van de Van, A.H. and Ferry, D.L. 1980. *Measuring and Assessing Organizations*. New York: John Wiley and Sons.

Vance, S.C. 1975. Are socially responsible corporations' good investment risks? *Management Review*, 64(8): 19–24.

Verbeke, A. and Yuan, W. 2007. Entrepreneurship in multinational enterprises: A penrosean perspective. *Management International Review*, 47(2): 241–58.

Veth, G. 2006. Strategy execution: Allocating resources to ensure execution. *DM Review Magazine*. December 2006. Available at: http://www.dmreview.com/article_sub.cfm?articleID=1069937/.

Vickers, I. 2010. Social enterprise and the environment: A review of the literature. TSRC Working Paper 22. Birmingham, England, Third Sector Research Center.

Vickers, I. and Lyon, F. 2014. Beyond green niches? Growth strategies of environmentally-motivated social enterprises. *International Small Business Journal*, 32(4): 449–70.

Von Hippel, E. 1988. *The Source of Innovation*. New York: Oxford University Press.

Wade, J. 2010. From tactical to strategic: Risk Management's next move. *Risk Management*, September 2. Available at: http://www.rmmagazine.com/2010/09/02/from-tactical-to-strategic-risk-managements-next-move/.

Wade, J. 2012. Strategic risk management not widespread in Europe. *Risk Management*, December 5, 2012.

Wade, J. 2013. Former Procter & Gamble CEO A.G. Lafley discusses risk and strategy. *Risk Management*, March 18, 2013.

Wall, R. and van der Knaap, G. 2011. Sectoral differentiation and network structure within contemporary worldwide corporate networks. *Economic Geography*, 87(3): 267–308.

Waltz, E. 1998. *Information Warfare Principles and Operations*. Chicago, IL: Artech House.

Wang, C.L. and Ahmed, P.K. 2007. Dynamic capabilities: A review and research agenda. *International Journal of Management Reviews*, 9(1): 31–51.

Waterman, R., Peter, T.J., and Phillips, J.R. 1980. The McKinsey 7S's framework. *Business Horizons* 23(3): 14–26.

Watson, T.J. 2001. *In Search of Management*. London: Routledge.

Webb, J.W., Kistruck, G.M., Ireland, R.D., and Ketchen, D.J. 2010. The entrepreneurship process in base of the pyramid markets: The case of multinational enterprise/nongovernment organization alliances. *Entrepreneurship Theory and Practice*, 34(3): 555–81.

Webber, A.M. 2000. New math for a new economy. *Fast Company* (News Letter), January–February 2000. Available at: http://www.cs.trinity.edu/rjensen/readings/lev/NewMath.htm/.

Weber, E.U. and Milliman, R.A. 1997. Perceived risk attitudes: Relating risk perception to risky choice. *Management Science*, 43: 123–44.

Weber, E.U., Blais, A.R. and Betz, N.E. 2002. A domain-specific risk-attitude scale: Measuring risk perceptions and risk behaviors. *Journal of Behavioral Decision Making*, 15: 263–90.

Weber, H.R. 2010. Blown-out BP well finally killed at bottom of Gulf. *Boston Globe*, Associated Press, September 19, 2010.

Weill, P. and Ross, J.W. 2004. *IT Governance: How Top Performers Manage IT Decision Rights for Superior Results*. Boston, MA: Harvard Business Press.

Weiser, J. 2007. Untapped: Strategies for success in underserved markets. *Journal of Business Strategy*, 28(2): 30–37.

Weiss, T.B. and Hartle, F. 1997. *Reengineering Performance Management: Breakthroughs in Achieving Strategy through People*. Boca Raton, FL: St. Lucie Press.

Welbourne, T. 2005. *Business School*. Ann Arbor, MI: University of Michigan Press.

Wells, R., Hochman, M., Hochman, S., and O'Connell, P. 1992. Measuring environmental success. *Total Quality Environmental Management*, 1(4): 315–27.

Whitney, P. and Kelkar, A. 2004. Designing for the base of the pyramid. *Design Management Review*, 15(4): 41–7.

Wikipedia. 1998. Hampel Report. Available at: http://en.wikipedia.org/wiki/Hampel_report/.

Wikipedia. 2009. Taking the lead: A50XWB presentation. *EADS* (December 2006). Archived from the original on March 27, 2009. Available at: http://en.wikipedia.org/wiki/Airbus_A350_XWB/.

Wikipedia. 2010. A 380 superjumbo lands in Sydney. *BBC*, October 25, 2007. Available at: http://en.wikipedia.org/wiki/Boeing_747/.

Wikipedia. 2011a. Boeing 747–8 Family background. *Boeing.com*. (November 14, 2005). Available at: http://en.wikipedia.org/wiki/Boeing_747-8/

Wikipedia. 2011b. Boeing partners expected to scrap Super-Jet study. *Los Angeles Times*, July 10, 1995. Available at: http://en.wikipedia.org/wiki/Airbus_A380/

Wikipedia. 2012a. The Boeing 747. Available at: http://en.wikipedia.org/wiki/Boeing_747-400/

Wikipedia. 2012b. A380 family press kit (January 1, 2012). Available at: http://en.wikipedia.org/wiki/Competition_between_Airbus_and_Boeing/.

Wikipedia. 2013a. Summary, [1]. Airbus (October 2013). Available at: http://en.wikipedia.org/wiki/Qatar_Airways/

Wikipedia. 2013b. Boeing 787 Dreamliner. Available at: http://en.wikipedia.org/wiki/Boeing_787_Dreamliner/

Wikipedia. 2013c. Pratt and Whitney – The free encyclopedia (October 8, 2013). Available at: http://en.wikipedia.org/wiki/Pratt_%26_Whitney/

Wikipedia. 2013d. Pratt & Whitney – The free encyclopedia (November 17, 2013). Available at: http://en.wikipedia.org/wiki/Pratt_%26_Whitney_JT8D/

Wikipedia. 2013e. Competition between Airbus and Boeing (December 2, 2013). Available at: http://en.wikipedia.org/wiki/Boeing_747-400/

Wikipedia. 2014a. Boeing 747–8. Available at: http://en.wikipedia.org/wiki/Boeing_747–8/

Wikipedia. 2014b. United Technologies Corporation (November 2, 2014). Available at: http://www.ask.com/wiki/United_Technologies_Corporation?long=en/

Wikipedia. 2015a. List of Airbus A380 Orders and deliveries. Available at: http://en.wikipedia.org/wiki/list_of_Airbus_A380_Orders_and_Deliveries/

Wikipedia. 2015b. Airbus A320 family (February 5, 2015). Available at: http://en.wikipedia.org/wiki/Airbus_ A320_family/

Wikipedia. 2015c. CFM International LEAP (February 8, 2015). Available at: http://in.Wikipedia.org/wiki/CFM_ International_LEAP/.

Wikipedia. 2015d. Pratt & Whitney PW1000G (February 8, 2015). Available at: http://en.wikipedia.org/wiki/ Pratt_526_Whitney_PW1000G/.

Williams, D. 2003. Explaining employment changes in foreign manufacturing investment in the UK. *International Business Review*, 12(4): 479–97.

Williams, L.S. 2008. The mission statement: A corporate reporting tool with a past, present, and future. *Journal of Business Communication*, 45(2): 94–119.

Winter, S.G. 2003. Understanding dynamic capabilities. *Strategic Management Journal*, 24(10): 991–5.

Woellert, L. and Chen, S. 2014. China's income inequality surpasses U.S., posing risk for Xi. *Bloomberg News*, April 18, 2014. Available at: http://www.tibet-europe.com/web/?p=768/.

Wolpert, J.D. 2002. Breaking out of the innovation box. *Harvard Business Review*, 80(8): 76–83.

Wong, S.K.S. 2013. Environmental requirements, knowledge sharing and green innovation: Empirical evidence from the electronics industry in China. *Business Strategy and the Environment*, 22(5): 321–38.

Woodcock, C.P., Beamish, P.W., and Makino, S. 1994. Ownership-based entry mode strategies and international performance. *Journal of International Business Studies*, 25(2): 253–73.

Wooldridge, B. and Floyd, S.W. 1992. The strategy process, middle management involvement, and organizational performance. *Strategic Management Journal*, 11(1): 231–41.

Works Institute. 2003. What is the competency? *Works Japan: Recruit*, 57(1): 1–47.

World Economic Forum (WEF). 2004. *The Davos Report: Highlights, Outcomes and Next Steps from the 2004 World Economic Forum*. Available at: http://www.weforum.org/summitreports/.

World Economic Forum (WEF). 2006. *Partnering for Success: Business Perspectives on Multi-Stakeholder Partnership*. Executive Summary. WEF Global Corporate Citizenship Initiative.

Worrall, L. and Cooper, C. 2004. Managers, hierarchies and perceptions: A study of UK managers. *Journal of Managerial Psychology*, 19(1): 41–68.

Wu, F. 2000. The global and local dimensions of place-making: Remaking Shanghai as a world city. *Urban Studies*, 37(8): 1359–77.

Wu, W-W. 2009. Exploring core competencies for R&D technical professionals. *Expert Systems with Applications*, 36(5): 9574–9.

Wymer, W.W. and Samu, S. 2003. Dimensions of business and non-profit collaborative relationships. *Journal of Nonprofit and Public Sector Marketing*, 11(1): 3–22.

Yahoo! News. 2010. Historic financial overhaul signed to law by Obama, July 21, 2010.

Zagotta, R. and Robinson, D. 2002. Keys to successful strategy execution. *The Journal of Business Strategy*, 23(1): 30–34.

Zaheer, S. 1995. Overcoming the liability of foreignness. *Academy of Management Journal*, 38(2): 341–63.

Zaheer, S. and Mosakowski, E. 1997. The dynamics of the liability of foreignness: A global study of survival in financial services. *Strategic Management Journal*, 18(6): 439–63.

Zahra, S.A. and George, G. 2002. Absorptive capacity: A review, reconceptualization, and extension. *Academy of Management Review*, 27(2): 185–203.

Zahra, S.A., Sapienza, H.J., and Davidsson, P. 2006. Entrepreneurship and dynamic capabilities: A review, model and research agenda. *Journal of Management Studies*, 43(4): 917–55.

Zhongyuan, Y., Rouse, W.B., and Serban, N. 2011. A computational theory of enterprise transformation. *Systems Engineering*, 14(4): 441–54.

Zink, K.J. 2007. From total quality management to corporate sustainability based on a stakeholder management. *Journal of Management History*, 13(4): 394–401.

Zook, C. and Allen, J. 1999. *The Facts about Growth*. New York: Bain and Company.

Zurich & HBRAS. 2012. *Risk Management in a Time of Global Uncertainty.* Available at: http://www.Zurich.com/en/news-and-media/news-release/2012/risk-management-in-a-time/.

Zwaan, L., Stewart, J. and Subramaniam, N. 2011. Internal audit involvement in enterprise risk management. *Managerial Auditing Journal,* 26(7): 586–604.

Index

For Product Safety Concerns and Information please contact our EU representative GPSR@taylorandfrancis.com Taylor & Francis Verlag GmbH, Kaufingerstraße 24, 80331 München, Germany

Printed and bound by CPI Group (UK) Ltd, Croydon, CR0 4YY

01/05/2025

01858393-0003